BY JOHN GREENWAY

DOWN
AMONG
THE
WILD MEN

DOWN AMONG THE WILD MEN

The Narrative Journal of Fifteen Years
Pursuing the Old Stone Age Aborigines
of Australia's Western Desert

JOHN GREENWAY

AN ATLANTIC MONTHLY PRESS BOOK

Little, Brown and Company — Boston — Toronto

FIRST EDITION

T 11/72

The illustrations on pages 39, 146 and 191 are photographs
by Norman Tindale. All other photographs are by the author.

Library of Congress Cataloging in Publication Data

Greenway, John.
   Down among the wild men.

   "An Atlantic Monthly Press book."
   1. Australian aborigines. I. Title.
GN665.G65   301.29'94   72-5522
ISBN 0-316-32680-1

ATLANTIC—LITTLE, BROWN BOOKS
ARE PUBLISHED BY
LITTLE, BROWN AND COMPANY
IN ASSOCIATION WITH
THE ATLANTIC MONTHLY PRESS

Published simultaneously in Canada
by Little, Brown & Company (Canada) Limited

PRINTED IN THE UNITED STATES OF AMERICA

for Norman Tindale,
with Whom the Fifteen Years Began
and Bob Verburgt,
with Whom They Ended

How these curiosities would be quite forgott,
did not such idle felowes as I am
putt them downe.

— John Aubrey (1626–1697)

CONTENTS

ILLUSTRATIONS

PROLOGUE

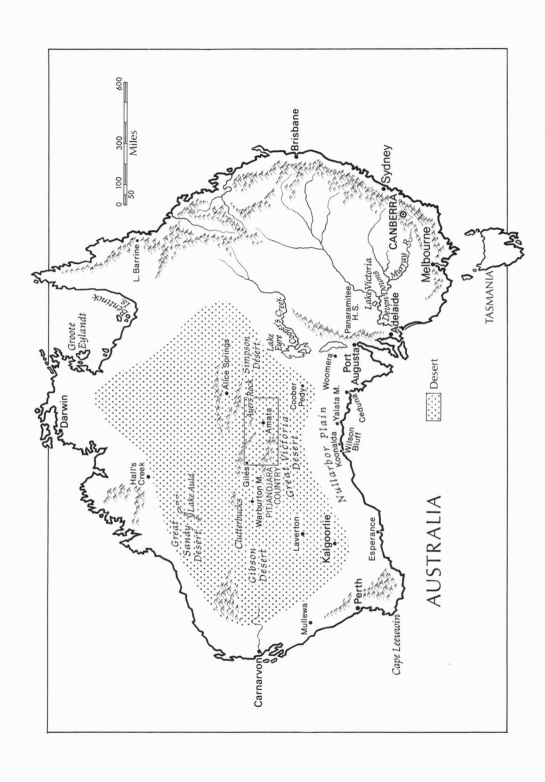

AUSTRALIA

The Making of an Anthropologist

In the western desert of Australia a boy becomes a man by having an upper central incisor pounded out of his head with a rock, without anesthetic, without permission to express pain or terror; by having his foreskin cut off in little pieces with a stone knife and seeing it eaten by certain of his male relatives, and as a climax of agony, by having his penis slit through to the urethra from the scrotum to the meatus, like a hot dog. At the same time the men singe into his brain with the white-hot poker of these memorable operations the first important knowledge, secular and sacred, of what he must know to survive in the world's most hostile inhabited land. He goes away by himself, bleeding, terrified, to prove he can live for a time alone. When he returns to camp weeks or months later, he is a man, a child no longer. The little boys throw toy spears at him. They break against his chest.

In America a boy becomes a man by living comfortably in the transitional womb of his parents' home until he reaches eighteen or whatever arbitrary age of maturity politicians whoring for his vote certify, by growing his hair long and his feet dirty, and, if he is masculine beyond the normal expectations in an attenuated civilization, by protesting one way or another against the natural order of things in the generation he is about to join. For our culture, our civilization, it does not matter, since technology has made human beings useless anyhow, but for the individual soul the American way makes trouble for its possessor and money for its psychiatrist. The American way of manhood lacks some essential if intangible quality — a failure of personal commitment, perhaps, a failure to reaffirm proved values — that someday will show that no man was ever made of the boy.

In the technetronic era the First World needs anthropologists no

3

more than it needs men. There, too, the inevitable drive toward entropy, as the Second Law of Thermodynamics commands, has its way. Therefore our new breed of anthropologists are made as easily as our men are made. A young man (or woman — I use the masculine inclusive until the raging ladies devise for us some acceptable unisex impersonal noun), too often merely aimless beyond his minority, attaches himself like a goose barnacle to a Fellow of the American Anthropological Association who pulls him thereafter through the warm academic waters. A series of weekends with a Navajo family, a summer's work among broken Hohokam pots, a thesis gestates into an advanced university degree, and the whole symbiotic complex of barnacles and neonatal anthropologist drifts off with the imprimatur of the Ethics Committee of the American Anthropological Association to find in a remote part of the shrinking Third World some disadvantaged people to help, thereby to expiate their profession's sin of being the vanguard of capitalistic imperialism exploiting the peace-loving peoples of the world.

As Sir Thomas Malory, himself the last magnificent anachronism of chivalry, wrote as he was rotting in jail and looking out upon his world rotting in modernism, *This is no wisdom nor stability, but it is feebleness of nature and great disworship whosoever useth this.* The old anthropologists were not so. They were wild men who went in great danger into the little worlds of wilder men because they were more content among people who recognized what manhood was. One of them whom I cherish as a personal friend and who writes books on anthropology for the same publishing house that is issuing this journal at least once to my knowledge strangled a man to death with his bare hands. Another of them, whom I did not like, was brained in New Guinea by a stone axe in the hands of a cannibal. In a house over which I used to look upon Sydney Harbour there once lived the excellent Baron Nicolaus de Miklouho-Maklay, who in New Guinea a hundred years ago handed a spear to a native braggart who had asked him whether he would ever die, and challenged the man to spear him. Still another, a revered teacher of mine who lived just this side of permissible violence, taught the Lenni Lenape Indians dances their grandfathers had forgotten, rituals now being danced for tourists, *ancient, White Brother, very ancient.*

These men whose hands I touched, and more whose hands I touched through the hands of others, were not interested in being social work-

4

ers. So far as induced culture change was concerned, they were most of them fundamental conservatives who followed John Randolph's first principle: *Never without the strongest necessity disturb a thing at rest.* They left the disturbance to the early missionaries, people whose greatest fault was trying to solve a problem they did not know was insoluble.

I do not say they were all good men, as men are measured today. Some of them were unmitigated rogues. Bronislaw Malinowski, for one example, the most influential of all anthropologists. He laid down the two basic laws for all of our profession who venture into other cultures: (1) infer nothing except from fieldwork of your own doing; (2) respect your native peoples as equals to yourself. Unhappily for his reputation today, he himself violated the most elemental rule of anyone who wishes posterity to think well of him: Do not keep explicit diaries, and if you must, do not let them fall into the hands of a second wife. Now we know that the only fieldwork Malinowski ever undertook was forced upon him by an indulgent Australian government while it was holding him in World War I as an enemy alien. And we have in his own hand the confession that when he was not reading trash novels in New Guinea, he was "coon-bashing" — punching in the face any native who dared contradict anything he as the superior man chose to say. And of course he was a lecher of impressive proportions — but that is a failing too widely shared to criticize him for.

Then there is Heinrich Schliemann, who created his own golden legend in his doctoral dissertation (his autobiography, if such a thing can be believed), written in classical Greek for the University of Rostock. We are told, and the tale has been repeated by endless anthologists of archaeological writings, how at the age of seven he promised his father he would one day find the lost city of Homer's Troy. Flapdoodle, all of it. The facts of his life are incomparably more fascinating. He was a modern Midas — everything he touched turned literally to gold. Fabulously wealthy from enterprises begun with a Russian partner named Zhivago, he moved into other areas. He went to California during the gold rush to settle the pitiable estate of his useless dead brother, got into the gold dust business, made four hundred thousand dollars in nine months, became an American citizen in order to divorce his frigid Russian wife, and returned to Europe bored to madness. He became a scholar for a while, picking up that amazing doctorate. Then to archaeology: he went to China, arguing along the

5

way about negligible expenses (once furiously with a monk at a lamasery about the cost of an overnight room), smashed down part of the Great Wall, and came home again, still hungry for new old worlds to destroy. He looked into Homer, memorized him, advertised for a wife (she had to be young, beautiful, to know Homer by heart), found her, bought the site of Troy, and began one of the largest acts of archaeological vandalism in the annals of that destructive discipline. He found and smuggled out the "gold of Troy" (stolen from Berlin in World War II by the Russians), went to Crete and haggled for the site of Knossos, representing himself as being interested in an olive grove thereon, and canceled the sixteen-thousand-dollar deal because the owner exaggerated the number of olive trees. Curious, one must concede, for a man who in 1863 cleared forty million dollars from his trade in indigo alone. Ultimately he died — ironically, without ever putting his hand on an object from Homer's Troy.

They were not all rogues, these workers in a better generation of the students of man. But they were all independent, thinkers of their own thoughts. John Aubrey, for example, whose remark about himself and other "idle felowes" I use to begin this book, remembered now as one of the promiscuous fathers of archaeology but disregarded in his own time as being "maggotie-headed," discoverer of the Aubrey Holes at Stonehenge, now being fed into brainless computers with stone angles by an American named Hawkins and coming out as unsullied astronomical nonsense. Before Aubrey, Sir Robert Bruce Cotton, another tolerable nut, who saved nearly everything we know from the Anglo-Saxon treasury of literature, a language Shakespeare could not read and a philosophy Shakespeare could not understand.

These men whom I so much admire were independent thinkers, so far as they could be in a world where no man is the master of his fate or captain of his soul. Like other, lesser men, they were tossed about in the crosscurrents of their culture, but they made that small struggle, now and again, to take themselves away from the tropismatic school of human fish. There was Augustus Lane Fox Pitt-Rivers, the British general who could have retired into useless contentment when he fell heir to a legacy. But instead he made a study of the design changes in the British army rifle — and found that it evolved through minuscule mutations its designers were not aware of. Living in the first excitement of evolution, Pitt-Rivers noticed that the inorganic rifle was evolving as inexorably as Darwin's finches or Mendel's garden peas.

With this astonishing discovery he turned his interest to weapons of primitive cultures and saw the same invisible process at work. Thus he became one of the original thinkers outside the herd smothering in received knowledge. Sir James George Frazer got hold of a "golden bough" anciently used in the rites of Adonis, something no one else was interested in, and by it pulled his way through the great tree of anthropological knowledge, producing finally a massive work that anyone pretending to education today should have on his shelves. Edward Burnett Tylor, in my estimation the greatest of all the students of man, was pushed away from easy falsehood into hard truth by being denied, as a Quaker, admittance into the great English universities. My friend Buckminster Fuller, with whom I have had delightful arguments when he intruded engineering into anthropology, nurtured his genius outside stultifying schools of conventional architecture; his concept of "tensegrity" came from the boats in the fishing village of his youth.

But however unorthodox the way they came by it, these men had education, wide education, to feed their imaginations. It was a mind-clearing joy to listen to those who were alive in my time or to read those who were dead. No one has conveyed the excitement of Darwin's observations better than Darwin, or the excitement of Cook's adventures better than Cook. And when Carleton Coon has gone, who will there be to pick up a common piece of undistinguished ancient sculpture and drawl on about it like Sherlock Holmes — what people it was admired by, whose hands made it, what stone it was formed from, what quarry the stone came from, what slaves — or freemen — hewed it from its matrix? How sad now to think that Carl like a great stag is being snapped at by the young hounds of our consensus anthropology! I had a note from one of these initiates a few weeks ago, a candidate for the doctorate at my university. *Dr. Greenway*, he wrote, *I would be extreeamly interested in T-A.'ing youre interim 104 if such oppertunity is available.* Still, what is one to expect from a boy at least a year away from American manhood when an official publication of the American Anthropological Association credits me with Mao Tse-tung's elegant borrowing, *Let a thousand flowers bloom, let a hundred schools of thought contend?* At the same time I had a note from Jo Birdsell, whom you will meet later, now of UCLA but on his way back to Australia where with Norman Tindale he established

7

scientific physical anthropology thirty years ago. Replying to a cynical note of my own, he wrote,

I would contend that the disintegration of your university has proceeded neither further nor more rapidly than that of my own. I personally am enormously alienated by the institutional trends shown here, and by the smart-ass attitude prevalent at all student levels, including the younger of the graduate students. The best years of the academic life passed some time ago.

I was lucky to have got into those best years just as the door was being slammed shut forever. I should like you to meet a few of the great men who made those years the best, some of whom are alive still and others whose bones are dust and whose names are memory. My life has been richened for the knowing of them. Even the dead ones, I felt, now and again reached across the years to me. I think Ernest Giles, the greatest of my Australian heroes, saved my life once, on that terrible desert where his companion Alfred Gibson died of thirst a hundred years ago. Nothing I will ever do will thrill me so much as finding with my own eyes and hands an object Giles threw away near that place. And yet I know so little of these men. I know the important things, yes, the things biographers record. But what made Giles hate the smothering humanity of cities, as I hate it, so much that time after time he plunged with the minimum of companionship into the deathly emptiness of Australia? Robert Burke, who died out there beyond Cooper's Creek — what nudged him into becoming a policeman in the Australian goldfields when policemen were hated above all other living things?

So rarely are they recorded, the little things on which lives and civilizations turn! Without considering those myriad currents and impacts from the outside that knock us about like motes in a sunbeam, look for a moment on the body itself, that confused, imperfect, unlovely thing a plumber friend of mine once said he could build better out of a load of three-quarter-inch pipe. At Waterloo Napoleon sat too long in a bathtub soaking his hemorrhoids. Five million years or more before, one of his Australopithecine ancestors discovered he could bash in baboon skulls better standing up than on all fours, as God intended him to ambulate. He stood up and the hominid rectal veins, not designed for the pressure, ballooned out into a loss at the

8

Battle of Waterloo. For a more respectable organ, consider the eye. The Anglo-Saxon King Harold Godwinsson looked up at the sky at Senlac, took a Norman arrow in his eye, and forever doomed England to being half French, God help us. Norman Tindale, who figures so largely in this book, lost an eye in an accident when he was young; he was wisely advised it would be better for him to be a one-eyed anthropologist than a one-eyed entomologist, so he became instead the greatest of all Australian anthropologists — though, to be sure, he still chases butterflies. The young anthropologist John Gwaltney is wholly blind; he has made his life's work the study of a village in Mexico, most of whose inhabitants are blind.

Or noses. Cleopatra's nose, Darwin's nose, my nose. A silly millimeter shorter for Cleo and she would not have had those great Roman lovers who sotted away on the Nile their integrity and that of their empire. One shred of nasal epidermis further toward the irresoluteness the phrenologist-captain of the *Beagle* already saw and distrusted in Darwin's nose, and a lesser unpaid naturalist might have followed evolution around the watery world without ever seeing it. My nose — if I had not struck it a great whack with my hammer while looking down upon my own Cleopatra as she worked at her desk below my scaffold in a Second World War defense plant, I would not have injured my brain to the extent of giving up a perfectly safe 4-F classification to talk my way into the Army so as to impress my way into her heart.* For that matter, if Joe Duffy, my first employer at carpentry, had not got the line of his right eye in the way of his nose he would not have put his end of a chalk line on the wrong plate point, I would have put in a line of ceiling joists level, we would not have had a hatchet-wielding fight, and I would now be a retired rich contractor with no knowledge or interest at all in Sir Leonard Woolley's finding on the foundation stones of Tutankhamen's temple a chalk line three and a half thousand years old, snapped there by some nameless stone mason erecting King Tut's walls.

Even the most misanthropic of us is influenced, often to great decisions, by others — so that we become a permutation of body, the nudges of our culture's Brownian Movements, and the aping of our betters. For myself there has been very little of the latter. I admire

* The sacrifice did not help. She married a fighter pilot and is now fifty, doubtless fat, and no longer sufficiently nubile for me to hit myself anywhere with anything for her.

Ernest Giles, Matthew Flinders, and Jonathan Swift of times long past; in high school one teacher; in university two professors; but of all the people I have met in books or life, only one has shaped to my recognition my own psyche — Joe Duffy, he of the chalk line. To know me and to know this book, you must know him. He took me off the idleness of my back steps and put me to work as a carpenter's helper, pulling nails at thirteen cents an hour from boards in the whorehouses of Bethel Court in the dirtiest city in Western civilization, Chester, Pennsylvania. Always he gave me assignments just beyond my expected competence, and within a year I was drawing first-class carpenter's wages. I stayed with him three years; no one else stayed with him longer than three weeks. He was, you see, a madman, far wilder than any wild man I ever met in Australia's western desert. I will give you one anecdote only.

He hired as a carpenter a giant from Trinidad, whom I got to know only as Bob. Bob was meticulous but slow. One day when Bob and I were working at a job requiring us to stand on our toes, Bob decided he had to have a stepladder — so he built one. It was a magnificent stepladder. When Joe returned just before quitting time he began to simmer ominously, for not enough work had been done by Bob and myself. Then he saw the stepladder.

"Bob," he said gently. "What is that?"

"Joe," replied Bob in that oleaginous dialect of the West Indian Negro, "that is a stepladder."

With no visible emotion, Joe asked, "Bob, lend me your hatchet, will you?"

"Yes, Joe, here you are."

Joe in an explosion of anger became an inhuman instrument of destruction, chopping and smashing the stepladder into flinderjigs. Then he walked off without a word.

Bob turned to me and began putting his tools into his box. "John," he said quietly, "I'm quitting. That man is crazy."

Two years ago, when my brother came unexpectedly from Spain (where he is a doctor of laws defending hairy American drug pushers), with a Mercedes-Benz, six intolerable children, and a tent he actually expected to erect on my lawn, I decided at once I had to get rid of him instanter, without violence if possible. I call him one of the grasshoppers of the world, a forty-four-year-old boy, with a history of impressive accomplishments and no sense of responsibility whatever. I thought it would be sufficient to exaggerate some of my less lovable qualities. The plan worked immediately. As he herded his brood through the door he gave me a last word: "You know what's wrong with you? You're just like that crazy Joe Duffy."

I had never recognized the resemblance consciously before the moment, but I suppose he was right. This book was full of pure Joe Duffy behavior before my editor persuaded me we had to stay within the demesne of civilized conduct. She also excised much of my natural profanity; women are apt to be like that, God bless their bloody souls. I do not know where I picked up my uncontrollable uncouth language — not from Joe Duffy, whom I never heard utter an unseemly word, even when he was running some idiot off the job with a hatchet. Possibly the Australians aroused the latency within me, the *baastids*. A bad influence, some would say of Joe Duffy, but I had from him much of undoubted value. I can still drive a nail into a board with my bare hand or put a fist through an ordinary plaster wall; I can still read the octagon scale on a framing square (ask the next carpenter you see whether he can do *that*); and, given the same number of laborers and the same crude tools, I could erect a Stonehenge as good as the original, to stand for another four thousand years. Joe taught me that neither fear nor inadequacy should ever enter a man's thinking. These attitudes of mind are lifesaving qualities in Australia's western desert.

If you are an astute reader — the kind of reader, say, who can detect in Whittaker Chambers's extraordinary autobiography *Witness* the presence of an honest monster — you will see unmentioned paradoxes and inconsistencies here and there. Consistency is the invention of an unreality. *That is the bare bodkin that makes calamity of so long life.* Huckleberry Finn's Jim said he wouldn't give a dern for a million of Solomon's half-babies; I wouldn't give a dern for a million wholebabies. Yet I still weep when I find behind a little-used book on my shelves a feather from a bloody parrakeet four years dead. My work among the whores of Bethel Court showed me first how near his animal ancestors man still is. Somewhere in Joseph Wambaugh's novel *The New Centurions* several policemen argue about where our society's trouble begins — black minorities or brown, rich whites or poor. One puts the quietus on the discussion with the unanswerable conclusion, "They're all assholes." I am therefore prejudiced — not especially against any particular race or society, but against all man-

11

kind, like Jonathan Swift. Prejudice is a precedent judgment, and greatly to be recommended. I will never be caught unaware in a dark alley. I have heard myself called after a public lecture both a Communist and a Fascist. When last I heard from them, Russian scholars were calling me America's most progressive folklorist, and I have been quoted in *Soviet Literature*. But I have also been quoted in the *Reader's Digest*. I will say for the rightists that they pay a man when they quote him. Perhaps for that reason, though I doubt it, I am the Show Fascist at my university. I say these things so that you will not disregard any of my distressing observations by calling me a racist, a Communist, a Fascist, or a pig (I am one of those, too). Give thought to what I say, and be prejudiced against the best-selling books in anthropology.

When I returned early from the Army in 1944, I tried to buy a supernumerary truck from Joe Duffy to go back to California and become a rich builder. Possibly he still rankled from our fight, but in any event neither he nor anyone else would sell me a truck when any kind of business vehicle gave its owner more gasoline ration stamps. So I went to the University of Pennsylvania, where under the influence of two great teachers I majored in English language and literature. Therefore, if I speak to you in Anglo-Saxon, do believe I know what I am talking about.

In 1938 I heard John Jacob Niles, the incredible howler, sing "The Coventry Carol." That sent me into the scholarship of folk song with my beloved teacher MacEdward Leach. Poor white trash turd-kickers in the Army had prepared the way by demonstrating their culture's one art — the performance of folksong. Out of necessity I became a practitioner myself with guitar, banjo, and Autoharp. I have made nine LP albums of this stuff, two or three of which are worth listening to. As the earliest of the second generation of folk-song revivalists, I became the academic proprietor of Woody Guthrie, the greatest of all American folk composers, successor of Joe Hill as the international labor martyr, father of Arlo Guthrie, whose skinny arse I used to kick as a child. Woody Guthrie was also a completely amoral bum who did not become a Communist like his companions only because the party distrusted him and rejected his applications for membership. Now that is what I mean about inconsistencies and paradoxes and calling me names. I also know Aunt Molly Jackson, the original pistol-packin' Mama of the Kentucky coalfields, a wilder woman than ever

12

I found in aboriginal Australia. She was a Communist. She also killed people. And she would weep over a dead parrakeet.

I scraped the bottom of English literature's barrel, getting more splinters under my nails than I ever had done in carpentry. When one young graduate student came to me to ask whether I would supervise his dissertation — a concordance to Edgar A. Guest — I fled into anthropology. There I remain, because in that discipline I can speak with authority on anything I have a mind to speak on. If I say Dr. Richard A. Gould of the American Museum of Natural History is full of prunes (a euphemism in deference to my editor's delicacy), you can be certain that an autopsy upon him (which should take place immediately after I next see him) will scientifically disclose an extraordinary medical phenomenon — that he was composed largely of prunes. *Do not argue with me in my margins about these things.* Anyone as controversial as myself cannot afford to deal in falsehoods or inaccuracies.

The Making of a Reader

That brings up the subject of a reader's responsibilities, which no other author in my immediate memory has spoken to. Just as the audience is responsible for at least 60 per cent of a concert's success, so is the reader responsible for much of a book's value — to him, at least.

When I was more mischievous than I am now, I used to ask my students what effect the discoveries of Gregor Mendel had on the study of evolution in the nineteenth century. Tropismatically they would scribble down the Mendelian Laws, often accurately. But the correct answer to my question was "none." Nobody knew about Mendel's work until it was simultaneously and independently rediscovered in 1900 by De Vries, Correns, and Tschermak. If those students had been proper readers they might have learned more about evolution and the progress of knowledge than memorization of the Mendelian Laws gave them. They might even have probed what Nägeli meant when he brushed Mendel off with the terse comment, "Try hawkweed." Possibly Mendel did go out and experiment with hawkweed; maybe that is why he gave up biology for church politics. In Mendel's case both he and consensus biology were right — and wrong. It is the search that teaches, not the finding. If I say something consensus anthropology disagrees with, it is your responsibility to *look it up*. I do not mean look up some other quaternary product of consensus anthropology; go to the earliest sources and use some common sense. If Montague Francis Ashley Montagu tells you aborigines do not know what makes babies, you need no one to tell you this is nonsense. Do not let his handsome physiognomy, his flowing silver locks waving across the TV screen, his elegant language, and his envied attractiveness to the ladies on the menopause circuit where he makes much of his living, distract you. I once doubted a declaration of his that an Australian blackfellow was his country's chess champion. Knowing a great deal about chess at the time and more than a little about the natives, I looked into the matter and found his aboriginal chess champion of Australia was at the first telling a part-blood aborigine who had competed in a Melbourne club's checker tournament without winning a single game. Recently on television Ashley Montagu played part of a chess game to demonstrate his polymathy. Fair enough. But he had the board set up wrong. All this should give you caution about Ashley Montagu. Take now this caution to the resounding UNESCO manifesto on race: Ashley Montagu wrote that. He also wrote that women are superior to men. There's a wicked notion for you. So do not listen to this gentleman on chess or the Australian aborigines or, not to put too fine a point on it, anything at all, even if the Great White Goddess of Anthropology herself — Margaret Mead — should come along to lend him authority. Do not listen to Margaret Mead, for that matter, whether she is speaking or writing in *Redbook* on the virtues of pot, rioting, or the need to select the best and hairiest of our youth and put them safely in a life capsule underground, there to propagate a new breed when the rest of us have been incinerated in atomic war.

Do not, ever, listen to bachelor anthropologists who tell you that the Venus of Willendorf and similar fat-buttocked Paleolithic sculptures are "fertility figurines." These innocent anthropologists must think babies are carried in the arse. Do not listen to Dee Brown on the Indians, even though you kept his execrable book *Bury My Heart at Wounded Knee* at the top of the best-seller list for nearly a year. I found forty-five errors on the first page of his introduction.

14

How can you find the truth? I cannot give any simple guide, for even our best reference works have besotted themselves into error as Antony besotted himself on the Nile. Watch out for any sign of righteousness in a printed work. Read Harvey Einbinder's *The Myth of the Britannica*.

All I can promise you for this book is what my rough Australian friends call the *good oil*. I will give you some common and uncommon facts about the last Paleolithic people on earth, and in doing so, indict as errors much of what is printed about them in consensus anthropology. (For one test of the latter's authenticity, if you find anyone speaking of the "Arunta" tribe, you will know he pinched his material from Spencer and Gillen.) There is no scientific anthropology here, for anthropology is not a science, no matter how much its young practitioners wish it to be. You can feed apples into a computer until the cows come home, but all you will get out of it is applesauce. I am defiantly an "eyeball anthropologist," a man with what might be called extensive knowledge in this sad age of rampant ignorance, with an insatiable curiosity and a visceral need to know the *whys* of human behavior, and the propensity to form a theory out of any two pieces of data. Watch out for that. I will not lead you down a straight Yellow Brick Road, but off into the poppy fields to look at this or that apparent irrelevancy, which will lead to another irrelevancy — but we will get to the Emerald City at last.

The book is, after all, the story of an adventure, one that perhaps may not be taken again in a world too full of civilization, and in this era of surrogate activity, it may be pleasant for its vicarious experience; but it is intended to be useful as well. We should study the Australian wild people the better to understand ourselves, so that like Candide, we will choose to tend our own garden and *leave things alone*. You will know a great deal more at the end than you do now at its beginning — without any doubt a lot more about the aborigines of inland Australia, more about life and the crazy way both wild men and civilized men live it, and, inevitably, more about me — perhaps more than I intend you should. You might grow to hate me — but hate is a far more reliable emotion than love, so that is something else you will learn. Hate will never abandon you, unless you are foolish enough to accept apologies for hurts done upon you.

I have had to take some liberties with the literal truth. Nothing consequential. A few names are changed, and a few conversations had

15

to be reconstructed, though most are taken verbatim from the daily journal Norman Tindale put a *geis* on me to keep — *no journal this day, no sleep this night.* Some of my shorter trips into the interior produced only one item of interest; in these cases I dropped the trip and put the item into a more consequential journey through the same region.

I have sacrificed some aesthetic orderliness to keep the narrative close to actual chronology. Some of the great moments came too soon for a perfect narrative pattern, but that is the way of great moments. We are lucky if we even recognize them. I close downhill, with a trip of great hardship and danger that did not achieve any of its objects. That, too, is the way of great efforts. Life should come, like expeditions of discovery, to a grand successful conclusion. It does not, for most of us. For all the people in this book it is ending as it should for only two of us: old Tommy Dodd, the rascal, lazing away the last days in the middle of Australia, tended by day and warmed by night, like old King David, by luscious maidens furnished him by the Amatapiti tribal leader, Kata; and Norman B. Tindale, in his seventies now, his monumental life's work in press, and still making mind-shattering discoveries in both anthropology and entomology. At this moment, if I project his expeditionary itinerary right, he is meeting again after thirty years the pygmies he first discovered in the jungles around Lake Barrine. I give him joy in his happiness. The only trouble is, so far as I know, he has not had enough unhappiness to recognize happiness. He chases butterflies. And how is your life going, dear reader, if you are far enough along to see the dark at the end of the tunnel?

There is an incident that keeps intruding into my mind as I let myself sink here into philosophy; I do not know its meaning, or why it should come back to me. It must have something to do with the real meaning of life, and I give it to you as your first problem in being a responsible reader.

My aborigines are stoic people, as they must be. As a fighting people they lose hands and feet as well as lives from wounds. They seem to recover from impalement as quickly as we do from scratches (the Ernabella Mission does not even treat nonfatal fighting wounds), but now and then part of a limb has to go, despite the knowledge of crude splinting. The most tragic of these footless men stumbling through the desert is Old Jacky, well known to the few white men who get into that most difficult country. Jacky was speared through the foot by

16

his brother — why, I do not know; a fight over a woman, most likely. The foot became gangrenous; Jacky cut it off himself with a stone knife and then crept up on his brother and blinded him permanently while he was sleeping. Jacky may be gone now, for he was not at Warburton any time I visited there, but many others remember seeing him (Len Beadell has a photograph of him in his book *Too Long in the Bush*) with his lost foot replaced by an enormous cocoon of kangaroo hide, string, and other bits and pieces of whatever he thought should go into his prosthesis, leading his blinded brother at the end of a long pole.

ONE

INTO
THE PAST

One should enter the most ancient continent in the most ancient way — by sea. Dropping down swiftly in a jet liner at Botany Bay is like landing at Newark, with sand here for swamp, and rushing to Sydney through the sedulous Australian imitation of American squalor. No one ever stopped permanently at Botany Bay, not even the convicts of two centuries ago, despite what you are told to the contrary by British street ballads.

But coming in by sea one passes through the Heads, those virile cliffs that break the raging Antarctic storms. One passage a few hundred yards across leads one from the ship-destroying ocean into what must be the most beautiful harbor in the world, its waters calm and warm, its gentle shores molded by an indulgent and repentant Nature into hundreds of little bays and inlets, here a white sand beach, there a soft hill furred with the inimitable green of gum trees. The first houses are all roofed in red tile, proper in a red continent. Past Shark Island (later you will find there are six species of man-eating sharks indigenous to the harbor); past Fort Denison, a stone battleship once called Pinchgut Island, where the worst of the convict settlers were put to sweat out their mischief; past the Opera House, whose roof is a cluster of stone sails to echo visually the small sailboats in the harbor; and at last under the magnificent Sydney Harbour Bridge to the heart of the city itself. When I first passed under the bridge in 1956, a worker in some bridge trade stood on the top of the steel arc, hundreds of feet above our ship, waving a good Australian welcome.

You may be pleased or disappointed to find Sydney an American city under the superficial differences, but that at least makes an easy transition, an insulation, against culture shock. No visitor could possibly accept the Outback directly from the boat. For a while at least, take residence in sight of the harbor — at Rose Bay, Double Bay, Watson's Bay, Woollahra, Vaucluse; later venture into Woolloomooloo, where as a boy Errol Flynn took more beatings than ever he

21

did in his motion pictures. Stay away from the eastern suburbs, where migrant males from southern Europe stalk through the narrow streets like dogs, panting for the prostitutes leaning in the doorways. Stay away from the slums like Redfern, which differ from inner-city American slums only in the dominant whiteness of their inhabitants.

You will suppose all of Australia is like Sydney, as all of the United States is fundamentally like New York. Your supposition is wrong. Nearly all of Australia's thirteen million inhabitants live in a dozen coastal cities. If you have the turn of mind that escapes the Cartographic Illusion, you will see inhabited Australia as a continuation of Polynesia, a few islands with the sea on one side and the desert sand on the other. Not many city dwellers ever go into either the sea or the sand. They are as different from the Inlanders of this book as Irishmen are different from Turks. Not one in several thousand has ever seen a full-blood aborigine, though three or four university students in every ten will march in protest demonstrations for aboriginal rights.

As cities go, Australian cities are tolerable, even to a hard misanthrope like myself. One of them, my Emerald City of Adelaide, I love. I will describe these cities briefly, each in its proper place, when my expeditionary paths took me through them. But my interest has always been in the Australian heart, the Inland, the Outback. Few first visitors from the civilized world like the Inland; its land is violently hostile to man, its inhabitants — plant, animal, and human — hardly less so. In 1971 the Australians produced for foreign consumption a film entitled *Outback*, which warmed my nostalgic heart. I was shocked to read the reviews of it; all the critics agreed it was a picture of brutal people engaged joyously in brutal life, wild men, with a travesty of proper human behavior as a standard of morality. At the end of the picture the protagonist, driven to the point of suicide by culture shock, flays one of the Inlanders for their crazy conduct. You will condone and admire criminals, brutes, bullies, murderers, wife-beaters, drunkards, human animals, he says, yet you will make an outcast of a man who chooses not to drink with you. The Inlander looks at him, beer can in hand, incredulously, and says at last, "Yer mad, y' baastid." I realized I could not evaluate the picture, since these were for so long my people, whom I loved — though I never drank with them. Of course I was a *mad baastid* for not drinking — never one of my vices — but I was accepted when I hit upon the excuse of stomach cancer. Still, I wondered; is it a humanly acceptable thing to do — to wrestle an old-man kangaroo and cut its throat? I did worse out there, and thought myself none so bad.

Yet my first year in Australia was almost wholly spent in the city, and within the city, in the Mitchell Library, where no kangaroo's throat was ever cut. Admittedly across the street, just beyond the statue to Shakespeare, a death adder once rose up from under an innocent flower and bit a gentle visitor; and a short walk away in the Rose Bay golf course, a golfing gentleman sank up to his gullet in a quicksand bunker. Altogether, a violent country.

I came to that country still in English literature, a visiting Fulbright research scholar, to collect its folksongs, then as little known by the city people as the aborigines. Even with the handicap of teetotalism I collected more than four hundred songs. I have them somewhere still, and once in a while (twice last year) I will hear on television documentaries of Australia my voice singing background to the Outback from the three phonograph records I made in the silent cellar of an old convict-built house. These things are of no consequence. My interest was not in folksongs or even in literature, but in anthropology. Reeling still from that concordance to Edgar A. Guest, I was trying to leap over the wall into a viable discipline.

How does a man make a change of that magnitude in life? By attacking obstruction's wraiths as Joe Duffy attacked the stepladder — with a hatchet of determination. Why are you young people who hold with the old ways remaining in a country that has given away its soul? Why are you not in Australia, where enough of the old America lives to be saved? There another illusion tries to slip by us — why do I speak here to young people? Why are you older folk, who suffer more from the national abandonment of principle, not on your way to Sydney's golden city? In this year of 1972 it is thought a wonder that George Blanda at the age of forty-four should be playing football professionally. Why should he not? Does a man die, like lesser animals, when he has fulfilled his species' requirements of reproduction? As you will learn at the end of this narrative, I am regularly in conflict, often violently, with the militant youth before whom our presidential candidates genuflect in terror, and I have not lost an encounter yet. I count myself in no way unusual — I am too old for vanity and do not speak with it — except in my habit of stopping for a moment to make acquaintance with an unexpected truth I blunder into. That is part of the theme of this book. You will meet in its pages men and women gloriously alive who in these United States would have obediently died had they been confronted by the same experiences, the way a horse in the western desert will die while looking at a water hole. When I tell you, a few pages on, what Ernest Giles told Alfred Gibson when he asked why men die on hard expeditions, listen to me. Gibson did not listen to Giles and he died two days later.

But that truth was years ahead of me when I decided to use my first Australian trip to move into anthropology. I went first and properly to Professor A. P. Elkin of Sydney University, so famous as Australia's only academic professor of anthropology that his book *The Australian Aborigines: How to Understand Them* had even been pirated by the Russians. I asked him for a list of bibliographies to find out what had been done and what within my competence had yet to be done. His reply was shocking: there were no bibliographies, beyond one made by Robert Etheridge in 1895 and a catalogue of holdings on the Australian natives in the New York Public Library assembled by G. F. Black in 1913. Well, then; there was my dissertation: make a comprehensive bibliography, read as many of the items as I could find, and analyze the published scholarship for a study to be titled *Anthropology in Australia*. But first, I asked Professor Elkin, how many items was I likely to find? About three thousand, he guessed. Fine; that was not beyond my power and time to compile. At the end of eight months of almost daily work in all the public and private libraries in Australia and speaking with all but one of Australia's scholars, I had not three thousand references but fifteen thousand. Had I not been so hopelessly deceived by Professor Elkin's estimate, I should not have undertaken so massive a job. Ignorance produces more results than genius.

But all along the way I stumbled into lucky decisions, like putting my references on slips of paper rather than the conventional cards. On cards, the bulk would have been too great for me to carry the work through Europe and the United States as I subsequently did — in a cabin bag tied to my ankle. I trust circumstances no more than I trust people. I had many adventures with that bag — like discussing the project and its problems with Turks in loud and slow French and being suspected in the Vatican of spiriting away some of that mass of golden trash the Popes assembled over the centuries. By the time I had typed the last item (a notice of the death of Albert Namatjira on 17 August 1959), I was relieved to say, as Dr. Samuel Johnson said two centuries earlier when he finished the harmless drudgery of his *Dic-*

tionary, "I dismiss this work with frigid tranquillity, having little to fear or hope from censure or from praise." So my work *Bibliography of the Australian Aborigines and the Native Peoples of Torres Strait* went to press in Sydney with 22,638 items. So much for listening to the advice of authorities. It remains the standard general reference, though the Australian Institute of Aboriginal Studies is still working out of the book for improved local lists. I caught them at it once — four people grubbing away with the book and thousands of cross-reference cards — and was greatly amused, since I had had in the meantime a fight with the Institute's director, who hid behind a door and would not see me. *Gone to China to help with the rice crop.*

It was this millstone on my back that sent me to Adelaide and one of the few real friendships of my life. While the Sydney University Department of Anthropology and its satellite, the Department of Anthropology at the National University in Canberra, received the attention, respect, and financial assistance of the rest of the world (that is to say, the United States), a small band of scholarship's most dedicated men labored in an almost unknown vineyard, the South Australian Museum. They gave me there a high stool and part of a table as a working area piled high with sticks and stones and bits of bone. On all my trips to Adelaide that has been my place, and I hope to sit there again many times before I become a contribution to the bones.

What fine men — some rough, like Peter Aitken, the burly mammalogist who would have wrestled and eaten a diprotodon, if diprotodons still lumbered over the Australian earth (I once saw Peter threaten to brain a fellow scientist with a whale's humerus in a dispute over where it should be attached to the whale's skeleton), to gentle H. M. Cooper, who worked at the desk behind me in all my sojourns at the museum. Dear Mr. Cooper! A man that nature should provide for our governance, if there was anything to natural selection. For more than thirty years he excavated by himself one principal site, Hallett Cove, repository of Australia's most ancient stone tools, discovering a few weeks before his death still another rich area of the earliest Kartan culture, laid down on that beach three hundred centuries ago. Very frail and weak in his last years, Mr. Cooper came daily to his desk to bury himself in the stone artifacts made by men too long dead to have left the merest fragment of their bones, looking up only at noon to nibble at a bit of bread and cheese, all he could afford to eat on his pension of ten dollars a week. In those days on the edge of his evening he was often felled by one of the cowardly blows of age, but instead of going into a hospital as we should have done in his place, he went always up to his mountain, discovered by his hero, the explorer Matthew Flinders, and named by one of mine, Governor Edward John Eyre. It is an arduous climb from its base, a circular pesthole of poisonous snakes, and in his place we should have gone there to die. But he always came back as full of health as if he had visited the fountain of youth. In his last illness Mount Remarkable was impossible for him; his eyes betrayed him and in his blindness, he died as he should not have wanted to do, helpless in his bed. We thought he had been forgotten, but in his cortege hundreds of cars followed to do him honor.

In the locked passageway to the large room that housed anthropology, T. D. Campbell worked with films or worked with teeth (there is a strong dental tradition among South Australian anthropologists). His gruff appearance and threatening cigar kept us from intimacy until much later, when I learned that at the University of Adelaide he had been a teacher of the woman who was to become my wife. He was a misanthrope also, but he always remembered her as one of the university's most brilliant and most beautiful students. But in 1956 she was ten years in my future, so he and I conversed only in growled greetings.

In that enormous room I was to know so well in the years to come were not only the remains of man (more than a thousand persons managed to get some of their bones into what immortality the museum could assure), but odds and ends and bits and pieces of anything man had held, or held any interest for the students of man. So many things here that it shakes out the mind to appreciate how the few workers the museum has had in its hundred years could have gathered them all, much less understood what they were and why they were. Sealed in a case to the right of my stool, a fossil bone of an extinct animal waiting for science to develop the means to ascertain whether the scratches on it were indeed what its collector believed — the tooth marks of a dingo (if so, then man with his dogs had been here when the diprotodons lived). Behind me the fragmented and mineralized skull of Tartangan Boy reposed, as dead today as he had been yesterday and two million yesterdays before that. Mr. Cooper sat at his desk behind me, moving as slowly as a tardigrade among his stones, cataloguing a boxful of flint implements brought to the museum a few weeks earlier by an amateur archaeologist. Over by the door an artist-secretary was drawing sketches of stone tools for an article to be published in the *Records of the South Australian Museum* and buried as Mendel's work had been buried. On a table directly behind Mr. Cooper was a crate of carefully wrapped artifacts just acquired by the museum — a priceless collection of aboriginal weapons gathered by explorer Charles Sturt in 1844 when he probed three thousand miles from Adelaide into the desert's red heart searching for the "Inland Sea." On the walls hung artifacts too large to rest elsewhere and paintings of notable aborigines and by notable aborigines, of which the most prized is Albert Namatjira's only representation of a sacred ceremony. In secret closed cases aboriginal *tjurunga* (sacred boards thought to hold a man's soul) and other objects from the *tjukurpa* (the aborigines' Dreaming), too holy for public exposure, waited for the visit of any properly initiated "oldman" — *wati yina* — who wished to see and revere the things given in trust to the museum so they would not suffer the desecration rampant in the changing world. So valuable, all these things, that one is not able to appreciate them as valuable — like thousand-dollar bills to a bank teller. Just to put one's hand upon them is an experience too rich to be forgotten. Imagine — a spear touched by Charles Sturt!

But of all these things and all these people, nothing will remain more firmly with me than Norman Tindale, then a generous man who gave me two weeks of his time in searching out obscure references for my bibliography in his own papers and in the South Australian Archives in an old building behind the museum, and in the years ahead my friend, teacher, companion, and benefactor. He and I were to travel alone more than fifteen thousand miles in aboriginal Australia, and never once in that distance, never once in fifteen years, did he display the least impatience or annoyance with me. To appreciate what that means one must know that the ordinary distance other persons can bear my contentiousness is fifteen miles or fifteen minutes.

Norman is unforgettable. On many occasions we would meet an aborigine with whom he had worked or talked for the briefest period years ago and he would be remembered; but the best experience of Norman's memorability belongs not to me but to my wife. She undertook the field research for her doctoral dissertation on Groote Eylandt far north in the Gulf of Carpentaria. Groote is fairly hostile tropical country occupied by the Wanindiljaugwa tribe, well reputed to be too inhospitable for the good of their visitors. For this and other reasons the island was not settled by white men from the time of its discovery in 1623 by a Dutch navigator until the missionary Warren in 1919 made a brief survey for a mission establishment. Norman Tindale was the first white man to spend more than a few nights there. In 1921 he and another missionary circumnavigated the island in a small boat, filling in the mangrove swamp breaks in the maps made by its first circumnavigator, Matthew Flinders, one hundred and eighteen years earlier. Norman stayed there for thirteen months, gathering data on the bugs and the aborigines. When my wife went there in 1968 she had prepared herself by virtually memorizing the three volumes of field notes lent her by Norman. I had better let her tell the story.

Old Charlie (Galiowa Wurramarrba, leader of the Iritja [moiety]) sent a message that he'd like to see me – simple curiosity about my role and status, really.

He was sitting on the ground under a tree with his wife and two youngest children. Another elderly man and his wife were in the same shade, the man lying down, dozing.

My conversation with Charlie, his wife as our interpreter, covered all manner of polite inanities until he asked, "Why you come here?"

"I was sent by a man who came here long ago."

"What man?"

"That man from long ago from the Old Mission. That man at Emerald River long time ago."

"No man."

"The first white man to live among the people. He was here when you had the ordeal by spears for killing a man to get his woman. You remember, Galiowa, you crept in the night to spear that woman's man in the back while he slept. You won, huh? Remember?"

"Maybe" — *eyes beginning to shine with memories of less docile days.*

"But you had to accept the ordeal — stand there while the dead man's kin threw their spears at you, dodging, ducking, twisting about." *Almost a smile but silent.*

"And this man of my people, this tall young man stood with you and called for peace. Then, as you jumped a spear, you asked him for tobacco — right there as you faced the dangers together."

Galiowa's eyes were glistening now with many emotions, but it was the other old man on the ground who sat up as I tried to press my claim to the position of heir apparent to those old relationships.

28

"Well, this white man, who was here then, he's too old to come back now [mental apologies to Norman], so he sent me in his place to see the people and talk with you of many things and learn with you."

Galiowa's companion, now bolt upright, suddenly spoke: "My name 'Borneo.'"

"Yes! He named you, Borneo, and many others, too — Aru, Badu, Banda, Java, Papua — and he wrote the name on a piece of wood and hung it around your neck so that you were special friends."

Both old men gave laughing, choking cries as they called together, "Tindalyiya, Tindalyiya!"

Forty-seven years — almost half a century — and remembered by people who had no writing, no reading, none of our devices to keep the past alive.

After his university studies in the other academic disciplines and his close acquaintance with Sir Baldwin Spencer (author with F. J. Gillen of the classic Aranda ethnographies), Norman joined the permanent staff of our South Australian Museum, thus becoming Australia's only professional archaeologist, a position he was to hold alone for twenty-eight years. It was in his capacity as an archaeologist that I first worked with him, several years after my bibliography quest.

Digging for the Dead Men

It was altogether proper that I should have made my acquaintance with the Pitjandjara dead. I lack too much in the social graces to have met them as my wife met the Wanindiljaugwa.

It is true, however reluctant laymen are to believe it, that better than 90 per cent of a museum's holdings are never put on display. Behind the locked doors of the South Australian Museum, in cavernous cellars and subcellars where the Hunchback of Notre Dame would have felt quite at home, repose hundreds of thousands of artifacts, brought out of the western deserts for the most part, but also from the edges of the sea and the eroded mountains to the east. I sometimes feel, in spite of all the valid objections to the idea, that laymen ought on occasion be made to see the enormous numbers of ancient implements recovered by archaeologists. We would have less trouble convincing the skeptical that sequences are based usually on massive redundancy of examples. Just saying there are hundreds of thousands of artifacts in the South Australian Museum is as futile in reaching the average mind as saying hundreds of thousands of Chinese were killed in this or that revolution. It would be good, too, to let the layman touch a stone tool from the intangible past. A man's soul must be dead if he can hold an ancient stone axehead and not think of the artisan who chipped it into shape so long ago that not a fragment of him remains, not so much as a stain in the earth.

And if only there were some way to communicate the ironies, the paradoxes, the incredible coincidences, and what I have come through seeing so many examples to call the Banal Impossibilities, of what perishes — and what remains for whose hand to find! My great teacher MacEdward Leach the medievalist, lying in a foxhole in the First World War, a bullet snapping into the mud and throwing up a small stone disc to hit him in the face; his taking it and recognizing it as a Celtic charm with the name of its maker inscribed upon it; his thought that he might leave in this hole part of his rifle for some later soldier to find — "I wonder what that man will deduce of me." Bones himself now, MacEdward, a man who should have been helmsman to Maeldun in the Celtic Dreaming. The Norse goldsmith, scratching his name and claim as craftsman on a pair of golden helmet horns — *Ek Hlewingastaz Holtingaz Horna Tawiba* ("I, Hlewinga Holtinga, made the horns") — could he have had the least spark of a forethought that he was writing what sixteen hundred years later would be the oldest fragment of the Germanic language ever found? And Ernest Giles, when he crossed the claypan Wrakina, could he have given any thought, for all his introspectiveness, that what he dropped there would be found in the next century by one of his strongest defenders, myself?

How little and yet how much man leaves behind him. Of himself, how little. Demographers reckon thirty-six billion people lived and died during the time when the entire world was in the Old Stone Age; but of all these human beings, fossils now in perpetuity, what remains could be lifted by one strong man. A football stadium filled with three thousand tons of living flesh, and what would be left for the archaeologist in ten thousand years? One tooth, perhaps. Only one tooth was found in the last hours of the great excavation at Choukoutien, but Davidson Black was able to extrapolate that into *Sinanthropus pekinensis.*

Of his works, how much remains after he has disappeared, and how capriciously the selection is made by whatever forces of preservation work upon them. We know ancient man not by what he treasured, but by what he threw away; from the oldest cultures, a few stone tools; from the beginnings of civilization, broken pottery, a bit of metal.

Consider the average band of my Pitjandjara; two dozen men, women, and children, foraging for edible plants and watching for an animal large enough to spear. What would such a band leave behind at their deaths to let a curious posterity know they once existed? None of their wooden tools would carry the message, for these are organic and would crumble into unidentifiable dust as quickly as the bodies of their owners. If they carried stone tools with them — no more than a possibility of that — these would endure, unless some later comers found them and fractured them into something different.

All the treasures of my wild men are ephemeral, carried in the mind. Left on the ground, nothing of value except as a thing to convey knowledge. Even alive the Pitjandjara have so little that an old-man, a *wati yina,* will know the whole of his culture. But not for many thousands of years has any Western man known more than the slightest perceptible fraction of one per cent of his accumulated civilization. Terenyi, my Bell Rock Jacky, naked and utterly ignorant of white man's civilization less than a dozen years ago, knows all of his people's material culture and most of its immaterial components. Old Kuta, head of the Malupiti Pitjandjara at Amata, knows all of both, and more of the white man's way of life than the Amata administrators suspect.

One of the innumerable paradoxes making anthropology so hard a subject for a student to master is the fact that savagery makes more use of knowledge than civilization, at least for any single individual. It is the way of whatever orders the universe that as humanity progresses through human intelligence, knowledge becomes less important than things. From the day that unremembered man-ape of ancient Africa took up the first bone club to batter the succulent brains out of a baboon it was inescapable that a computer would make the multiplication table a frivolous piece of useless knowledge. Even more ironic is the probability that as soon as near-man became intelligent enough to begin constructing culture with his club, he marked the physical decline of his own intelligence. My wife believes Neanderthal Man was more intelligent than ourselves. It must be so, for with the Neanderthals began the preservation of weaklings in body, mind, and spirit, the perpetuation of imperfect genes against the struggle of natural selection to make men perfect.

The materialism deplored by philosophers (comfortable in their materialism) is neither good nor bad in the grand scheme of nature, where man is the demiurge whose destiny is to make things to replace him. In his most primitive state he has next to nothing; he is little more than an animal with a high intelligence his restricted way of life will not let him develop. Ninety-nine per cent of the time the human species has spent on earth so far has been lived in the Old Stone Age, in a culture no more advanced than that of the aborigines in Australia's most remote deserts. Only very lately, when with the discovery of agriculture man became able substantially to change his environment, did he advance to what we agree is real humanity. Not without difficulty, even today, when it is fashionable for bored housewives and aimless men to interest themselves in "saving the ecology." The mountain town where I am writing is now considering an environmental ordinance that will prohibit a man from grubbing out his dandelions or exterminating his termites. Our council would be better employed indicting that Australopithecine who — or which — with his club altered his ecology and made a man of himself. Instead it condemns DDT, which my friend Dr. Thomas H. Jukes of the University of California Division of Medical Physics calls "one of the safest compounds ever to be placed in contact with human beings." Even an agency of the United Nations admits nearly a billion — a billion — deaths of human beings were averted by DDT's conquest of malaria, and not a single human fatality has been successfully charged to DDT. Yet the Director of Information for the National Wildlife Federation calls DDT "a global insanity." Perhaps it is — saving another billion lives. Things like this have driven many scholars in general anthropology — some of them my own friends — into the relative safety of digging up the dead. But on the general point of my wild men, their environment is intractable to change, and it therefore forced the desert dwellers to rely on their own adaptability rather than on the tools and impediments of material culture.

My earliest archaeological trips with Norman Tindale were to the earliest of Australian cultures, incongruously close to our museum. Just south of Adelaide, and now being engulfed by the growing city, lies a mass of sites once occupied by Australia's first inhabitants, none of whom left us a stone tool less than eleven thousand years old. At Moana on a day when the bibliography bored us both, Norman traced for me the barely perceptible meander of a stream long dead (and long since buried by a housing development). Along its sinuous banks we found several little scatterings of fractured stone — the waste of a beach boulder some aboriginal warrior smashed into a tool he carried away. Lying on the surface of the earth, this evidence of an ancient stoneworker's presence must have been passed over and stepped upon by thousands of people walking for a swim in the Southern Ocean. It is all there, everywhere, but as Dr. Siegbert Tarrasch said for the brilliant combinations in a chess position, *it must be seen.*

To do archaeology — surface archaeology at any rate — with any hope whatever of success, one must focus one's eyes naturally at one's feet. My eyes, unhappily, focus at eight miles without glasses and eighteen inches with their assistance. I once led my wife-to-be, when I was courting her away from her affluence and fame as South Australia's first lady of television, into a fine microlithic site to show her how archaeologists work. The site was what we call a "blow-out," a circular sand valley where winds frequently expose areas ordinarily covered by sand to reveal the heavier stone artifacts below. Joan is, as you will see — and you will have to forgive my speaking about her now and then — one of those know-all people (as the Australians call them) who actually do know it all. Not understanding this at the time, and wishing to save her the disappointment inevitable to beginners when we began looking around for the tiny stone implements of the period Tindale called the Mudukian, I told her the truth, that all the Museum's archaeologists and amateurs privy to the site's location had been over this ground literally on hands and knees many times, spending the whole of a day to find, if they were lucky, one little curved point known as a *bondi* or a thumbnail-shaped serrated knife-tooth called a crescent. It was, I said, not at all unlikely that the winds could blow around this bowl until our Savior came again and she would not find anything of human manufacture. Just look around, I told her, and appreciate standing where primitive man worked at his tool-making three thousand years ago while his women fished over in that nearby depression, where a limb of the sea once intruded. She looked, and within half an hour found half a dozen classic *bondi* and as many crescents. I should have been alerted immediately to this new threat to my territoriality, but I was, like Caesar and Antony, too besotted to see anything of that insignificance. Way led on to way, we married, I brought her to the United States, she gave up television for anthropology, took her A.B. in 1968, her M.A. in 1969, and her Ph.D. in 1970, with an unblemished "A" record all the way, and presently believes she knows more about all these things than I do.

Unlike the massive lump of ordinary university students she had already accepted the fact of tool classifications. My own students will not allow the validity of the tool samples I show them and tell me they can pick those things up from their driveways. The *tula* adze blade is an example; it does indeed look like an ordinary bit of stone — unless you have seen several of them, all as near to being identical as makes no difference. Its subtle angles are visible in the many and invisible in the few. A new book by an eastern Australian archaeologist shows a page of photographs of *tula*, not one of which in fact is a *tula*, yet I have seen Mr. Cooper sitting at his worktable buried over his elbows in hundreds of them, alike as so many bottle caps. But trying to convince students that these things have a complex of characteristics unmistakably identifying them is like trying to convince them that Willie Z. Foster had a complex of characteristics unmistakably identifying him as a Communist.

Within walking distance of Moana Beach — and accessible only by walking, the ancient cliffs overlooking Hallett Cove (Mr. Cooper's favorite site) juts almost perpendicularly out of the sea. For geologists this fifty-one-acre area is one of the earth's most interesting small terrains, for the variety and classic sharpness of its strata. During its six hundred million years of existence Hallett Cove was in turn, as the South Australian Museum's geologist J. M. Scrymgour summarized it, "a tidal flat, part of a mountain range, covered by thick ice, submerged beneath the sea, and cliffs overlooking a vast alluvial plain." In the time of its deposition Australia was still part of the macro-continent of Gondwanaland.*

But little of its six hundred million years is of any interest to us as archaeologists. The cove's history begins with the early settler John Hallett, who found the place in 1837 while searching for strayed stock. Its human prehistory begins rather earlier, with the first aborigines who sat down here and broke sea boulders into tools toward the end of the Ice Age about forty thousand years ago (though the great body of Pleistocene Ice lay over the northern hemisphere, a small hand of ice pushed its fingers across parts of southern Australia). The tools lay undisturbed and unseen until Mr. Cooper found the first assemblage in 1934. About that time Norman Tindale and Brian Maegraith discovered similar artifacts just across the Backstairs Passage on Kangaroo Island directly off the southern coast and were calling them "Kartan Culture Implements" from *Karta,* the mainland aborigines' name for the uninhabited island. Such things were seen and recorded at Fulham in 1893 by Samuel White, but that was long before anyone knew that sequences could be determined for the native cultural evolution.

During the next thirty-six years Mr. Cooper made two hundred visits to the cove (and nearly that many to Kangaroo Island sites), gathering stones and making observations, and between his work there and others' work elsewhere, Norman Tindale's first projected phase of Australian aboriginal culture, the Kartan, was established not only

* Some time after the Carboniferous Period Australia split off from its now distant neighbors South America and Antarctica. Not long ago this great continent "Gondwanaland" was rubbished by serious geographers, but now highly sophisticated instruments and scientific methods have established its prehistorical existence as fact. The hardest evidence is appropriately geological — the Gondwana rock system, almost identical in South America, Australia, and Antarctica, is one example, but other more ephemeral things point also to a common homeland: fossils of many kinds in Antarctica; the one rabbit form that established itself so devastatingly in Australia and the virus that nearly killed it off both derived from South America; the Argentine ant (*Iridomyrmex humilis*), a serious pest in Western Australia; several species of freshwater fish, very ancient in evolutionary history; Amazonian psittacosis in certain wild Australian parrots; a number of molluscs and crayfish (the crayfish family *Parastacidae* is found only in South America and Australia); and the prickly pear cactus (*Opuntia* spp.) and its lethal parasite *Cactoblastis cactorum* — not to mention entire families of insects the entomologist Paramonov calls "Paleoantarcts" — bind South America and Australia together in bonds almost as tight as the geological evidence of affinity. Students do not believe any of this, though they believe in Atlantis and the Lost Continent of Mu.

35

in South Australia but as far north over the sea as Malaysia and Thailand.

The Kartan was the culture of the first Negrito immigrants, and a poor thing it must have been. The type artifact, called a *karta*, is a horsehoof-shaped chopper made in the crudest fashion from stream boulders of quartzite or some similar stone hard enough to hold an edge. Imagine an extremely rough-skinned pomegranate with its lower third sliced away and its edges trimmed along the flat bottom, and you have a fair image of a *karta*. Some have been resharpened so often as to appear almost spherical. Students will not accept the *karta* as anything more than an ordinary rock, such as they throw at police, though on one especially frustrating class occasion, I chopped through most of one leg of my lectern desk to prove its utility. One of these days I expect to chop through most of one student to make the point. I will concede I have my own doubts about the *karta* as having been simply a hand-held chopper — that extraordinarily flat bottom puzzles me. Norman tells me in his gentle way, "the cleavage surface," and I give him in return a disdainful look.

A second characteristic tool of the Kartan assemblage is the *sumatralith*, most simply described as a smooth stream boulder a bit smaller than an ostrich egg, shaped the same, and broken in half along its broad axis, leaving a rough chopper about two pounds in weight. The rough undersurface is trimmed by percussion to give a cutting edge of no impressive sharpness. Stone flakes broken off during its manufacture were used by the Kartan folk as knives.

The *sumatralith* is named for an identical tool type found in Sumatra and intervening places; its congeners link the Kartan culture* and its makers with their ancestors' original hiving place in mainland China. The "boats" of their primal southward migration did not have to be more than the simplest flotation devices, for open water between Australia and the Asian mainland during the final phase of glaciation did not extend more than twenty miles — probably much less, for even the latest official charts of the Torres Strait–Gulf of Carpentaria waters show far fewer islands than are actually present. The difficulty of migration postulated by consensus anthropology is still another ex-

* "Culture," used generally and capitalized where there may be ambiguity, means all the things that the human species owns to distinguish it from lesser animals; a "culture" is that portion of the whole identifying a named society. The latter is recognized by a selection of characteristic implements peculiar to that society.

ample of what I call the Cartographic Illusion, the fallacy of believing that what is on maps is also on the earthly areas they purport to represent. With land always in sight, these island-hopping migrants could have made the journey without imagination, daring, or advanced technology. In the coastal areas of northwestern Australia today aborigines tie branches and small tree limbs together in the roughest kind of raft and allow the tides to take them well out to sea and off-shore islands, and back again. The natives do not even use paddles. Nothing to it.

In every part of the tropical Old World the first comers after the hominid near-humans about whom we still know so little were Negritos, small and simple people so poor in material culture and so insignificant in physique as to suggest to racists that they were children playing at being men. Though they had the land first, there was no recognition of ownership through possession in the savage era of man's development, and they were accordingly and inevitably displaced everywhere by the larger later comers — in Africa by the Negroes (except in South Africa, where they ran into the Dutch about a hundred years before the large Negroid invaders arrived), in Asia by the Mongoloids, in Australia by the Australoids. Everywhere they were driven into what we call "refuge areas" or "culture pockets," places where no sensible human being would enter without the most compelling reason (Oklahoma before the oil, as a North Temperate example), and forgotten until modern times. The near identity of culture in African pygmy societies living in hidey-holes a thousand miles apart is sufficient to prove the general process. These isolated and unimportant peoples lived on in their remoteness. The one significant exception to this general law of demography was Australia.

Significant exceptions ought always to be an urgent question for scholarly resolution. What I like to call the "Suspect Singleton" is intolerable in science — even social science — when important theoretical conclusions hang upon it.

In 1935 Norman Tindale found a handful of old photographs at the Warburton Mission which purportedly had been taken in the far northwest of Western Australia. One picture showed a line of naked aborigines of a rather infantile physique standing in front of a brush-and-leaves shelter. By anthropological detective work more appropriate to 221-B Baker Street than the edge of Australia's southwestern desert, Norman deduced that there was too much foliage for the Great

37

Sandy, where Colonel Egerton Warburton was supposed to have taken the pictures in the few periods when he was not worrying about death from thirst. Moreover, it seemed to his one eye that the leaves of the shelter were banana leaves, and if they were in fact or probability banana leaves, the photograph could not have been taken in the northwest but about two thousand miles away in the northeast in the only place wild banana plants grow in Australia — specifically in a small tropical rain forest around Lake Barrine on Queensland's Atherton Plateau. He pushed his hypothesis further: if these were banana leaves, the people by comparison of size were pygmies. He could have allowed the leaves were extra-large banana leaves, but this would have required the postulation of another Suspect Singleton instead of the resolution of the one already to be accounted for. His own intelligence as well as Occam's Razor — the logical prohibition against unnecessarily multiplying entities — made him opt for the pygmies. His announcement of the hypothesis was rejected by his colleagues in Sydney — the tail that wags the anthropology dog in Australia. So there was nothing for it but to go up to Lake Barrine and find the pygmies. In 1938 Tindale and Jo (Joseph B.) Birdsell, whose dispiriting letter to me I quoted earlier, went up into Queensland jungle (taking as you will see, the ten-thousand-mile western perimeter route) and found them. It was that simple. Just a comparative handful of a few hundred souls remaining from what once had to be a continental population. These people were not unknown; indeed, most were living on isolated mission stations, but they were hidden like a lost book in a library. Some Australian anthropologists and at least one important American subscriber to their school still ignore the existence of these people or dismiss them as a tribe of dwarfs — which, if true, would constitute a genetic miracle – but the fact of their presence allows the only reasonable explanation of the peopling of early Australia.

Before the discovery of these negritoid Barrineans, as Jo Birdsell named them, the theoretical prehistory of Australia was based on intuition — some brilliant, some erratic, some brilliantly erratic, some crazy — like the postulation of an ancient web-footed race (they needed these here now webbed feet, you see, to swim down from Malaysia). That delightful old rascal Franz Weidenreich, proprietor of Sinanthropus pekinensis, *had always persisted in the theory that the modern Australian natives descended right*

38

Professor Joseph B. Birdsell and adult male Barrinean native,
Atherton Plateau near Lake Barrine, Queensland

from his fanged Pithecanthropus *through* Homo soloensis *to the fossil* Wadjak Man, *whose morphological credentials as an Australoid forebear are good. The Doubting Thomas of American paleoanthropology, Aleš Hrdlička, was not convinced of the alleged primitiveness of the aborigines, and disposed of the Tasmanians as simply a local deviation. Giuseppi Sergi was just as certain that the Tasmanians were a separate genus of hominids — "Hesperanthropus tasmanianus" — a classification hardly flattering to the much abused and now extinct people and certainly not in accord with the compassionate principle of* de mortuis nil nisi bonum. *One would think it sufficient for the Tasmanians to have been exterminated in 75 years of contact — a bit more than that, actually; Norman Tindale (again with a discovery!) found that the last of the Tasmanian race, the tragic Truganini, was outlived by two Tasmanian women in the Kangaroo Island harem of an American pirate.*

The sequence and process of Australia's prehistorical settling seem clear now, despite the occasionally flashing but decreasingly illuminating fulminations of some scholars too publicly committed to opposing positions. Some scholars persist in the profitless enterprise of living on after their theories have been killed. Toward the end of the last glaciation three waves of distinctly different people surged down the Indonesian corridor into the country at two probable points of entry: Cape York on the east (by land from New Guinea across the emerged Sahul Shelf) and Cape Croker on the west (by sea from Timor and other islands in the Sunda chain). The first of these people were the Negrito ancestors of the Lake Barrine folk, simple hunter-gatherers, pygmoid in stature and infantile in general physique, resembling in many respects their Bushman cousins in Africa. Presumably they spread over the continent in accordance with recognized principles of population movement (Birdsell has charted this meticulously). Radiocarbon datings of undoubted human occupation are moving the date of their arrival to forty thousand years before the present.

The next wave of immigrants carried in the true Australoids (or primitive Caucasoids, as some prefer to call them) to displace their tiny predecessors, exterminating most in obedience to the biological Law of Competitive Exclusion; driving others to dismal refuge areas in Queensland's jungle, southeast Victoria, and southwestern Western Australia (where Norman and I found a few strongly persuasive descendants); and intermarrying with the remainder. To these robust but primitive-featured people Professor Birdsell has given the name

"Murrayian," for the Murray River separating Victoria from New South Wales and cutting its weary way to the sea through dry South Australia. On the Murray is located the cave shelter known as Devon Downs, where Norman Tindale discovered the *pirri* points and other implements typical of the culture of the Murrayians. These are the classical Australoids of fact and fiction. Their miscegenation with the indigenous Negritos produced the dihybrid race of Tasmanians, who possibly fled southward into that cold refuge island while Bass Strait was still a land bridge.

The dominant artifact of these early Murrayians was the *pirri*, a handsome projectile point worthy of comparison with the best products of more advanced — or at least more generally admired — Paleolithic peoples in the Old and New Worlds, very like the Yuma Point of America and the Solutrean Point of Europe. It is a thing hard to find, since it looks like the leaves of several of the more common dry-country eucalypts. After picking up a few hundred gum leaves with decreasing eagerness, one does not even attempt to pick up real *pirri* points. I admire the *pirri*, but for no good reason. It is an example of the beautiful products of time-wasting found at deteriorating periods in the evolution of all societies: it is handsome, but it breaks easily and is far less utilitarian than a spearpoint made of mulga wood. From the Murrayian culture my favorite tool is the *tula* — an adze blade, a parallel segment of a discoid usually about two inches long and three-quarters of an inch wide, shaped in a smooth concave curve worked out of the flint bulb of percussion on the cutting edge. This implement was fixed to a handle with *keti* or a similar resin gum, like the adzes of the present-day aborigines. I suppose what I like about the *tula* is that smooth, gently curved back; held in the pocket it makes an excellent worry-stone — a function I doubt the original fabricators had in mind. But then they did not have the worries I have.

Finally, some ten thousand years ago, to put an arbitrary date on the movement, the third wave of "Carpentarians" (named for the Gulf of Carpentaria, around whose shores they currently flourish) entered Australia. Tall, black, proud, ferocious, these folk are well represented by Joan's Wanindiljaugwa friends. We do not know much about their ancient tools — archaeology has not prospered in the tropical north.

All of these people — the pygmoid Barrineans, the hairy golden

Murrayians, the part-blood Tasmanians who remain, and the tall black Carpentarians — are physically distinctive and can properly be called "a people" as distinguished from "a culture." Unfortunately, there is a persistent tendency, honored by tradition, in all anthropologists, Norman Tindale and myself included, to use the two terms interchangeably and sometimes to suppose a new culture (as determined by a different complex of artifacts) necessitates a new people. Australia is not the only place this mistake is cherished; it is universal wherever old things are dug up. In the American Southwest archaeologists divide the general Anasazi culture (named so by the Navajo, who know nothing at all about it) into a "Basketmaker" and a "Pueblo" dichotomy, partly because of a fairly sharp artifactual change and partly because the "Basketmakers" had long heads and the "Pueblos" broad heads. Cranial indices have been used too long by physical anthropologists to be abandoned now (though they are almost wholly useless for anything), so one must imagine this new broad-headed race coming into the Mesa Verde region and exercising early American genocide upon the hapless Basketmakers. But everybody knows the long heads became broad when, about eight hundred years ago, some dominant nut decided back-flattened heads should be fashionable. No doubt of it — fashion can change the human anatomy astonishingly. See Gina Lollobrigida in her old pictures on television before breasts became fashionable — or Raquel Welch before silicone. Let us go hastily back to the Anasazi. At the end of their deteriorating evolution, there appeared in San Ildefonso Pueblo a master potter, Maria Martinez, who began producing a unique black-on-black ware. Had this happened in the unrecorded past, we might well have had another new people, the Black Pottery Makers — or in a simplification admitting another ambiguity, the Black Potters. No exaggeration here: those folk who built all those barrows on the Salisbury Plain around Stonehenge and buried their dead in them together with their equivalent of beer cans are known to archaeologists as the Bell Beaker People. If we persist in this confusing business, some of our professional posterity a few thousand years from now might be writing books about a ferocious, genocidal Automobile People who invaded the North American continent from France (*vide* linguistic evidence like *chassis, carburetor, coupé, sedan,* and the various tribes — *Cadillac, Chevrolet, Renault, Citroën*) and exterminated the indigenous Horse People (though miscegenating with some in the back seats of their principal artifact), who retreated to refuge areas, culture pockets, in the hostile western regions, where they are known as Cowboys.

Let us therefore distinguish the "peoples" from the "cultures" clearly and summarily. Ignoring any adverse argument emanating from the Sydney School, here is the culture chronology from wide areas of Australia:

KARTAN: From possibly 40,000 years BP (before the present) to 11,000 years BP. Associated with the Barrinean race, a pygmoid people, greatly diminished in number, but still existing. In the Post-Pleistocene period when this culture flourished, there was great variation in climate and topography; during the Tazewell Phase (17,000 BP) the eustatic level was lowest — about three hundred feet below the present level of the sea — much seawater having been drawn up in ice. Principal archaeological sites are Kangaroo Island, Hallett Cove, Sellicks Beach, Fulham, Moana, and other places in South Australia, but other isolated sites have been identified in the extreme north and south parts of Western Australia, and in a narrow geographical band running from South Australia into Victoria, New South Wales, central Australia, and south Queensland. Artifacts include the karta sumatralith, kodj (a two-element axe, hammer and hatchet), worimi (a specialized cleaver), flake knives, and hammerstones.

TARTANGAN: Floruit 8,700 BP, but with a range presently dated from about 10,000 BP to 6,570 BP. Associated with the Tasmanoid race (the culture very like that of the Tasmanians at the time of white contact), with one certain fossil remain — "Tartangan Man" — discovered across the Murray River from Devon Downs by Norman Tindale. Climate extended from the end of the cold period to the warm period of 5,000 BP, the time of extinction of the giant birds and large marsupial mammals. Sites have been found from the eastern part of Western Australia to Cape Bridgewater in Victoria, from Lake Menindee in southwestern New South Wales to Mount Harriett in northwestern South Australia. Artifacts include the jimari (a flat, gum-hafted general-purpose knife, one edge worked, unifaced; in Tasmania, the tronatta), burren (an adze blade differing from the tula in having concave-convex edges, whereas the tula is a stepped-chip edge on the concave side of a percussion cone), and other flake stone tools; but the Tartangan culture seems to have been mainly a wooden tool culture.

PIRRIAN: Extended from ca. 5,000 BP (dated by the Mount Gambier eruption of 4,710 BP) to ca. 3,000 BP. Associated with the Murrayian race, the

43

Australian archaeological sequence, collected by author. From top down: *Kartan, Tartangan, Pirrian, Mudukian, Murrundian, Modern*

"classic Australoids." Climate begins with the very warm period, represented almost everywhere in coastal Australia by the Ten-Foot Terrace, to nearly present conditions. Sites nearly everywhere in Australia, excepting the eastern coast; the Type Site is Devon Downs on the Murray River in South Australia, dated for the Pirrian Culture at 4,250 BP. Artifacts include the pirri (a symmetrical projectile point about one and a half inches long; survives into modern times with the Wanman tribe of northwestern Australia, who call it a karu), the tula, and undifferentiated blades.

MUDUKIAN: Extending in time from around 3,000 BP to 1,000 BP, but may have persisted in coastal Victoria until approximately 500 BP. Carried, like the Pirrian, by the Murrayian people. The climate of the culture period was like the present, Post-Ten-Foot-Terrace. Devon Downs is again the Type Site, but other sites have been found all over Australia. Artifacts are very like those of other microlithic cultures — in Europe, for example; in the microlithic periods all stone artifacts were very much smaller than their predecessors or successors. In Australia these include the bondi point (resembling the microburins of Africa and Europe), microlithic discoidal adze stones (crescents are differentiated in being specialized to toothlike cutting implements set in jaw-sticks), Woakwine points (larger and heavier than the bondi), scrapers, a knife four or five inches long set in a skin haft, called by Tindale a juan and by McCarthy an elouera, the perfected tula, and a large assemblage of bone tools, of which the most important is the muduk, a toggle fishing hook.

MURUNDIAN: From 1,000 BP to the time of white contact. Its people were Murrayians, its climate modern. Once again the Type Site is Devon Downs, but similar sites are ubiquitous — though concentrated for historical and environmental reasons in South Australia. Artifacts are of the modern assemblage — adze stones for spear-throwers, cleavers, chisels, hammerstones, knives, grinding stones, scrapers, and as a curiosity, some edge-ground ("Neolithic") axes. Wooden tools and weapons are dominant.

How easy these periods are to summarize, how easy not to read! But the hard, grubbing, generally unproductive, and massive work that went into their identification can be compared only to the immense mathematical, astronomical, and physical effort that produced Einstein's $E = MC^2$. The opposition, controversy, and acrimony from consensus knowledge Einstein experienced are also paralleled in Australian archaeology. The human target, of course, is Norman Tindale, who established the sequences. He is not bothered by the storms drifting blackly westward out of the eastern skies. His view was that recommended by Benjamin Franklin: one launches one's work upon the world as one launches a child; what happens to it then is pretty much the work's business. From time to time, nevertheless, Norman raps an opponent so sharply across the knuckles that the bones will ache during low barometric pressures as long as the opponent lives. One Sydney archaeologist went to print with his "proof" that Norman's sequence was *blown* — this fellow had found two sites less than a hundred yards apart in the same geological stratum but with quite different tool assemblages. Norman gently replied that what he had got into was the same site at the same time and that he had overlooked the small fact that one part was the men's camp where men did men's work with men's tools and the other part was the women's camp where women did women's work with women's tools — the kitchen assemblage versus the garage assemblage.

On one of our archaeological trips Norman and I visited a "dig" where a European archaeologist was desperately trying to substantiate a theory of universal stability of cultural evolution by finding European sequences — Abbevillian, Acheulean, Mousterian, Perigordian, and the other elaborations the Gallic genius exercises itself upon. Of course neither we nor the visiting professor ever found any of these things, but we did pick up a couple of sherd-bags full of microlithic (Mudukian) points around the entrance to the cave. Later Norman asked the visitor's assistant how much work they had done on the microlithic site. "What microlithic site?" he gaped. The two of them had walked over the ancient encampment at least twice a day for three seasons and had never seen it.

There is a second irony in that story. If the Frenchified visiting archaeologist had dug at Port Lincoln instead of where he did dig, he would have found enough French Paleolithic implements to astound anthropology to its collective soul. The South Australian Museum has an impressive display of unquestionable French *coups de poing* sieved out of the Port Lincoln silt. Such things cannot be; one does not find Model T Fords waiting for our astronauts on the moon. The explanation is mundane: in the last century merchant ships used the port to discharge earth ballast loaded in France.

Archaeology is the easiest of the anthropological sub-disciplines to master. Dead men *do* tell tales; what they *don't* do is argue with you. Scarcely a statement can be made in the field of religion or social

46

organization without some contentious counter-scholar using it to identify its maker as a fool or scoundrel. God only knows what any man is capable of doing when he is alive — but dead, he is capable of nothing but decomposition. The archaeologist digs up what is left of him, analyzes it, studies what tools went in the hole with him, and writes up his findings. Still — even here — there are those persistent Banal Impossibilities. On my first visit to Australia I found near the South Australian coast in a Mudukian stratum an axehead made by grinding and polishing. This is a solidly characteristic tool of the Neolithic period, which the Australian aborigines never reached. I didn't know that at the time, so I found the axe. Later I was accused of having faked the find — and being that kind of difficult person, I went out and found another one. Both are lying on a shelf behind me as I write — both impossible. Years later, fossicking around Mount Harriett in the central Australian desert, I found a microlithic site — no doubt of its identification. But there was an incongruity: the *bondi* points were made of porcelain. I have never told Norman Tindale of this; let him learn of it here. But what does it do to his date of 1,000 BP for the end of the Mudukian period?

It was a single bit of porcelain embedded in the foundation wall of Zimbabwe that in an instant removed that city from its legendary identification as the great Biblical metropolis of Ophir to a medieval community of no particular importance. Will my porcelain *bondi* destroy the Mudukian age? Almost certainly not. Archaeological sequences are not often made nor destroyed by the Suspect Singleton. Here archaeology is like litigation; as Mr. Dooley observed, what looks like a solid wall to the man in the street is a triumphal arch to the corporation lawyer.

Anthropology is the dustbin discipline; it intrudes into law, music, chemistry, physics, literature, linguistics, and everything else man has put his mind and hands to, and though it generally snaps up the un-considered trifles, they are no less interesting than the discoveries we are assured change the world. Consider the problem Norman Tindale accepted when he first put his shovel into the floor of the cave shelter at Devon Downs; he thus began in a systematic way to determine the entire cultural evolution of a people who had been in Australia for tens of thousands of years but who had left no writing or any other clear chronicle of what they had done and what had happened to them in all that time. I am convinced he has built from his work a structure that can never be seriously altered. The problem of cultural evolution cannot be set apart from the question of what people made the tools, how they came to the huge Australian continent, how they behaved toward earlier and later immigrants, and whether there were contacts and intrusions from other places by people who did not remain.

That unaccountably low percentage of fossil man's remains in the rest of the world obtains as well in Australia. My guess as to the total number of aborigines who lived on the dry continent before the arrival of the white convicts in 1788 is a hundred million; the figure is wrong, of course, but the error is in gross underestimation. From these hundred million people we have four fossil skulls of major significance recovered from the Australian earth; they are joined by three ancestral skulls from the islands to the north. Scholars know the indigenous fossils by the names of the places where they were found—Talgai, Queensland; Keilor, Victoria; Cohuna, Victoria; and Tartanga, South Australia. To make these petrified bits of bones more recognizably human, we speak of them in more personal terms — Talgai Man, Tartangan Boy. Regrettably, none is anywhere near so important as, say, Dart's Child, the first Australopithecine from South Africa, in giving a link of evidence in constructing evolution's chain. We Australianists defend their importance because they are Australians, as the British defended their improbable Piltdown Man because he was British. Only one of the Australian skulls — the boy from Tartanga — was recovered under scientific conditions; the others were accidentally thrown up by workmen digging ditches. We shall never know much more about the strata of the earth in which they were found (for instance, whether the original burial was intrusive) than we know now for any of these fragmentary people. There was a chance for this still at Keilor, but that archaeologist who foolishly tilted against Norman Tindale with the bipartite site undertook an almost criminally inept excavation, a sudden rain fell, and the entire site was pitched down into the Maribyrnong River. Of these fossil fellows I am fondest of Tartangan Boy — principally because of our acquaintance at the South Australian Museum. I held his poor broken head in my hands as Hamlet held his old friend Yorick, and have persuaded myself I knew him well. It must be admitted he is not in the best condition — in hundreds of pieces, to say the truth — but I doubt I will look half so well when I am in the sod six thousand years.

Two of the significant skulls found outside Australia are representatives of Wadjak Man, discovered by Eugène Dubois, the man who started serious protohuman fossil-hunting by his recovery of *Pithecanthropus*. Known for eighty years now, Wadjak Man is not yet firmly placed in geological time, but the probability is that he came in after the end of the glaciation. His evolutionary importance is his resemblance to what the earliest Murrayians must have looked like. Here I must mention something Norman Tindale has not yet written of: his belief that his Kaiadilt tribe on Bentinck Island are living Wadjak Men. Stated so, the identification seems absurd; it did to me — until I saw his photographs of the Kaiadilt people. I shiver still to think about them — they *are* an ancient type, no question whatever about it.

The most important of all extraterritorial remains of the oldest Australoids is the Niah Cave Skull, found a dozen years ago in a large cave at the northern tip of Borneo. The Niah Woman is so embarrassing to consensus anthropologists that they have hurriedly put her bones into the closet with a few other inconvenient skeletons and her credentials have been impounded, judging by what you will read of her in the current textbooks. She is awkward to received knowledge because morphologically she is not only *Homo sapiens*, but Australoid; she was laid to rest with Kartan implements; and she lay among associated organic remains dated by Carbon 14 tests at 40,000 BP. The small, cantankerously dissident school to which I belong is delighted with the lady and would gladly shake her hand, if that were possible, for she tends to prove a number of minority assertions: that the Kartan phase for the first Australians is correct, that the Kartans were ancient Australoids, that the ancient Australoids were a branch of ancient Caucasoids, that the Kartan folk came into Australia along the route we had guessed, and that in being contemporary with the Neanderthals, she takes the latter out of a necessary phase of human evolution.

Since my own archaeological interest is in the near past rather than in the oldest periods, I wonder more than most about the people who, just before history began to be written, visited Australia and did not stay. It is curious that this great continent should have remained culturally isolated for so long. One has to look closely to see in Australian native culture any influence from the outside world. But the evidence is there. It used to be asked why the Polynesians as fearless

49

and foolhardy mariners could have got to the Antarctic ice to their south and to Madagascar to their far west, and somehow missed Australia. The answer is prosaic: they didn't. Along several eastern Australian rivers Polynesian sailors considerately left for us to find a few greenstone (*pounamu*) adzes originating nowhere else in the world but New Zealand. They also taught the South Australian aborigines how to play the fascinating "Kangaroo Rat Game" (Hawaiian *pahe*) and showed them how to make the *wit wit* sticks with which it is played. Norman Tindale and I picked up at Yalata on the eastern Nullarbor a half dozen of these curious implements. To these certainties I am compelled to add two banal impossibilities because they are my own ideas. One I found in a collection of sacred *tjurunga* boards Norman Tindale assembled from a pre-white contact situation. Among the conventional incisions symbolizing rather than representing in a realistic way the wanderings of the totemic Australian ancestors, I noticed the textile design known to anthropologists and others as the Greek Key. Incidentally, this is one of those strange self-inventions, this one deriving from a discovery, probably made many times, of a master weaver playing with his art. Instead of using a one-over-one warp and woof technique, the experimental weaver may try different alternates; one of these produces the Greek Key design. All the inventor has to do is notice the pattern — then he can transfer it to other media. I saw it occurring polygenetically in the grass-woven wall of a native house in Samoa on a visit there a half dozen years ago. Its significance in central Australia is its testimony that one way or other the desert aborigines had come into contact with textile-weaving people. Possibly this ties in with my second impossibility, the most outrageous suggestion I will make in this journal: that the Aranda tribe of the center, neighbors to my Pitjandjara, are descendants of miscegenation of Murrayians with Polynesians.

First Probes

In that evanescent moment of archaeological time when grant money flowed out of Washington like a river of gold to scholars who poured it into grand expeditions all over the world, there grew up an instant tradition that it had always been like this. After I had done with the *Bibliography* and settled down at the University of Colorado in my new career in anthropology, I got in on some of this new archaeology. In our continuing work at Mesa Verde we would mount digs staffed by general archaeologists, geochronologists, physical anthropologists, linguists, botanists, zoologists, geologists, and geochemists — and the more specialized dendrochronologists, climatologists, palynologists, parasitologists, osteopathologists, osteologists, museologists, glotto-chronologists, ethnobotanists, agronomists, ecologists, entomologists, pedologists, and even scatologists, whose work, they used to say, was "not bad once you got into it." Our department worked a site along the Nile in the days of the Aswan Dam, when the whole region was laid out like building lots, each assigned to some American university. At any time we would have two or three men at least on leave, digging somewhere in the world. The truth we would not accept lest it presage a barren future was that it was never, except for that insignificant period, like this.

In the last century's golden age of archaeology the classic fossil discoveries supporting Darwin's evolutionary theory were made in Europe, not because that was where the Neanderthals evolved into or were displaced by modern man, but because the archaeologists had no money to go anywhere else. The Dutchman Dubois revolutionized knowledge of man's most ancient prehistory in Java not because that was where his *Pithecanthropus* had crept out of the Garden of Eden, but because the Dutch owned the place and Dubois got himself sent there as military surgeon. The British made the great discoveries in early civilization because their empire owned most of every other place.

There had been exceptions, surely. The first considerable archaeologist, Nabonidus, who 2,500 years ago recorded on tablets his joy at finding a foundation stone laid down for King Narim-Sin 2,200 years earlier still, probably did not want for expense money — but then he was king of Babylonia. Heinrich Schliemann was another digger who did not have to scrimp — though knowing him, we might suppose he did. Nevertheless digging for the past was overwhelmingly done on weekends in pits and caves and mounds near the digger's home.

On my second year-long visit to Australia (the first as an established anthropologist) my friends at the South Australian Museum were as poor as those old hunters of Neanderthal skulls. Norman

Tindale had fifty dollars in his research account, and Mr. Cooper was digging his Kartan sites on one or two dollars a week. I fell in with their way of life, rediscovering the contentment of simplicity. I spent most of my days at my worktable learning from the museum's treasures, and absorbing the Australians' variation of Western civilization — eating boiled pumpkin instead of potatoes, meat pies instead of hamburgers, distinguishing the wild white men of the Outback from the effete city dwellers, understanding the peculiar vocabulary and pronunciation of the Aussies, and wallowing in their affection for Americans. Without moving far from Adelaide I did a fair amount of anthropology and archaeology, for the wilderness begins within the limits of the city. One typical short trip came out of a telephone call from a station [ranch] owner just across the South Australian border in New South Wales.

In his long tenure as curator of anthropology at the museum Norman took about a dozen calls a day from people who wanted a good aboriginal word to name their houses with or who had found bones in their gardens. In Australia more discoveries are made by the amateurs than by professionals, and it is usually worth one's while to listen to their telephone calls. One day as I was grubbing through old books and stones and bones Norman came over and asked me whether I would like to go on an archaeological investigation with him for several days. *Would I what!* He had taken a call from a man who had led him to a few good things in the past, one Doug Bannear, who ran an orange grove at Cobdogla one hundred and thirty miles up the River Murray. While fossicking around Lake Victoria another fifty miles east of his property he had found some bones he thought might be of interest.

We gathered up Mrs. Tindale and some gear and set out in Norman's old Holden station wagon and set off up the road paralleling the Murray, stopping the first night at Berri in the rich citrus area called with typical Australian infelicity "Sunraysia." One of the advantages of doing casual archaeology without carrying the burden of scatologists and other archaeological organization men is the delight of digressing into anything you wish. Confident that Doug's bones would keep a day longer, Norman took me around this region, of which from my own historical work I had some previous knowledge. The district was developed by George and William Chaffey, the men who established California's modern agriculture, building the first irrigated settlement in that state and making Los Angeles the first city to be lighted by electricity alone. While they were founding the city of Ontario in California they were visited by Alfred Deakin (later prime minister of Australia) and persuaded to come to his country and get it some water. They came and, despite massive criticism, made the region centering on Mildura into so rich an agricultural center by drawing water from the River Murray into the barren mallee country that its inhabitants now feel so superior that they are agitating for secession. Their first great river water pump was still in use when we went through Mildura. But for the Chaffeys things did not go as well as they should have done; they were prime examples of what I call the Sacrificial Pioneer. A concatenation of circumstances at last discouraged George Chaffey and he went back to California to build the Imperial Valley. William had made a stronger commitment to Australia; he remained to become one of Australia's most honored men.

At Loxton, one of Sunraysia's smaller communities, we dropped Dorothy Tindale off to visit her daughter and grandchildren. Norman's son-in-law grows several fruits at subsistence profit or less, in poorest times supplementing his income as an insurance salesman, and thereby elevating himself to a better position than the man who a year or two earlier had sold him several hundred sheep on the hoof for a shilling (eleven cents) each. All were moribund from thirst and starvation; Ron had to kill them and bury them under his trees as fertilizer. Poverty on the desert, riches in Sunraysia, and everyone on the edge of economic death. Both Sunraysia and the rich wheat country on the other side of Adelaide suffer from a poor market in a grievously underpopulated land. Another adamantine truth gone: Australia's inadequate water is a psychological set: more water, more produce, more poverty for the grower. It is a philosophical bad penny all of us hold to tightly — that progress means more people, more water on the land, more crops growing. Progress may mean none of these things. Sheep selling in South Australia for a dime apiece; their skins, cut into coats, selling in America for a hundred and fifty dollars.

Norman wears many hats. He is chairman of the Nature Preservation Committee of the National Trust, so we deviated for half a day to look for koala bears at Martin's Bend on a Murray backwater. Not wild ones here — they are all gone now — but four zoo-grown animals released here some months earlier by Norman's committee. We found three of them, all sitting like sloths in tree crotches, and giving me again wonder how they survived so long in a land of supernally proficient hunters; the koala alone is enough to cast doubt on Darwin's theory of the survival of the fittest. Fat, shy, cuddly, covered with fur soft and sensuous beyond your imagination, it sleeps all day in sparsely leaved gum trees. One can bring them down with thrown rocks, but somehow they persist. I was to see them in the wild in Queensland, where aboriginal population in pre-contact times was heavy. Why the early pioneers called them "bears" I cannot say; as well call them elephants. But "native bears" comes easier to the tongue than *Phascolarctos cinereus*.

On the other side of Berri we looked in at an aboriginal flint "mine" few Australians in that area know about, the prosodically satisfying Wilabalangaloo. This is a scarp leading down into the valley which was intended to hold the waters of the Murray caught by the great Chowilla Dam, then being planned, now abandoned. Sterile place, this Wilabalangaloo. We kicked about through billions of bits of broken flint; I found one *pirri* and Norman found nothing — the only time that distribution of finds was ever to occur in our trips together.

We followed the Murray here and there to places of prehistorical or historical interest, usually where no roads existed. The Holden rattled on, breaking off pieces of itself, but no matter. I think the American notion of planned obsolescence gets into the minds of American cars as well as into the minds of their timid owners. An American car would not make this journey. It would lie down like a discouraged horse and die.

On our second day out I told Norman I would like to make camp early by the river to savor the rare Australian comfort of throwing down one's swag by water. Norman teaches his companions by many means. One is by letting them learn through their own folly. We had just established camp when the mosquitoes hit. They even drove the ubiquitous swarms of bush flies away. I was able to record the whine of their wings on tape, sticking the microphone outside of the swag-cocoons we slept in, designed by Norman and sewn by Dorothy. (Its cheesecloth sides let in the air and kept out everything but the smallest of Australian winged demons and ants; the canvas top kept out the infrequent rains.) In that camp I deduced another reason why aboriginal campsites are found a little distance away from water — the mosquitoes. Later in the desert itself I learned that the aborigines, for all their adaptation to a hard environment, like biting, stinging, and bothering insects no more than we do.

I was learning, too, almost without knowing it, quite a bit of practical knowledge. I used to think Australian anthropologists lived off the land, shooting animals and plucking fruits. Some do, now and then, but more for the adventure than the sustenance. I envy Peter Aitken's experience of having eaten a Tasmanian Devil (*Sarcophilus harrissi*, meaning "flesh-loving"), the most ferocious of the native animals, now entirely extinct on the mainland. But camp food is a dreary succession of camp pies in tins, pumpkin in tins, plum pudding in tins, lamb in tins, stale bread without butter, and the omnipresent billy of tea, which I grew so much to love. Every stop, even to relieve oneself, is occasion to "boil the billy" — the billy being a fire-blackened quart can whose name derived from French canned beef imported into the bush during the gold days — *boeuf bouilli*. Boiling the billy is the base of Australian Outback culture; if civilization falls when the Colosseum falls, Australian civilization will vanish when the billy disappears. It is a threat in both cases. The Colosseum is in bad shape and the Australian city dweller knows nothing of the billy. When I first came to Australia one had to carry the billy to the grocery store to buy milk; by the second visit, milk was being sold in bottles.

On our first swag-drop Norman taught me a practice I recommend to all who go into the bush. Before he did anything else he would walk around the campsite and break off at the trunk any dangerous branches. One could easily lose an eye by walking in the dark into a jagged limb, and Norman could not afford to lose his one remaining eye. But can anyone afford to lose one of two eyes? I break off branches.

Up at dawn the following day before the bush flies came out of their sleep, we plunged into surprisingly heavy bush and emerged around midday at Rufus Creek, a wilderness now with but one habitation — a general store, one-roomed, its stock mainly tea, flour, and sugar, and selling gasoline out of a forty-four-gallon drum. Norman pointed out to me an overgrown area where, many years ago, there occurred the worst attack by aborigines upon settlers and the worst of the punitive expeditions. Now there are neither whites nor aborigines in this place. A notorious incident, seen from either side. Here our muffler dropped off, Norman found two australites (meteorites), and I found a *karta* of classic fabrication. I was beginning to appreciate how true was Huxley's remark: "To a person uninstructed in natural history, his country or seaside stroll is a walk through a gallery filled with wonderful works of art, nine tenths of which have their faces turned to the wall."

Late that afternoon we reached Lake Victoria, where Doug Bannear met us at a prearranged rendezvous. We spent the rest of that day and part of the next circumnavigating — rather, circumambulating — the lake, whose shores must have been the chief burial ground for aborigines from an immense area. One did not have to dig for bones; they protruded from the ground like mulga stakes in the desert — femurs, tibia, radii, ulnae, patellae, and crania. A quick examination of a sampling of the latter told us these folk had been deposited too recently to be of paleontological interest — though I found one fossil, a four-inch piece of humerus. To touch a fossil is to touch ancientness ineffable; like the fur of a koala, it must be touched to be known. No way of telling how old this bone was, for the process of fossilization proceeds at different rates in different places. All we could deduce from it was the probability that once there had been heavily mineralized water here.

In this great boneyard we made only one valuable find: a secondary ocher burial. I am fascinated by ocher, red ocher (hematite, earthy iron ore, Fe_2O_3), its history and prehistory; why did this material in almost every religion since Neanderthal Man invented that institution become the most spiritually rich and magical of all substances? We know the Neanderthals had religion because tens of thousands of years ago they rubbed ocher over the bodies of their dead, whose bones it settled into after the flesh had gone. And here on the shores of Lake Victoria in Australia we had the bones of a person dug up and cleaned after a temporary initial burial and put down again permanently in a neat little ochered package. Norman painted it with a shellac preparation to hold the insubstantial fragments together and removed it with the carefulness of a cardiac surgeon. There is no end to the myriad uses of ocher. I will speak of its mythical importance later, when we get into the deserts. Among the American Indians it marked them as the red race. I have worked among the Indians off and on for as long as I have been in anthropology, and the only red ones I ever saw were blushing — a condition to which they are not overmuch given. Indians became members of a nonexistent red race when their emissaries to the first white discoverers tried to pro-

56

tect themselves against the alien devils by rubbing their bodies with magical red ocher. It did not help them against white men who had even forgotten it was the substance from which the Easter ashes of Catholics had so long ago derived. Ironically, by applying an inhuman color to their skin the Indians made it that much easier for the whites to treat them as less than human.

Not long after we returned from the Lake Victoria expedition I was off on another casual trip with Bob Edwards, who was to succeed Norman Tindale as curator of anthropology at the museum. There are others in the specialized archaeological field of rock carvings more famous than Bob, but fame in this endeavor is acquired like fame in any other — by being obsequiously present in the centers of fame. Bob did his work in the bush, where there is no curious living thing but emus to admire him. For years before he gave up moneymaking as a fruit broker and went out of love into the starvation profession of archaeology, Bob made weekend trips into the northern drainage basin leading into the River Murray. Calling this enormous stretch of semidesert a "drainage basin" is justified by its terrain, not by the actual water the term implies. Bob's interest is the area's rock engravings, and for years he was the only man to study these unique marks. Since most people, including archaeologists, look on rock engravings as equivalent to graffiti on lavatory walls, I will give him here a term for his specialty designed to raise its status: *riparian archaeology.*

In the barren country one hundred and seventy-five miles or so north of the Murray, all settlement disappears. The names you see on maps in that region are produced by one force: the cartographers' abhorrence of a vacuum. Between Peterborough, one hundred and fifty miles north of Adelaide, and the crazy town of Broken Hill, one hundred and seventy-five miles along the eastern track, there is nothing Americans would accept as a settlement. In the center of this line stretch a half dozen pastoral stations large enough to enclose Rhode Island. These ranches run sheep, but far more numerous than the woolly scourge are kangaroos and emus, which the citified Australians have seen only as purple-dyed dog meat. A mob of 'roos gliding along in great ripples or a flock of emus bounding is a sight to see, but we saw enough of them on this trip to bore us. We bounded along after both 'roos and emus in one of the museum's

Toyotas (the best damned vehicle General Motors ever made — in Japan or Detroit) at their terror speed of thirty miles an hour. I have had my Mustang well over a hundred miles an hour on lonely Colorado roads, but that speed is nothing for thrills like thirty on the South Australian plains.

On the way out to Panaramitee Station, our locus of operations on this small venture, we stopped for a few hours at the abandoned copper mine at Burra, from which the struggling settlement of Adelaide in the 1840's drew the illusory wealth every new city on the frontier must find to lure settlers. Burra's lifetime production of five million pounds' sterling worth of copper did not begin to match the money made by selling worthless things like shoelaces and meat pies, things whose trade make a wilderness into a metropolis. Adelaide has three-quarters of a million people now; Burra has thirteen hundred sitting there for reasons best known to themselves.

Cutting east from Peterborough on the border of South Australia's frontier, we pulled at last into Panaramitee Station and met its owner at the gate — the "flamin' gate," as pastoralists all call these devices, because it is a matter of personal pride and integrity for visitors and transients to leave them open for the sheep to get out and the dingoes to get in. Panaramitee's proprietor, Charley Wade, is probably a millionaire; his land is bloody worthless and I never saw on it a single sheep, but anything is good for fifty cents an acre and Charley owns so many worthless acres he is rich. This is a business I cannot explain. Australians live at a good standard of American living on a third the American cash income. I do not understand it; Joan claims she does not understand it; and anything one or the other of us cannot understand about Australia, nobody can understand. Yet it is a fact, a certified Mystery like the Trinitarian nature of God. Probably Catholics have the right idea about Mysteries: the human mind cannot apprehend them and therefore the human mind must not try.

Charley is a husky moustachioed man, right out of a movie on India during the days of British imperialism. His great tree trunk of a chest is always carried at attention; his favorite expletive is "Strike me!" but he makes it sound so oozingly obscene one knows one is in the company of an extraordinary man. Charley in his Land Rover led us over the sterile sandy acres to his homestead, a sprawling flat barn of a house, on whose veranda his "Mum" sat among the dogs and the wool listening on the wireless to the England-Australia Test cricket match in London. Another Australian Mystery. One of my greatest intellectual achievements was learning to play cricket, but I still agree with the American who said "watching cricket is like watching a man collecting stamps." Stamps? Stumps? We left Mum and a batter out "at stumps" with something like a thousand runs, and the teams all went to tea for several days. No part of this queer game is simple. A Yorkshire announcer gave a score "at stoomps" and was corrected: "You mean 'at *stumps*.'" "Nay; *stumps* is wot 'un poots on letters."

Charley led us to the shearers' quarters, where we found to our great pleasure we would be able to sleep that night in the luxury of iron cots and iron mattresses. Just beyond the sheds I saw a chicken-wire cage ten feet long, five feet wide, eight feet high, with a three-square-foot opening at the top. I had read about this sort of contrivance years before in an Australian's journal of his childhood. This was a crow trap; one put a dead lamb in the cage as bait, the ungainly crows would drop down through the top opening, gorge themselves, and find they could not become airborne again in the short run. Then the boys of the station would come in and beat the crows to death with sticks.

Next day the fossicking. We were all distracted from the rock carvings lying some miles ahead of us by a talus slope from which poured the unnatural "Devil's Dice," cuboid pieces of black limonite crystallized into shapes the Devil indeed might have made. Alternative explanations for their occurrence seem less credible. Every station in this country has some particular uniqueness; Panaramitee has two: these "dice" and some of the most intriguing rock carvings in the entire continent.

After filling several sherd-bags with dice and chasing emus and 'roos and poking around on a couple of surface archaeological sites (on which I found two microlithic adze slugs), we came to the dry beds of the Murray drainage system and its slabs of rock — carved or, rather, pecked, by aborigines two and a half thousand years ago, if patina dating can be relied on. The engravings have no interest for untaught eyes and that is just as well. Any archaeological feature the average layman thinks good enough to photograph another average layman will think good enough to destroy. As editor of a state archaeological journal for four or five years I warned our amateur pothunters through reporting vandalism in other states, but at the

59

first opportunity of raiding a site inadvertently disclosed by the news-papers, one chapter of the state amateur archaeological society cleaned the place out entirely in one night. In Australia the destruction that most aroused my violent emotions was the burning down of the Burke and Wills "Dig Tree" by tourists who somehow got out into that remote and tragic camp.

The tourist would not recognize, even if they were pointed out to him, several extraordinary representational carvings among the pecked tracks of kangaroos and emus which comprise about 70 per cent of the Panaramitee markings. These almost unaccountable en-gravings represent a saltwater fish, a possible *Diprotodon*, tracks of long-extinct kangaroos, and an unmistakable head of a seagoing crocodile, *Crocodilus porosus*. This crocodile head was not at Panara-mitee when we visited; it was in the South Australian Museum about forty feet from my worktable. Such a thing was too valuable to leave out where tourists and erosion could work their damage upon it. These things pose a problem with a number of equally different ramifica-tions: the fish and crocodile are not found in southern Australian waters; the nearest possible place they could have been seen is a thousand miles north. Although many animal tracks are found in the peckings on the rocks, there are no dingo tracks, which suggests the people who engraved with stone on stone came into Australia before the dog. This negative evidence joined to the positive evidence of extinct animals in the drawings point to a very ancient occupancy by these riparian people. Bob Edwards showed further that the less interesting designs comprise a pattern of motifs unlike those in other parts of the continent. By mapping the old stream beds where they occur he was able to hypothesize a people who chose to live along rivers thousands of years ago.

I was drawn many times to sites along the River Murray for most of its westering meander through the South Australian plain, growing to love the river as Twain loved his erratic and affecting Mississippi. Twain had to concede some treacherous hostility to man in his great river; not so the Murray. It is too lazy to hold any harm for man. My wife remembers the time years ago when she crossed it in an old-fashioned ferry — still running — near Renmark. As the ferry raft creaked across the river, hauling itself hand over hand along its cable, its path was crossed by a river tramp drifting by on a flatboat with nothing aboard but indolent comfort, a dog, and the tramp himself. He must have seen the envy in her eye, for he called out, "Don't you wish you was me, lady?" The tramp flatboats were gone when I made acquaintance with the River Murray, but the ferry was there, and many times I leaned over its bow, watching the minuscule waves slapping the eucalypt hull. How many of our all-knowing youths know ferryboats? Sometimes my generation comes close to pitying them in their wild innocence.

At those times, watching those lapping waves, I would think of the Murray's history: the contention of the first steamboats, so long delayed because the pioneer explorer Charles Sturt said the Murray was not navigable; the first steamboat captains Randell and Cadell (who learned his profession on the Mississippi); of the incredible races these two men ran against each other, more fierce and bloody than the Mississippi knew; of the improbable floods on the Murray, when the river became forty miles wide; of the boats that lost their way in flood time and steamed out into the desert; of all the great men whom I admired and who had to cross it to get into the northeastern interior. One could argue that the greatest of these was Charles Sturt, wrong though he was about the Murray's navigability. A most remarkable man, of whom I shall write at length one day.

On one of those rare occasions when one's workbox is suddenly cleared of the usual mountain of urgent but inconsequential work, Graeme Pretty, a young archaeologist being groomed then with Bob Edwards to share as a team Norman Tindale's place, invited me to help him find Sturt. Find Sturt? Sturt was in England in his grave these many years. "Sturt?" I asked Graeme. "What Sturt?"

"The town Governor Eyre was going to found and name for him."

"Never heard of it. Ain't on the maps."

"We wouldn't be going to look for it if it was on the maps, would we, mate?"

"Fair enough," I conceded; "where we going to look?"

"On the Murray south of Blanchetown."

"Good-oh! You want me to take my vehicle?"

"That's why I'm bloody inviting you."

At Blanchetown, a hundred miles or so up the River Murray, we cut south across pastoral country, rich enough to be heavily populated, but in fact empty country. All we had to go on — Graeme, myself, and one of Graeme's young friends — was an old sketch map and an engraving from the last century showing an avenue of new river gum trees (*Eucalyptus camaldulensis*). Regularity of any kind being an eye-striking rarity in nature, we found the place quickly after driving a few dozen miles south along the trackless river bank. But there was nothing of man's making in sight; all we saw was the river a hundred yards wide, the eucalypts drowning on its edges or thriving on the river terrace, and the soft wild grass among the blue-bush. A lovely place for a settlement, I thought; but where was it? Had a hundred years and the river in flood carried everything away?

We walked in a flat spiral from the middle of the avenue of now ancient trees with our eyes at our feet, and ultimately found the barely perceptible remains of two walls running about fifty feet from the raised bank to the river's edge. With that base line to work from, we found smaller things — bits of building stone and flat places where once something had been built but was no longer. The town we sought reduced itself, as we traced the possible perimeter of settlement, to one large house site, with no artifacts and nothing of estimable worth except one stone in the skeleton of the wall containing a shell fossil. A wonder that Eyre, himself an explorer of substantial accomplishment and a man observant beyond the ordinary, had missed this. All the probity impressed upon me as a responsible scholar could not keep me from putting that stone in my pocket. I suppose every archaeologist has his price.

We had one small event worth remembering on our drive westward to intercept the Adelaide road without going the long way back through Blanchetown; crossing a meadow I gunned the vehicle across the shallowest of streams — and bogged solidly into something as tenacious and insubstantial as quicksand. There was no chance to dig our way out of this in a hurry, so I sent Graeme to look for help at the nearest homestead shown on our maps, about fourteen miles away, while our companion and I took shovels and diverted the creek so that the vehicle would not disappear entirely, like the town of Sturt. Graeme came back toward dusk with a farmer on his tractor; the farmer threw us a cable and pulled us out. Aside from the delay, the only real unpleasantness was experienced by our companion: the mud sucked his shoes off and he pulled his feet out covered with leeches, surely among the world's most unlovely creatures.

I never got back to dig Sturt systematically. That is the sad story of most archaeologists: to find a place worth digging and have to put it aside for a time, and the opportunity to return never comes. Some time later I got hold of a copy of Charles Sturt's *Narrative of an Expedition into Central Australia,* and there, at the end of chapter 3, is an end-of-page engraving of *Mr. Eyre's House at Moorundi.* We see the house from across the River Murray, a grand mansion for its time, with two stories, all alone on the river plain, no town attached, with two short embankment walls on either side of the house, running down to the water. So "Sturt" was Eyre's home at "Moorundi." *Moorundi?* The *"Murundian"* phase of Australian prehistory? Of course — both named for the tribe that once inhabited this region. The blackfellow and the whitefellow both gone now; Eyre himself left to play out his tragic end in Jamaica.

TWO

HEROES IN A HOSTILE LAND

Of the two greatest inland explorers of Australia, Ernest Giles and Charles Sturt, one went into the Western Desert and one stayed out. Sturt knew the better part of valor, having nearly died in his brave but tragically unsuccessful attempt to pierce the smaller but equally terrible Simpson Desert to the east. He went to the edge a century ago, looked in, and predicted (correctly, as this estimable man nearly always did) that *"the great desert cannot have a less breadth than from 1,000 to 1,100 miles, or a length from east to west of less than 1,200. It would be difficult to determine from what point any attempt to survey it should be made, should such an attempt be considered necessary, for I believe the desert extends with unvarying sameness to the south coast, and that any anticipation of good from an exploration of it would end in disappointment."* Giles had failed bitterly to cross it in 1874, turning back when his companion Gibson died, but in 1875 tried again on a southern route traversing two thousand five hundred miles across the inland edge of the Nullarbor Plain. Pushing west from the central salt lakes region, he took note of the fact that the last waterless stretch had run a hundred and fifty miles and that the country ahead was clearly worse. Perhaps remembering Gibson, he made a grim decision. Lacking nothing in courage himself, he made his chances less by offering his men the choice of going ahead with him or taking rations and camels and striking south to the coast, whence they could make their way back to the outposts of civilization. As he recorded in his journal, *"I represented that we were probably in the worst desert upon the face of the earth, but that fact should give us all the more pleasure in conquering it. We were surrounded on all sides by dense scrubs, and the sooner we forced our way out of them the better. It was of course a desperate thing to do, and I believe very few people would or could rush madly into a totally unknown wilderness, where the nearest known water was 650 miles away. But I had sworn to go to Perth or die in the at-*

tempt, and I inspired the whole of my party with enthusiasm. One and all declared that they would live or die with me." Then followed seventeen days without water during which they were to plod 343 miles. At the 190-mile point his Afghan camel driver, Saleh, spoke the plaint of all: *"Mister Gile, when you get water?"* Giles with apparent flat unconcern answered, *"Water? pooh! there's no water in this country, Saleh. I didn't come here to find water, I came here to die, and you said you'd come and die, too."* Saleh persisted, as if in persisting he could change Giles's mind and the character of the country as well: *"I think some camel he die tomorrow, Mr. Gile."* "No, Saleh," corrected Giles, *"they cannot possibly live till tomorrow. I think they will all die tonight."*

"Oh, Mr. Gile, I think we all die soon now."

"Oh, yes, Saleh, we'll all be dead in a day or two."

Once, in the heart of Pitjandjara country, in the middle of an even drier desert north of where Giles made his decision to go on, I wondered what drove us all to this madness. There we were, Norman Tindale and I, with six university degrees between us to prove before the world that we had some sense, choking in the calid brick dust whirled off the desert floor into our faces by the furnace wind, afraid to breathe through our mouths for fear of swallowing a loathsome bush fly, and stepping carefully between the spear-sharp blades of the spinifex, as if walking through a minefield, so as not to disturb one of the deadly snakes that think of that hateful grass as a home. *We were all bloody mad*, I thought. *Bonkers. Crackers. Every man who had ever come into this infernal bloody country.* My eye catching sight of a hairy something oozing through the sand, I stopped. It was a tail-to-nose procession of hairy caterpillars. As he always did when we came upon some new thing, Norman observed through teeth clenched against the bush flies, "Waṇka. Starvation food for the aborigines. The last thing you eat before you die. Among those fluffy hairs are barbs that tear your throat and poison the wound — but it is food when there is no other."

Revolted by this ultimate horror, I asked him, not expecting an answer, "How can people live here, like this?"

"John," he said, "you have to realize that life exists where it is possible, not only where it is comfortable."

I had to accept that as reason enough for the aborigines who had lived for hundreds of generations in this desolation. This was all the world, so far as they knew. Tied to it body and soul, they loved this land — but they did not always like it. The idea of one getting used to hardships reminded me of Mosquito, an aboriginal police black-tracker in the early days of settlement who became an outlaw when he discovered the profitability of crime. Eventually he was caught and sentenced to be hanged. On the scaffold he made an ethnological observation to the hangman.

"Hangin' no bloody good for blackfella."

"Why not as good for blackfella as for whitefella, if he deserves it?"

"Very good for whitefella; he used to it."

Mosquito's logic about hanging was no better than mine about the environment. The natives have never grown used to it. I saw them once sitting in naked misery as a cold winter rain poured over them. I have often seen them slashing small branches across their faces in madness at the bush flies. I remember a tiny desert man squatting with his head in his hands moaning like a song the bush whitefella's complaint, *"Poor fella me poor fella me poor fella me poor fella me poor fella me poor fella me poor fella me."*

There is death on the desert. From thirst, for everyone not well prepared against it. From poison in eating unknown fruits and berries, for the ignorant. From the bites of snakes and insects, for the unlucky. It is easy to be unlucky with snakes. Nearly two-thirds of Australia's snakes are poisonous, some unnecessarily so. Reckoning lethality in the sheep-killing power of one bite, there is the cobra, which can with the poison of one fanged snap kill 31 sheep; the tiger snake, 118; the taipan, 200. More lethal still is the sea snake of northern Australian waters. Every person known to have been bitten has died. The sea snake can be deterring to swimmers on the occasions the aquatic serpents choose to congregate; they have been seen thick as spaghetti. One does not worry about sea snakes, though. They generally keep well away from swimming places — out of fear of the sharks. Of all Australian reptiles the most feared is the brown snake, not so much for its lethality as for its ubiquity. It is everywhere. "New chums" — beginners in the bush — wear knee-length boots against attacking serpents, not knowing that one species of the brown genus can hurl itself over your head — and will, with no more provocation than its having got up on the wrong side of its hole that morning.

But people rarely complain about death, even in the bizarre forms it takes in Australia. Complaint is something one uses against annoyances. No one who has entered desert Australia and come out again to write about it has failed to complain about the flies, the ants, and the spinifex. Giles sought out hardship as if it were necessary to living, but in his journal he would at times go on for pages about the bush pests. Under the date of 23 April 1876 he wrote, "*The flies at the camp to-day were, if possible, even more numerous than before. They infest the whole air; they seem to be circumambient; we can't help eating, drinking, and breathing flies; they go down our throats in spite of our teeth, and we wear them all over our bodies; they creep up one's clothes and die, and others go after them to see what they die of. The instant I inhale a fly it acts as an emetic. And if Nature abhors a vacuum, she, or at least my nature, abhors these wretches more, for the moment I swallow one a vacuum is instantly produced. Their bodies are full of poisonous matter, and they have a most disgusting flavour, though they taste sweet. They also cause great pains and discomfort to our eyes, which are always full of them.*" God knows what the function of the bush fly is; no one else does. Entomologists have gone little further with their study than to name them — *Musca sorbens*. They do not bite, they do not drink water (though they do appreciate a bit of blood if it is made available to them), they seem to have no purpose in life except to fasten themselves on your face until an earlier-coming fly has vacated its position in your eye or until you make the mistake of opening your mouth — and then down they go, with all claws scraping. Clearing your throat does not relieve the nauseous feeling. Norman put it best: "You don't recover until you see it wriggling on the ground."

Ants are the dominant group among the fifty thousand species of Australian insects. There are nearly a thousand species of ants swarming under and on and above the Australian earth — thirty of them introduced by man. Hardly any are useful; fewer are benign. Leaving the northern tropics to Joan, I have never personally experienced the camouflaging tree ant, *Oceophylla virescens*, which drops in masses of green flame on incautious passersby to ignite them with a degree of pain at the top of the scale of human agony. I will accept the northern explorers' word for this, but I cannot imagine the green tree ant to be worse than the meat ant, *Iridomyrmex detectus*, which deals with the human skin the way heated pincers of medieval torture chambers were said to do. One could walk through the whole of

Australia and find between each breath at least one of the eighty species of this ferocious genus. Yet they are gentle creatures compared to the *Myrmecia*, which have bred themselves into sixty species, all peculiar to Australia. They have not only size as a weapon (some are an inch and a half long), but unreasonable aggressiveness; they will not simply repel human intruders, but chase them. And do not suppose you can shade an Australian ant you do not know; some of these little baastids run so fast they cannot be photographed at ordinary shutter speeds. Others are so fierce that naturalists have not studied them. Some jump, some hop, some dance; some build precise duplicates of birds' nests; on the ring of the Australian frontier, some other ants build tunnels up, around, and over tin foundation barriers so they can eat wooden houses. In my various journeys into the desert I have camped many times where Ernest Giles felt sufficiently beleaguered to make an entry in his journal about the ants: ". . . *here we had to remain for another day, in this Inferno. Not Dante's, gelid lowest circle of Hell, or City of Dis, could cause more anguish, to a forced resident within its bounds, than did this frightful place to me. Even though Moses did omit to inflict ants on Pharaoh, it is a wonder Dante never thought to have a region of them full of wicked wretches, eternally tortured with their bites, and stings, and smells. Dante certainly was good at imagining horrors. But imagination can't conceive the horror of a region swarming with ants; and then Dante never lived in ant country, and had no conception what torture such creatures can inflict. The smaller they are the more terrible.*"

Nevertheless, everything has its use. The Pitjandjara and other desert natives are very fond of the honeypots — principally the *Melophorus bagoti* and *Camponotus inflatus* species — because the huge specialized abdomens of these ants are filled with the sweetest substance available to the aborigines. But in my view these make poor compensation for the suffering that is the daily — and nightly — punishment for sitting or lying down within a few feet of the nearly undetectable entrances to underground nests of hordes of savage ants of one species or other.

Many of the noisome creatures of the Australian desert have set up some kind of symbiotic housekeeping with the chief scourge of the continent's flora, the spinifex. "*I am told,*" wrote David Carnegie, the most persistent explorer of the western deserts, *that the term 'spinifex,' though generally employed by those who have the pleasure of the acquaintance of the plant, is wrongly used. I do not know its right name, and have seen it described as 'Spinifex,' 'Porcupine Grass,' 'Triodia,' 'Triodia pungens,' and 'Festuca irritans.' Why such a wretched, useless plant should have so many names I cannot say. . . . I can imagine any one, on being suddenly placed on rising ground with a vast plain of waving spinifex spreading before him — a plain relieved occasionally by the stately desert oak, solemn, white, and mysterious — saying, 'Ah! what a charming view — how beautiful that rolling plain of grass! Its level surface broken by that bold sandhill, fiery-red in the blaze of sun!' But when day after day, week after week, and month after month must be passed always surrounded by that most hateful plant, one's sense of the picturesque becomes sadly blunted."*

True spinifex is a genus of beach grasses — *Spinifex hirsutus, Spinifex longifolius,* for example — but no one ever calls beach grasses "spinifex." That abominable stuff is *Triodia pungens* to the botanist, but to the poor baastids who have to go out into it, it is *Triodia* bloody *irritans.* I speak of it at length here because on our last desert expedition, Bob Verburgt and I labored through two thousand miles of it. What is wrong with it? Why is it so maligned? Because it is needlessly hostile beyond anything else in this generally malicious land. Its blades will take the leather off your shoes if you walk through it for any distance, and on the end of each blade is a tiny barb with some noxious substance in it to enter your hands, legs, and arms to give you the poison and subsequent irritation of a gnat bite. Have a bit of sensitivity training: go up into your attic and in that privacy strip naked and roll around in the Fiberglas insulation between the ceiling joists; you will come out with some idea of what a roll in the spinifex will do to you. You will be safe in the attic as you would not be on the desert, for each clump of spinifex is an autonomous floral hell, repugnant in itself and a yellowed sepulchre of worse — venomous serpents like the brown snake *Demansia nuchalis* and the mulga snake *Pseudechis australis,* lizards such as *Amphibolorus reticulatis, Tiliqua branchiale,* and the ferocious-looking *Moloch horridus;* scorpions, grasshoppers, ants, and flies. Like vampires at dawn, but with nocturnal habits reversed in this upside-down land, the denizens of the spinifex ordinarily retreat into it at nightfall. This, I am convinced, is what made the aborigines into a night people. When the unbearable sun and the insects go down, they come out to sit around their little campfires to talk, fight, laugh, sing, and copulate.

In accord with the general rule, spinifex is not quite useless. It is the principal source of the aborigines' hafting gum — *keti* — and the common covering for their brush shelters (*wiltja*). To the white man it gives at certain times of the year fodder for cattle in the marginal pastoral areas; for the white bushman, it makes a nice mattress if canvas is put between it and the swag. Much too can be said for the sadistic fun of sprinkling a handful into a companion's sleeping bag.

Most of the men with whom I have gone into the desert would do that — and worse. The inland is no drawing room where subtlety is understood or appreciated. During the Second World War, when the American jungle troops were being trained by Australians to live entirely off the land, they were instructed to use in place of toilet paper leaves from the stinging nettle — whose touch is like a jolt from a 240-volt power line. Since humor is the most ephemeral of literature's genres, little of it is recorded in the old journals of the explorers (the large exception is Giles, and partly for that I love him above the others). But around Alice Springs Burly Bob Buck, the most outrageous of the belting bushmen, is well remembered in folklore. Bob succeeded Bill Harney, the cattle-rustling anthropologist, as custodian of Ayers Rock, the world's second largest single pebble. Walter Gill repeats several tales about his friend Buck, whom he met first in 1931 after that grizzled bushman returned from "pouring Harold Lasseter into his grave" (Harold Possum Lasseter is also legend in the Centre for "Lasseter's Reef," a lost gold mine, and for using his full double set of false teeth as a removable magical device to frighten the aborigines). One of the Buck tales recalls his putting a couple of drops of battery acid into an abscessed tooth to kill the pain — and embarking immediately on a magnificent run to nowhere across the gibber flats. Bob Verburgt once at our campfire told me an even better Bob Buck story. In the time of Buck's authority over the Rock some hardy tourists came down from Alice Springs on camels, those equivocal beasts beloved by some and detested by others. One of the latter was a hard-nosed spinster upon whom the camel threw up his vile cud — this animal's most effective expression of disapproval. The lady took instant action, and Buck hurried over as the camel shot in frenzy toward the horizon. "What the bloody baastidly hell did you do to that rotten animal?" shouted Burly Bob. "The filthy beast chundered on me and I just ducked under him and bit him on that bag under there." "Well," said Bob resignedly, dropping his trousers, "you'd better have a nibble at mine, too, so I can catch the baastid."

The explorers in whose time I should so much have liked to live have not been honored by posterity, for whom they labored. People nowadays appreciate neither their humor nor their stern necessities. Canning and Carnegie, who tried unsuccessfully to open north-south trails through the Victoria, Gibson, and Great Sandy deserts, were in their own time persecuted and prosecuted by city people for torturing, as the lawyers put it, the aborigines. Both men captured desert natives and chained them to trees, feeding them there on salt pork until, crazed by thirst, they led the explorers to water. This behavior for Carnegie was a stern necessity; he had found after bitter experience that the aborigines when simply asked where water might lie, always pointed in the wrong direction. (They may, in fact, have feared the fouling of their water holes.) Not once, Carnegie recalled, in three thousand miles on foot through the western deserts, had he found water on his own. On our long trip in the same deserts, 2,885 miles, Bob Verburgt and I found only one water hole we did not already know about.

In his memorable book *Spinifex and Sand*, Carnegie recalls the words of Colonel Peter Egerton Warburton, another torturer of natives: " 'We tried to cross [the Great Sandy] but had to turn back. . . . Country very bad, dense spinifex, high, steep sand-ridges with timber in flats. Any man attempting to cross this country with horses must perish. . . . A strong easterly wind prevailed, blowing up clouds of sand and ashes from the burnt ground. Truly this is a desert!' " Carnegie, himself writing for us more than seventy years ago, adds this comment, "This was written when I was two and a half years old. The writer little thought that an infant was growing up who would have no more sense than to revisit this ghastly region; nor as far as I remember was the infant thinking about sand! Dear me! how easy it was to get a drink in those days — merely by yelling for it — but the strongest lungs in the world cannot dig out a native well."

Like Carnegie, all but the first explorers knew the dangers they would have to face, and for this alone they deserve to be what I call them — heroes, whether their actions appeal to us or not. The desert was ringed with names of past tragedy and present warning — Lake Disappointment, Ruined Rampart, Mount Unapproachable, Mount

Misery, Mount Dreadful, Mount Despair, Mount Deception, Mount Destruction, Mount Hopeless, Mistake Well, Madman Outcamp. Even Giles is rubbished now by smart-assed apprentice anthropologists (who had to use Giles's trails) for defending himself against the natives and failing to make profound ethnographic analyses. In all his harrowing exploration through Pitjandjara, Jangkundjara, and Ngadadjara territory Giles and his small parties were attacked almost constantly, sometimes by hundreds of natives at once. Without his good humor (which put courage into his companions) and his own audacity, he would have died out there, like so many others. That he should be criticized for never using craniometers or chi-squares upon aboriginal warriors with spears fitted into their *miru!* Ah, what a wonder it is — how a hundred years of convincing savage spearmen that they must confine their savagery to their own kind can free young modern minds from any suspicion that there can exist conditions in which ethnography does not enter one's consciousness! In 1874 Ernest Giles had about as much interest in aboriginal marriage patterns as a tethered goat has in the social organization of Bengal tigers. Let Giles speak to the overriding requirements of exploration: *"The explorer indeed should be possessed of a good few accomplishments — amongst these I may enumerate that he should be able to make a pie, shoe himself or his horse, jerk a doggerel verse or two, not for himself, but simply for the benefit or annoyance of others, and not necessarily for publication, or as a guarantee of good faith; he must be able to take, and make, an observation now and again, mend a watch, kill or cure a horse as the times may require, make a packsaddle, and understand something of astronomy, surveying, geography, geology, and mineralogy,* et hoc, simile huic.*"*

The two men to whom I have dedicated this book, Bob Verburgt and Norman Tindale, satisfied all Giles's requirements and more he could not have conceived of in 1874. I will speak of Bob Verburgt when in his time he appears in my narrative; for the moment I will say simply that with him as my companion, I had no fear of any danger in the worst situations — one time only excepted. Norman must be spoken of now. If I say much about him in these pages, it is because much should be said about this man.

We met first when I was compiling the *Bibliography* that started it all. Thinking him then to be just an ordinary extraordinary man of whom I had met so many, I officiously informed him in the fresh fulsomeness of my bibliographic knowledge that a group of cave paintings he was reported to have discovered three weeks previously had been discovered at least twice before. I also had the impudence to tell him he was not keeping his field journals properly (a morsel of unrequested advice he noted in his Foreword to my *Bibliography:* "More than one researcher was led, by his persuasion, to prepare title pages and define the scope of his field notebooks, so that generations to come might know what to expect in these books"). Eleven years after that initial meeting Norman stood beside Supreme Court Justice Tom Clark and heard the citation by which he would become an alumnus of my own university:

Norman Barnett Tindale, Visiting Professor of Anthropology at the University of Colorado, achieved distinction as an entomologist early in his career, and then, changing his field, became the outstanding anthropologist of Australia. In fifty years of absolute dedication to scholarship he has made important contributions to anthropology, archaeology, geologic and geographic sciences, and many branches of biology in more than two hundred publications. His discoveries range from the oldest fossil lepidopteron to the pygmy race that first inhabited Australia. At the beginning of the Second World War he commanded in Washington an intelligence unit of the highest sophistication and importance. His work and his services in the tradition established by Lafayette saved incalculable thousands of American lives. For the last decade his guidance and counsel helped build the Department of Anthropology at the University of Colorado as one of the chief centers of Australian studies in the United States. For fifty years Norman Barnett Tindale has given unselfishly of himself to others in service to science, the United States, and to the University of Colorado. Mr. President, in recognition of these services and to make the University of Colorado his university, it is an honor to present Norman Barnett Tindale for the degree Doctor of Science, honoris causa.

How poor a summary of Norman's accomplishments! Many scientists have labored the whole of their lives and become famous for what they did in the corner of a garden on the gigantic ranch Norman Tindale took as his province. After the loss of his eye, he took refuge in anthropology and became the most knowledgeable person who ever accepted the Australian aborigines as a special field of study and opened new regions where no reliable guidelines existed. Still in his vocation-become-avocation he achieved enough to make himself the world authority on the *Hepialidae* and the *Rhopalocera*; in Australia he discovered the most ancient fossil lepidopteron (Triassic) and in the Colorado Rockies he found a new species of ghost moth for which he had been searching in this area for the last thirty years. In this field no less than others more lighthearted, the genial humor that makes human his scientific achievements subtly emerges, often well above the heads of those toward whom it is directed. During the Second World War in Washington (where his greatest service to this country was done) he found in a collection of butterflies sent him from Tennessee a new species of lepidoptera which he named for an important event in the intellectual history of that state: *Sthenopus darwinii.*

Norman was brought to Washington after the attack on Pearl Harbor because of his intimate knowledge of the Japanese language and people (his parents were missionaries, his mother the woman who brought the Salvation Army to Western Australia). It was his small Unit in Intelligence, largely staffed by Nisei, that cracked the Japanese naval and military aircraft production codes, so vital to the war effort that his achievement of stopping (by detective work reminiscent of his Barrinean discovery) the only enemy attack on the continental United States — the fire-bombing of the Pacific Northwest — seems insignificant in comparison. A day or two ago, while conversing with a student who had the two of us as teachers, I suddenly recalled that Norman had invented a Japanese typewriter. She told me that he has just been appointed once more — at seventy-two — a visiting professor at the University of Colorado. Norman is an exception in thus prospering in his edge of evening. Most of his predecessors did not. Giles died alone and in poverty. A few died in disgrace not of their own making. Edward John Eyre, the man who built that house at Moorundi, is the most tragic of the latter unfortunates. He was an explorer, too; he broke the trail across the southern Nullarbor where the Eyre Highway now lies. His magnificent work in Australia as protector of aborigines, described by Henry Kingsley as "eminently kind, generous, and just," was rewarded by having peninsulas, lakes, and rivers named for him, and eventually secured for him the position of governor-in-chief of the West Indies. During his tenure a bloody rebellion occurred; Eyre put it down the only way such things can be put down — with massive force. Safe from violence three thousand miles away in England, soft-headed men including that over-honored booby, John Stuart Mill, turned public opinion viciously against him.

Though acquitted in two trials, Eyre died a broken man, "the hero as murderer," as his latest biographer, Geoffrey Dutton, called him.

The hostile land itself punished with death many more of these heroes for errors of judgment, ignorance, or simple bad luck. Many places on the land are named for their perishing, but most did not have even that memorial. The most dramatically tragic of all Australian exploration was the Burke and Wills expedition to strike from Melbourne on the south coast to the Gulf of Carpentaria in the north. Alan Moorehead has recounted the story, largely in the words of the doomed men themselves, in his enthralling account, *Cooper's Creek*. Robert Burke and John Wills departed from Melbourne with perhaps the largest and best-equipped party ever to undertake land discovery on the Australian continent, and they died with nothing left but their clothes. The one survivor of the summit dash, John King (who was saved by the aborigines), did not even have his clothes — only a few rags and part of his hat. Burke and Wills were heavily to blame for their own misfortunes and death, surely, but the country they crossed was well named by Moorehead as "the ghastly blank." And yet it was traversed in 1883 by Australia's chief ambulatory nut, George Morrison, who walked the entire distance of two thousand miles alone in a hundred and twenty-three days. An even more remarkable walking madman known now only as the "Hatter" frightened away hostile aborigines by walking on his hands through aboriginal country.

Alfred Canning, the man who established the Canning Stock Route and who was born the year Burke and Wills died, had a few impressive strolls himself. He could not understand why other people could not see the western inland as he saw it — not as a thousand miles of nearly impenetrable desert, but as an elongated Garden of Eden. Who needed water? he asked. Certainly not himself; and if not himself, why anybody? "*I have lived all my life in a hot country,*" Canning wrote in the London *Daily Express*, "*and have gone a day or two days without water and have not felt any the worse. Once I lost a camel and walked 210 miles in five days carrying my own water and again I went for 80 miles without a drink.*"

Why, really, did these people go into the hostile land? I have given much thought to the question, having gone in there myself and having suffered the anticipation of untimely death without its release; I have read the journals of the explorers; I have looked beyond the reasons given me by my companions; and I can find no common denominator in any of us except bloody madness. Of course we all offered reasons other people might understand, but they are all as specious as the reasons given by policemen for choosing their profession. Giles said he wished only to open a path for later settlers. This is a common excuse. Len Beadell, who bashed useless tracks through the bush with a bulldozer, said he only wanted to lay down a path a traveler could not cross without noticing. Canning, as a lunatic's lunatic, was not obliged to give a reason for persuading the government to undertake what surely must be the craziest enterprise in all colonial history, the Canning Stock Route. But he too went before the public with a reason: *"There is a tract of 600,000 square miles capable of supporting a great white population. It is untrue to say that it is not a white man's country. The days are hot but the air is dry and one can easily work in temperatures of 120 degrees. Great colonies of farmers will one day flourish in what was popularly supposed to be a desert. They will send their produce to the countries of the world."* The Canning Stock Route and the desert it traverses are as empty of human beings today as they were when he wrote that prediction in 1910.

Some people will not believe this, but what it is, this madness for a desert once entered, this compulsion in some men to go again and again into empty places — the Australian Outback, the polar ice fields, space — is some inborn error of metabolism, possibly an autosomal recessive like diabetes mellitus, whose pathogenic clinical features are latent until the propositus enters an environment that can activate the malady. Right. Given the propensity and the stimulus, the ill is inescapable; like Montezuma's Curse in Mexico, you go in there, you get it. And like *Herpes progenitalis*, you get it, you do not get rid of it. One bite by a six-inch centipede, one mouthful of ironstone sand ground between your teeth one night in the swag, one thirst slaked by a billy of soupy water drawn from a rock hole full of drowned snakes and rotting birds, one bush fly scraping down your gullet, and you belong to the desert forever. I say in this book that I spent fifteen years pursuing the aborigines of Australia's western desert. Believe that if you can, for it will make my narrative better. But you will have to forget that statement was written by a misanthrope who would not cross the street to meet all the candidates for President, Democratic and Republican, together with all the crowned heads of Europe, much less the bloody wild men of the Pitjandjara tribe or their wilder neighbors. I did not know this thing

79

at the time, but I contracted my own activating infection twenty-five years earlier on California's Mojave Desert when there was nothing out there but soldiers and scorpions. From that time it was the desert I was after, and the past; a steadily growing dislike for this worst of all centuries and a wish to know those heroes who opened my desert. Not only the survivors, but those who perished, too — Charles Wells and George Jones, as a last example, men whose trail Bob Verburgt and I crossed when we were deepest in that terrible desert that claimed them. They died undeservedly but bravely, looking for a water hole their predecessor Warburton inaccurately noted in his charts. In his diary Warburton admitted carelessness in mapping, but added, *"What matter in such country as this?"* David Carnegie, with far more experience and bush nous than the Wells personnel, caught Warburton's mistakes on his own:

Many things go to prove that Warburton's positions are incorrect; I think I can show how, by moving his route bodily on the chart about eighteen miles to the East, a more accurate map will result. My own experience alone would not be conclusive, except that my work fits in with that of Forrest, Gregory, and Tietkens, where my route crosses theirs, but taken in conjunction with others it proves of value. . . . Considering the hard trials that Colonel Warburton and his party went through, there is small wonder that he found great difficulty in keeping any sort of reckoning.

Poor Carnegie — for all his knowledge, he was to die of a native's spear in Africa a year after this was printed, while he was looking for another desert.

Bob and I were to have our own disappointment, in part because of Warburton's cartographic errors, but ours was nothing set against the termination of the Calvert Expedition, named thus by the Wellses for their wealthy English sponsor. Even the survivors suffered frightfully, themselves making it to the safety of the Fitzroy River on the coast with only one bucket of water left. Larry Wells tried to fight his way back into the desert as a man will go back into a burning house where his family is trapped, but he did not find his cousin's body until the following year. *"I could see,"* he wrote on his arrival at Discovery Well, *"my cousin's iron-gray beard and at last we were at the scene of their terrible death and its horrible surroundings. Where Charles Wells lay, half-clothed and dried like a mummy, we found nothing but a piece of rag, a piece of rope hanging from a tree and some old traps hanging to some burnt bushes which held the brass eyelets of a fly which had either been rifled by natives or burnt by fire which had been within a few feet of his body. Where Jones lay, and near his hand was a note-book with a piece of paper fastened outside it with an elastic band. It was addressed to his father and his mother. . . ."*

My dearest Mother and Father,

I am writing this short note the last one I shall ever write I expect. We left the main party at the well and after 5 days travelling had to return being away 9 days as we were both far from well and I had hardly any strength. After 5 days spell we started to follow the main party after severe trials some of the camels died so we have had to walk we are both very weak and ill the other two camels are gone and neither of us have the strength to go after them I managed to struggle half a mile yesterday but returned utterly exhausted. There is no sign of water near here, and we have nearly finished our small supply have about two quarts left so we cannot last long. Somehow or other I do not fear death itself I trust in the Almighty God. We have been hoping for relief from the main party but I am afraid they will be too late. Any money of mine I think I should like divided between Eve Laurie and Beatrice. Now my darling parents I will wish you goodbye, but I trust we will meet in heaven. You both have always been so good to me I should so like to see you again. Mr. Charles has been very good indeed to me during this trip he is not to blame that we are in this fix. It is Gods will and so we should not object. Goodbye to Evie Jo and Beat and all our friends. And now darlings God give me strength till our next meeting. God's will be done, I remain,

Your loving son,
George Lindsay Jones

There are many further examples of divine improvidence in the narrative of Australian inland exploration, but I must not speak of these, for we must not have too many banal impossibilities, lest the skeptics be driven closer to inconvenient belief than I should like them to go. Let them abide with me only to the understanding that whatever force was to set Bob Verburgt and me not only out there where Jones and Wells died, but in another place where a still more memorable explorer died in circumstances of incredible coincidence, whatever force had set our so-much-revered predecessors in their several destinations before us, made us all alike in the ways little regarded by the more sensible and civilized world — fatalistic, wryly humorous in

81

things that do not bear humor in other places, strongly devoted to others like ourselves, and above all things else, bloody mad; and eternally complaining even in prayer: *Dear God, pity us in our unhappiness, that we may retain the strength to go on pitying ourselves.* Hear the first man to penetrate after terrifying hardships the precise center of our dear hostile land, John McDouall Stuart, as he lay on a stretcher between two horses, suffering beyond the enduring of pain, yet faithfully keeping his journal: "*My right hand nearly useless to me by the accident to the horse; total blindness after sunset . . . and nearly blind during the day; my limbs so weak and painful that I am obliged to be carried about; my body reduced to that of infantile weakness — a sad, sad wreck of former days. Wind variable.*"

Bē swa lēofan men, licʒan ðence. Oh, the dear men; I think to lie by them, to go with them into whatever Dreaming is ahead. Good on you, cobbers, good on you.

THREE

INTO
THE BUSH

I was working through my bibliographic sources still when I saw my first full-blood desert aborigine. Although we had the words (I had a few of his, he had many of mine), we did not know enough about ourselves or each other to understand that we could not even establish a ground for communication. We grinned at each other in that social fear of the impossibly different stranger that makes American and Russian track competitors hug each other and exchange medals. His name was Mike McHale and he could not say for sure whether he was Scots-Irish or Irish-Scots. I was happy to tell him we must be distantly related, because I was Irish-Dutch with the Irish part black — though not quite so black an Irishman as he appeared to be. Much later I learned that was the proper way to initiate acquaintance with aborigines — talk about relationships. In America we talk about the weather, a harmless subject. In aboriginal Australia a discourse on relatives used to end in death for the intruder who could not prove a relationship close enough to provide a pattern of expected social behavior. An utter stranger in the aboriginal world was a possible homicidal lunatic; one could not be sure what he might do in any situation. He might use a word containing a syllable in the name of a person recently dead, or walk close to where the clan's *tjurunga* were secreted. Capital offenses. Kill the baastid. I did not know any of this at the time. I did not know anything at the time. I knew thousands of items of scholarship in my *Bibliography*, but even there I had no conception of how much error there was in scholarly writing. *"What country youfella,"* he asked. America. *"Teiwa? Ngamu? Long way way? Close up?"* Long way way, my bloody oath. *"What way youfella country?"* Oh, Christ. Where do you point for America when you are halfway around the world? I swung my arm out in one direction or other and put the question to him. No harm in that. What way youfella country? He turned and pointed pursed lips to the north. Jesus Christ, I thought, that's the way Mexicans point direction. A thing learned already and never to be explained. We did not get very far with our dialogue.

We were at the small and desperately poor Umeewarra Mission just beyond the outpost town of Port Augusta on the northern edge of the South Australian frontier. Norman had sent me there after I picked his brains on the bibliography. I wanted to see some aborigines; I had not seen any in Sydney or Canberra or Melbourne or Adelaide. "Go to a jail town," he advised; "go to Port Augusta." When it becomes unavoidable to arrest an aborigine for what we know as a serious crime, he is taken to a border jail town, and his family walks down hundreds of miles after him.

That was another thing learned. It is practically impossible for any white person, Australian or American, to meet a full-blood aborigine. For one thing, there are no more than a half dozen passable tracks leading into aboriginal country, from any direction. For another, the few tracks that do exist are on prohibited land. For a third, you cannot get permission to travel these tracks unless your credentials are such that ignoring you would be a matter for the United Nations. For a fourth, if you do get into aboriginal country, you are not allowed to do anything — you are enjoined under the gravest penalties from trading with the natives, employing them, interfering with flora or fauna or rock hole or soakage or watering place (no tying aborigines to trees and feeding them salt pork, like Carnegie and Canning!), photographing aborigines, giving them liquor, transporting them, or attempting "to induce change in any sphere of thought, beliefs, or actions of the Aboriginal residents, or in any way [to] interfere with the traditional character, behaviour, spiritual beliefs or ways of life of Aboriginals." Not much danger of that, since you are also forbidden to proceed more than sixty-six feet from any road or track. Moreover, you must obey any order of any commonwealth or state officer whatsoever, which order often is to take your arse out of here.

But there is more than one way to skin a dingo. Tindale's method of getting things done in a country where it is not permitted to do anything is to employ the legal precept of *numero unius, exclusio alterius*, which is to say, "do anything not listed." The overburdened legal system never got around to revoking the right of a mining prospector to enter any land he wished, so he carries a gold miner's license. There are other devices to which I am now privy.

In 1956, for the short time I could spare from my bibliographic work, Norman's jail-town device was enough. At Port Augusta the authorities were troubled not only with crazy white men going into the forbidden Outback but aborigines coming out — for liquor, then entirely forbidden to them. Every day the Adelaide newspapers told of dreadful drinking debauches in the bush. A policeman seeing a native with a bottle of booze in the streets would try to confiscate the gargle. Having learned in his first few days in civilization essential English, the aborigine would resist, saying, *"Fuck off, you fucking trap — I ain't no fucking blackfella; I'm a fucking Australian,"* followed by a wobbly attempt to sing *Waltzing Matilda*. I saw no drinking disorder in Port Augusta and so remarked to a white resident. "Look," I said, "all they're doing is carrying around bottles of orange soda." "Yair — they mix that with gin." Another thing learned. White Australians, being more civilized, drink rum and raspberry.

At every place I stopped on that first Australian visit I had my head knocked free of another of those crystalline truths I was sure I'd die with. In Hawaii I discovered all the Polynesians were Japanese. In Fiji I saw what happens when a country permits unrestricted immigration (Indians — the turbaned variety — had come in and driven all the native Fijians to refuge pockets in the centers of the two islands, and were carrying placards reading YANKEES GO HOME — FIJI FOR THE FIJIANS). In the Australian coal-mining region around Newcastle, where I did some down-in-the-mines research for an article commissioned by the American *United Mine Workers Journal* (for which I used to write in my liberal days) I saw there were only two ways for the government to achieve industrial peace: (1) shoot all the miners, and (2) give the workers the mines and open new, fully automated mines in the lignite country. The government sentimentally inclined to the former, but at last settled for the latter.

And my notions about missionaries. Anthropologists as a first article of received faith must hate missionaries. I hate easily, but I couldn't hate the dear ladies at Umeewarra. Granted, they had a house stuffed full of native children taken, in violation of the United Nations charter, from their parents; there were no amenities at all; in the periphery of the mission adults squatted in squalor; altogether the place was a mess. What, I asked as a first question, were these missionaries doing with all the money? What money? I learned that the Umeewarra Aborigines Mission was one of those autonomous Christian charities known to Australian inlanders as "faith missions." Inde-

pendent as they are dedicated, fundamental in doctrine and fundamental in purpose, they have little in common except a raw Christianity, the work of helping aborigines as they know best, and abject
poverty. The "faith" missionaries live on a subsistence as bare as the
aborigines who come to them in desperation as refugees. I never met
one who earned in currency more than five dollars a week; many received no cash at all. Harder than poverty, as I look back on them
now, was their dissociation from a great Church to give them com-
radeship in Christ. They exist in spatial and social isolation, clinging
to their aborigines as the aborigines cling to them. At Umeewarra the
missionaries were women, strong sisters of the poor, worn by hardship to rawhide; and yet I criticized them for "conditions." In a day
I learned the children had not been taken from their parents; the
parents had brought them in and abandoned them. I was shocked to
see the children lying in dormitories on beds set together as tight as
squares on an inlaid chessboard. What would the children do in case
of fire? Fire indeed. As well worry about the wetness of the water in
a bay full of sharks. Take out alternate squares on the chessboard of
beds and you take out alternate children. Well, what about getting
some sort of decent shelters for the adults who come in from the
Centre to squat outside the mission? They showed me a small settlement of minimal but quite livable corrugated-iron huts. Empty. "Why
dempella 'ouse he empty?" I asked Mike McHale. *"Pella him pinis in
dem 'ouse."* A man had died there. Of course. All over the primitive
world the place of death is contaminated. One wonders whether our
belief in haunting does not derive from a universal fear, overcome in
our case by the unbearable expense of evacuating a home worth a
lifetime of labor. It takes a strong religion, one overcrowded with
inimical spirits, to intimidate the pocketbook.

I came eventually to admire, even to like, the missionaries — not
all of them, of course; that would be too great a strain on my small
resource of love for mankind. But on the whole, vastly more than the
do-gooding city people who criticize the only group of whites who put
their own lives on the line without any thought of monetary — or,
more common these days — political, gain.

What a terrible thing is the interfering charity of ignorance! The
last word I have heard from my informants in Australia is that American civil righteousness has been imported, and aborigines are being
brought in from the Outback to demonstrate in the streets of Sydney

(not one in fifty thousand of whose residents have ever seen an aborigine), raising fists and screaming *"BLACK POWER!"* Black power to my golden people? Afro wigs over their curly golden hair? *How long, O Lord, how long?*

Not that my profession, even the scientific part of it, is much better in avoiding the sins of ignorance. Look into the medical literature of the aborigines and you will see summarized cases of natives brought in from the desert and incarcerated in asylums for indisputable insanity.

Item: A young aboriginal woman named "Grety, alias Cranky" was committed to a mental prison. "The reasons for certification were that she was continually moving about, never for a minute at rest." She died, still incarcerated, two years later.

Item: "Delusional insanity — Jacky Jacky, alias Jimmy, aged 56, a widower of no occupation. . . . The reasons for certification were that he stated that he was a white man (in colour, not quality)." He died incarcerated within a year.

Item: "Diagnosis not stated. . . . No details were given of his previous history except that he was delusional, thinking that he had just been operated upon and a piece of stick removed from his head. . . . On the mental side he was exalted and had delusions of persecution together with the delusions mentioned above. Restlessness and suspicion were marked features. During the next six years his condition varied between phases of restlessness, noisiness and troublesomeness and of others when he was more settled, quieter and would work well."

Item: "Diagnosis not stated — Waubin, alias Ross, aged 40. . . . He was certified as insane on the grounds that he did not answer questions but gesticulated, laughed and behaved absurdly. . . . He was noticed to have curious shy habits and in July relapsed into a restless confused condition and was discovered lacerating his penis with a piece of glass." Waubin died in two years.

The more deviant the conduct in these cases, the more it conformed to proper aboriginal deportment. The penis-cutting, for an extreme instance, is the basic socio-religious rite among tribalized natives, no matter how little the practice appeals to us. I know the man who certified the diagnosis of insanity on Grety, Jacky Jacky, Waubin, and others of their misfortune. He is very old now and very much honored.

So he should be; he is an honorable man. His only fault is his rampant altruism, and for that he will be damned, if there is damnation for any of us.

On another trip into the bush a few years later with Norman Tindale as my companion I stopped at Umeewarra again. The mission ladies were still there, skin and sinews a bit more like beef jerky, still caring for their children, tolerating a new mob of visiting desert people in back of the compound, and teaching fundamentally from the Bible. At that time they had a young girl among their de facto orphans named Winnie Bamara. Winnie had been brought down nine years earlier at the age of seven from Ooldea (Ernest Giles's Youldeh, the base water camp on that Fourth Expedition). Trachoma sent her to the Adelaide Children's Hospital first; later she was found to have polio also. Whoever her parents were, there was no finding them at the time of her release, so she was sent to Umeewarra. In her early education at the mission school she was too remote, too uncommunicative, to do well. Nothing organic hindered her, except a left arm thinned by the crippling disease; she had just withdrawn into her own mind when there were no others to cleave to in that critical time of her life.

Winnie's life was opened by art. The schoolteacher at Umeewarra showed me several of her watercolors, bursting with artistry unapproached by the other children, yet Winnie was untaught and unteachable. The ladies brought in a professional artist from Adelaide who caught the potential in Winnie's watercolors and showed her she had the shadows all wrong. After he departed Winnie drew better shadows, but she drew nothing else — just shadows, shadows, till the schoolteacher, in that desperation few adults can long repress when confronted by a stubborn child, tore up her papers and let her work as she wished. When the learning of art stopped, the exercise of art began. She painted landscapes in the white man's fashion (her own people had no artistic tradition at all) but somehow unlike white man's landscapes. I think the transforming element in Winnie's work was the red ocher permeating it. As Grandma Moses's seven coats of white lead shone through even her thunderstorm landscapes, so did the aboriginal ochers illuminate Winnie's watercolors — the ochers and their magic.

In 1959 the most famous of all her people — Albert Namatjira the painter — died in a canvas-and-tin humpy on the dry banks of

90

the Finke River in the Red Centre, under sentence of imprisonment for giving liquor to the aborigines (honored with citizenship, he fell under citizens' laws). In that year, a few months before Albert's passing, this little girl had twenty of her paintings placed on special exhibition in the outstanding art city of Adelaide, a show opened by one of the nation's leading citizens, Sir Lloyd Dumas. I do not know what happened to Winnie afterward. She would have had to leave the mission when she came of age and go out into some kind of world. I hope it was a better world than Old Olga lived in. Olga was one of the last of the Dieri tribe, come down to Umeewarra when her own people died away, and kept there as a special resident. She had almost no English and she had lost her Dieri tongue in the years away from her tribe. Anesthetized by her cultural muteness, she grinned at visitors and thought what thoughts I could not imagine. I hoped then there were no others in her plight, but I was to see many later on my journey along the western fringe, their humanness destroyed by an intrusive religion.

But our destination on this particular bush penetration was another mission, the Yalata Reserve on the eastern Nullarbor. This anomaly among missions is at once a South Australian government aboriginal reservation and a mission of the Evangelical Lutheran Church. A clear enough connection of church and state to stir up all the cranks who write letters to the Adelaide *Advertiser*, an embarrassment to the government, and a worry for the church under secular assault, Yalata survived because it was more than anything else a wise abandonment of principle for practical good. From its foundation it was a triumph of sensible expediency over rigid philosophy.

Yalata is a million and a half acres of utterly dry land in an expanse of saltbush, bluebush, insignificant lesser brush, and mallee (semi-desert eucalyptus) merging to mulga (desert acacia). The only good water in this vast region provided by unassisted nature is at Ooldea. Giles had been drawn here to "Youldeh" by the water, and he was followed much later by the transcontinental railway; finally, the railway drew in the aborigines from mutually hostile tribal lands to a chaos of intermingling but internecine bands who were not only killing but eating one another when Mrs. Daisy Bates came to save them from themselves and from the railroad whites.

Daisy Bates stands out among a nation of outstanding women. A year old when the American Civil War began, she lived until 1951 — ninety years, of which the best were spent in a small tent on the

91

Nullarbor. Early photographs show her to have been a willowy Irish beauty when she came to Australia as a traveling journalist. She married a John Bates of Bathurst, New South Wales, probably while she was too ill of incipient tuberculosis to know what a nuisance a spouse would be to her. After coming back to her health and her senses she left Mister Bates and Master Bates, the latter a son who evidently bored her as much as her husband bored her. In Western Australia near the dread Ophthalmia Range she took up a pastoral property of nearly two hundred thousand acres, the strongest memory of which was her hatred of cows. "I loathe their whitewashed faces," she wrote in *The Passing of the Aborigines* (1938), her astonishingly slim story of "a lifetime spent among the natives of Australia." One would have thought it was their other ends she loathed, for she rode behind them three thousand miles by her own estimate — seven hundred Hereford behinds, by actual count — in driving the largest mob of cattle ever taken down from the northwest coast. After various kinds of nomadic work in outback Australia she settled at Ooldea to become the *kabali* (grandmother) of a mob of man-eating savages. Nothing they could do annoyed her — murder, cannibalism, filiophagy, incest, and impudence to one's elders. They had all been tried, convicted, and doomed for crimes done, still to be done, and never to be done. Her office was that of a death-house chaplain — as she said over and over again, "to make their passing easy." She has been called a missionary, but in all her years among the natives she confessed to having spoken only two sentences of religion to comfort a dying woman out of this world to the Dreaming. In *The Passing of the Aborigines* she tells of the woman, Jeerabuldara, in the ugliness of desert death seizing her hand and whispering in terror, *"Yaal wanning?"* ("Where am I going?"). Daisy Bates asked in return, *"Kabbarli balya?"* ("Is Grandmother good?").

"Kabbarli balya." ("Grandmother is good.")

"My Father is sitting down where you are going, Jeera, and as soon as I let go your hand, my Father will catch hold of it. He will take care of you until I come."

"You Father, *Kabbarli?* Then I shall be safe."

Daisy Bates came back to civilization in 1935 to write up her lifetime's knowledge of the desert people, but strangely, she did not have much to say. I dug up from various obscure papers two hundred and seventy-four published items written by her, none of any consequence.

92

She has in her book a few words about her first bath in twelve years on her return to Adelaide and the surprise she gave the city in walking its streets in clothes a quarter-century old, but her disapproval of the changes civilization allowed itself to suffer in her absence shows she did not think it worth her while to say much to civilization on anything at all. She tried to return to her desert people in 1935, but poor health and age kept her in Adelaide, a Commander of the British Empire with little regard for the British Empire. I was to meet a few

Ruins of chapel at Eucla, W.A.

old aborigines who had known her at Ooldea; each remembered her as frail in body and strong in spirit, the person to whom they most owed gratitude for having established as national policy rations distribution, and withal, a woman a "li'l bit wonky."

Her community or congregation at Ooldea was taken over by the United Aborigines Mission, the cooperative of Faith Missions, which held it until 1952, when the mission moved down to the old sheep station of Yalata on Fowler's Bay.

Our arrival at Yalata had been anticipated for a long time, and we expected to be greeted like Germanicus bringing the lost eagle back to Rome. But at Yalata there was no one running madly out of the shade, no children crying for lollies, no barking dogs, no adult men with hands clasped behind their backs and beards thrust forward in studied dignity to bid us a formal "G'day!" A couple of aboriginal garage hands stared at us from the open garage. Apart from these and the superintendent, Barry Lindner, emerging from his house, the compound was deserted. We looked around, identifying the buildings: across the hard sterile gray earth of the empty acre to the southwest were a half dozen small living quarters for the staff; next to them in our direction, storage sheds and doorless garages; behind us a schoolhouse, the schoolmaster's cottage, and a large recreation ground, concreted in futile hope as a water catchment; and at the northeast of the barrio the superintendent's house and the commissary. As mission and reserve establishments go, this was a large community.

Barry Lindner came over to us, smiling warmly, genuinely pleased to see us instead of exercising Christian hospitality as a duty and a discipline. Guests we were to him, not intruders upon Samaritan reputation. Barry is a small man with compensative wiriness, the typical Australian battler. He is not in professional fact a missionary. The assigned Lutheran minister, he told us, had left some months ago, principally to give the mission its best chance to survive the determined minor government officials' policy of dragging the aborigines into twentieth-century civilization by the bloody black ears. Barry's mind was full of this worry. Obviously he loved his mission and the people, and he was sure any speeding of acculturation would destroy them.

Where were the aborigines? we asked. Out in the bush, about five miles north, most of them. A few of the older and more sedentary people who worked at little jobs around the mission were sitting down on the other side of the compound to the south. He kept no permanent camp because the aborigines cleaned out an area of all vegetation and game so long as water was available. Water, he said, was his carrot; he needed no club to move the aborigines from one place to another. He had the water tank on a truck, and when it was time to move to a fresh camping place, he simply had the truck moved off. The more indolent men, anxious to catch up on thirty thousand years of sleep lost in Paleolithic exertion, grumbled about unnecessary removals. Nevertheless, water had to be followed, and there was nothing for it but to grab up their bits of canvas, empty milk-powder cans, fragments of clothing, and other whitefella detritus, slam the lot on their wives' heads, and walk after the water truck shaking their spears in annoyance.

On our first day at the mission we worked on background material. The reason for our mission was Barry's hope that Norman in his great knowledge would draw from the native craftsmen's minds the memory of how artifacts used to be made for themselves before they were made for tourists, with kangaroos and emus scratched all over them. One does not work hastily with aborigines. Let their curiosity build to the point where they will silently investigate you first, and then make yourself available. Without their goodwill nothing can be done except blunder. So we spent our time going through Norman's *Register of Yalata Natives*, one of the many genealogical data books he had compiled for most of the continent.

Next day we offered ourselves to the people. I weaved my Toyota Land Cruiser — the best of the small desert-worthy vehicles — through the mallee to a clear place about a half mile from the aboriginal camp, roared the motor a few times as a signal of our presence, got out our groundsheets and swags, and sat down to await their emissaries. This was the old way of meeting between an outsider and the owners of a country before the white man came. In those fair times if a man fled or was driven from his own tribe he would seek attachment to some other in just this way: approach their camp, sit down, and wait for a delegate. As I said earlier, the first talk would be about relatives. If the visitor could establish social affinity, he would be welcomed. If not, he would be killed. Nothing cruel or unreasonable; aboriginal individual behavior is almost entirely determined by social placement. Integration had to be immediate or not at all. In these latter days when white men have shown stern displeasure toward the old and easy solutions of sociological dilemmas, a receiving group may just place the visitor arbitrarily into one of the subsections among them. In the deepest bush, however, a stranger has an excellent chance still to be killed.

Bimeby little bit close-up— a half hour or so — an old man approached from the camp. Though neither of us is an addict to the sotweed, we lit up cigarettes. The man ambled over, taking no more notice of us than if we had been a couple of logs. He sat down. We puffed our cigarettes and laid them down near him. Just as casually he picked them up, pinched the glowing end off one and put the stub behind his ear along with his quid of native tobacco, *mingulpa*, and stuck the other cigarette butt in his mouth with commendable aplomb. Nothing spoken.

Bimeby Norman said, *"Ngayulu Aranda Mbitjana."* ("I am an Aranda man of the Mbitjana subsection.") True enough; during his expedition to the western Aranda in 1929 he was placed in this one of that tribe's eight divisions.

"Uah." ("Yes.") The man did not have to make any reciprocal yabber about who he was; we were the ones who had to establish ourselves.

"Wati nyanga teiwa pitjangu," Norman continued, telling him I was a man who had come from far away.

I was not having any of that. It had been the custom for many years — ever since the aborigines learned by hard experience it was not expedient policy to treat the *walypela* (whitefellow) as themselves — to accept an adult white man at face value, since his penis value was not up for examination. If you are male, obviously older than voting age — the old voting age — and do not have your thumb in your mouth, the Australian natives will accept you as equivalent to a fully initiated man. But with so many Americans abroad spreading the mischievous democratic nonsense of *liberté, égalité, fraternité* even unto the desert inland of Australia, there was no telling what this mob might do. So I introduced myself proper loudfella: *"Ngayulu Ngala; wati nyanga ngayuku mama."* ("I am a member of the Ngala subsection; this man here is my father.") Among the Aranda *mama* is the papa. Thus at one stroke I became proper-fella man for the aboriginal camp, saved my working parts from religious mutilation, and put Norman into a social relationship with myself that would forever keep him from making goo-goo eyes at my wife.

Thus were the important points made. After a few more phrases of small talk and a few more cigarettes put behind the ear, the man got up and slowly walked back to his camp. Nothing more for us to do this day. The man would report. Tomorrow we would come here again and we would see whether we had been accepted. We waited until the man had been out of sight for some minutes; then we threw our swags and groundsheet into the Tojo (the Toyota's inevitable nickname among Australians), and drove off miles farther in the bush, to spend the rest of the day fossicking around old aboriginal camp-sites. There were plenty of them, going back ten years and more, judging time by the degree of natural attrition. "Archaeology in the making," Norman called these sites. What impressed me most was the amount of biotic destruction around them and the reluctance of the bush to regenerate itself. In this area just over the mallee line, the only significant trees were the skeletal mulga; in the old camps they had been burned or hacked down for firewood or artifact-making. The thin grass had been kicked out by hundreds of rough bare feet, the desert pavement had been broken, there was no regrowth at all. Total devastation.

Apart from the destruction which no other animal than man could have caused, the evidence of occupation was meager and already turning back to its entropic elemental components. We saw carbonized ashes of campfires, each with one or more bits of clothing rotting away (the natives will leave clothing where they throw it in warm weather; sometimes they will pick it up again, sometimes not). On the windward side of the campfires hardier limbs of *wiltja* structure lay where they had finally collapsed. At some of the campfires too many mulga chips told us that artifacts had been made for barter to the mission. A mission camp, therefore, these *ngura*. Here the natives had chopped hard mulga slabs into dark brown, yellow-striped boomerangs, clubs, and rough figures of kangaroos, lizards, and serpents — the things overseas visitors to Adelaide would buy as genuine aboriginal crafts. A day of leisurely chipping and gouging of nontraditional designs with a sharpened screwdriver instead of the old stone adze, a boomerang for an American tourist, and five shillings for the maker at the Yalata commissary. The face of the poor ground again and yet again, saith the letters to the *Advertiser* six hundred miles away; but out here a week's tobacco, a can of powdered milk, lollies for the children, some tinned food as a frivolous delicacy. Riches undreamed of for a day's doodling. Many of them remembered when keeping alive allowed no doodling at all, when a phratry of families had to trot to reach the next water hole in far better country than this.

At dinner that night with Barry and his wife (who had made as a treat a large quandong pie) we talked about the background and present plight of the mission-reserve. In all its territorial vastness the only habitable part was the few walkable miles surrounding Barry's movable water tank. No other water, standing or running, existed anywhere. The Mirning and Wirangu tribes that inhabited the Nullarbor before the coming of the white man were gone — the Mirning entirely, the Wirangu all but a few anomic families. The vacuum they had left, abhorrent to demography as well as to nature, had been filled in the last two generations by remnants of other tribes shifted by a movement of the Pitjandjara.

When a terrible drought in 1916–1917 forced the Pitjandjara out of the west into the eastern Musgrave and Everard ranges, the shock of their thrust went through the other tribes like a wave. The Jangkundjara were blasted out of their country into the homeland of the Arabana, the Arabana fell upon the Kujani, and so around a circle skirting the south-central dry lake chain and then west again along the coast. And back in America my colleagues laughed with their students at the Domino Fact as if it were a theory.

This part of the Nullarbor was not really habitable to the newcomers, but here is where their domino fell. The resourceful Mirning, masters of the esoteric craft of discovering water where no one else would think of looking for it — in certain roots of certain trees and brush, in aestivating frogs, and other improbable places — had been able to exist here, but their successors, fitted by their culture to drink as human beings were supposed to drink, had neither the knowledge nor the inclination to suck water out of taproots. They became entirely dependent on the white missionaries who carted water in from places better favored by Jupiter.

Yalata now was bringing its water in from Koonibba, its declining sister mission some seventy miles east. Only three inches of rain had fallen here in the last year, and evaporation had taken most of that before the catchments could carry it into the tanks. The staff had drilled a bore for underground water, but what they pumped up was so heavily mineralized it could not be used for anything except washing down the garage floor. Men could not drink it, sheep would not drink it, it could not be used even for washing clothes or bodies. One of the least forgettable sights I retain from Yalata was of a gang of children whose hair had been washed in Yalata bore water; they looked as if they had grown stalagmites on their heads.

The four hundred and thirty tribespeople at Yalata were dissociated elements of the Ngalia, Kokata, and Pitjandjara from the desert to the north and a few survivors of the Wirangu. They lived in tranquillity such as I was not to see again among so many aborigines. It was Barry's peace. He was neither permissive nor silly. All aboriginal rifles had to be checked into his strong room, removable only with his permission for stated purposes at stated times. No one took a rifle into camp at night. If any spearing occurred, he promptly moved the water tank an inconvenient number of miles away. Aborigines have grown tired of walking through their Paleolithic millennia, and if a couple of contentious men bring on a camp move through their indulgence in truculence, they can bet their bloody boomerangs they will be on the receiving end of a good punch-up from the uninvolved men, who will also institute a period of watchful probation with no appeal to a higher court.

When the sun rose high enough the next morning to stir up the bush flies, making sleep impossible for the rest of Australia's tormented creatures, we went out again to our sitting-down place. Immediately the men came in; we had been accepted. One factor in our favor was the presence in camp of two oldmen whose lives Norman had saved a few years earlier. They had dropped and broken a stone *tjurunga* — a capital offense. Norman restored the sacred stone with epoxy and the custodians escaped punishment. Such debts are remembered.

Religion is nearly the whole of life among the aborigines; war, peace, sex, food, and entertainment all flow from it. Since the invention of the tape recorder Australian field anthropologists use sung myths almost exclusively to establish communication with the aborigines. Both Norman and I had our own portable tape recorders. Our practice was to have Norman conduct the formal taping while I set up my machine twenty or thirty yards away under a jacket with other gear, the microphone well disguised. Turned on at a speed of fifteen-sixteenths inches per second, I can get at least four hours of song and conversation without touching the recorder for adjustment. By this method Norman would get good-fidelity recordings of whatever our informants wanted us especially to hear, while I picked up everything at the cost of a little clarity. Invasion of privacy? It is the science of trespass.

On this field trip we saw our first case of simony in the south country. One man who came in with the group this first day, a queechy little sour-faced baastid, demanded money for singing the sacred

99

songs. "Me money man," he grumbled. "Me not silly. Me wantim like money." "*Nyuntu ma kumpurowa*," I told him — 'Go piss up your leg." He was a soul lost to himself, lost to his people — rubbish. He was the kind who sold *tjurunga*, the spirits of his totem, for sixpence in the old days. The other men ignored him.

Not to mince the matter, we gave these men more than money and they repaid us in the same treasure. Knowing them all to be fully initiated *wati*, we let them hear and learn the sacred songs of the desert country, songs and mythic cycles they knew only fragments of in their own *Inma*. The men's delight was fearsome. As soon as the first few phrases were played they looked around wildly for possible eavesdroppers and motioned us frantically to turn down the volume to a whisper, though we were a half mile from the camp's hearing. Our songs inspired the men to sing their contiguous continuations; in this way we would ultimately be able to patch out a quilt of the continent's mythic songs.

One day when we all had a surfeit of sacred singing, Barry Lindner took us deep into the bush to see a ceremonial ground. Norman was as excited by the place of dramatic ritual as if he had swung a new species of butterfly into his net. In a way what we saw was in fact a new species, for this part of the continent at least. It was a *bora* ground, classical as the great but forgotten scholar Robert Hamilton Mathews described it for New South Wales three-quarters of a century earlier. Two dancing grounds, one circular and one elliptical, cleared of all brush, just over three hundred yards apart, each with several entry paths made for each of the several religious classes of participants. The southern, circular ground was an antechamber, the nave of this aboriginal unroofed cathedral, where women (properly hidden under blankets) could witness the preliminary dancing. A straight path led north to the chancel where the climactic ritual took place. Both grounds had a concealing altar of brush, both forty-two feet long, both six feet high, both approximately six feet broad; in these were the tabernacles where the holy objects and materials for decorating the dancers were secreted. We grieved that we had missed the ceremonies, which had taken place a few days before our arrival.

The tracks left by the dancers looked regularly irregular to me, so on a second visit we took along a knowledgeable informant, the most fluent speaker of English among the aborigines, whose whitefella name was Peter Pepper. I had him and Norman shuffle along the track, Norman recording while Peter sang the dancing song, as I was up a tree photographing the path as their shuffle outlined it and timing the movement to join in space and time the sacred song on the tape. Putting the photographs together later, I saw that the path was a representation of the ubiquitous rainbow serpent.

Later Barry took us a hundred yards off the joining path and showed us the *tjurunga* concealed beneath a cover of leaves and brush. The

Tjurunga ("law sticks") at Yalata, south of Nullarbor Plain, S.A.

men had given him permission to show the sacred boards to anyone he judged worthy and eligible to see them. This is the kind of missionary-administrator Barry is; one so sure of God and the many paths to Him to believe that every good road, white or aboriginal, leads to the same salvation. The very few successful missionaries to the Australian aborigines I know approach religion this way.

A few of the *tjurunga* were quite unlike any I had ever seen or

101

heard of — anatomically accurate (if ambitiously large) subincised penes made of mulga wood. We photographed them (one photographs everything, including ants and butterflies if they are up to anything in the least out of the ordinary), but Norman coveted one for the museum's collection. The next time we sat down with the men we broached the subject. No sign of answer to the unspoken question was made by any of the men, but in that night's pre-dawn two men came into our camp, each with a mulga penis for our purchase. The things were unconsecrated rubbish with no more religion in them than rosaries on Roman stalls, but we bought them for the effort.

Out in the men's singing ground we had established identification of the important people, whose names would go into our genealogies and ultimately into the schema we would make of the social organization. There were the *wati yina* Ornandu, Wongin (also known as Teddy Wongi), Kugena, and men who would not give us any but their *walypela* names — Edgar Stewart, Bobby Minn, Kenny, Kelly Brown, Peter Pepper, Mickey Chamberlain, and the taciturn Freddy Windlass. This Babel of alternate names is confusing, doubtless the source of bitter accusations of inaccurate reporting among different ethnographers working in the same regions of Australia at different times. Kugena was also Harry and Jarrie; the old rascal Freddy Windlass whom we were later to come to know very well was also Tommy Windlass; Ornandu (a Pitjandjara adopted by the Ngalia tribe) was also Charlie Tunkin; and Teddy Wongi was Wongin. We thought at first there was no difference between "Wongin" and "Wongi," but the man's severe agitation at having the former said aloud led us to the discovery that somehow we had got hold of his secret *tjukurpa* name, which a man does not himself learn until he is high in his religious hierarchy. "Wongi" and "Wongin" are indistinguishable to untrained ears, but to Teddy they were as different as "Negro" and "nigra" in the American South before both those appellations were tabued. And in his case one could let one's tongue slip easily into "wonky" — bush yabber for "crazy." *"Better youpella callit TEDDY!"* Bobby Minn was also known as *Tjinakukatji*, a secret name we thought, until we separated the syllables and made the phrase "meat foot" out of them. It was a nickname alluding to his unfortunate loss of toes in some campfire one night in heavy sleep.

There was another "meat foot" in camp — and she was wonky also. Ordinarily male anthropologists do not talk to women — not because of anyone's fear of seduction, but because in religious matters women are rubbish, and any *walypela* seen talking to one would not be spoken to again by the initiated men. But Belita Queama was judged sufficiently off her chump by the other aborigines to make her eligible as an informant. She was no mine of ethnographic information, but she had a few peculiarities worth her appearance in our journals. First of all, she was a thrasher asleep, and in her nightly gyrations had burned several toes off as well as roasting patches from other parts of her body. She was cheerful nonetheless. For me Belita's main attractiveness was her addiction to hillbilly music. She had an agile tongue; she sang, not only hymns, but country-western songs, rather well, too. She also imitated birds and banjos. She told us she had been on stage with Buddy Williams (a famous cowboy singer in the Australian bush) and had been offered a contract to go on tour with him until it was noticed that she was short several toes. Alas! The physical deprivations keeping so many of us from fame and fortune!

Belita was not the only aboriginal admirer of cowboy songs. All the men appreciated American country-western music, though not in the context of their religious singing. No guitar masses in the bush. And the children! When their schoolteacher told them one of the two whitefellas was a famous American cowboy singer — that is how my function as a folklorist was translated at Yalata — I was commanded to give a performance. Orright. I had my big Martin Dreadnaught in the Tojo against such a situation, so I sang to them with unbounded applause. The kids — all of them pure aboriginal and all of them blond — received me with the same brainless hysteria American teen-agers at that time were pouring over the Beatles. Fair enough. One does not look appreciative screams in the mouth.

Their repayment in kind was more memorable to me than my entertainment could possibly have been to them. It had been laid on ahead of time, no question. Lights were suddenly dimmed, shades drawn, a little fire built on a tin sheet in the center of the cleared schoolroom, and a circle of little boys decorated in flour and lipstick formed around the campfire to sing. To appreciate their composition one has to understand that all aboriginal song, sacred and profane, consists of a succession of disarticulated phrases, each lasting one cascaded breath. Tjinakukatji's myth about the spinifex wallaby, for example, has the repeated line

Mala   li   bidi:n   paṟu pardui
Spinifex wallaby goes separated long long way

as its main message. The Yalata schoolboys, little fellows of seven
to nine, sang their own song of a subsistence totem, beating out the
rhythm with desk rulers in place of their fathers' tapping sticks:

Weet-Bix-pa   Weet-Bix-pa   panikinta ngarinji panikinta ngaringi
  Weet-Bix   Weet-Bix   panikin lying-down panikin lying-down

Weet-Bix-PA!   Weet-Bix-PAAAA!   Brrrrrrrrrrrrrrr
  Weet-Bix!   Weet-Bix!   [labiopalatal sound of approval]

Weet-Bix resembles straw threshings pressed into bite-sized blocks
like our Shredded Wheat, and similarly held by some to be edible.

Looking from the children to their native teacher was turning from
heart-warm comedy to heart-cold tragedy. I had watched Billy Stewart
appraisingly as he worked at giving all the children of different tribes
a common language; there, I thought, was a born teacher. Patient,
humorous, tolerant, competent, cheerful, he molded the children together as if with his hands. I had never, however, seen him out on
our groundsheet with the other men. Talking about him later with
Barry, I found out why. He was twenty-five years old, ten years past
the normal time for initiation, but he had never been "cut," and was
therefore unmarried and ineligible to hear the songs we heard. It was
unlikely now that he would ever reach manhood in aboriginal eyes.
To the *wati yina* he was *tjitji*. If he had dared come near the sacred
singing he would have been beaten, his bones perhaps broken. No
prejudice here; no punishment for working in the whitefella's school;
just immaturity in the aboriginal sense. Every hour he spent away
from the native camp to learn the white man's culture was an hour
irretrievably lost. So he stood astride the two worlds, now forever
unable to stand with both feet in either.

*The ceremony of man-making is strenuously discouraged by mis-
sionaries and other whites now, and this most important of all aboriginal rituals is conducted secretly in the bush, well away from
walypela eyes.*

It is not a subject I should like to come back to, so let us look in briefly on a typical climax of the life crises of a native male, and then put the matter as much out of our minds as we can.

Life among the desert people of Australia is not as biologically simple as it is for us. The road from birth to death is no smooth path, a freeway with no intersections, but a series of positions for which the individual must qualify. True life does not begin with birth. If the child is a twin, it and its sibling are killed, smothered in sand. Although twin-killing is an ecological imperative (a mother cannot spare more than one arm to carry an infant), religious sanction fortifies the secular necessity and makes the hard act easier. Twins are thought to be mamu tjitji — malignant spirit children. In this as in so many other things the desert people share a concept with ourselves; the mamu tjitji of the aborigines is the changeling child of European folklore.

If the infant lives until the umbilical cord dries and falls off, it is brought back into camp from the secluded place of birth by its mother, its father recognizes its existence, and it is deceived into thinking life is unbounded joy. The fact that an ordinary spacing of births every four years (by contraception, sex-activity tabus, abortion, and infanticide) eliminates much sibling competition is certainly a factor in the affectionate treatment of children; they are cuddled and rarely chastised. Indeed the whole Freudian concept of the Oedipus Complex — based as it is on father-hating — does not appear in Australia, for without chastisement in childhood and competition for women on adjoining generational levels in adulthood, there is no reason for a child to hate its father. Freudians get around this difficulty by creating "father surrogates." They are an agile bunch; one must concede them that much.

Weep not, my wanton, smile upon my knee; When thou art old there's grief enough for thee. Aboriginal children are happy beyond the understanding of our children, though they have no adjuncts to joy like our imagination-stealing toys; they are made acquainted with the hardships of nomadic desert life as soon as they can be made conscious of anything, and they know there is no solace in complaining. It is the complaining about ills that makes us unhappy — not so much the ills themselves.

Children are sexually undifferentiated until they enter that universally critical decade of life we call the teens. A tjitji pilyirpa is an infant, carried by its mother or laid in the wira cradle. When it begins *to crawl it achieves the first stage of independence and so qualifies for the title* tjitji maṟamaṟa, *the "crawling child." Ambulation is literally its next step, and the youngster becomes with that accomplishment* tjitji tjinatjina, *"walking child." Bodies and abilities grow, and the child becomes a boy or girl. Though all races and cultures guide their children in ways commensurate with their culture's needs, it is still hard to be objective when you see a group of Pitjandjara preadolescents at play. Boys adumbrate their fathers, making* miru *with neither craft nor artistry but well enough to hurl a reed spear with impressive — one might say frightening — accuracy. Three or four ten-year-old boys can make an unwary lizard look like a pincushion in a few seconds. One has to recognize in their acts and emotions the eradication of that weepy sentimentality over animals we seem to regard as instinctive in children. Pitjandjara boys are playing, but their play is a training for manhood. They will have to hunt to live, so there can be no hesitation whatever to kill and overkill when food animals come within range of their weapons.*

In just as cold a way we notice in the different nomenclature of Pitjandjara girls the function assigned to them by the male-dominated society. No unisex nonsense on the desert. Girls are not named for what they can do, but for what they are. A girl in the age group of the young male spear-hurlers is ipi tuntumba, *"young girl with small breasts." But she too is learning the skills of her mother and her mother's sisters, and she can winnow seeds in a toy* wira *as well as her brother can throw spears. About the age of fourteen a girl is* ipi longkara, *"girl of well-formed breasts," and soon thereafter she becomes* kungkawara, *"unmarried girl with large breasts and pubic hair."*

The adolescent boy is tjitji mutilya, *nearly ready for his initiation into the first phase of becoming a man, when he becomes* tjitji myi: ṉka, *"nose-pierced child." After that the climax.*

A great amount of dancing, singing, and other preparatory ritual precedes the climactic acts of circumcision, subincision, and tooth evulsion. Some anthropologists hold that the boys are anesthetized by these ceremonies. They are entitled to their opinion. Circumcision is not much more than a grab and a quick circumpenal slice. Not pleasant, but worse coming. The boy sits over a small fire dripping blood while the men hop around naked in a penis-flapping dance that has

106

some masturbatory elements. (When women sing, they sit on the ground and beat time with their cupped hands against their pudenda.) Sex is part of religion, part of the need to channel all emotions into the most important thing, the religion.

In a few weeks, during which time the assembly of delegates from neighboring tribelets continue their dancing and singing while the women gather food, the young man is sufficiently healed to be cut again. A bewildering amount of social imperatives is impressed upon the subinitiate, the tjitji mu̱rdilda. For a time he wanders in the bush as a maliki *or* ta̱rdata, *learning from two male guardians. He hears the sacred bull-roarer, the* mantaruki, *a wooden tjurunga strung at one end with a length of human hair twine, rather like the rulers we used to mutilate in elementary school. In the Australian desert, as in other distant parts of the world, the whirring, roaring noise of the bull-roarer is said to be the voice of the spirits. After his initiation the boy will be disabused of this notion, but for now it does not hurt to scare the spirit of God and the Devil into him. And the women, too; if they so much as hear the* mantaruki, *they are killed. These cere-monies are inviolably* meilmeil — *tabu to women. Well before the rituals begin old men are sent to warn the women away —* "Teiwa teiwa njina!" *("Long way off camp!")*

Of the dozen or so male relatives the initiate meets in this time, the most important is his puruka, *the man who sat on him and held his penis during circumcision. At a brief ceremony of great emotional tension this man and this boy embrace —* puruka tjunguri nganji; *they will never touch each other again, unless circumstances of almost unimaginable social crisis require it.*

Finally the walu puruku, *the ground on which the subincision —* Inma murduni — *is to be performed, is prepared, and the operating table sets itself up — literally, for it is made of certain male relatives of the initiate resting on their hands and knees. The boy is laid across their backs, another relative holds the boy's penis (which by this time has shriveled through fear to the size, shape, and color of a Brazil nut). Officially the man who makes the long cut is the boy's* puruka, *but in fact his office is honorary. One slip of the knife and the boy bleeds to death — a fate duplicated at once upon the malpracticing surgeon. The cutter is therefore a specialist, a professional. Jews may recognize in this a reflection of their circumcision ceremony, at which the boy*

107

sits on the knee of his sandek (*godfather*) *while the professional circumcisor, the* mohel, *does the cutting. The age difference of the initiates in the two cultures is easily accounted for: among Jews, the important event is becoming a Jew, so circumcision occurs early; among the aborigines the important event is becoming a man. The Jewish rite of* bar mitzvah *is much less important to the society as a whole; it is a familial rather than a societal ceremony.*

Why most anthropologists wish to find improbable reasons for the surgical rites of initiation is beyond my explaining. Ashley Montagu insists still, after my quarter-century effort to set him straight, that penis mutilation is performed by men out of envy for women's menstruation. Hoo boy. Several young anthropologists in the wisdom of their generation say subincision is done to make the human male's genital organ resemble that of a kangaroo. These young anthropologists should be apprehended and the contents of their minds impounded and examined. Besides, the kangaroo's penis, in the way of marsupials, is up its arse. A few older anthropologists, persisting in the odd notion that every human act is logical, say the aboriginal penis is slit to hinder procreation. I do sympathize with the intent of their explanation, but it is wrong. The married woman, without any ceremony, is cut to accommodate the man. Nor is the man in any way disabled. Subincision makes for rather startling erections in the aboriginal male, and in the lateral dimension, decidedly enviable. So far as the pleasure of sexual intercourse is concerned, we may infer from the constant bloody fighting over women that the aborigines suffer no measurable loss.

The reason for subincision (and circumcision and the last act of surgery, tooth evulsion) is as simple as Columbus's egg. It is a mnemonic, a memory aid. During the associated religious rites (which are continuous) the initiate learns the fundamental elements of the myths by which he will live. These must be remembered. On a long trip into the west which Norman and I were later to make, we met a half dozen of the boys, now grown into old men, whose initiation he had witnessed and filmed in 1932 and 1933. They not only remembered him, but even such little things as his being given a dingo pup at the time and its name, even though the poor beast had died almost immediately. If any gentlewoman, too shy to ask the question, wonders why a mnemonic operation is performed on the penis instead of some other somatic locus if the purpose of all this fiddle-faddle is just to tattoo a mythic memory on a boy's mind, let me say to her, Lady, that is where it hurts.

The operation is literally bloody awful. Using a stone knife, the cutter slits the initiate's penis from meatus to scrotum. No physical restraint is put on the boy; he is not held, except by the requirements of proper behavior. He must not show any sign of pain beyond a silent grimace. But when it is over, as all things pass, the boy has become a man. A man. He endured the worst ordeal a human male can imagine, without scream, cry, or snivel. Nothing can frighten him again. He can go into this most hostile of all environments naked as he was born and survive.

In Norman's 1933 motion picture of subincision among the desert aborigines one can see an event that will never be photographed again. One boy, well past the normal age for initiation, disqualified till then for being an obviously genetic homosexual (physical anthropologists who maintain homosexuality is entirely cultural may write rude words here in the margin), is accepted on the special plea of his father. But the boy cries out, screams in agony, and sits sobbing long after the deed is done. The father, suffused with shame, tries to make light of the blasphemy. Norman told me the boy was kicked about and ultimately speared to death for having rubbished the sacred ceremony.

Billy Stewart had no defects of body or soul to disqualify him from the pleasure of manhood's pain. In choosing to work for his people by bringing the children painlessly into the inevitable world of the white man, he missed too many classes in his own courses of education. He failed life.

I will not speak here of the hundreds of other things I learned in this first substantial trip I made with Norman Tindale into the bush, for I wish to sustain the subject of religion, the integument of everything the aborigines do. Of course Norman put in many hours with the craftsmen, persuading them to stop incising boomerangs with bloody kangaroos, incising instead the geometrical designs of the old times. His efforts came to nothing, for the new traditional boomerangs Barry sent down to Adelaide did not sell. Tourists want kangaroos on their boomerangs, and kangaroos they will have. We carried back with us sacks of rejected artifacts kept in Barry's storeroom, all of them excellent examples of genuine traditional craftsmanship. Most amusing to me was the craft director's selling us *wit wit* sticks cheaply because the bloody aborigines had made them with the "tails" bent. Should be straight, he said. Tourists won't buy warped artifacts. We did not bother to tell them that tails of the kangaroo rats are supposed to be bent. Let ignorance be its own punishment.

FOUR

THE ANATOMY
OF RELIGION

The human brain is like Mrs. Murphy's arse, as it was described by her adulterous lover who was holding it when Mr. Murphy came in with his shillelagh: *Sure and it's a beautiful thing in itself, but it's not worth a damn in a fight.* We forget the truth of the cliché that life is a struggle, whether one is an illiterate nomad in the Great Sandy Desert or a hyperliterate aerospace engineer in Seattle. It is worth reflecting on the sad fact that the principal difference between the two is that the one with the big brain is out of work. Of all the mistakes in natural selection's evolution by blunder, the brain is the worst. We rubbish the dinosaurs for their pea-brains, but these creatures knocked about the earth for three hundred million years. If *Homo sapiens* makes it to his first million even the optimists will be confounded.

When culture developed civilization through agriculture it gave man time to apply reason to religion. His thinking destroyed his religion and hastened his own inevitable entropic end.

What I have to say in this chapter will be thought iconoclastic; it is not — it is iconodulistic. Moreover, despite the received error of millennial analysis, what I have to say is right. It is based upon adamantine, indubitable theory, and all contrary evidence is spurious, all contrary argument is specious. I know more about religion than the Pope. To argue otherwise would be to impute to the Pontiff a degree of diabolical mischief he is patently not capable of. Consider the work of Angelo Giuseppe Roncalli. When he was elected Pope he chose the name John, the twenty-third of that lamentable series. Acknowledging the Johns as the worst of Popes, he accepted the name to rehabilitate it. John XXIII was the author, among other mischiefs, of ecumenism, founded upon the New Wisdom. History will remember John XXIII and his successor Paul VI as the wickedest followed by the weakest. Their thinking made irreversible the collapse of their Church. Reason is the death of religion; so beginneth my catechism.

Religion is a social institution. It is society sanctified for the pur-

113

pose of making its members observe the only morality: *whatever conduces to the preservation of the group.*

All religions have all of the following components, placed here in arbitrary order, without any imputation that one is more important than another. All are essential. If an institution lacks one or several, it may be a philosophy, a way of life, a pattern of holy and wholesome behavior, or cabbages, or sealing wax, but it is not a religion.

1. *A concept of the supernatural*
2. *Myth*
3. *Ritual*
4. *Powerful emotion as motivating force*
5. *Dogma manifest in secular behavior, with means for its enforcement*
6. *Specialized practitioners* (*priests or shamans*)
7. *The concept of a transcendent spiritual power* (mana)
8. *Regularized means of obtaining spiritual power for secular purposes* (*prayer or magic*)

All peoples, since the Neanderthals built their first altars of bear skulls, have religion, though in some unhappy societies (notably our own) the institution may be attenuated beyond recognition. Often the discrete components are hard to see (who, without being told, would see Christ in the Traveling Salesman?), and for most people what is hard to see does not exist. Without being told about it, the concept of *mana* is not visible to Americans, though no other explanation accounts for such mysteries as why Samson lost his strength when he lost his hair, why Mary had to go to the temple to be "purified" after she had given birth to God the Son, why Uzzah was struck dead on the spot when he saved the sacrosanct Ark of the Covenant from imminent desecration, and why Denver policemen take their service revolvers to the priest to have them blessed. Many religions are said to have no dogmata, no rules of secular behavior, no *lawnorder*, but what is actually lacking in such cases is the unequivocal Decalogue our understanding requires as a code of law. Modern Jews are liberal enough to admit a depleted supernatural to accommodate *YHVH*, deprived like no other deity on earth, below the earth, or over the earth, of supernatural associates. If you ask them about Lilith, Hasdiel, Samael, Asimon, Naamah, Quastimon, Igarth bath Mahalath,

Afrira, the Seraphim and Ophanim, the Golem, Senoy, Sansenoy, and Semangelof, they become as unreasonably petulant as if you had asked them where exactly in the cosmos Elijah was headed when he blasted off in his fiery chariot.

My succession of visits to Australia became without my intention a series of expeditions into religion — of all kinds: fundamental denominations of Christianity of various degrees of ferociousness, gentlemanly sects of Christianity like the Church of England, and of course the aboriginal religion which pervaded everything the aborigines thought or did. All of these religions had in common the listed components, unities disguised by superficial variations. But let us confine this analysis to the religion of the desert aborigines.

The Supernatural: Totemism

How droll it was, thought the early colonizers of Australia, that on this strange continent there should exist people who traced their ancestry to kangaroos! They did not suspect their own origin in the mind of an ineffably superhuman God, so firmly held in 1788, would in less than a century be destroyed and their ultimate ancestors degraded to insectivores. An outsider does not have to stay very long among the Pitjandjara to see totemism as a satisfying religious system — imperceptibly abrasive to the brain and highly pleasing to the senses. Hold a young 'roo in your arms for a moment and you will not greatly mind sharing a spirit with it.

The Australian aborigines are thought by many people (ironically most of them strenuously anti-racist) to be dumb. They are not dumb. One reason they are held to be deficient in cranial marbles is their aboriginal habit of running around naked. As Mark Twain said (improving upon Carlyle), naked people do not have much influence upon society. Montague Francis Ashley Montagu, as suggested earlier, has some jocose notions about the aborigines. He thinks they do not understand physiological paternity because they say children come from totem pools. Joan's Wanindiljaugwa friends are on the Pill. My mob use more primitive contraceptives. Here in Colorado one of my do-gooding students runs an abortion clinic of some sort; he tells

115

me his group had in one recent month more than two hundred inquiries from pregnant girls. I infer from that intelligence that Americans do not understand physical paternity.

It is not reasonable to believe people and koala bears are produced by the same spirit of the koala totem. But whosoever submits his religion to reason ain't gone have no religion pretty damn quick, by Chrise. The Christians' first grave error was in letting their God set his feet on earth; that led to iconoclastic questions like, "Why did Jesus play with frivolous things like healing the sick and causing the lame to walk when He could have made human beings perfect to begin with?" No. We cannot have that. *Religion is strong insofar as it is uncompromising nonsense.* The further a religion's gods are from reality, the stronger they are. What Mexican was ever foolhardy enough to criticize a Tlaloc? I will make a prediction: the Tlalocs will be back one day when God has been driven out of Argentina.

The Australian gods are animal spirits in about 90 percent of the cases, or more accurately, spirits pervading a totemic animal and all descendant members of that totem. Totemism, though almost infinitely complex in its functional intricacies, is pretty much just that in essence: it has nothing to do with bloody great utility poles carved with grotesque faces for tourists or hairy two-inch rods to simulate erections in detumescent plants. As with everything else in the view of the world through the anthropologist's eye, we have unrecognized remnants of ancient and primitive totemistic beliefs — intellectual dysteleologies. I know a couple of football players (not many more than that, unfortunately) at the University of Colorado who would die (or kill, which is more to the effective point) to defend our totemistic mascot bison, Raalphie. And in the Australian desert people do not cannibalistically eat the flesh of their totemic animal except during religious occasions of great solemnity; then they must take a symbolic portion of its meat — *to increase the spirit within them.* I was thrown out of that great liberal university, UCLA, in 1961 for suggesting this was a polygenetic phenotype of the force producing the communion service of the higher Western religions. "Because of our communion service," said the Episcopalian 'chaplain' of this church-separated state school, "a professor on this tax-supported campus says we are cannibals." I tried to mollify him by saying it was not Episcopalians who were cannibals; it was the Catholics who are cannibals. Or, to state the situation more accurately, theophagists. I can say

116

anything I bloody well please about the Catholics, having been reared as a good little Catholic boy who sang and played the organ in church, and who still has a soft spot in his head for Catholicism. I know enough Latin to say the Mass old-style, and I can play the guitar well enough to play the Mass new-style. Believe me, if I were Pope, I'd shape up the Catholic Church. I would not make Paul's catastrophic mistake of making Holy Communion easier for Catholics by rescinding the sunset-sunrise fast; I'd make the communicants go without sustenance for a bloody week before taking the consecrated Host. And I'd have the ceiling of the Sistine Chapel whitewashed. I might not have many communicants left when I finished, but I'd have a Church, by Chrise, *nungkarpa*.

Myth

Myth still is best defined as Malinowski saw it when he was punching his New Guinea "niggers" in the mouth: *the narrative charter of a religion*. In these libertarian times there is no federal law or local ordinance to my knowledge forbidding an ethnoliterary writer from considering myth as literature, just as there is no law to prevent him from hanging a pepperoni pizza on his wall and admiring it for its inutile contribution to the room's decor. The mischief of such behavior comes from the next degenerative step in this usage — of supposing that the primary function of pizza is to serve as pendent art; this leads to aesthetic criticism of pizza, which makes as much sense as berating a paint brush because it will not drive nails.

When a culture can produce books titled *The Bible Designed to Be Read as Living Literature* its priests might just as well hang up their vestments and go into the streets with placards demanding an end to environmental pollution. Australian aboriginal myths are *relevant*, as our young people would say if they had enough sense to say anything sensible, because, for instance, they unite the two dimensions of the MacDonnells as a range of ironstone mountains and a congealed river of totemic blood. These mythic song cycles establish the basis for things as they are now and how they may best be lived with — a world of hardship and little romance; of the constant quest for water, food, and women; of the religious ceremonies; of the making of tabus, cicatrices, and water holes. No marvelous adventures of Celtic magic will be told by a Pitjandjara. True enough, most of the totemic spirits go eventually into the sky to become stars, planets, and constellations, but their ascension is matter of fact and poorly motivated.

There are thousands of myths in the wasteland as there are thousands of species to hang them from, but there are no characters of any memorable sort, since the totemic spirits' function is the same whoever and wherever they may be. Take as an encompassing example the myth of *Wati Kutjara*, the Two Men. Norman Tindale once traced the path of these two ancestral beings from a point seventy-five miles northwest of Laverton, a ghost town at the end of the gold trail in Western Australia, to the central Rawlinson Range near the site of the present Giles Meteorological Station. His information, gathered song by song from individuals each of whom had a small part of the whole, allowed him to fit together the tiles of a huge mosaic showing the meandering path of the Two Men over three hundred and eighty miles of desert. It is not a story with plot, unstable situations, unresolved conflict, symbolism, philosophical theme, or even character development. In briefest summary the myth tells of the erratic creative wandering of Kurukadi and his nephew Mumba. They come first to a place called by the aborigines Panatapia (Red Hill); here they made the ceremony of piercing a large vein in their arms to draw ritual blood of secondary holiness. The excess flow of the blood can now be seen as a seam of red ocher. From place to place they went, few of which can be identified on the maps, until some distance past Jambiri (named Empress Spring by David Carnegie) they met another spirit named Kulu. Kulu is fitfully chasing seven sisters, wives to the Wati Kutjara. They try to send him off in the wrong direction, but he is not to be fooled so easily. They all drift off in their aimless separate ways, Kulu not pressing for his desires with any urgency and the Wati Kutjara not showing proper attention to the plight of their women, going on as before, creating water holes, artifacts, rock shelters, trees, damper, fruits, and ceremonies. Eventually the paths cross again and the Wati Kutjara kill Kulu with a large boomerang, the *walanu*. Kulu rises into the sky to become the Moon; the Kungkarungkara sisters follow him to become the Pleiades. Ultimately, after other adventures, they pass out of the knowledge of Norman's informants, heading northeast into Aranda country. On my last long trip with Bob Ver-

118

burgt into the heart of the Gibson Desert in the far southwest, I found the last resting place of the Wati Kutjara — in the double-peaked Mount Everard.

With a knowledge of world myth and the supernatural one can detect in the adventures of the Australian totemic spirits the antipathetic functions present in all anthropomorphic gods — the Culture Hero and the Trickster. The Culture Hero is a being neither entirely human nor supernatural, uncertain which world to choose. At last he uses his divine powers to give to the mortals some of the good things from the spirit world; for this he is punished by the hierarchy of gods. Prometheus would be the classic example if we were not directed away from seeing Jesus Christ as a more nearly perfect instance — coming to earth part mortal and part divine, choosing mortality and dying for mankind after providing salvation — that is, entry into the spirit world — for mortals — and then being taken back into the divine dimension again. The Culture Hero is also the Trickster — a poorly named divinity whose identifying characteristic is not cunning but stupidity, gullibility, amoral behavior, and omnipotence. The best-developed example in world myth is perhaps the Polynesian Maui, though the Culture Hero–Trickster pairing is seen in the oldest story in the world, the Gilgamesh epic of Mesopotamia, first written down two thousand years ago. The North American Indians have scores of Tricksters; so also do the Africans, one of whose Tricksters burrowed his way into our own children's treasury of story as Br'er Rabbit. On a more adult level, the American Trickster is the Traveling Salesman, whose outrageous sexual exploits with the farmers' daughters parallel the principal activity of all other Tricksters. The pursuit of the seven sisters by Kulu is only one of many Australian examples. Some will object that there are no Trickster elements in Christ. It would be more nearly correct to say there are no Trickster elements surviving in the Bowdlerized myth in the New Testament. Few theological students are aware of how select the Gospels are. Let them go to a branch of story never directly touched by theological censorship — oral folklore, in which the character of Christ is exactly opposite that of the canon. As a child, Jesus is a terror to his highborn playmates, dozens of whom he kills daily with no more motive than Caliban needed to kill crabs.

There are no synods in aboriginal Australia to clean out any unseemly stories or to bring consistency to a myth; therefore a myth will vary considerably from place to place. This worked to our purpose when Norman and I were at Yalata. Norman would get a new variant of an old myth by telling the men, "We want your country one; 'nother country one li'l bit cranky." At Yalata we were told the Wati Kutjara went at last into the earth at a place called Tukuntjara; another clan's ending takes them into the sky as the classical twins Alpha Gemini and Beta Gemini. But in Ngadadjara country they are in the stone tomb of Mount Everard. Kulu also ends variously; I like the transformation of the old lecher into the Moon, but he is also petrified into a conical boulder nearly four hundred miles east of where he was supposedly killed. It is a poor believer who cannot accept six impossible things before breakfast.

Ritual

Ritual is the means of recharging the battery of faith. All religions use it for this purpose — if they are viable; if not, their ritual attenuates into entertainment, becomes metapaegniac. I know a Catholic priest (who, I pray, will not be chained near my destined corner of Hell) whose brilliant ecumenical contribution to Catholic ritual is the packaging of consecrated Hosts in plastic Baggies to be picked up at his drive-in church and consumed with pickles and relish, if the communicants like. On 4 February 1972, another priest was arrested in New Mexico with a carton of Baggies — and lo! the bread had transubstantiated into marijuana!

Without regular and compulsory participation in dramatic replications of a religion's important mythic events, the religion dies. Whatever is not used is lost. The Host in a Baggie might as well be a potato chip. Solemn High Mass in a cathedral celebrated by a mitered bishop lets the good Catholic relive Christ's Last Supper and the nucleus of his belief — the doctrine of transubstantiation. With all his senses the communicant knows it — knees sore from kneeling, nostrils tingling from the waft of incense, palate tasting the unique flavor of the Host, hands rubbing the patina worn into the pew by thousands of believing hands before him, the spectacle of the Mass behind an altar rail insulating him against lethal holiness, and hearing the solemnity of Latin, not the vulgar vernacular. When the priest used to intone *Ite, Missa est*, there was religion in his utterance. Moreover, nobody knew what he was saying, so they stayed for the post-missal elaborations grown up over the centuries. Today, when the priest yells "Split!" the communicants are likely to drop their roaches and get in the wind, man. To draw a better example from the Roman Church to illustrate the meaning of Pitjandjara ritual, consider the Stations of the Cross. It used to be that a good believer would from time to time perform this ceremony: he would enter the church, stop at the first represented scene (statuary in rich churches, watercolors in poor) of Christ's Passion on the right wall near the door — the condemnation of Jesus in Pilate's court. Here he would contemplate the sight and meditate its meaning, say prescribed prayers, and then move on to the next, and so on until reaching the door again and the plaque on the left wall, the Pieta, the taking down of Christ's body from the cross, the end of the central element of Christian myth. His belief would be renewed and he would leave the church a holier if not a better man. C. P. Mountford, a long-time associate of Norman's whom I used to see occasionally in the South Australian Museum, once filmed an astonishing parallel to the Stations of the Cross on the central MacDonnells. We see the Aranda priest, the *inkata*, sitting in a sandy circle with a large *tjurunga* held reverently in his hands. On these most sacred religious implements are inscribed geometrical figures representing the wander-paths of the totemic ancestors. While the lesser men on the periphery of the circle sing and beat out the rhythm of the mythic song, the *inkata* sits swaying in a religious trance, running his thumb over the engraved lines to follow the spirit's movement. The stations of his god's cross, as near as one could imagine.

Powerful Emotion as Motivating Force

"You don't have to talk about it; you can feel it in your soul," says an American hillbilly sacred song, conveying more truth than any number of sophisticated modern ministers who think all one needs to intrude into adult affairs is to put a collar on backward. Emotion

121

and reason, as I have said, are antipathetic; between them there can be nothing but strife. A person either feels religion's power working within him or he disbelieves. Paradoxical too is the fact that the more a religion demands of its believers, the stronger it is. Take away all a man's natural vices and appetites and pour their energy into a religion, and the faith will sweep the earth. A man can be persuaded by emotion to die for even a mediocre faith; reason may keep him alive in many circumstances, when keeping alive may be fatal for his society, his culture, and his soul. Nothing is reaffirmed by reason. Apply reason to religion, rationalize each day of Biblical creation into a billion years, and it comes out even — but the stone of religion's foundation turns to powder.

On the Australian desert religious emotion makes every man offer his penis to the stone knife – what greater faith than this? The desert people have been trained by hardship to control all emotion in secular things except anger, which has direct survival value. Acts of love are rare; seduction is accomplished by magic, not by kindness. In an environmental situation where spouses die often before their time it is best not to invest too much of oneself in them. What affection an adult has for his children is shared, like mutual funds, among the children of all his kin. A person does not even care overmuch about himself; it is not unusual to see someone take a small stick, set it afire, and casually burn doodles into his flesh — for no particular purpose and with no particular consideration of the incidental pain. They train for ill, as the poet said.

And yet times of religious ritual bring a drop in the bars of emotion; the great store of feeling is released in a debauch of religious emotion. I have been present at rites only partly sacred — "playabout corroborees" — at which grown men wept. I wept too — the first time in a religious ceremony since the day a priest hit me alongside the ear for throwing spitballs at choir practice.

Dogma and Its Enforcement

Meager cultures have meager crimes. A society that does not count beyond "five" has little use for accountants; the Pitjandjara do not even get to "four" easily (*kutjara kutjara* — two two). Some commentators on religion believe the religion of primitive societies does not intrude upon behavior, and they extend this erroneous inference to suggest our religion should also stay out of the business of conduct between assenting adults or dissenting children. I do not hold with those who say religion is freedom from fear — of death, of the unknown; or a probing of primitive science, or similar projections of our own psychologies. Death be not proud; few people really fear it. The ordinary rational man can be persuaded to die after a few hours of conditioning. These basic instinctive drives are fraudulent. Take reproduction: who needs kids? Nature understands man; if there were any instinctive compulsion to reproduce, nature would not have made the initial action so pleasurable. Nor is primitive man all that fascinated with the question that leads to the establishment of science — *Why?* Primitive man is no more interested in the origin of the universe than he is in the origin of his foot. The function of religion is to control the fearsome human energy that has made him earth's dominant animal.

None of the myths as they are sung on the desert include any directions toward virtue or prohibitions of evil. Aboriginal law is communicated by precedent, not precept. What the Culture Hero, acting in that capacity, does, human beings must also do. If he cuts his penis — without any explicit reason – so must men. When he becomes the Trickster, his actions are negative; a man must not do these things. His function here is to provide vicarious sinning — people laugh about his outrageous incest, but they had better keep their pleasure in their totemic surrogate.

Religion is the most backward, most conservative, most retarding of all institutions. It must be so, since it preserves the situation obtaining when it was founded. Everything connected with religion is behind the times — and when it is not, you can be certain the religion

123

is moribund. St. Patrick's Cathedral smothered by secular skyscrapers and the Anasazi *kivas* (pit-house ceremonial chambers) among five-story residential structures — in each independent case religious architecture half a thousand years behind secular building. Priests orating in Latin, Vedic priests chanting in Sanskrit, *inkata* singing totemic songs full of archaic language. Ancient Roman street wear from the time of Christ worn before Catholic altars until John XXIII, nuns in medieval street wear until Paul VI, aborigines painted with ocher. Steel knives and screwdrivers among the aborigines for hunting, cutting, and cooking — but the stone knife for subincision.

Nevertheless religions and their dogma change when the culture gap between technology and behavior changes. The agent of change is the dominant male. Most anthropologists will not have this; they like to imagine religion is unchanging (at least for the primitives), that priests never make errors in their ceremonies. Consider: if you are a Navajo priest on the eighth night of the Yeibechai nine and your tongue slips, do you go back and start over with night one? Like bloody hell. You either deny the error or ignore it, and once ignored it can become the new orthodoxy. One of the myths Norman and I recorded among the Pitjandjara is firmly embodied in their tradition, though it is the *Inma Rabita*. If rabbits can infiltrate a strong religion in three generations, more imposing totemic beasts can invade the pantheon also. We are close enough to the actual event to identify those elders of the Pitjandjara who deliberately made major changes in the mythic complex in 1917 when drought moved them into country that had for them no spiritual significance. Their decision was transferred to totemic ancestors, and in another two or three generations the ancient canon will have vanished as completely in the memory of the common man as the Arian heresy has disappeared from Christianity. The Wati Kutjara in one of their exploits open a path through the MacDonnell ranges for their people to escape by. I have on tape the new version — with the Wati Kutjara opening the hole with an atomic bomb.

No law exists without force, exercised frequently whether there are sinners or not. So it is in the central and western deserts and on the Nullarbor Plain. No fond fathers there with the unused twigs of threatening birch. The most terrifying physical inquisitors in aboriginal Australia are the little-known Red Ocher Men, whom we shall meet in their proper place. They are such powerful overseers of the native religion that Christianity has no strength at all against it, for all the hymn-singing at missions where one must sing to eat. Psychological punishments for infractions of dogmatic laws are feared as much as the physical punishments, and these are available to any man sufficiently injured by another to risk the use of their dangerous power. Crimes and torts are not named in the Paleolithic world, but they are recognized.

Religious Practitioners — Priests and Shamans

The undoubted phenomenon of polygenetic shamanism is probably the greatest of all anthropological puzzles. The shaman is a complex figure, and therefore he should be a result of diffusion; but he appears so often among people who have no knowledge whatever of other shamans that he must be considered in almost every case an independent invention. My thought on this paradox is that the shaman at base is a biological phenomenon, not cultural; if that is right, then probably religion itself is a biological constant. All religions of which we have any knowledge begin with shamans leading new movements Kroeber called Nativistic Endeavors — like the American Ghost Dance, the scores of Cargo Cults in Oceania, Judaism, Christianity and all its sects, Islam, and the hundreds of new faiths challenging the orthodox from brush arbors, revival tents, and inner-city slums every few weeks. No illiterate snake-handler in backwoods Kentucky knows anything about the shamans of the Tungus, Chukchi, Samoyeds, Kukukuku, or the Old Testament (despite his thumping of the text), but he is indistinguishable except for clothing from any other shaman.

The shaman, wherever he appears, is emotionally (and often mentally) unstable, subversive of the dominant established religion, a tramp (as one irreverent wit said it, Jesus was supposed to be a carpenter, but the first nails he ever had in his hands were hammered in), a bringer of a sword instead of peace, a user of esoteric language ("talkin' in tongues" to the hillbillies, glossolalia to the linguists), an exhibitionist and showman of great skill (a dancer, singer, demagogue, and prestidigitator), a healer of the sick and raiser of the dead, a direct mediator with the other world, a self-suggestible man for whatever god he creates. Priests are fundamentally different. They are products

125

of a tamer time, docile, quieter, the servitors of highly organized religions; trained for spiritual power and ordained to it; men who know their personal powers are feeble and who draw their strength from their cult; firm supporters of orthodoxy; and supplicators of the established gods.

No two elements of any culture move forward in their evolutionary course at the same speed, and no two components of religion are progressing at the same pace at any time. The totemic religion of the Australian aborigines has elements the Neanderthals might have invented, yet it has priests instead of shamans. Admittedly some Australian *inkata* work magic at times, but so do Catholic priests in the syncretic religion of the American southwest. Sorcery is a boondoggle, an affair of the moonlight, in the desert. You can be cured of any illness, somatic or psychic, by the *mapantjara*; they can bring rain for the community, kill for you, seduce for you, or cause your death; but their primary function is to administer the religious ceremonies. Some sorcerers are apprenticed to proper *mapantjara*, but they know their inferiority; they just do not have the personal power that shamans must have. In this bifurcation we can see the evolution of shamanism into priesthood.

Old *mapantjara* are the mafiosi of Australia's deserts, working for good as for evil. But power corrupts as surely in the Mann Range as it did in Acton's England, and terror brings hatred as well as respect. The *mapantjara* is mortal and every man's hand waits for his throat. The man who is whispered about by other men is the man most likely to receive a spear through his back. But fear of assassination never deterred an American presidential candidate and it does not deter a potential *mapantjara*. Few men with the power to inspire terror can resist using it, for the human reason that the drive for prestige is stronger than the imagined instinct for the preservation of self.

Mana: Power from the Dreaming

One day on an expedition into the desert's heart, a Pitjandjara man with whom I had grown friendly (though he had not a word of my language) unwrapped a small packet of rotted cloth and leaves to

126

show me an object of great spiritual value: an incised disk of pearl the size of his palm made from the shell of the oyster *Meleagrina margaritifer*. I had seen disks like this in the South Australian Museum in Adelaide, the Western Australian Museum in Perth, the Australian Museum in Sydney, and the Queensland Museum in Brisbane. It was a *longka longka*; with its braided human hair belt it was sometimes a phylocrypt covering a man's penis (itself a source of religious power), and its projective functions were in all the areas where human knowledge is impotent. It cured the sick, lured reticent women, opposed sorcery, and was beyond price. Those in the museums doubtlessly came from dead men. It radiated power like a laser.

In a culture whose material technology is hardly more puissant than the human hand, artifacts augment human strength by drawing from a greater energy — the universal spiritual force anthropologists call *mana* from its name in Oceania, where the concept is strongest. From its first description a century ago it has been likened to electricity. Its power is invisible and amoral. Electricity will run a toothbrush with the same impartiality with which it will run an electric chair or a new-style votive candle. It is just power, flowing from the spiritual dimension to energize sacred and secular tools in the terrestrial dimension. Certain objects and certain people are the earthly batteries of *mana*; all shamans have it by right of their special personal qualities; all priests have it by right of their ordination. Those who have it hold it in their penis or in their hair (hence Samson). Women have it not at all, except by participation in a few spiritually powerful acts, like childbirth (hence Mary in the temple). Commoners of either sex cannot touch it without being melted like a thin wire struck by lightning (hence Uzzah). Objects and acts possessing *mana* are tabu. Those not spiritually grounded must not meddle with them, not because the chief forbids it, but because such people would be killed on the spot by a surge of spiritual electricity.

The Pitjandjara share with other peoples a great body of the same concepts, though with us these things are hidden in words once chosen for their secretive euphemism. Objects with *mana* have "luck," good or bad. People with *mana* are blessed in a state of "grace" or have "charisma." The oldmen, the *wati yina inkata* or *mapantjara*, glow with *mana*, topped up by contact with the oldest and most powerful tangible source of spiritual energy, red ocher. Scientists, who know so little about the deeper significance of things, dismiss red ocher as "hematite," Fe_2O_3, iron sesquioxide, in rhombohedral crystals or earthy form. As well call love estrus.

Ayers Rock is the Pitjandjara Ark of the Covenant, a mass of *mana*, ocher-red in the sunset. It lies southwest of the MacDonnells, the northern barrier between the Pitjandjara and the Aranda, a stone stream of totemic blood nearly two hundred miles long, most of it old, dried, and rust-colored, much of it fresh, pulsing, arterial. The rock is the dominant feature of central Australia, one tremendous unbroken pebble six miles around and a thousand feet high, rolling in color under the sun as if it were lit by internal fire, like the burners of an electric stove, until at sunset it turns into a gigantic mound of glowing vermilion, igniting the surrounding plain to the horizon. Ironically the rock is now off limits to all aborigines so as to prevent harassment and injury to tourists flying in from Alice Springs to climb and gawk — another stern necessity; my wild men customarily hit tourists with boomerangs when tourists refused to buy boomerangs.

I was gratified to find in Norman's Pitjandjara lexicon the word *mapaṇpa* defined simply as "red ocher," for I do not often get to score on his whelming knowledge. But here he had run aground on a synecdoche, taking the part for the whole. Red ocher it is, but it is more than that; it is *mana*, and the priest who handles it for good or evil is a *mapantjara*, "man of spirit power"; the bundle of sacred objects he uses in his religious functions (the "medicine bundle" of the American Indians) is also *mapaṇpa*.

Blood is liquid *mana* — and why not? Who could live without it? Congealed blood is ocher. Those who think this is all cleverly tenuous should be apprised that one of the objects given to the South Australian Museum by the last living Dieri priest, Dintibani, was a mass of red ocher named *Kututu Darina*, which translates literally as "the Sacred Heart of Darina." Put *that* in your tabernacle, O ye of little faith.

Man-made receptacles of *mana* in Australia can nearly all be subsumed under the generic term *tjurunga*, which we have badly translated as "soul sticks." Every man has one, though he rarely sees it, since it is too holy and therefore too dangerous to be exposed. *Tjurunga* are kept hidden in a *pulpa tjukurpa*, whose location everyone knows but avoids. Some few men of courage may carry their *tjurunga* with them, like my desert friend with his pearl-shell *longka longka*.

128

Prayer and Magic:
The Means of Obtaining Mana

Mana does not flow from the spiritual dimension — the *tjukurpa*, the Dreaming — any more than electricity flows from the Columbia River. A means of generating the power must be devised. In all religions the means of securing this spiritual electricity inherent in the current's flow is either supplicative or coercive. In the usual evolutionary phases of religion, simple cultures coerce the spirit dimension by magic — the shaman does this and says that, and the power comes as surely as if he had thrown an electrical switch. In the higher cultures one deals with the source of *mana* as we deal with the electric company — in short, one must supplicate the owners of the power to release it, and one usually has to pay for it. The electric companies take an arm and a leg; in strong religions the whole body is taken in sacrifice.

The Pitjandjara stand again somewhat apart from other cultures in this aspect of religion — doubtless because their environment demands an unusual strength of social organization and therefore a parallel strength of religion. Their means of securing *mana* is supplicative, a praying. Prayer to our minds is debasement to the deity — kneeling, bowing the head, pressing palms together in symbolic impotence, holding the hand palm up like a defeated chimpanzee before his Alpha superior, expressing profound devaluation of self and utter worthlessness to receive what is asked for. Pitjandjara religion is based on an honest appraisal of the supplicant, for he too is part of the totem, and his relations with the *tjukurpa* spirits are like those he has with his fellow men — equals or near equals, not creatures at either ends of a seesaw.

The outsider will not come very close to understanding the worlds of the Pitjandjara by restricting reality to what the five senses perceive. There is another dimension to aboriginality one must learn and which few outsiders are taught. Old Tommy Dodd, son of one of the first explorers of his country and an aboriginal woman, speaks fairly good English (if you will accept the change of the fricative *f* into the bilabial p and make similar equations of sounds the western desert people have not mastered) and he makes excellent sense. Tommy can talk to you about the geology of the Musgraves at two levels above your head — but suddenly he will come upon an outcrop of stone in no visible way different from any other, and at that instant Tommy Dodd will vanish and you will be talking with Tjonduga, the religious custodian of stone that is not stone but the remains of food eaten in the Dreaming by Wanambi Kutjara, the Two Sacred Rainbow Serpents. There is no conflict between what we must call dimensions in Tommy's mind; the geology and the Dreaming are both equally valid matters of fact.

To know the Australian aborigines, the outsider must somehow see their world illumined by the invisible light of faith — their faith. It is not enough to accept their intangible cosmos as a mere complex of elaborate symbolism, as so many of us do with our own moribund religious belief. Things in the natural world — plants, mountains, animals, stars — are not equations with counterparts in the supernatural world; they are identities. In the Roman Catholic Mass the consecrated bread and wine did not weakly symbolize the body and blood of Christ; they became in literal fact the body and blood of Christ, and Hell was open for him who did not accept it so.

An analogy in our experience for the two realities is the phenomenon of fluorescent minerals. Any visitor to a geological museum has seen the curious spectacle of certain stones suddenly changing not merely in color but in fundamental essence when visible light is turned off and invisible light (darkness to our mundane eyes) turned on. Opal, fluorite, willemite, calcite, curtisite, and wernerite are in their natural state rather dull representatives of the mineral parts of our world, moon rocks of uninteresting grays and browns. Fluorite is whitishly translucent and poor opal has unencouraging oozings of color; neither would inspire the layman to look twice upon them. But in an ultraviolet environment they are in an instant transformed — were it not for the sacrilege we would say transubstantiated — into flowing sources of greens, blues, and purples so bright that one could find one's way through the dark by them. Some living things, too, exhibit this weird and still unexplained property — the firefly or lightning bug is the most common example, though the unique aquarium in the Baie des Citrons above Nouméa in New Caledonia has incredible fluorescent corals, not only alive, but flaunting their animation by waving tentacles of curved pink, red, and yellow light.

Our physical ultraviolet is the metaphysical ultrareality of the Australian natives. Fluorescence is only an analogy, so it takes us no deeper into the Pitjandjara mind. To approach as far as we can into the unreality, we must go into the transformational reality — into the physical form of the *tjukurpa*, into the Dreaming.

FIVE

INTO
THE DREAMING

I made my first trip into the Dreaming in 1965, when I returned to Australia with a government research grant whose magnitude we shall not see again. I bought my own Tojo, had it rebuilt to desert worthiness with extra tanks for gasoline and water, a top rack to make the vehicle into two storeys, augmented suspension, unbendable "roo bar" to shunt kangaroos as the cowcatchers on our old locomotives used to shunt cattle and automobiles, and similar amenities. In the back I had sacks of money which would let me repay Norman for what he had done for me in less prosperous days.

"Where would you like to go?" I asked him. "Any unfinished work you want to do? Any problems to solve?"

Yes, he said, there were — many of them; but one in particular he fancied now, especially since it would change my mind about the historicity of myth. Norman has the strange illusion that oral tradition preserves historical fact. Encourage him a little in this vagary and he will cite new traditional remembrance of the Ice Age. My years as a folklorist had taught me otherwise. Dull illiterates cannot tell you what they were doing last Friday night, much less what they had done back in the Pleistocene. Smart illiterates will remember Creation itself for a drink. I like to remind Norman of the old folk-singing North Carolina analphabetic mountaineer who announced to the tape recorder that his next song, an *ole ballit* from the time of Christ, was going to tell about a son of the Virgin Queen Victoria named King Napoleon who led his navy south by boat across the Alps to capture a group of nations near Moscow called the Bonny Bunch of Roses-O.

What the hell. No matter what one's primary reason for mounting an expedition into the Australian interior, one does everything in any way anthropological, from picking *pirri* points out of the sand to making scientific observations of sexual intercourse. My only apprehension was about where he wanted to go. His interests are conti-

135

nental, and I do not care for the humid tropics and their crawling and slithering inhabitants.

"I want to take you into the Dreaming. For an unbeliever you have a strange interest in religion, and I've got a good problem for you."

"What Dreaming? *Alchera* or *tjukurpa?*" *Alchera* was its name farther north than I liked to go.

"*Tjukurpa* all the way from the Musgraves to the south coast." He explained that he wanted to follow a myth flown on the wings of a totemic bird out of the far northwest, across the desert home of the Pitjandjara, and south to a sea unseen by any man of that tribe.

"This particular myth cycle," he said, "I tape-recorded two years ago up in western Pitjandjara country, about seven hundred miles north from Eucla as the bare foot walks. I got on to a new informant, Tjipikudu, only a couple of years from uncontacted tribal life, no English, who sang me a sacred song about a turkey bustard . . ."

"Bastard."

". . . the turkey bustard, the bush turkey . . ."

"*Ardeotis australis.*"

"*Eupedotis australis.*"

"*Arde . . .*"

". . . the bush turkey, blackfella *keibara*, keeper of fire-flints."

Like all these mythic songs, Norman continued (with interruptions like the above, a harmless form of contention we somehow invented), Tjipikudu's myth had gone on for hours, with the usual kind of indirection and irrelevancies, but the main story line had to do with the Keibara flying out of Pintubi country southeast into the land of the Waljuna Pitjandjara. Where he came from originally Norman's man did not know, since he had only that part of the myth belonging to his clan. Keibara was being chased all the way by fireless desert spirits who were after the fire-flints he held in his head — another of those variants of the universal tale of the covetous keeper of fire. Keibara's main activity in Pitjandjara land was getting *arungoli* to eat. At last he flew south and west, across the Nullarbor Plain, and to a sea cliff — his home, evidently — and rested there until he saw two fierce pursuers coming. These were the brown hawks, *mbitjana.* "I think I got this myth," Norman said, "because I told Tjipikudu I was myself a brown hawk, put into that totem by the Pitjandjara back in 1933."

Keibara had no further retreat, and being characteristically churlish, he dived into the sea to drown the fire rather than let the others share it. But just as he was about to strike the surface, the hawks swooped in and snatched away the fire-flints, and jammed them into the cliffs, where they were still supposed to be. "Do you see anything very unusual about that so far?"

"Naw. Just a version of the worldwide story of the keeper of fire. A Culture Hero robs him of the fire and gives it to the people."

"Fire-flints."

Well, yes, there it was. There is no historical or ethnographic record of aborigines making fire with flint and pyrites, only by some form of friction — wood drill and hearth, stick rubbed across the edges of a *miru*, or a fire-plough. He had made a point: the tale went far back to a time when striking fire was known. I remembered something else.

"Are you thinking of those flints you found in 1938?"

"That's it; you have it."

From my bibliographic work ten years earlier I knew a little of Norman's find in the Eucla sands, just over the state border in Western Australia. (It is wondrous strange how a memory that can utterly fail to register where you put your goddamned car keys an hour ago can recall something about each of twenty thousand bibliographic references.) What Norman had found was a small thing to the eye — a cache of several hundred flint implements, a few knapped to perfect tools, all the rest in rough, do-it-yourself condition. They lay close together as if they had been in a wrapped parcel, which was undoubtedly the case, though the parceling material, being organic, had vanished. These implements were the trade stock of some aboriginal artisan-merchant, a naked incipient capitalist, who had hacked flint out of the earth, fashioned a few pieces well as models for the rest to be perfected upon, and was making the whole ready to be carried — probably through a series of trading partners — hundreds of miles east or west into country where such fine stone did not exist. What happened to him, why he left the cache in the Eucla sands, we can only guess. The notion of trade in the Paleolithic world surprises people who suppose Americans invented profit-taking and capitalism, but throughout the world from the very earliest times great trading routes existed.

"You reckon the trader was selling these flints off the Keibara story, Norman?"

"Probably. In any case this flint is nearly the only material of its kind good enough for percussion-firing. If we find the flint mine we'll find the cliff of the Keibara story."

"But Jesus, Norman, the whole Nullarbor is solid cliff down to the ocean — how will you know?"

"Because most of it is sheer; we're looking for a place accessible to people without structural technology. It will be near Eucla, because that's where the Nullarbor cliffs end."

Unless one is looking for certain trouble one traverses the Nullarbor by the "Eyre Highway," a dreadful road only partly stabilized, though it is the one transcontinental east-west highway. The country from Adelaide west to Ceduna, the last substantial town on the South Australian frontier, is unmistakably within the borders of civilization, though many of the things we regard as necessities disappear one by one. The milk line, as one example, ends at the settlement of Penong; after Penong for a thousand miles west you must do without fresh milk. At Ceduna everything ends; the sign facing the traveler at the western edge of town is hardly meant to send him on his journey with confidence:

LAST RELIABLE

WATER SUPPLY

FOR 770 MILES

It was the twelfth of October when we reached Ceduna; we planned to stop there for the last proper dinner we would have for some time, but Norman let fall the information that this day was his sixty-fifth birthday — an important life crisis in Australia, a *rite de passage*. On this day he would be retired from the South Australian Museum as a regular member of the staff (moving thereafter into an honorary position), and on this day he would begin to draw government pension. All these things considered, I decided we must mark the occasion. Against his protests, I registered us in the new Ceduna motel, declared this a night of civilized conduct (which prohibited any anthropological work or talk), took him to the best dinner in town, and afterward to the Buddy Williams Show.

Buddy Williams is one of about a half dozen Australian country-and-western performers who tour the Outback settlements with a band of musicians who double as comedians in sketches of "good clean family fun" — which in present-day rural Australia means what it did in the United States early in the century: risqué dramatic fragments in a genre somewhere between Huckleberry Finn's *Royal Nonesuch* and burlesque routines. I greatly enjoyed the nostalgic echoes — and the singing, too, since my musical tastes peak at country-western music; Norman seemed to appreciate it as well. So he might bloody well do, for Ceduna did not often have entertainment at so high a level and in any event it was the only show in town. Anthropology intruded, despite my precautions. Ceduna had a substantial minority of aborigines in its 1,400 population, some of them rather bushy indeed. These wilder natives sat in the large open space between the first row of chairs and the proscenium, a disposition loudly identified as manifest prejudice by the emptier heads in the city, but in actuality a concession to the aborigines who preferred their traditional bush supination to the imprisoning posture of the white man's chairs.

Next morning we had breakfast at the motel and were off at last into the virgin bush, with the next stop the Yalata Reserve once again. Our purpose in dropping in at Yalata was to look for a man among the four hundred aborigines then sitting down in the reserve who had some knowledge of the Eucla region still far to the west. We found one; he turned out to be Freddy Windlass, one of the men who sang us mythic songs on our earlier visit. I wished we could have had someone less taciturn than Freddy, but out here the beggars were the choosers.

Beyond Yalata the Eyre Highway identified itself for what it truly was — the last insult to Governor Eyre's name. Just awful, just that almost imperceptible measure better than the untracked bush to keep us on it.

Freddy was hardly the native guide one is acquainted with in adventure fiction. In the best Outback tradition, he spoke only when he had something to say — and that rule kept him completely silent for hours at a time. Nor did he carry the material goods one associates with the best guides; he had a hat of sorts on his tonsured pate, clothing barely identifiable as such, and the most elemental swag — a blanket wrapped around his billy. But he had one knowledge to redeem his myriad defects as servant to Bwana: he knew where behind the road-bordering wallaby grass the old sandalwood trees were. I knew all this coastal country south of the Nullarbor had been scoured by sandalwood traders before the Chinese edict against joss houses was promulgated in the early years of this century. Western Australian sandalwood was thought to be among the best of the world's species, and in fact was sought even after the joss-incense trade collapsed for pyre wood, since its powerful fragrance overwhelmed all other odors. Dear reader, can you know what it is like to lie a-swag on an Australian plain, in the certain knowledge you will not see any other human being except your companions, with no access to the communications media rat-bag of hawked troubles, in front of a roaring fire of burning *sandalwood?*

The perfume of sandalwood became a necessity after the second day out of Yalata, for then we were in that narrow stretch of the southern Nullarbor which is the last range of the hairy-nosed wombat (*Lasiorhinus latifrons*), a beaver-sized burrowing creature occupying the econiche which in the American plains region is held by the prairie dog. Next to the incomparable koala, the wombat is the most heart-winning creature in Australia's ancient clime. Freddy liked them even more than I did — preferably in an earth oven. So we had to kill wombats for him and breathe the stench while he knelt by the track and drew out their guts. Opened thus, all animals smell alike. So sandalwood was a double blessing.

The southern rim of the Nullarbor is lovely country to the Australian eye — so long as you have water in your tanks and can put out of your mind the suffering of Giles and his men when they labored through this barren region, sure they were walking to a dry death. A little imagination will bring the ghosts of Giles's words out of the breeze hissing through the thin mallee — *"Oh, dear reader, if you have never suffered thirst you can form no conception of what agony it is."* Giles wrote that when he still had another hundred miles to trudge over the moon-dry earth before he found water.

Westering, the country grew more frighteningly desolate. No rich reds here; grayish-brown loam somehow supporting a cover of dull green vegetation capable of drawing moisture out of the Sea of Tranquillity, and all blown over in your mind by the judgment of its first explorers. The French navigator D'Entrecasteaux, searching along the southern coast in 1792 for the lost mariner La Pérouse, logged his opinion on the failure of the first comer, the Dutchman Pieter Nuyts, one hundred and eighty-five years earlier, to say anything about the land: *It is not surprising that Nuyts has given no details of this bar-*

140

ren coast, for its aspect is so uniform that the most fruitful imagination could find nothing to say of it. Summarizing the conclusions of Major Egerton Warburton about the land between the sea and the heart of the Nullarbor, the president of the Royal Geographic Society of South Australia said in 1917,

The major says the country is an irretrievable desert; to traverse it would be dangerous; to occupy it impossible. . . . [He] distinctly declares that to the best of his judgment the country behind Fowler's Bay is unfit for occupation. With respect to the country beyond the head of the Bight there can be, he says, no question. Neither man nor stock could live upon it. . . . At Cooeyanna two sheep had been purchased, which were cut into strings for the purpose of drying, but unfortunately whilst remaining in camp a tremendous sandstorm arose, which converted the mutton into a kind of fossil — a circumstance bitterly deplored by our travelers.

R. T. Maurice, who put his foot onto the Nullarbor at the beginning of the century, concluded his criticism with the observation that *"one who would travel this country for pleasure would go to hell for a pastime."* As I write this account the newspapers are full of the "Nullarbor Nymph," a white girl seen running across the plain in the company of kangaroos. On this Keibara trip and other penetrations of the Nullarbor I came to know all the women who have even been known to stop in the region, and I can certify that none is by any extension of the definition a nymph. This is not a country for nymphs or any other form of natural divinity.

At 1,568 miles from Adelaide by the Tojo's odometer we threw the gear into low-low and turned into the Eucla sands. Of all the metropolises created by imaginative cartographers to fill the empty spaces on their Australian maps, Eucla is the most wonderful. In 1877 when she first investigated this place, Daisy Bates said there were sixty or seventy people here, the families of telegraphists for whom the settlement was made. Today there are two ancient shells of the old telegraph stations, filled to what remains of their roofs with drifted white sand. Out in the dunes Norman and I found a few scoured studs of what apparently had been a chapel, though I was never able to find on later research any record of it in the old descriptions. Daisy Bates said too that at the time of her visit to Eucla in 1912 about thirty natives had a camp here, only one of whom remained of the Eucla (Yirrkili) tribe, the last of his people. But 1912 was a lifetime ago, and now no one full-blood of the Mirning people, who once held all the southern Nullarbor country, is known to be alive. The last man died in what for him must have been paradise enow — on the banks of the Murray nearly two thousand miles away.

Retracing Norman's lucky wandering through the Eucla sands thirty years before, I came upon a wind-cleared area. Such places often hold australites, sifted down through lighter materials. I had not then found an australite with my own eyes or picked one from the ground with my own hands, so I spent an inordinate time at this blowout, looking for what must have seemed to an observer nothing. I had an observer — old Freddy Windlass looking down on me from the top of a sand dune. I felt rather foolish. The old baastid must think I am bloody mad, I thought, down here looking for something where there is obviously nothing. Freddy, I had to assume, was a lame-English speaker. As a Jangkundjara man he should have known the Pitjandjara tongue, but in all our time together he did not utter many sounds beyond a snore in the night and a grunt in the day. For my part, I did not then know the Pitjandjara had several words for these tektites believed now by astronomers to have been blasted off the moon when the Tycho meteor struck nearly three-quarters of a million years ago – *mapunpa, ku:ti,* and constructive nouns — so I asked him weakly, "I look for demfella black shiny stone, he fall from sky; you know datfella? *Yabu katu maru?*" ("Black sky stone.")

"Um. *Uah.*" ("Yes.")

"What name you callim datfella? *Eni na watjala?*" ("Name tell?")

"Um. Meteorites."

I rose to my feet and slowly walked over the far dune.

We made no great discoveries in the sands this time, except the chapel. That will be my cache to dig one day, that and the remains of the houses that must have adjoined it, now buried like the kingdom of Ozymandias. The chapel and the tracks of an ox cart at least sixty years old, estimating from historical probability. A sixty-year-old cart track preserved in loose sand? Yes; nature will do these things. A track in the desert makes a depression; if the depression is not leveled by wind before the next rain, even a slight sprinkle will draw under-lying minerals up in solution; these will form a crust to last centuries after the ox, the cart, and the driver have vanished. In southwestern Arizona one can see a better memorial to General George S. Patton, Jr., than any brass cenotaph: the tracks of his tanks engraved in the desert during maneuvers in 1942.

Our archaeological fossicking done, we fought our way on foot through the deep sand to the southern sea (no chance of driving a vehicle through an erg desert of this purity) and looked east to the cliffs. Running hundreds of miles for the length of the Nullarbor, they showed like the side of a broken layer cake the composition of that vast plain — porous limestone, hard in its strata of calcareous rock, soft in its chalk built of the remains of centillions of Mesozoic marine creatures. The plateau-top patina of soil could not be seen from where we stood, and as for the two-hundred-and-fifty-foot height of the cliffs themselves, there was nothing to hold water except the useless chambers and caves into which the infrequent rains were precipitated. Somewhere out there was the flint cliff into which the brown hawks drove the fire-stones snatched from Keibara. Not far from here, surely; perhaps in sight, for we could see thirty miles down the coast. It would have to be that close to account for one man's carrying his hoard of trade flint back to Eucla.

So we went back — not along the Eyre this time, since the track deviated quickly inland — but probing along the cliff edges, hunting a way to climb down to the sea. For twenty-five miles on the odometer, a hundred miles in our imagination (very rough country), and perhaps ten miles as the brown hawks flew, we roared the Tojo through all its twelve-gear combinations until at last we found one steep parting of the cliffs, a trough down which some great cloudburst must have poured once upon a time. We fossicked around the cliff tops on foot for an hour, determining by the flint flakes whether this was close to the point once used by the aboriginal flint traders. It was, we decided, and began our descent. From this point on in the composition the plural personal pronoun does not include Freddy. He had spent all his sixty years of life on safe flat ground and he was not planning to take up topographical acrobatics now. He was much too old to die, as he looked at the matter. Besides, he did not know anything about any bloody turkey and all he remembered about flint hereabouts concerned an aborigine named Reuben, ancient when Freddy was a boy, who used to haul flint in an ox cart. So Freddy curled up under a ti tree and wished us Godspeed.

The descent through the trough was more annoying than dangerous. For every foot solidly planted, two more would slide down the scree, cutting and bruising our ankles. But a person can always get to the bottom of a mountain, one way or other, and in an hour we were on the narrow beach and walking east — the direction pointed to us by the cliff-top flint distribution.

I will not say how far we walked nor how many flintless cliffs we passed along this broken edge of the Nullarbor plateau, because I do not want any new adventurers mucking up our territory. But we walked long enough for suspense and drama to build the proper tension for discovery. We were ready to stand with stout Balboa (it was not stout Cortez, Keats old buddy) staring at the Pacific on that peak in Darien, to offer our hand in stout good fellowship to Dr. Livingstone along with stiff Stanley, to look over Clyde Tombaugh's shoulder when Pluto swam into his ken, when we rounded a large dark promontory and saw it, sparkling in the angled sun. Yes, dear skeptical reader, there was in truth an overshadowing peak between us and the Keibara cliff, and the mythic mountain did in truth sparkle. All discoveries should be arranged so. Only the brown hawks were missing; surely their totem master could have assigned a couple of them to sweep around the cliff, just for the drama of it.

The sparkling came from dozens of strata of edge-broken flint, layered between chalk and limestone, struck by a cooperative sun. No mistaking this place; if there had not already been a myth to account for its origin, I would have made one. What point is there in being a folklorist if one cannot make a needful myth? My myth would have dealt not with grubby flint but with diamonds — they are more convincingly sparklers and accord better with my materialistic nature. Still and all, flint of this quality must have been like diamonds to the vanished Mirning traders.

For the rest of this day and the next we climbed and clambered over the Keibara cliff, sifting through the talus for lost stone tools, edging along the suicidally narrow paths the aboriginal miners had made to reach fresh areas of flint outcrops, wondering what sort of Paleolithic scaffolding some imaginative miner had built to reach nodules twenty feet away from any foothold, scrabbling out wind holes for bones. Norman spent most of his time sliding very slowly down the scree adjoining the cliff, picking over the debris left by many generations of naked miners.

Only the most dedicatedly Christian of Norman's many companions in the last half century must not have let the unkind thought slip into his consciousness that everyone else was lucky Norman had only one eye. If he had two, no one near him would ever find anything. In this unpromising rubbish heap (over which I had myself gone on hands and knees) he found a large flint knife, unapproachably the largest and most symmetrical specimen of its kind ever found in all Australia. Nine inches long it was, a triangular blade with its three planes split off by the Levalloisian technique from a rounded boulder whose bottom was left to form a base for its user's palm. Some poor bloody native miner-craftsman had found the raw stone, cleaved it like a diamond cutter into this exquisite knife, pushed it point down into the scree while he worked at something else, and then could not find it again in the mass of useless rounded stones. Poor bloody baastid! He must have lamented the rest of his life over the loss. Think upon it: the Nullarbor Koh-i-noor, mislaid forever — or until Tindale with his lonely eye came along. I groused over the discovery myself, though I gave him grudging congratulations. Then I sat down in the talus and picked away at rounded stones. All I found was rounded stones. Norman came back *bimeby*. He comforted me. "Don't feel bad, John; you'll find something."

"Go to hell, Tindale."

I could not get over the damnable paradox of the thing. He should not have found it. Knives do not come with rounded bottoms. He was a damned fool to pluck rounded stones out of the rubbish. I told him as much: "You shouldn't have found the bloody thing. Knives do not come with rounded bottoms. You were a damned fool to pluck rounded stones out of the rubbish."

He turned the knife slowly before my eyes and grinned. "There's proof of the plucking. A national treasure."

"Answer not a fool according to his folly," I muttered, "lest thou also be like unto him. *Proverbs 26:4.*"

"Answer a fool according to his folly," he countered, still grinning and turning the knife, "lest he be wise in his own conceit. *Proverbs 26:5.*" I had forgotten for the moment Tindale was the offspring of bloody missionaries. Baastid.

But it was for all that a joy to be, with Norman, the first anthropologist to find the source of Australia's best flint, blue-gray-black, like obsidian in its pure translucence, so metallically hard that it would break steel (as I discovered on a later visit), so dense in structure that it rang like a bell when one piece was struck against another. No

145

The author trying to break flint boulders with a ball peen hammer
at the foot of the Keibara Flint Mine on the shoreline of the
Southern (Indian) Ocean, S.A.

Freddy Windlass with rifle at the *Kapi Pina,* inland from the
Keibara Flint Mine, S.A.

wonder this was traded over a third of the Australian continent before the *walypela* came along with his flashy inferior knives to show that Gresham's law obtains in flint as well as in currency.

Late afternoon on the second day we walked back up our trough and packed up for the return to Yalata and the east. I had made a fair estimate of the distance from the trough to the cliff, so I was able to edge the Tojo to the cliff margin, where we lay prone over the precipice to photograph the mine from above. Then off through the brush, circuitously following the line of least rocky resistance. A half dozen miles toward the Eyre from the Keibara cliff Freddy (who had during our absence collected about fifteen pounds of good flint from the chips strewn around the cliff top) called out sharply, "*Teitu nara!!* 'Top here. *Kapi pina!*"

I braked the Tojo sliding through the soft earth and saw about thirty yards away through a clearing a small claypan ringed at its south side by a barrier of stone slabs. A stone dam, obviously; but these things do not exist — in the literature, at least. We swung down from the Tojo and surveyed the phenomenon. "*Kapi pina*," Freddy had called it — "water ear." An ear-shaped dam at the bottom of a claypan's slight declivity. Aboriginal effort of unusual degree; most of the several dozen stones were ten feet square in area and held upright by large backfill stones. At one time this structure must have been made nearly watertight with brush and mud, all of which was gone now, of course. And on the higher ground around the dam, flakes of quartz microlithic tools. Quartz here, so close to incomparably superior flint? And microliths in an obviously historical stratum? The microlith users — the carriers of the Mudukian tradition — were supposed to have disappeared a thousand years ago. And why a dam at all? The historical occupants of this region were mallee-root drinkers. I could understand that a fall of rain might have shown them that water can be drunk from a pool, but dam-building implied long acquaintance with falling or running water, not at all characteristic of the Nullarbor. We had solved Norman's thirty-year-old mystery; now I had one of my own to solve some day.

Years later, I am still assembling data on aboriginal dams; my notes list dozens of them now, and one day I will expand our kapi pina *into a dull and scholarly article to be published in a dull and scholarly journal to refute the Hydraulic Civilization thesis of Karl Wittfogel —*

the theory that civilizations begin when dams and irrigation channels enable a people to hold a sedentary existence.

We returned Freddy to Yalata along with seven or eight dead kangaroos and wombats to feed his clan, and then I let Norman drive us back to Adelaide while I drowsed and reflected on the myriad meanings of what we had experienced in the last few weeks. Principally, of course, the Keibara myth for which we had made the journey. On our groundsheet I saw for a fact that the old gods were alive and living in the desert; the pale Galilean had not made much impact on those robust totemic heroes of the Australian Dreaming. One day perhaps a revitalized religion will come from them to carry the aborigines to a destined greatness, as the displaced Aztec and Toltec and Olmec gods, now peering out from the edges of the jungle, will rush out and strike the deathblow to staggering Christianity. This is where new religions and reborn nations come from — the old gods sulking in defeat but growing strong again as their titanic conquerors become effete. Barry Lindner saved his mission by not letting the upstart members of his own pantheon contend against Keibara, Waluwaru, Walpurdi, Mala, Mako, the Kungkarungkara, the Wati Kutjara. The promised bliss of heaven has caused no rush for harp lessons, as Mark Twain cynically observed; but for the aborigines *tjukurpa*, the Dreaming, is not the remote if pleasant improbability heaven is for our truest believers. It moves all things in both dimensions.

SIX

INTO THE HOMELAND

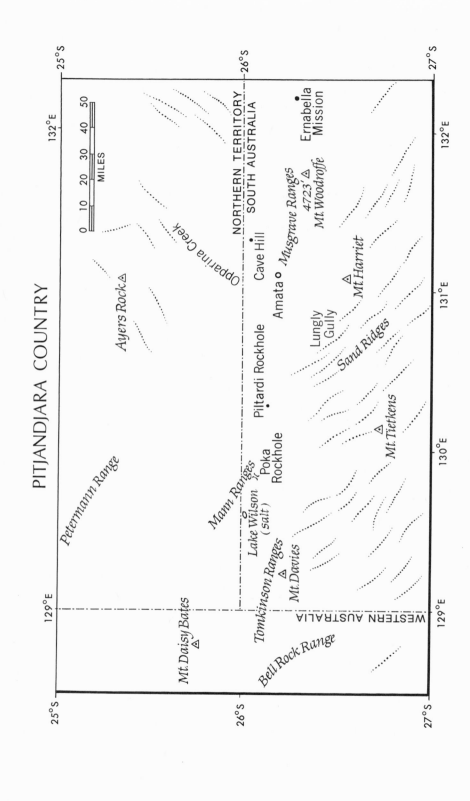

PITJANDJARA COUNTRY

Petermann Range

Ayers Rock △

Mann Ranges

Lake Wilson (salt)

Poka Rockhole

Piltardi Rockhole

Opparina Creek

Cave Hill

Amata ○

Musgrave Ranges

4723′ △ Mt Woodroffe

Ernabella Mission

Lungly Gully

Mt Harriet △

Sand Ridges

Mt Tietkens △

Tomkinson Ranges

Mt. Davies △

Mt. Daisy Bates △

Bell Rock Range

NORTHERN TERRITORY
SOUTH AUSTRALIA

WESTERN AUSTRALIA

0 10 20 30 40 50
MILES

25°S

26°S

27°S

129°E 131°E 132°E 130°E

The Sweat Quest

Early in January 1966, when the Australian summer was stoking up its solar furnace, three of us — Norman Tindale, Professor W. V. (Vic) MacFarlane, and I — met for a long evening at Norman's home in Blackwood on the near slope of Mount Lofty above Adelaide. We had gathered to plan some of the logistics of a new expedition. An expedition it was to be, proper-fella, no more gammon. We had three vehicles to move out of the Adelaide area: my Tojo, further rebuilt for a rougher trip, out of Blackwood with Norman as my offsider; a Land Rover out of the South Australian Museum with Peter Aitken, curator of mammals; and a third truck from the Waite Institute in Netherby, carrying Vic and his assistant, Dr. Robert Seamark. We would rendezvous at Port Wakefield, about fifty miles north of Adelaide on the Gulf St. Vincent, where traffic would drop off and allow us to proceed in a motorcade to Woomera, where we would be joined by Native Patrol Officer Bob Verburgt in his big International 1300 truck. Meanwhile a gigantic bush-bashing Bedford truck owned by the Waite Institute would leave Alice Springs towing a large mobile biological laboratory lent to the expedition by the national Department of Agriculture; this was to meet us at our operations base at Musgrave Park, as the Amata Reserve was then called. There we planned to load aboard as many aborigines as the vehicles could carry and take them far enough into the dry country south of the Musgrave Range to discourage them from walking back to the reserve camp and its easy living.

Though we had lists of normal desert expeditionary necessities to work from, it took us from late afternoon until early morning to anticipate our needs. About midway we agreed that each vehicle would have to pull a supply trailer. While Norman and Vic were totting up the last of the ancillary oddments — like a two-gallon jar of lollies (hard candy) as payment to aboriginal children for hunting biotic specimens — I figured the net weight, excluding the vehicles, of what the eight or nine of us would require to enter and stay alive in the desert for the few weeks necessary for Vic's work came to about fifteen tons. We would add to that additional fuel cached out on the Northwest Reserve, water from the Musgrave Park compound, and some additional supplies from the last pastoral station, Victory Downs. Two tons a man — just what David Carnegie loaded on his camels for his journey from Wiluna to Hall's Creek seventy years before. Apparently that was the minimum. A. W. Canning, that bushman so tough that he felt going without water for days in shade temperatures of one hundred and twenty degrees to be no hardship, paralleled the route of Carnegie in 1909 with a caravan of seventy camels, five hundred goats as ambulant food, and even more gear than Carnegie.

"Norman," I broke in, "do you realize it's going to take us two tons of supplies and equipment apiece to stay alive out there? How much would an aborigine need?"

"A stone knife, a woomera, and a few spears," said Vic.

"Nothing," Norman concluded. "He could go in naked, find a piece of quartz, make a knife in a minute or two, use that to cut his spears and woomera, and he's in like Flynn."

"We represent progress?" I asked, philosophically.

"Of course," said Norman, "don't talk rubbish."

It became unpleasantly apparent also, as we talked over our material needs, that our work on the main project would be much heavier than I had hoped. Those of us who had an unrelated discipline could work at it in our spare time, but in joining Vic's expedition, we were his to use, each according to our ability. And much was expected. Except for Vic himself, who would be making the scientific observations, all the white men were to be guinea pigs, like the aborigines, but with this difference: we were expected to perish first.

What were we to perish of? Whatever it is that causes death on the desert. Beyond the immediate threat of thirst, not much is known about it. The expedition was being financed by the United States Army which, possibly for a contingency plan of fighting somebody in the Near East, wanted to know what it was that killed so many of our aircraft crewmen in Second World War desert crashes. Vic's work was titled "Water and Electrolyte Metabolism of Nomadic Aboriginals" and his interest was entirely scientific, not crassly technological; but the Army was free to interpret his results for its own purposes.

A month later the expedition began its move, north along the road to Port Augusta, then by track to Woomera, and beyond that by bush trail to the Centre. We were bogged several times when the road disappeared in the sand; I gave up the illusion that the lowest gear of a four-wheel-drive vehicle could negotiate sand bogs. It was back to the days of the camel expeditions — the elemental process of digging around the bogged truck as the early explorers dug around their camels, filling the hole with brush, and then *Haul away, Joe.* Bogging in sand and bulldust, trailer-hitch wrenching, staked and blown tires, bolt-snapping, and similar gremlin troubles now became constant, and since repair parts distribution made the vehicles interdependent, a delay to one was a delay to all. One did not mind such things, since they were expected. If Vic snaps a spring, Vic and Bob will fix it, Peter Aitken will find some foolishly curious animal to decapitate for the museum collection, Greenway will chase an emu, and somebody will put the billy on boil and call Norman in from the bush where he will be chasing butterflies.

We pulled into the portcullis gate of Woomera, officially the Weapons Research Establishment of the national government, after being allowed to cross the glacis and moat. This place is perhaps the largest settlement on its concentric ellipse over the entire continent — 896 numbered buildings and five thousand residents — and as hard to get into as the NORAD cave under Colorado's Cheyenne Mountain. Built out of nothingness for the purpose of hurling rockets into the northwestern nothingness, Woomera at this time was agonizing over the internationally shared ELDO missile conceived to show to the Third World that it too could put together an ICBM. What they had achieved so far was a Gantry of Babel. The French second-stage responsibility was so reliably unreliable that the Australians had taken to calling it De Gaulle's *force de fart.*

Woomera had an unexpected satisfaction for me. Our permits, long arranged for, were supposed to be at the outer gate guard house. As the senior member of the party and the best known of us (it was he who suggested to the government the name "Woomera," Aranda for "spear hurler," so precisely appropriate), Norman gave his name and asked for the passes. None such, said the guard. A great fright, be-

153

cause these permits cannot be reissued in any tolerable time. We suffered, contemplating the necessity of having to reapply through Parliament for a special Act of Admission. And then the chief guard found the permits under the rubric of "Professor Greenway plus four." From that moment until they dragged me off the reserve I had a bloody marvelous time, ordering the others to follow me here from this radar complex to that gantry, to perform menial and humiliating tasks of servitude, and to give me no reason to exercise displeasure.

The vast Woomera secured area is pretty bad country — I had a tire mulga-staked on the main road — but it is not a fair preparation for what lies beyond. That is the hundred-thousand-square-mile stretch of gibber plain, poor Sturt's "Stony Desert." Gibbers are fist-sized pieces of sharp quartz or siliceous ironstone, covering the ground like stucco pebbles on a California roof. No use digging them out to make a flat place for your swag; they extend right down into the earth until they melt in the magma. In fact, if you disturb them on the surface, those underground will push their way up to help their companions. They tend to revive in any reasonable man's mind the old theory that rocks copulate and reproduce.

At Woomera Bob Verburgt and Tommy Dodd (native name Tjonduga) joined our caravan. We had not expected Old Tommy; it seemed Bob had taken him in to civilization for the first time in his seventy, eighty, or ninety years. As a Native Patrol Officer with full police authority, Bob was a useful fellow to have along as we drove through the last settlement, Coober Pedy, north of Woomera. Coober Pedy is the opal center and a deal wilder than Boot Hill ever had been in fact or fiction. Opal mining is an intensely individual enterprise in which only men utterly devoid of sense engage. And only the most unlucky find anything of value, for the first discoverer of an opal seam in his burrow is more than likely to find a "jelly" (gelignite) bomb tossed in with him to effect a rapid transfer of ownership. When we belted through Coober Pedy there was not a single policeman to keep order. Australian travel books are not to be relied on for communicating the real Coober Pedy. Take for only one example its name: the guidebooks say it is an aboriginal phrase meaning "place where white-fella lives underground." Like so many other aboriginal place-names, its name is an obscenity. Oodnadatta, another opal warren northwest of Coober Pedy is translated "Flower of the Mulga." It is correctly translated "Yellow Shit," a perfect description as well as a perfect

154

translation. There isn't any mulga on the gibber plains; there is nothing on the gibbers but gibbers, and whitefella lives underground in his burrows because there is no wood to build with.

We followed the 1861 trail of explorer John McDouall Stuart through familiar sand-ridge country beyond the Stony, through the Everard Range, into the Northern Territory and out again, and thence on a westward track to the Musgraves and the Pitjandjara homeland.

Incredibly, some of this border territory is officially designated pastoral country, and leases have been taken up; but the land is now worthless, its natural vegetation destroyed by a brief period of sheep-running which broke the matzo-thin crust — the "desert pavement" — that keeps the inland from blowing away like the Oklahoma dust bowl. Mulga Park, for one example: when Ernest Giles, the first explorer into this region, saw it in 1874, he wrote, *"Here I found a spot where Nature truly had 'Shed o'er the scene her purest of crystal, her brightest of green.' This was really a delightful discovery. Everything was of the best kind here — timber, water, grass, and mountains. In all my wanderings, over thousands of miles in Australia, I never saw a more delightful and fanciful region than this, and one indeed where a white man might live and be happy."* Now it is blasted desolation with nothing organic to interrupt one's view of Ayers Rock sixty miles northwest.

I was told by my reading in the explorers Carruthers, Gosse, Wells, and even Giles, that the country immediately south was better, but that was the pastoral lease of the Ernabella Mission, so we fixed our route to avoid it. Visitors, especially anthropologists, are not welcome at Ernabella, for reasons that did neither the anthropologists nor the missionaries credit. I later came to know the present missionary, Bill Edwards, and found him to be altogether admirable, but at the time of this expedition he was still suffering from the rumors adhering to one of his less venerable predecessors whose interest in the aborigines was more corporeal than spiritual. The only criticism I make of Ernabella nowadays is its inability to recognize in me the exception I know myself to be among anthropologists —that and its teaching the natives to make for sale in Adelaide the most hideous textiles ever conceived by the mind of man.

Halfway between Ernabella and Amata we pulled off into the bush at Norman's direction to look in at a ritual place of a much older and more persistent religion than Ernabella's Presbyterianism. Cave Hill, the place was called, very secret, so we stopped the caravan on the track and walked circuitously through the mulga and saltbush to the ancient shrine. A *pulpa tjukurpa* it was — a sacred cave shelter where the symbols of myths were painted and repainted in the uniquely Australian reds, yellows, and blacks. At this place the totemic lecher Kulu was killed by the Wati Kutjara — there he was, a few yards from the cave, petrified into a phallic cone. Here the seven sisters flew up into

Norman B. Tindale and Dr. W.V. MacFarlane at Cave Hill, S.A., where the Wati Kutjara killed Kula, pursuer of the Pleiades

the sky to become the Pleiades and manifest aboriginal Australia's version of the universal myth of seven sisters pursued by a satyr represented by the star Aldebaran (Arabic: "the Follower").

Not many miles beyond Cave Hill I saw my first purely desert nomadic aborigine in his own country — riding a camel. One family: the *pater familias, wati kuritjara;* his two wives, one of some residual nubility, the other very old and apparently senseless, tied into a bundle on her camel saddle; three camels, the distant posterity of some early expedition; and dogs, which one counts out here no more than one counts bush flies. I braked the Tojo and walked out to meet the fellow. We grinned at each other, gestured in friendship (fists pointed, fingers down), murmured a few purr words in Pitjandjara, and parted — he the richer by a handful of cigarettes, I by a half dozen photographs.

The only things of interest in this scorched country grew out of our preliminary knowledge of the land and its people — Cave Hill, the aboriginal family, the perfect *tula* that fell out of the first shovelful of sand I dug out of a dry bog the Tojo sank in, the wave line of worked flint flakes marking a Murundian campsite at the arid Wantapela Swamp, and best of all so far, Peter Aitken's discovery of a flint tool originating in our Keibara cliff in a camp site at Emu Plains, not far, incidentally, from where Australia's first atomic bomb was exploded.

At exactly one thousand miles from Blackwood we pulled into the station compound at Musgrave Park (Amata). This was the administration center for the vast North West Aboriginal Reserve, 27,620 square miles in the northwestern corner of South Australia, matched by a nearly equal-area contiguous reserve in Western Australia and the Northern Territory: three sprawling cottages of corrugated iron and Transite, residences for the seven whites who comprised the staff; a sideless garage; a hut for the gasoline generator; a one-room commissary shanty; a chapel built of brush and thatch; and a two-room cottage for the Old Aboriginal Identity, Tommy Dodd, built for him by Bob Verburgt when Bob was superintendent here two years before.

A mile or so north of the compound the native camp was located. It comprised a floating population of about three hundred and fifty persons who stayed as long as their stomachs could endure the novelty of white man's food rations. Then they would leave as they had come, in small bands of a few families, to live the old way in the bush.

Our Alice Springs contingent had come in earlier — Godfrey McPherson and another fellow I had better identify only as the Other Fellow, since it will be necessary to report of him some rather discreditable behavior, and their huge Bedford truck (the largest mobile thing ever to enter the bush, apart from the Blue Streak rockets that did not make it out over the Indian Ocean) pulling the mobile laboratory, through whose equipment most of our blood would run in the following weeks. We had already chosen the base of our operations, so after a shower, shave, shine, shampoo, and surfeit of lemonade, we satisfied the civilized proprieties of reporting to the isolated staff the progress of the outside world (three new illiterate emergent nations in Africa, wolf children in India, octuplets born in Afghanistan, Panama and Guatemala conscripting soldiers over a soccer dispute, a Russian peasant dead at the age of two hundred and eight, trouble in the Punjab, and fighting among the Irish), and then rumbled off across the trackless bush into the southwest. Our progress on this last leg of the journey was slower so as not to pitch off any of the three dozen aborigines (nine piled into and atop my Tojo, already carrying me and Norman) who had volunteered for whatever was going. No dogs. I wasn't having any goddamned dogs, and Vic saw no imperative need for the baastids either. The natives grumbled, but could adduce in debate no reasonable arguments in favor of bringing any bloody dogs.

Our operations camp was excellent. It lay in a little valleyed plain formed by the half-billion-year detritus of Cambrian mountains ringing it like the lip of a five-mile saucer. There was — *mirabile dictu!* — enough water here to supply the entire reserve; a government work crew had been brought in to drill an artesian well from which a windmill now was drawing water into a concrete tank eight feet high and twenty feet in diameter. *By Chrise!* I thought, *we could swim in this thing!* Vic got the idea at the same time and sternly reminded us that water was off limits to all personnel between sunrise and sunset and that we were not out here to swim but to find out why people perished in hot dry deserts. We had to keep our priorities straight. Die first, swim later.

This saucer of land was to be known henceforth as Twenty-Five-Mile Bore, in recognition of its distance from the Musgrave Park compound and in appreciation of the general ignorance of the old maps (I held the only one in the entire region) which identified it as Lungly Gully. At 26° 18′ S — 130° 53′ E, it lay between two named "mountains," Morris and Caroline, and thus fell into the path trod by Ernest Giles and his excellent aide W. H. Tietkens on 10 September 1873, when Giles was in a midsummer night's madness after repelling a mass attack by the aborigines. Some strangely named places remain on the maps from this time of Giles's fanciful aberration — *Fairies'*

Glen, Mount Oberon, and, at the head of Lungly Gully, *Titania's Spring ("Dry")*.

We worked that afternoon in a frenzy of cooperation we were not to share again, and by sundown our camp was well and truly established. The official expeditionary tents holding equipment and supplies and the mobile laboratory were placed according to Vic's master plan. For our individual needs we were on our own, like peasants on a Russian collectivized farm. Norman and I had our swags enveloped in our large gauze cocoons, his placed near the generator lamp in the middle of the compound so he could work all night on his journals and catch moths the while, mine set as far away from the others as bush etiquette would allow. I do not hold with communal sleeping. Over behind their own ironwood tree the two genuine bushmen, Bob Verburgt and Tommy Dodd, had their swags on great canvas groundsheets whose edges were all rolled in upon themselves so that the night-creeping creatures — scorpions, ants, centipedes, and snakes — would always be turned away. Peter Aitken threw his swag on the bare ground; he had already been bitten on the balls by a giant centipede and had nothing more to fear. Vic and Bob Seamark appropriated the air-conditioned laboratory, rank having its privileges, and the two men from the Alice chose to reside in the storage tent, too green in the ways of the bush to know a tent is insufferable in hot country. They would learn.

Preparations completed and the sun down, we had a good wash and a feed, leaving time only for the big yawn and the swag. But we were to get no sleep that night. A couple of the aboriginal men walked up from their camp ground a hundred yards away and whispered that there was to be a *proper big-business corroboree* in the bush well north of the Musgrave Park station and everyone would be delighted if we could attend. Moreover, they would be enchanted to accompany us in our vehicles and guide us safely to the dancing grounds thirty miles away. *R.S.V.P.*

My oath. No question of our refusing. Aboriginal ritual has an irresistible magnetism drawing upon an atavistic part of our natures. The need for sleep vanished, we piled the aborigines back on the vehicles and bounced through the rocky darkness, guided by shouts of the natives and their directional pounding on the cab roofs — an adventure in itself.

159

With the familiar northern hemisphere constellations the wrong way about and ourselves lost in a pool of our own headlights, we had little sense of direction. Later, after puzzling over the maps, I located the dance ground in the sand plain between Opparina Creek (dry) and Cave Hill, facing an appreciable northern rocky upthrust that must have been Mount Woodward. For the last mile we were guided by the singing, easing the vehicles very slowly to a place where a hundred tiny camp fires glittered like the Pleiades themselves around the southern periphery of a great sun-like ritual fire. At least half the entire population of the Musgrave Park camp was there — not only the men, but women and children and dogs as well, which meant this was not a proper big-business corroboree, but a semi-sacred ceremony, a "playabout."

After our eyes adjusted to the darkness above and the sparkling little fires below, we could see that the orientation of the ritual was skewed away from the north-south line I first projected. Crux — the Southern Cross — hung low over a mulga tree to our left and a little behind; the mountain lay northwest; the great fire north; and the congregation southeast. To the left side of the large clearing, across which a single man walked (the priest tending the fire), there was a rectangular brush fence about fifteen feet long, very like the one Norman and I had seen at Yalata. On the edge of the acre clearing sat the men, singing and beating sticks, and behind them at the conjugal fires away from the ceremonial center, sat their women and children and dogs.

Thinking it the better wisdom not to ask permission, I set up my tape recorder about sixty feet behind the congregation — an ideal placement, as it turned out, for I caught on my sensitive microphone not only the mass singing but all the intervening conversation. For the whole of the night my tape recorder turned slowly upon the alternate singing and talking, leaving me free to move around, sitting now with this group of men, then with another, learning from each a little more about the ceremony. There was confusion about its meaning, as one might expect among the laity in any religion's rituals. All were agreed this was the *Inma Pabelo*, the Sacred Song of the Dreaming Buffalo. But it could not be a true *tjukurpa* song, for women were present, and there were no buffalo in Australia except those imported by missionaries in the most distant tropical north. So I had a serious doctrinal problem to begin with. Well; sufficient unto the night is the virtue thereof; we would nut these things out later. The grass-swept clearing and the brush barriers promised dancers, but where were they? *Teiwa, teiwa — kantillytja waṟara;* long way, long way, beside the mountain range. And indeed on the farthest horizon of the mountain's foothills there was a tiny spark, the fire of the dancers. Hour by hour and fire by fire they approached, till the sun's spears struck the mountain — then they would be here, to leap upon us from the brush altar. So said the men.

What a way to build dramatic suspense! We watched through the night, seeing one fire wink out and another (a little larger, for it was a little closer) flare up, as the unknown dancers came toward us, unseen. Tension built in the congregation, too; in the early night the men left one by one for their family fires, to take their wives into the dark bush to copulate. But as the night grew older and day neared, the singing lengthened and the conversation shortened. I had returned to my recorder and lounged drowsily on my swag. Once I was startled by a thing utterly beyond my dulled imagination — a kitten jumped into my lap, settled down, purred. *My God!* I thought, *the bloody thing's purring just like an American cat!* Another problem to be solved later — whence cats in the Centre?*

With false dawn the singing became continuous, the beat stronger, the women's voices nearly hysterical. Suddenly — dawn: the top of the mountain ignited with sunlight and at once from behind the brush screen two dancing men leaped out and danced sideways in the knee-shaking, Charleston-step, characteristic aboriginal way, over to the big fire, where they paused for everyone to see them in their guised glory. To the usual painted body decorations was added to each man a pair of enormous down-turned horns, like great arms growing from their heads and hanging nearly to the ground, made of bits of grass and other vegetal fibers, cotton string, and emu feathers, and painted in alternate stripes of red and white. Before any of us could really take them into our visual consciousness they ran toward the seated congregation and sank to the ground. At that instant, which I learned

---

* The solution was prosaic: house cats, ferociously efficient carnivores for all their deceptive indolence in houses they have taken possession of, spread over the continent as fast as the rabbits. One does not see many of them because they keep their own population controlled — and because the aborigines hold them to be gourmet delicacies, food for honored men. I was to see one cat fondled in the afternoon and eaten in the evening. In some parts of deepest aboriginal Australia not only the cat but its name preceded the white man — *putjikata,* "pussycat."

was a transubstantiation from secular men to sacred animal, all the women sprang up and ran off toward the Musgrave Park camp, howling like keening banshees. The children screamed and ran with their mothers, and the dogs, yelping for an unknown fear, bounded off with them. All the men remained, like communicants after a High Mass, some sobbing from the unbearable emotion of the ritual. I found myself weeping too, though I did not even believe in their bloody religion.

We all stood around for a half hour or so, drawing in the scene, planting it in our memories. In small groups we were invited, whitefella and blackfella, to go behind the screen and touch our hands to the horns, now removed from the dancers and laid on the ground, to draw from them their *mapanpa*, their *mana*. Later these horns would be ritually burned, like a respected flag.

Most of the anthropological work Norman and I did during our stay in Lungly Gully was concerned with ritual singing and social organization, mainly because Vic's work did not allow the natives to forage and hunt as they ordinarily would do. Day by day we picked up more information about the corroboree, not all of it consistent. Norman quickly twigged the "buffalo" heresy as a recent importation imposed by whites and natives willing to be influenced by them. What we thought were horns were really symbols of *bardi*, the *witjuti* grubs, larvae of great moths, so essential for the protein needs of the aborigines. I should have guessed it myself, but I did not think to wonder why buffalo would be striped. The stripes of course were the segments of the *bardi*. The ceremony itself, the men agreed, had the social function of honoring the alternate age generations, *Waltunduru* the elder, *Tjanamiltjana* the younger. Our most importunate informant, a young fellow we knew only as George, insisted the ceremony was something different altogether — a ritual associated with the mysterious Red Ocher Men and relating the mythic wandering of the totemic possum, *Waitjuta tjukurpa*. This interpretation prompted the other aboriginal men to declare that George was full of shit (*kuna pulka*), and while I should not presume to rule upon his contents, I shared the opinion that George was without question a pain in the arse. On another trip, when heat and thirst did not abrade my nerves so badly, I was able to see George more objectively — an aborigine trying to make it in the white man's way but damned to failure because he lacked the rare qualities of personality to effect so great a transition. He thought he had charisma, but it was only *chutzpa*. His *waitjuta* was an echo in his memory of *witjuti*.

In Lungly Gully he was trying to usurp the camp leadership from Kata, the proper *pu:rpa*, head of the Malupiti Pitjandjara, from whom dominant authority exudes. Kata wears a symbol the white men at Musgrave Park do not understand — a pair of eyeglasses, or more accurately, a pair of frames with one lens missing and the other scoured into opacity by wind-blown sand. Between the confused image produced by the two orbits he stumbles in authority. But Kata had not only hereditary authority, but the personal power of a super-Alpha male.

On the white man's path another aborigine in our group stood immovably in George's way — Teddy, a rough and ruthless man who permitted George his assumed liberties simply because he couldn't be bothered killing him. Teddy's naturally dominant qualities were augmented by his education — he had been in jail and had learned essential English (imprecations, ejaculations, obscenities, and the like). He had brought into Lungly Gully an innovative replacement for the traditional *walanu* status staff — a portable crank phonograph and one record — "Adeste Fidelis," which he played constantly with a nail as a needle. Both George and Teddy had two wives, another mark of status, though one of Teddy's spouses was at the moment in the Alice Springs hospital recovering from a broken forearm, snapped by Teddy across his thigh, a more or less regular chastisement he provided for cheeky wives. Teddy fell into the category of dangerous men *True Grit*'s Rooster Cogburn meant when he spoke of rats: "All you can do with a rat is kill him or let him be." We let Teddy be.

Thinking back now upon the two score people, white and black, whom Vic MacFarlane assembled in Lungly Gully for his "sweat quest," I am impressed by how many strong personalities and men of superior accomplishment were among this random sample. Of the handful of whites, there was Norman Tindale, the polymath, master scholar in a dozen disciplines; Vic MacFarlane, narrower in his interests despite his two doctorates but probably as eminent in the judgment of world scientists; Bob Seamark, a young physiologist of great promise; Peter Aitken, a highly respected zoologist whose knowledge went as far beyond mammalogy as Lamarck's had gone past his assigned invertebrates; and Bob Verburgt, Master Bushman.

163

Our outstanding aborigines included not only Teddy, that magnificent rogue male, but several other men and women who would be memorable in any group. If Teddy was the aboriginal John Wayne turned wholly misanthrope, Bell Rock Jacky was the dusky Audie Murphy, the little man of unplumbed ferocity and depths of darkness. What a punch-up we would have had if these two could be fired at each other! Jacky, a miniman all of us pulling together could not have stretched to five feet, had the reputation of complete fearlessness in a spear fight. He had also the foulest temper of any human being I can remember. He knew not a single word of English, and in his own language his vocabulary seemed to be limited to an unrelieved stream of curses and obscenities. Bob Verburgt (who had once been a professional fighter) told me he had had to twist Bell Rock Jacky's nose once when he was slashing his wife's face to ribbons with a hooked wire. My personal favorite among the aboriginal men was the inimitable Tjipikudu, transmitter of the Keibara myth, as much a man as Teddy or Bell Rock Jacky, but without political ambitions. Tjipi was a natural actor and comedian who sensed exactly what to do before a motion picture camera, though he had never seen a movie; a mighty hunter who could spear eagles on the wing (he impaled one in Lungly Gully); a great hand with the ladies, by all accounts and by the scars of spear wounds in his thighs; the best of our informants despite his total ignorance of English; the Errol Flynn to Teddy's John Wayne and Bell Rock's Audie Murphy; and withal, a cunning rascal who was shining up to me for the single purpose of getting by one means or other my leather-handled, stainless-steel *tameha* ("tomahawk" — hatchet).

Though the cultural and environmental deprivation of the desert aborigines does not offer many opportunities to women for achieving distinction, we had two at least who will be long remembered: Nia, Bell Rock Jacky's nubile daughter, who would cause aboriginal blood to flow before we left this camp; and Lucy, George's first wife, who had magnificent teeth, a beautiful singing voice, and a coruscating personality that shone right through the language barrier.

The children of our people, like all children, were worthless little devils, though it must be conceded for this lot that they were outstandingly worthless little devils. One apocalyptic day one of them no doubt will become Australia's Jomo Kenyatta. I wonder whether he will be my Willie, the seven-year-old who used to nuzzle up to me for

Terenyi (Bell Rock Jacky) at Lungly Gully, S.A.

lumps of over-sweet lollies the way Tjipikudu did for the *tameha*. The little rascal had learned some English, and when he put his arm around me he would say, "Me your pren."

"Fine bloody friend you are," I would answer. "You're a bloody lolly pren."

"Me no lolly pren — me your *true pren*" — with that enormous aboriginal smile.

Sitting around the testing tables with the aboriginal men in the century heat on those alternate days when Vic's work consisted mainly of sticking needles into us, making us drink heavy water (I was surprised to find it wasn't really heavy), forcing fluids of one kind or other from us, and making us step up and down on boxes (an exercise we thought every bit as senseless as the natives did), Norman and I recorded a wealth of aboriginal mythic songs.

Though no women or children were allowed within earshot when this singing was going on, everyone knew generally what was being done, and on "Ladies' Days," when the women were tested, we took down some marvelous feminine singing, drawn from the special sacred world the women had to themselves.

Late one afternoon the little boys came up to us after their fathers had departed and announced through their spokesman, my pren Willie, that they would like to sing for us also. I do not know what they expected from us in return besides lollies, for we had been careful not to play back any of our recordings. Well, what the hell. Expecting another composition on Weet Bix, I drew them around the microphone and told them to pitch in. A few giggles, and then —

Bornana mouta toppa Tennetee,
Greena tate inna lanada pree;
Bornana wooda toh e newebree tree,
Kilima ba enewa onee tree —
DABY, DABY CROCKA, KINGADA WILE PRONTEE! *Brrrrrrr!*

After I had shaken my head vigorously two or three times the way Norman does when he meets anything absolutely astonishing, I played back the tape for the boys. Their astonishment was the square of my own. They shrieked and squealed and jumped up and down, demanding that I play it again and again and again and again. I was very

Tjipikudu with speared eagle at Lungly Gully, S.A.

Puntaru, Tjipikudu's son, at Pidul Rockhole, Mann Range, S.A.

happy to do so. As some explorer said before me, *It is the special privilege of an explorer to work miracles.*

Still more delight would come from that tape. I knew Tom Blackburn, composer of "Davy Crockett," and when I got back to the *lanada pree* I sent him a dubbed copy. I think it pleased him more than all the other recognition he had received for his fine song to know his composition had penetrated to the most remote inhabited place on earth and was being sung by bare-arse–naked Old Stone Age children who had no acquaintance whatever with movies, television, or radio.

In those lazy days I also put time into the hopelessly knotted question of aboriginal society. Since the last great Dominant Male in anthropology, A. R. Radcliffe-Brown, told us all the proper study of mankind was social organization, my colleagues and predecessors and their forebears have been devising charts and genealogies and inventing ugly macaronic terms and imagining hypothetical filthy human relationships to prove the absurd proposition that every man relates to another in a prescribed invariable way. It is part of the literal discipline of anthropology to do several hours of social organization every day, like five-finger exercises. All of us have to put in this prentice work — until we are established at least. Some go on with it, for various reasons. Claude Lévi-Strauss does it for the fun of pulling the legs of his sycophants and those whose sense of humor is too weakly developed to see what he is up to.

I am no Dominant Male. I am no Pied Piper to the hairy generation. I will establish no departments of anthropology nor found any emergent nation. But I sit here and say to the world, lay and scholarly, that it is all a lot of *crap.*

I do not mean to suggest that peoples, primitive or civilized, do not have elaborate systems of marriage patterning. They do indeed. And one of the most ingenious mathematical devices in that scientific branch of anthropology called population genetics is the Hardy-Weinberg Formula. *But they do not work in real life.* There is no such thing as random mating or inviolable patterns. They do not work for the same reason: men and women, since the time the first handsome slack-jawed Australopithecine man-ape looked with desire on the first pretty slack-jawed Australopithecine maiden, have been marrying spouses they were not supposed to. If the insistent lover is an Alpha and the properly installed leader of his clan, horde, moiety, tribe, nation, or commune, he will change the rules to vindicate his gonadal urge. If the man does not have a sufficiency to dominance or authority, there will be fighting and killing and an eventual accommodation to take care of the child (the implantation of the child precedes all the other mucking about). In either event the tidy rules will be scrambled. The only strange thing about the whole business is its ease of accomplishment. If a few noisy demonstrations of hairy youth can convince the Church of England that it should marry fairies one to the other in holy matrimony, what social tradition is safe?

For years I tried to pull the infinitely varied rules of social relationship in aboriginal Australia into a general unified field theory, certain that if I succeeded I would have in my hands and notebooks the materials to construct a New Decalogue to govern the human race until its next mutation. After Lungly Gully I thought I had it. Its basis was the Fry Framework.

In 1929 eight Adelaide anthropologists (four of whom I had the honor to know) formed an expedition into western Aranda country. Because they were eight, one of them (H. K. Fry) devised a schema for patterning the social relationships of a tribe so ingenious and yet so simple it can be compared only to an abacus. I will not discuss it here. It is too damned complex. I first saw a Fry Framework covering twenty-four square feet of a worktable in Norman's corner of the South Australian Museum's Department of Anthropology. I labored over that thing for hours, trying to make some sense out of it. Norman finally came over to comfort me. "John," he said, "you have to understand this is only a two-dimensional representation of Kenneth's framework. The actual structure must be seen as a cylinder in two planes simultaneously."

The important thing for our purposes is to know that there were eight men. Had they gone in a hundred years earlier, there would shortly have been no men and the problem of their being fitted into the Aranda organization would not have arisen. But because the Aranda in 1929 had learned a little about whitefella behavior, they put our eight men each into one of the eight subsections of their tribal structure — *Pananka, Purula, Ngala, Knuraia, Bangata, Kamara, Paltara,* and *Mbitjana.* After Norman and his companions had exhausted the explorers' miracle-working of removing their teeth and striking matches and that sort of thing, they turned to more desperate forms of passing the time, like playing with their new relationships. "Could

I marry your sister?" one would ask. "Stay away from my sister," he would be admonished. "No, I mean according to the Aranda system could I marry your sister?" "I told you to stay away from my bloody sister, y' baastid." From what I have been able to get out of Norman, Kenneth Fry stayed out of these hypothetical and philosophical discussions, and instead set about to place all the possibilities in what is now known as the Fry Framework. My derived schema illustrates only the marriage patterning, but it should suffice to prove the difficult intricacies of aboriginal social organization. In the paradigm below, the butt of the arrow represents the man, the bend of the arrow the woman

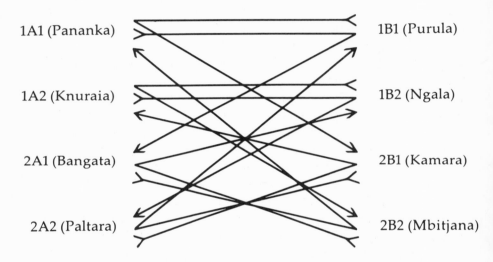

1A1 (Pananka)	1B1 (Purula)
1A2 (Knuraia)	1B2 (Ngala)
2A1 (Bangata)	2B1 (Kamara)
2A2 (Paltara)	2B2 (Mbitjana)

he properly marries, and the point of the arrow the subsection into which their children fall. The initial number indicates the two alternating generations between which marriage is absolutely forbidden, the letters *A* and *B* — capitalized to signify males, though we will understand that the bend of our arrows changes the letter to lowercase to recognize the wife as female* — indicate the two moieties between

---

* Three incidental points must be made here: (1) Fry at first let the ladies have the capitals but he was informed by higher authority that he must not do things like that; (2) there is homosexuality, but I will not speak about it; and (3) the subsection names are all so ancient that no aborigine has the faintest memory of their ever having semantic meaning.

which marriage is compulsory, and the terminal numeral indicates the subsection divisions.

This is great stuff for classroom instruction. The trouble with it for me is that I pursued these schemata of marriage rules all over the bloody Australian continent, like a silly ass. All I can say in thoughtful conclusion is that the aborigines do not understand the rules but recognize their existence and the necessity for enforcing them — note well that I do not say "observing them." The merest schoolboy can see at once that this impossible paradox will lead to spear fights. Among the people we had at Lungly Gully, the schema looked like this:*

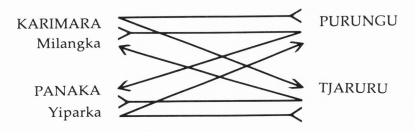

KARIMARA
Milangka

PANAKA
Yiparka

PURUNGU

TJARURU

I went on to construct a beautiful theory of invariable cultural inevitability to account for the difference between these two nearly contiguous tribes, but Norman assured me both the ethnographical record and the extensive genealogies he had compiled for forty and more years prove that before their movement east into Jangkundjara territory the Pitjandjara had no concept of moiety, section, or subsection divisions. Nor did some other desert tribes. The coming of the white man precipitated incalculable trouble in this area of native social relations by allowing, encouraging, and even forcing the integration of traditionally isolated peoples on the mission stations. Tribes that had no elaborate rules of marriage felt an inferiority and yarked some up quickly, together with an unshakable conviction of rectitude and tradition going back to the Wati Kutjara. Men who were too old to fight over women now fought over marriage theory.

* See also p. 244.

And for all your theory, what are you going to do with those sexual witches whom the psychiatrist Leopold Stein wrote about in his *Anatomy of Eve?* They do exist, these females that live to lure males into fights; they have been observed even among domestic cats. I personally will go so far as to suggest the reason Irishmen spend half their time in pubs on the gargle and the other half throwing bombs into pubs: Irishwomen. Celts were always regarded by their unfortunate neighbors as being a witch-ridden people.

Nia, Bell Rock Jacky's daughter, was a witch. Every move she made with any part of her body from toe to eyelid was an invitation to several contending men at once. Nia's sexual magnetism had at least a twenty-five-mile range — it reached from Lungly Gully right back to the main Musgrave Park camp. One night, very late, Bell Rock Jacky pulled me and Norman awake and told us Nia had run off to Amata with some fucking son of a bitch he was going to push a fucking spear through. Now would we get the hell up and drive him there? *"Wia ma pitja, nungkarpa lara pupinpa!"* (Freely translated, "Come you, God damn it son of a bitch!")

Many many years ago in the innocence of my youth I once intruded into a family dispute of this nature. I came out of it pretty well — only some bruised knuckles — but I learned to stay right out of these things in future. Norman did not need that experience to direct him to the same course of expedient inaction. So we both mumbled in feigned stupidity, *"Na? Na? Puru watjala — putuna kulinu. Na?"* ("What? What? Say it again — I did not understand. What?") We correctly relied on Bell Rock's volatility to take him away quickly, and he tramped off into the bush, shaking his spears, and muttering *"Nung! Nung! Walypela nung! Kumpu! Kuna!"* ("Idiots! Idiots! Stupid whitefellas! Piss! Shit!")

We never found out what happened; we got on the blower to Musgrave Park next morning and told them that Nia had better be brought back here pretty damned quick, by Chrise, and in something resembling virginal condition, or there was going to be smash-up dead fella he fall all 'roun. Nia was trucked back to Lungly Gully, smiling innocently and seductively as usual. Musgrave Park told us by radio that a man had been speared to death in the camp that night. We do not know whether Bell Rock had anything to do with it, but I do know if he didn't, it was not his heart that hindered him.

As the weeks went on, Nia somehow became increasingly pretty in

172

our eyes as well. All permit-holding intruders into reserves are sworn to vows of chastity, but to several of the rougher men in our party Nia's appearance in the lab compound meant sudden cessation of all other stimuli. The Other Fellow from Alice Springs, in whom racism and randyism fought a bloody struggle, became more and more interested in Nia. He also became dirtier and hairier — this, remember, in a time when even Bowery bums did not cultivate unkempt filthiness. From the day he arrived he neither changed his clothes nor washed them, no razor was drawn over his rough face, and in observation of the expedition's purpose, water had touched him through the throat only — except for one occasion which must presently be recorded. The stench of him was as vile as his appearance; he had brought severe gastrointestinal illness down from the Alice with him, and for two weeks he vomited almost constantly over everything, including himself. All this led to the most memorable remark of the expedition. One afternoon toward the end of our stay he was standing on the steps of the mobile laboratory when Nia sauntered by. He followed her with his eyes from the moment she came in sight till she disappeared into the bush on the other side of the compound, and then remarked in angry frustration, "If they only weren't so *fucking DIRTY!*"

This gastric illness was a dreadful thing. We all caught it, recovered slightly, and caught it again, evidently reinfecting one another. We could not die of it, but we wished we could. Strangely, I was least affected; I had only one bad day. Peter Aitken, the strongest of us, was the sickest. The Other Fellow one day vomited his way over to the water trough draining from the storage tank and flung himself into it — an act of irresponsibility that infuriated the rest of us. Vic and Bob, angrier than I thought scientists could be, scrubbed out the trough. Of course it could not again be used for drinking water. But it was so used by the aborigines and they caught the bug. And still the ailing children multiplied our agonies with their bloody lizards.

The lizards were Norman's doing. The South Australian Museum's herpetologist suspected in this region the presence of a rare species of small lizard and gave Norman the responsibility of finding one. Norman in turn gave the job to the best lizard hunters, the native children, offering a lolly for each lizard delivered to the storage tent. Dear God! No one could have guessed how many lizards there were in this desert, nor how adept the young hunters were at finding them. The stream of children coming in with lizards and going out with lollies was unending. One day the Other Fellow, trying to sleep off his illness in the tent, went berserk (I use the word figuratively) and threw all the lizards out, screaming at Norman, "One of your bloody lizards *bit* me! If one more of those bloody kids comes in here with a bloody lizard, the lizard is going to walk off with the lolly in its bloody mouth! Why the bloody *hell* don't those bloody abos go off and starve or whatever they do in the native state?"

Thereafter the children carried the lizards to any of us who was not hidden, not to the storage tent. The afternoon of my worst day they pestered me until I shouted at them, *"Ma pitja! Ma pitja!"* ("Go away!") They paid no attention; since aboriginal children are almost never chastised, they do not obey any adult instruction they do not want to. I alternately moaned and shouted at them in their own tongue to cease and desist holding their lizards in my face, until at last my legendary sweet disposition broke and I screamed, *"FUCK OFF!"* At this they looked at each other in wild surmise and walked away, repeating, *"Puck opp! Puck opp!"* Another new word in their vocabulary.

For three days Norman was deathly ill — literally, I was sure. He would arise dutifully in the morning, stagger to the table, eat something bland, turn away and spew it up, and return to his swag. The bush flies by this time had become clouds, and every time we lifted a side of our mosquito net they blew in by the hundreds. Our cocoons allowed us to spray them with Flyaway, which stuck to the net gummily and caught the blowing desert dust until both of us were imprisoned in a thin brick-walled furnace. One day Nia appeared, not with sensual temptation, but holding a lizard by the tail and her head bearing an aureole of bush flies. She pulled up the side of Norman's net and stuck her head in, releasing upon him the flying cloud. Norman told me later, "John, that was the single worst moment of my entire life."

Vic was as ill as any of us, but in the best tradition of the imperturbable British expeditionary leaders, he did not show it. After he began to push his hypodermic needles clear through our veins we put him under restraint and stopped the water metabolism testing. With all the fluids lost by ourselves and the aborigines, his work became suspect anyhow.

The aborigines kept the virulence alive by their lax — I am tempted to say laxative — behavior. After a couple of weeks in Lungly Gully they were fouling the drinking water by using the trough area as a latrine. Another insight: in the state of nomadic nature, aborigines do not pollute their water supply, but instead camp one or two hundred yards from it, use it quickly and respectfully, and go away. Religious reasons are offered for this conduct; they say the water holes are the dwellings of the Rainbow Serpent Wanamba, who does not like any mucking around in the area of his creation. Water holes in fact are often called "snake-possessing places." But in environmental fact, that is just what water holes are — places where one is sure to find snakes. Any man who squats his naked rear around a water hole is liable to get it bitten, and he may join the Rainbow Serpent in the Dreaming. The religious prohibition simply reinforces one of the facts of life, another example of culture at work trying to keep man alive in spite of himself.

The days were growing unrelentingly hotter now as the summer waxed stronger and the desert drier. We could rely on the century mark every day, a base exceeded cumulatively by three or four degrees a day as we pushed into the desert. I had a very sensitive thermometer from an Adelaide supply house to record not only the atmospheric temperature but altitudes as well. So far as I could determine, altitudes on the maps had been taken by plane-borne altimeters and therefore were subject to gross errors. To figure the altitudes at our various camps I had first to convert Fahrenheit to Centigrade (subtract thirty-two, multiply by five, divide by nine), then measuring the boiling point of water. The formula is $100°C$ times (0.0367) $(P-760)-0.00023$ = height of Hg laid off against a table of figures from the Smithsonian Institution, which, unfortunately for the science of the thing, did not have a correction for the boiled centipede and bush fly content. Another difficulty was the tendency of the lead in a pencil to slide out as its surrounding wood desiccated in the near-zero humidity. I have the figures and will work them out one day according to a list of priorities. Any day now. *Koara.*

Water was the subject of almost monomaniacal interest in camp. All talk grew out of it, all talk led back into it. Our big storage tank was a demon, untouchable, set there to taunt and tempt us. The desert sun was a white-hot poker driven into our brains. Like horses running for safety back into a burning barn, we were sometimes taken by a compulsion to run — anywhere — to escape from it. There was no hiding place. Every other day Vic gathered all the men, white and

175

aboriginal, sealed off our arms in plastic bags to catch the sweat, and set us off on what quickly got the name "perishers," long walks at a vigorous pace.

We never found any water on these journeys; this was indeed dry country. Bob Seamark and I put to the test a new form of water-getting much publicized in outdoorsman magazines that year. We took a large sheet of unbroken plastic, laid it over a hole about ten feet in diameter and three feet deep in the bottom of which we set a pannikin, and set a stone in the center of the sheet so that interior drippage would fall into the cup, finishing off the job by burying and sealing the sheet's edges. The theoretical idea is that the sun's evaporative force will draw subsurface water to the underside of the plastic and run down into the pannikin. Lovely. In two days we got two table-spoons of water.

Do you know how much water a man needs in the desert to stay alive? One canteen — or a sip from a canteen — as we see on tele-vision dramas of desert distress? I will tell you how much water a man needs in the desert every day to stay alive. Two gallons is an ab-solute minimum. That is how much he needs to stay alive. An average-sized man has about four gallons of water in his body. In extreme desert conditions, with low humidity and high exertion, he can lose as much as three gallons a day — more than a pint of it just by breathing.

Without a Moses to strike water out of a rock, the aborigines learned how to strike water from frogs and tree roots, and to conserve water by avoiding Baptist revival tents and other prodigal sources of water waste. If they need water or a similar solvent for utility, they use blood, urine, and even sebaceous grease squeezed from their noses.

We lost these liquids, too, in Vic's laboratory. Bush flies were so gorged with our blood drained out of the lab's sinks that they had taken to walking around and getting underfoot.

The camp was not what explorers call happy. If one of us did a silly thing, the others twitted him about it. I am legend in central Australia now for washing out my clothes in peanut oil, thinking it to be soap. A dietetic and political rebellion simmered over the discovery that Peter Aitken had laid in stores of black Communist sugar instead of good white capitalistic sugar; he was not popular in any event, having brought heaps of rotting animal carcasses into camp for maceration. Lungly Gully was a dust-swept brazier. The red desert dust swept out during the day and back in during the night, so that we woke every morning with our mouths and ears full of grit. Vic's constant watch upon us in voiding any liquid — even spit — began to get on our nerves, especially since it was our responsibility to run over and lay violent hands upon any male aborigine who stood with his back turned to camp — the native male's position for micturition. Women we couldn't watch, since they squatted for that and everything else. Nevertheless Vic assembled great masses of data.

This material is still being studied; Vic is returning every year for more. He has published some preliminary conclusions, and we spoke together about the work at length when he stopped in Colorado four years after Lungly Gully on his way to Alaska, where he was going to study human water metabolism in a cold desert environment; but I still cannot make a satisfactory summary of the research. It is all extremely complex, having to do with the metabolic behavior of sodium and other salts. However, I can say that aborigines studied are more puzzling than aborigines imagined. Logic demands the desert dwellers to be less needful of water and more conservative of the substance by urinating and sweating than persons living in humid conditions. One might anticipate biological rules dealing with this logic — something like the rules of Gloger, Bergmann, Allen, and Rensch, which account for differences in function and form of the same animal species (human as well as lesser mammals) occupying different environments. Surely at the least an approximation to the equation Vic once thought of working up into a popular article: CAMEL IS TO HORSE AS ABORIGINE IS TO WHITE.

So much again for logic. The weeks of testing and months of analysis showed that compared with the white men in Lungly Gully the aboriginal men and women drank more water and drank it *ten times* as fast, sweated *twice* as much, had *63 percent* greater body turnover of water, and urinated up to *twelve times* as much. I remembered David Carnegie's observation of an aborigine he had sent for water after discovering Empress Spring: *"He drank a great deal more than any of us and yet had been a comparatively short time without water, whilst we had been walking and working on starvation rations for a good number of days."*

I have always had doubts about the presumed physical superiority of the Noble Savage. In physique, only the West Africans and the upper-class Polynesians have enough muscularity to keep beach bullies from kicking sand in their faces. During the 1904 Olympic Games tribesmen from all parts of the primitive world were brought in to participate in the "Anthropology Days." Their performances were risible. If I remember aright, the high jump was won with a leap of two and a half feet. Do not offer as argument the case of the seven-foot leaps of the Nilotic Watusi. I can rise from this chair right now and clear a seven-foot crossbar if, like the Watusi, I took off from a four-foot platform and had lying Italian ethnographers to record the feat (it was the Duke of Abruzzi who faked the Watusi high-jumping). The Watusi are so effete for all the talk to the contrary that when the ordinary-sized Bahutu rebelled against them a few years ago they would have been killed off to a man, had it not been for the help of their Batwa allies, who saved their elongated skins. The Batwa are pygmies.

We had corroboratory evidence on this point during our perishers. On the worst of these, two men collapsed into unconsciousness and without help would surely have died. And who were the two men? *Tjipikudu and Bell Rock Jacky!* The two aborigines most recently in from the uncontaminated Old Stone Age! So much for the wild men.

I don't enjoy walking; no point to it. Given a distance, I'd rather cover it at a run, even now. Day before yesterday I was running across campus and a hippie shouted solicitously, "Don't run, sir, you'll have a heart attack." I shouted back, "Mind your own goddamned business, Seed, or you'll have a head attack." The run and the language do not accord with professorial conduct, but both are legacies from my unconventional life. On our perishers out of Lungly Gully Godfrey and I used to team up, since we had the same opinion of leisurely ambulation. Not running, but walking fast, the two of us were generally back in camp when the rest of the party was still over the horizon. Eventually the ambitious young George twigged the situation and decided he had to show physical superiority. He and Andrew, another young aborigine with incipient ambition, stayed with Godfrey and me on the next walk. The next time George tried to outwalk us I went along on his terms until we were a half mile from camp; suddenly then I slapped him on the behind, yelled *"Langari! Nyuntulu wanala!* Come on, you rascal, RUN!" Except for the Pitjandjara, this was the device Roger Bannister used to beat John Landy in the British Empire Games mile in 1954. I began with a sprint, a good method of breaking the other fellow's spirit (used so well by Vladimir Kuts against Gordon Pirie in the 1956 Olympics 5000 meters), and then settled down into a long stride. I did not give George any psychological assistance by looking back. I sprinted into camp alone. Godfrey told me afterward that George, thirty years younger and fitter, ran only about fifty yards and died. Well, now, what do you make of that, Jean Jacques, old buddy? I will give you from the Jamaicans one of life's most useful truths: *Hog run fo' him life — dog run fo' him character.*

I was soon to travel, as you shall hear, many thousands of miles among the fringe-dwelling aborigines who squatted on the edges of white settlements. Mostly they were beaten people — beaten, I think, not so much by the whites as by themselves. I could never bring myself to laugh along with their old men, forty years exiled from their tribes to save their penes from the stone knife, when they bragged with their characteristic high giggle, "I nebber bin cut. Dey nebber catch me!" They nebber bin cut. Rubbish they were thought to be by the desert people, and rubbish they were.

For George and other aboriginal men, they were bound to fail in competition against white men. Too much was going against them in the situation, whether it was intellectual or physical. To start with, they had never read Stephen Crane, all of whose good work tells us another useful truth for the combative man: the other fellow is just as scared as you are. I learned this on my own in the Army. As a corporal, I had the distasteful job of assembling men for work detail. One day I chose a huge Pittsburgh Pole, a rough recruit with hands truly like hams. He gave me the bad mouth, and in my appointed authority I told him he would thenceforth be in every goddamned detail I called. Before the squad he told me he would meet me behind the latrine after retreat and beat the shit out of me. I had to meet him, of course; there is no way out of that. And when I got there that evening, *he did not show up!* Possibly he feared my knowledge of judo (I instructed in judo at the time), but if so, that was a rationalization (as indeed learning judo and jujitsu and karate and all such ritualistic flapdoodle is itself a confession of poor self-confidence). He just was frightened. After that he never gave me any more trouble — and neither has anybody else since that day. I commend the discovery to my readers. The other son of a bitch is as scared as you are; if you

179

augment the advantage of that knowledge and hit first, you will win every time. Run fo' yo' character.

The aborigine has other disadvantages. He cannot help being awed by the cultural superiority — in things, at any rate — of the white man, and inferring from that physical superiority. The white man does in fact have an advantage: his gods are competitive and give him precedent for aggression; the aborigines' totem spirits are not, in spite of the clubbing and spearing of *kvetcherim* like Kulu, much for serious combat. Like the unfortunate bear who fell afoul of a Kentuckian in the days of Dan'l Boone and after a scuffle was lucky enough to be able to limp away with nothing lost but an eye and part of his nose, the aborigines are "not much fer bitin' an' gougin'." Perhaps most important, the distillation of their various disadvantages requires them to plead in one way or other for relaxation of ordinary rules (like being allowed to throw the first spear), so that even if they win they lose. We see the same process now in the special advantages given to racial minorities in our universities. It is a kindness that takes away more than it gives. George quit in a footrace with an old white fart, and for that one act he was doomed, as all his fellows along the fringe of white settlement are doomed. Their only hope lies in men like Teddy, who — perhaps because of his practical education among the white felons in the Adelaide jail — will meet white men as the Sioux Sitting Bull met white men. Probably, like Sitting Bull, he will be killed, but that is really the better part of valor.

Travels with Three Friends

About a year later I was back in the Homeland again, the sweat quest (and a particularly bad return journey) far enough in the past to have been transformed by the pearl-making of time into a pleasant memory. Bob Verburgt and I were sitting in an Italian restaurant in Alice Springs, valiantly consuming what I suppose must be identified as spaghetti, if only because it was nothing else. After all, it was the last civilized dinner we would sit down to for some time to come. And shredded pasta swimming in mutton fat was in itself a gustatory adventure. We were conversing about the joys of our civilization, trying to persuade ourselves they were worth the price. The talk among the spaghetti was largely about that straddler of centuries and cultures, Tommy Dodd, Tjonduga. Old Tommy, Bob was saying, had recently missed out on an opportunity to share in one of the pleasures of civilization. *"Well,"* said Bob, in traditional bush monologue,

I pulled up in front of the store there in Andamooka, I had old Tommy with me, I was down in Andamooka over this opal stir-up. And this was about nine o'clock in the morning. This sheila [girl] kept staring across to the side of the truck — she wasn't a bad-looking piece, either, she was about, oh, she'd seen the best part of thirty, I suppose, but she still wasn't a bad-looking girl for an abo. And she stood there looking at me and she said, "You're a bloody patrol officer, are you?" And I said, "Yeh." She said, "Well, I want a ride to Pimba and you're gonna take me." And I said, "Yeh?" So I said, "If you're here in the morning, with your suitcase, in front of the store here, I might take you." She said, "Aaaaah!" She said, "You can call me Darlin." She said, "My name's Annabel." And she said, "Who's the old baastid you got in there?" So she walked around the other side of the bus and she rubbed old Tommy Dodd on the side of the face and she said, "By Chrise, you'll go all right here tonight, old man!" She came back around to my side and she said, "Hey! You have a beer, hey?" And I said, "Ah, yeh, sometimes, not while I'm working." She said, "You come down tonight, I got plenty beer down there." She said, "Where you goin' to camp?" And I said, "I'm going right out that Marree track somewhere." She said, "Ah, you're silly, you don't want to go down there, I got a caravan [trailer] down there." I said to her, "Yeh, well, no, we got to go down the track." She said, "Ah, my caravan, proper big one, you know? Two beds in it. You and me could sleep in the top one and that old bugger can sleep in the bottom." Anyhow, that night about eleven o'clock, you see, we're camping and the mossies [mosquitoes] were fairly thick, we were on a creek out of Andamooka, it was a hot night and we had the groundsheets pulled up over our faces, the mossies were thick, and old Tommy, he'd roll over and he'd say, "You know, mate," he'd say, "I tink we might ha' been more comportable in dat caraban."

We would see old Tommy Dodd in a couple of days, when we got down to Musgrave Park. He was to be my adviser, guide, back-up interpreter, and liaison man with a mob of aborigines for a small expedition I had yarked up on my own hook. What I wanted to do in this penetration of the Homeland was to revisit, a generation later, elements of the Pintubi, Ngadadjara, and Pitjandjara tribes Norman

Tindale had discovered thirty-five years earlier. With the handicap of poor equipment, cheap black-and-white film, and desperate working circumstances, he and E. O. Stocker had nevertheless made a series of remarkable motion pictures of what life was like in the Old Stone Age at the moment of first white contact. I would have the children of his subjects, now grown to desert middle age, corrupted in some cases and refined in others by contact with the few whites who intruded themselves into their desert homeland in the Mann and Musgrave ranges. With my 16-millimeter Bolex motion picture camera and several thousand feet of commercial Ektachrome color film I wanted to get on permanent record what had changed and what had remained the same under the impact of more than three decades of traumatic culture shock.

Because of his dedication to bush hospitality and since it did not make much difference to him where in his quarter-continent police beat he ran his patrols, Bob was providing the transportation. He had met me at the airport just over the ring of fiery mountains making a cozy saucer for Alice Springs, where I had flown from Adelaide. His vehicle this time was another brute of a truck with an open metal bed to facilitate the hauling of a mob of aborigines, who lose vast quantities of body fluids through all apertures because of their susceptibility to motion sickness.

So many people should be in these pages besides those who appear — but one cannot afford these days to publish books the size of The Golden Bough. *I have been very lucky in having all of them as my companions, for each had something unique to help me know my gentle wild men. But Bob Verburgt must stand out, for he was the master bushman who taught me practice as Norman taught me theory. He knew something unpublished about every thing and every place, as Norman knew something published. Since so much of Bob's treasury of knowledge was unpublished, it was largely unpublishable. It has never been written before, as an example, that Dodd's Creek in the southern slopes of the Musgraves came onto the map when Old Tommy walked off into the bush to take a piss. Bob knew all the Outback Identities, even so respectable a bushman as Arthur Upfield, Australia's most popular detective novel writer, who created the half-blood Detective Inspector Napoleon Bonaparte while riding dingo fence on camels. Bob told me "Agar's Lagoon" in* Sinister Stones *was*

the ghost town of Innamincka, where Bob once played pub piano be-
fore its total abandonment, and which in fact was a desert lagoon
ringed by a five-foot-high reef of broken beer bottles, like Upfield's
fictional settlement. The lake in Bony Buys a Woman *is Lake Cala-*
bonna, north of Lake Frome in the dry Eyre chain. And the unforget-
table description of the effect on the prey-hierarchy of living things
by the rapid drying-up of a desert rain-lake in the novel Death of a
Lake *was pictured upon Lake Victoria in northern New South Wales*
(not the southwestern New South Wales Lake Victoria, from whose
banks Norman and I had dug human fossils).

Talk to Bob about himself and you get nothing unless you ask
leading questions, then you get, "Yeh. Aw, yeh." Everyone else to
Bob is more interesting than himself, more entitled to respectful
deference, especially if they are well educated. I like to think that
acquaintance with me was good for his self-esteem. I had more degrees
than a thermometer, and I tried to wash my clothes in peanut oil.
"Wha de good o' eddication, ef 'e got no sense?"

Bob had little formal education, but he had a hell of a lot of sense —
and experience. He knew everybody in the Inland, aboriginal and
white, and everybody liked him for his decency, honesty, and practical
knowledge. Admitted, he was an aggressive, profane, and rough-edged
little baastid who altered my language so much for the worse that I
am afraid to converse with decent people, but what the hell. Spend
your life as he did — run off from home to be a Johannes Factotum
to the bush, a jackeroo, professional prizefighter, brumby (wild horse)
hunter, dogger, piano player in the Finke, superintendent of a reserve
holding the largest and wildest bloody mob of bloody aborigines in
Australia, prospector, one half of the entire police force of a third of
the continent, and gifted master of bush hyperbole ("the baastid
was shivering like a constipated cat shitting razor blades"), and the
Duchess wouldn't often be having you in for tea yourself.

We camped just far enough out of Musgrave Park to make an early
morning arrival, a good run southwest from the Alice. After paying
the briefest of formal salutations to the administration people there,
we bounced over the scrub back of the compound to the little cottage
of Tommy Dodd. Old Tommy oozed out with a rawhide rope looped
in his hand and bade us "g'day," the invariable greeting between
aborigines and *walypela*. (Between *walypela* and *walypela* in the bush

there is more volubility — "*Ow y' goin' mate orright?*") I was pleased to see Tommy was still natty, the dandy of the bush; no matter what the temperature, he wore his tan business suit (with a tie on formal occasions) and soft hat, the latter always replaced by the hand-me-down when Bob bought himself a new one every few years. Of course the suit had not been cleaned since he acquired it — sometime in the 1930's, I should guess. Once again I tried to determine his age — the most controversial question in central Australia — and I still held out for the mid-seventies. Norman wants Tommy to be in that range also, partly to tie him in with a white party that went through this country three-quarters of a century ago. More romantic Inlanders want to push Tommy back another twenty-five years to bring him in reach of his centennial. Tommy is agreeable, and if gently suborned, he will tell you of his experiences as a volunteer soldier in the Boer War.

From his aboriginal mother Tommy inherited his golden skin and puckish grin; from his white father, the added stature to bring him up to five and a half feet; from time, his white hair; and from the bush, wiriness. Whatever his actual age, Tommy had a mountain of years in his tough old body — yet he had gone into civilization only once, a few months earlier, when Bob carried him to Woomera. The scientific staff was prepared to honor a man of his fame and allowed him into their politest company — once. Tommy made the social error of offering to them his idea of urbane conversation. On the sonic boom of the warcraft shooting by above the settlement, he observed, "My word! Dey shake d' teacup outa your puckin han." He could not understand the sniffy reaction of those puckin people. Baastids.

We told Tommy what we were after — a small mob of aborigines, three or four families, who were close to the bush ways and who could be relied on to get along well together. He drove with us to the aboriginal camp and within an hour he had assembled the perfect subjects for my filming. Candidates at first were a glut on the market, though we cut down on them some by limiting personnel: only one wife per man, minimal complement of children, no dogs. We had some argument on the ration of wives, but I insisted — I wanted this mob to hunt and forage, not to puck.

After the usual delay in getting away from a native camp — losing time in scraping children off the truck and kicking dogs out of the

184

way — we roared down the dusty track to the west with our cast of characters bouncing around in the back, to wit:

Jacob, a man of about thirty-two, his wife *Tinimai*, and his two children, *Wally*, twelve years old, and an infant, not yet named but for immediate purposes referred to as *Ian*.

Jimmy, thirty-eight, his wife *Munadji*, and his three-year-old boy *Paul*.

Tjipikudu, about forty, his spouse *Djimiungul*, and his son *Puntaru*, aged six. Tjipi will be remembered as the Keibara singer.

I complimented Tommy Dodd on his efficiency in rounding up these people and persuading them to undertake the trip. "Tommy, you must be the big chief of this Amatapiti mob." Bob grumbled, "Yeh. Big Chief Shitstick." Tommy pursed his lips up against his nose and accepted the accolade by translating his title into Pitjandjara, "*Pulka Kata Kunapurunga.*"

The three of us rode in front, the mob in the truck bed. Riding in the cab when there are natives in the back is like sitting in a tin belfry when a carillon is pealing out a Bob Major. The frantic banging on the cab roof is continuous. They bang as a signal to stop whenever someone is truck-sick, they bang whenever someone has to urinate, they bang whenever they think they see *kuka* (meat animals). Since all these crises are going on all the time simultaneously, the din is skull-shattering. We stopped early to teach them all how to chunder and piss over the sides of the truck, but the hunters still saw an unbroken parade of dingos and kangaroos (most of them in the Dreaming dimension) and the noise persisted. There is not much use stopping the truck to shoot 'roos, for the roof-banging sets the sharp-eared animals bounding immediately for the horizon. By the time you can skid the vehicle to a stop and get a rifle on them, the 'roos are out of sight.

Nevertheless we got in a good bag of *kuka* by catching a few 'roos dozing too close to the track. On one occasion I saw a kangaroo before the aboriginal watchmen did, and Bob picked him off with his 30-06 through the cab window, right through the heart at a hundred yards. If that is not a sufficiently shocking indictment of the infallible hunting ability primitive people are supposed to have, consider that

Children returning from *witjuti*-grub hunting expedition beyond
Lungly Gully, S.A.

when we swung down out of the cab to pick up the dead kangaroo
I saw another one, not more than ten yards from us. Our hunters
missed him too. Bob popped him through the head with his pistol.
So meat for the hunters that evening at our first camp, Piltardi Rockhole, fifty-three miles west of Musgrave Park and seventy-four miles
east of the Western Australia border. Kangaroo makes bonzer tucker,
no matter what the sheep-eating city people say.

Tommy Dodd and I were up first next morning, an hour before the
sun. By the time the bush flies had driven the others out of their
warm sandy nests between their bush windbreaks and little belly
fires, I had photographs of him burning acacia and using the ash to
prepare *mingulpa*, the native tobacco. That day gave me a richness
of film, still and motion picture, for Piltardi is a picturesque spot, and
in historical fact the location of Norman's 1933 film, *A Day in the
Life of Pitjandjara Natives*.

Bob Verburgt, Norman B. Tindale, and aborigines with game at the
Amata Camp, Musgrave Range, S.A.

A few hundred yards into the gorge, a sacred place tabu to the
women, we found the Piltardi rock depressions full of water, an
unusual condition. Tjipikudu, Jacob, and Wally began spear-making
activity, one of the tasks I requested of them. How quickly a white
man would go wrong here; he would look around for straight saplings,
forgetting that spears must primarily be flexible. Later I caught with
several quick shots of my 35-millimeter still camera a good spearman at Amata, one Mundjandji, slinging a spear with his *miru* ninety
yards into a two-foot target; as the spear left the spear-thrower it
bent nearly double, like a vaulting pole. The white man's stiff javelin
would have broken in two before it had gone five yards. Nevertheless
our psychological set about how spears should be makes it awfully
hard to see spears in the aboriginal spear tree, a twisted tecoma bush
the natives call *urtjanda*.

As we walked back through the Piltardi gorge and debouched again on the rocky plain, I noticed a pile of about a dozen stones, each about five pounds in weight, not looking quite right. I called Tommy over. He knows everything not originating with the whitefella. "What's the matter with those stones, Tommy? They look li'l bit crook."

"Oh, dem *Wanambi kuka*. Dem d' meat lep' by *tjukurpa* women por dat big snake. All dis place Wanambi place. When we in rockhole all dem women — Munadji, Tinimai, Djimiungul — dey all wash dem stones. Hab' to do dat." At Piltardi as in Rome, women in religion are the menial servitors to the clergy.

Tommy now became for an hour the compleat aboriginal oldman, showing Jacob, Tjipikudu, and Jimmy (Wally excluded; too young) two large bent trees and summarizing for them the essential motifs in the myth of Wanambi Kutjara, the two water snakes. When Tommy touches his religion, he is Tjonduga, no devilish grin on his face, no glint of mischief in his tobacco-brown eyes; he is then in the Dreaming dimension, a proper-fella *wati yina*.

Piltardi had no more game now than it had when Norman's mob left it for greener pastures so long ago, so we left it too, though much faster. Into the truck went our swags and the aborigines' rags, uneaten pieces of 'roo, kids, men, and women, lacking only chickens and dogs and guitars to resemble an Okie family migration to the peachbowl of California in the dustbowl years, pounding ever westward. Forty miles from the Western Australian border, just where the Mann Range swings up into the Northern Territory, we turned north off the track through Trew Gap toward Poka Rockhole.

I would have to call this the roughest country I have ever traversed in a vehicle, since this break in the mountains was the only place where I had to walk in front of the vehicle to push insurmountable boulders out of the way. This is also where the aborigines became as dumb as the racists would have them be. Catch any of them getting out of the truck to help me roll rocks away!

I would have to say, too, that this place produced the most shockingly dramatic incident with which I was even indirectly associated in all my pursuit of the desert aborigines. To this place, thirteen months earlier, thirty-seven aborigines had tracked a rain cloud, only to see it pour itself out in the sands beyond the two rockholes Malara and Erinjerinja, just this side of Poka. All these stone catchments were dry; they had crossed the tire marks of Bob's truck on the track (evidence, they inferred, that he had gone through on his monthly patrol a few days before) and since neither Bob nor any other white man would be at all likely to come along the track, they cut their hair for the death ceremony, dug their graves, and were lying in them when Bob came through. The tracks they thought were his were actually those of the other Native Patrol Officer, Wal MacDougall, on a special run to the Giles Meteorological Station in the far west. Bob had seventy gallons of water in his tanks — life for them now instead of death. But to people accustomed to accepting either with little emotional distinction, it was all one. They rose from their graves, ambled over to the truck, and asked Bob for a *kapati* — a cup of tea. One of the women in the band was Anmaneri, middle wife to Bell Rock Jacky; that morning she had given birth to a child.

Poka is a pleasant place to sit down; a dry creek bed of fine sand makes a comfortable location to nap, work on spears, and broil *kuka* during the day. At evening the people move to higher ground; no one takes the chance, however remote, of drowning while asleep in a flash flood. Here the men began the spear-making, lazy work of turning the shafts in a fire to boil the sap and then straightening them across tree boles, their knees, or over their teeth. I put several hundred feet of film into this and into the evisceration and cooking of a dog which had nosily ventured into range of Bob's Enfield. Exactly here in 1933 Norman filmed the man-making of the boys. I had no chance of duplicating that in this expedition, though young Wally in my opinion was ready for his initiation. At Poka and Pidul and Piltardi and in other *ngura* we watched him demonstrating to his elders his knowledge of manhood's skills. He did excellently well, and when this trip was done, I would pay him man's wages.

So much there was to know to become an aboriginal man. Even the best of anthropologists a generation ago maintained the vocabularies of primitive men were limited to a few hundred words. Think now of how few names any of us know for maggots, and then put our taxonomic knowledge over against that of Jacob, Jimmy, Tjipikudu, and Wally on that insignificant wriggly creature, the *witjuti* grub:

bardi: generic term for grubs.

mako: edible grub; word common in the west and southwest.

189

mako ilkoara: any of several species of grub found in the roots and stems of the *"witjuti* bush," *Acacia kempeana.*

iwiri: One of the *A. kempeana* grubs.

muṛtu muta: another *A. kempeana* grub.

mako laṇgi: grub found in the roots of *wardanka,* another acacia.

mako tu:ta: grub of *Trictena argentata* moth found in the roots of the red gum tree (*Eucalyptus camaldulensis*).

mako tjilkatjilka: grub found in the stem of the roly-poly bush, *Salsola kali* (*tjilka:* sticker).

mako pundilpundil: grub in species of saltbush.

mako pundi: grub found in stem of the *pundi* shrub (*Cassia phyllodinea*).

mako natunba: grub found in *natunba* bush (*Acacia strongylophylla*).

mako nalta: large longicorn larva in roots of dead kurrajong trees (*Brachychiton populneum*).

mako jaranpa: grub of the *Cnemoplites* family, found in the *yaralye* tree.

Tommy had his amusement in another *walypela* ignorance — his thick-tongued ineptitude with the stranger sounds of the desert language. Pitjandjara and its linguistic relatives have phonemic clusters we cannot even distinguish without training, and confusing these words knocks the most polite aborigine off his feet in hilarity. Witness the trouble the missionaries have with *wangka* and *waṇka* and *waṇka*. *Wangka* means "language"; *waṇka* means "life"; *waṇka* means "hairy caterpillar." The silly *walypela* "god-men" thought they were touching the chords of a childlike longing for heaven when they soberly intoned amid gleeful aboriginal roars, "Believe on the Lord Jesus Christ and ye shall have everlasting hairy caterpillars." But as my missionary friend Wilf Douglas says, "To learn the language you must become a fool."

This list of grub-words is only fragmentary. Had Norman Tindale been with us, he could have multiplied that lexicon several times on his knowledge of coccid moths and their floral hosts.

Witjuti (Hepialid) larva in adult aboriginal hand; important source of
protein for desert aborigines

Honey ants with abdomens distended with a sweet substance much relished
by the aborigines

The natives use a six-inch twig, a *wintu* (I like to call tools of this sort "found artifacts"), to winkle stem grubs out of their holes. They find the grubs by listening with their ears against trees for the tiny sound of grub-boring, or by searching for the little piles of sawdust left by the larvae. These methods may sound incredible to us, but it is a photographed fact that the aborigines hunt the native stingless bees by following the bees' dung spoor. I doubt that many of us even knew about bees dropping dung, much less about tracking the stuff.

Our men ate grubs as we eat peanuts, tearing up man-high saplings to get two or three grubs. I should like to confront our ecology idiots with the agonizing paradox of sacrosanct livers-with-the-organic-land inflicting such rape upon the environment.

As for the grubs themselves, I say *eck*. I will eat dogs, if it helps to reduce their population, but I would not touch a *witjuti* with a ten-foot *wintu*. My bush-culture friend, H. A. Lindsay, insists *witjuti* grubs are not only the perfect nutritional food, but delicious as well. I will listen to him on other things, but not on this. He has for the other things an encyclopedic knowledge of what is edible and what is not among the thousands of wild vegetables in Australia. Few flowers here are innocent. Our literature's subsistence means in the wilderness is eating "berries." One of the popular natural food nuts the other day declared there were no inedible plants that tasted good; nature does not deceive, he said. Well. As a teacher of American jungle fighters in northern Australia and the islands in the Second World War Lindsay propounded his Four-Hour Test for edibility:

First crush it and smell it; if it has the characteristic smell of peach leaves and bitter almonds, this reveals the presence of prussic acid, a very deadly and swift poison. If it smells all right, crush some of it and rub it on the skin inside your elbow. If it doesn't raise blisters or make the skin red and sore, try a bit on your tongue. If it doesn't sting or burn and the flavor seems all right, chew a little, gargle the juice in the back of your throat, and spit it out. Now wait to see if your throat becomes sore. If it doesn't, eat a LITTLE of it and wait for four hours, to see if any ill effect in the way of vomiting, giddiness, internal pains, or purging follow. If there are no ill effects it may be safe to eat a quantity of it.

Collecting vegetable food — *mirka*, as distinguished from *kuka*, animal food — is usually women's work and the largest part of native sustenance. Their knowledge was also great, including a discovery I could never understand possible — squeezing and washing poison out of certain lethal plants to make them edible (Amazonian Indians also had this knowledge).

But there was neither *kuka* nor *mirka* at Poka, so we packed up and moved to Pidul, near Piltardi, where a mass of 'roo tracks established the presence of *kuka pulka* — and where there are kangaroos, there is *mirka*.

Kangaroo hunting is nearly impossible to film, for the 'roos distrust the whirring of the camera, as well they might, and begin their long-striding hops before the aboriginal hunter can creep up on them. I remembered that Norman had to fudge on this in his own filming — the one kangaroo he shows being speared had already been crippled.

Tjipikudu is our best hunter. I followed him quietly at the distance he indicated on one of the forays our men made for *maḻu kuka*. A half dozen years earlier Tjipi would have been naked, carrying spears and a spear-thrower; now he had a .22 rifle and a pair of white jockey shorts, a gift from the good-hearted Woomera ladies via Bob, pulled up over his red trousers. Who could accept a motion picture of that, even if he had brought down a kangaroo? I had gone a little bit crook on Bob for distributing these clothes before my filming.

Our men are not proficient with the *ripela* (to the old timers, *muketa* — muskets). *Here is an interesting case of traditional motor habits offsetting the lethal potentialities of a weapon and so saving the aborigines or primitive hunters in other parts of the world — over-killing their game. The aborigines used to stalk their prey with spear in spear-thrower, held somewhat as we hold a rifle before aiming, and shaking the spear for the feel of its flexibility, as we hold a dart before throwing it. When the distance and the feel were right, they hurled the spear as now they fire their guns. The wonder of it is that they ever hit their targets. We who intrude into the country and culture of the desert aborigines see quickly the* miru *and think ourselves wise in knowing it by the whitefella name "spear-thrower" or the common bush name* woomera, *the name used by the extinct Dieri. But every part of this artifact has a name. Wilf Douglas, missionary, linguist, and creator of Irish bulls, under whom I studied the western desert language, conceived the device of bringing us into the language by way of the desert tools, hanging the abstract terms on tangible objects. Thus the* miru:

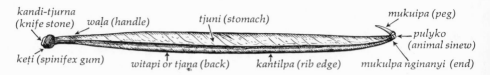

kandi-tjurna
(knife stone)   waḷa (handle)   tjuṇi (stomach)   mukuipa (peg)

                                                                          pulyko
                                                                          (animal sinew)

keṭi (spinifex gum)   witapi or tjaṇa (back)   kaṇtilpa (rib edge)   mukulpa nginanyi (end)

kurku (mulga wood, acacia aneura), apu piranpa (white rock, knife edge material),
malunguru (peg from kangaroo), malutjina nguru (kangaroo leg)

The process is a deception, of course (where are the verbs, those Pitjandjara verbs which are the hardest things to learn in all tongues of the earth?), but a student must be lured into the desert language. No language is easy. When Neil Armstrong spoke the first words from the moon, what did he say, exactly? Received Knowledge now certifies, "That's one small step for man, one giant leap for mankind." He did not mean to say that, if that is what he said, for the missing definite article in the first clause robs sense out of the second. The television interpreter Frank McGee, echoing immediately the statement, garbled it. The other man on the moon, Edwin Aldrin, balled it up another way. And Joan thought that Armstrong's second adjective was not "giant" but "vast." After listening over and over to my taped recording of it, I cannot be sure. One day I will feed it into a voiceprint and find out whether the hundred million are right or wrong.

That was in my language; what then for Pitjandjara? God only knows how many times I made an utter ass of myself among the natives. Wilf used to play skillfully on our knowledge and confidence, which varied wildly in us. "Repeat after me," he once challenged, when I thought I had scored a point by saying a little bit (tjuku tjuku) of sugar (tjuku) would be "tjuku tjuku tjuku," "this sentence meaning 'The person saw us all' — 'anangungkungananananyunyangu.' " No use your trying to pronounce it. No English-speaking tongue on earth can handle that correctly at first or tenth attempt. The sentence contains

194

*three nasal consonant clusters not present in English or any other
language I have any acquaintance with.*

Tjipikudu is a marvelous stalker in an enterprise where skill of
stalking is nearly everything. He glides through the bush, his upper
body as nearly unmoving in any but the forward plane as the head
and torso of a good high hurdler. Hips swing in the sinuosity of a
ballet dancer, so that when he stops (and he must stop often when
the ears of a 'roo twitch on the edge of wakening) there is no shaking
of a disturbed bush to draw the animal's wary attention. Animals see
only when there is motion, and even a man becomes part of the unseen background when he is still.

Tjipi got his 'roo on the occasion I watched him, well out of position to interfere with his stalking. His stalking with spears was a swift
thing, darting, stopping, darting again, until within closest possible
range and then striking explosively. This last, fast approach is another device of effectiveness we might not think of, because the
wakened kangaroos explode also from sleep into great but aimless
leaps, giving the hunter a second shot if he is quick about it. Our
adverbs were not made to describe such hunting, so once again we
find the best descriptions in the aboriginal tongue, and even to some
lesser extent in the fractured English that serves in the bush in place
of the northern islands' pidgin. Bill Harney, one of the legendary
masters of the bush, gave us an example from one of his aboriginal
friends:

I bin go, I bin go, I bin go I bin go I bin go I bin go — orright! Ah! [Hand
signal for spotting kangaroo]. *I bin sneaka, I bin sneaka I bin sneaka I bin
get spear, slow, close up, slowpella, I bin sneaka — MISSED 'IM. Him bin
race away. Orright. I bin move again, I bin tracka, I bin go, I bin follerim,
I bin follerim, I bin follerim I bin follerim I bin follerim I bin follerim I bin
follerim I bin follerim I bin follerim I bin sneaka — CAPPED 'IM, by Chrise,
proper good one, no more gammon!*

Pidul was a rich *ngura* and I bin put into the can all the footage
I was likely to use to show game preparation as the men came in with
their *kuka* — rabbits, 'roos, dog, euro, wallabies (even a nail-tailed
wallaby, *Onychogalea lunata* — very rare). I would make use of an
event not often seen by white city dwellers — a joey, baby kangaroo,

hairless, pink, blind, wriggling on the earth among the voracious meat ants after one of the men pulled it from its dead mother's pouch.

The ethnographic film maker does not have the luxury of retakes. He gets his picture first time around or not at all. And since he cannot be sure that he is getting anything when he uses, as I did, a bloody French-made camera, he gets back-up shots with his still cameras. As I worked at this Bob sat under a tree laughing — he reckoned, he said, the best action wasn't being filmed, me hopping around from animal to animal and hunter to hunter with Bolex, Pentax, Rolleiflex, and Uher. Hopping literally, with one leg crook from a hematoma arising from whacking my shin against the roof of the truck. Roof? Yes; I had nearly perfected a running cat-climb up the side of the truck to pull out our twenty-foot transceiver radio antenna every day.

What I photographed was precisely what Norman had filmed thirty-five years before. None of the techniques of *kuka* preparation had changed, for white intrusion did not touch upon this in any way, except for the substitution at times of tinned food. When a man kills a kangaroo he throws the dead animal on its back and immediately disembowels it, a memorable business for eyes and nose. After the visceral opening is cleared, the hunter pins the opening closed with a sharpened twig (another Found Artifact), ties the four legs together with the animal's entrails the way a cowboy ties up a thrown calf, and heaves the sixty-five pounds of meat on top of his head for the walk back to camp. Gutting prevents spoilage; it is the inordinate time entrails are left in white-hunted kangaroos that turns the meat bad and certifies their bad reputation in cities.

In camp an oven is dug for each animal, just deep enough for it to be covered by the embers of a fire lit the moment a hunter returns with his quarry. Branches are first thrown into the pit, shaken into a roaring fire, and the animal is thrown on to singe off its fur. It is then removed, the fire is stoked, and the animal has its legs broken and the sinews removed. Aborigines with a kangaroo in the earth oven, broiling under a heavy mound of hot ashes, are as impatient as Charles Lamb's Dootsy Bobo when he invented roasting pig by burning down his house. Aboriginal *kuka* consequently is cooked only within the most tenuous definition of the word. Like a Frenchman's *biftek Americaine*, the meat appears raw to any decent human being. Only the outer half inch of a kangaroo could be said to be truly roasted; the rest drips blood. One of the good shots I missed when my camera wind ran out (as it always does when something good is going), was Tjipikudu holding up a cooked wallaby to his mouth and drinking the pouring blood like a Spaniard with a bagful of wine.

With a naturally organized group of Pitjandjara — which I did not have — the meat would be distributed according to a rigorous pattern based on the schema of social organization. This sharing of food persuades some willful people that the aborigines are primitive communists incipiently inventing the best of all possible governments in the worst of all possible worlds. Not so. Native food-sharing is nearly the opposite — a device that does not merely distribute food, but also simultaneously reinforces the small-group selfishness of tight relative cohesion. If our animals had been carried to the Amata camp, the choice loin of a 'roo would have been given to the hunter's wife's father and mother. His elder brother would have got the heavily meated hind leg, his younger brothers and sisters the foreleg, the head, and a portion of the thigh. Mother and other elder brothers, if the hunter had several of such, would have been given the breast. The tail, another choice part, is for his wife's elder brother. The hunter himself would have received the kidneys and liver. And if no one more important covets the crackling, the skin would have been thrown to the family dogs — which would, having no parallel distributional organization, have had to fight over it with their fellow communists.

Wally tried to fetch up some dessert by digging for honey ants, but they had vacated. The women, however, had prepared sweets from some dozen kinds of lerps in the area. Bob, Tommy, and I ate 'roo stew with canned beef and tomato sauce and passion fruit and Christ knows what else thrown in (Australian bushmen hold atavistically to their remote British origin by mucking up good food), with Rice-cream for dessert, damper and marmalade, and good billy tea. We did little talking in the Pidul nights — too full of food for that — but sat against our swags in front of the fire, patting our haunches, making rude gastric noises, and watching the moths immolate themselves in the flames. Surely this must be a gene-ingrained contentment than which there has been no better since Neanderthal times; only our women were lacking.

This laziness continued as long as there was this unusual abundance of food. During the day Bob and I would go off fossicking, he for minerals, I for archaeology; the aboriginal men worked on their spears, straightening and scraping and engraving them, pissing around one way or other; the women went off to gather berries and nuts in May, and Old Tommy, with his wisdom of seven or eight or nine decades, slept.

What a story and songs there are in Tommy Dodd! Norman Tindale is probably right in identifying Tommy's father as a member of the Carruthers expedition into the Everard and Musgrave Ranges in 1891–1892. Carruthers, a government surveyor, believed in large expeditionary parties, so the precise responsibility of Tommy's paternity is diffuse. No matter. John Carruthers's men were attacked only once by the natives, whom he conceded to be treacherous, crafty, but otherwise friendly. Friendliness in explorers' accounts has a narrow meaning — hence Tommy.

By happy accident I turned up some corroboration of the Carruthers hypothesis. During one long evening at Pidul Tommy sang into my tapes his natal myth, the *Inma Malu Kutjara*. Back at his Amata shanty at the end of this trip I pressed him into drawing the track of his Two Dreaming Kangaroos with colored crayons on paper. Ordinarily in having aborigines make drawings of this kind one uses typewriter paper — another whitefella psychological set. But the great length of the myth as I had it on tape gave me the idea of supplying Tommy with a larger base to work on — a piece of brown parcel-wrapping paper, three feet wide and four feet long. By the time he had put in all the places where the Two Dreaming Kangaroos had their earthly adventures, the sheet was covered with symbols of actual topography, and swinging across the top margin was a creek bed. I had been writing down on the map both the native and English names of the places marked, so I asked Tommy what creek that was. "Tietken' Birt'day." Bless his bloody old heart! Tietkens' Birthday Creek! In Ernest Giles's first expedition through this country he noted in his journal on 30 August 1873:

In about an hour Mr. Tietkens came and informed me that on his return to the camp the other day he had found a nice little water, six miles from here, and where the party was, and to which we now rode together. At this agreeable little spot were the essentials of an explorer's camp — that is to say, wood, water, and grass. From there we went to my clay pans, and the next day to my lonely camp of dreams. This, the 30th of August, was an auspicious day in our travels, it being no less than Mr. Tietkens' nine-and-

twentieth birthday. We celebrated it with what honours the expedition stores would afford, obtaining a flat bottle of spirits from the medical department, with which we drank to his health and many happier returns of the day. In honour of the occasion I called this Tietkens' Birthday Creek, and hereby proclaim it unto the nations that such should be its name for ever.

By these fortunate accidents I have acquired possibly the most detailed myth chart of a Dreaming song, located precisely to known topographical features, but like other bedeviled creatures who constitutionally cannot leave well enough alone, I am not satisfied. If it were not for the awkwardness of having to make Tommy Dodd just on a hundred years old, I would emulate that great Procrustean archaeologist Heinrich Schliemann and hammer hard fact into malleable truth, giving Ernest Giles the parentage of Tommy. Much of what I admire in Tommy are the virtues of Giles — wry humor even in the most difficult situations, intelligence, resourcefulness, dominance, and courage — qualities not found together in many men. Tommy in legend would be the Australian *bel inconnu*, too rich in his own character to be the offspring of an ordinary man.

Tommy's strongest first memories are of his employment as a camel boy to the explorer Frank Hann, a sour and superficial man who went through the Everards and Musgraves early in the century, looking for land he could destroy with stock. He did serve a good purpose by delaying other intrusion with an influential newspaper article in which he described the Pitjandjara country as a "plague spot in a realm of despair."

Tommy had good cathexis to implant these early years in his mind. He was caught between two violently contending worlds — the employee of rough men of white society clashing with rough men of his own people. Besides the mundane position of camel tender, Tommy filled the office of bait. Whenever a new mob of savages screamed out of the mulga waving spears, Tommy had to meet them, naked, without even a white handkerchief to wave back. He says the natives believed the white men to be *mamu*, devils, come into the desert to hunt aborigines for food, with horses and camels as their hunting dogs. Tommy's job was to persuade the aborigines of the real purpose of the white man's intrusion — which did not make even good nonsense to the natives; the cannibal inference was more credible. Tommy insisted the white man was orright, that he had plenty tucker (the camel and horse were tucker also, if other food became scarce), and his unfortunate white skin was an injury he had received because he had come from a land of ice. Tommy had other incredulities to overcome in arranging a *détente;* for instance, he had to assure the aborigines that white men had women in their own country. Like the Polynesians of earliest contact, the aborigines believed the whites were a race of men and came to the desert for women. It did not make good sense, they held, for men to come alone, without women to send out to gather *mirka* and to *puck. Spear the lying baastids.*

Tommy remembers well one spearing. Kata, brother of the present Amatapiti leader, hurled a spear into the eye of a surveyor at the Gnarlbo Rockhole (a small catchment not far from Lungly Gully). The conflict was unfortunate, like the sword slash at the serpent which began King Arthur's last battle; the surveyor, alone, saw the native warriors approach and fired off his revolver to summon his companions. Kata thought the man was shooting at him and threw his spear. The surveyor's companions, hurrying up, cut off the shaft of the spear, leaving the point embedded in his eye, and had him carried first to Henbury Station, where Tommy had been fishing (using his trousers as a net). Tommy made him a *kapati,* the station owner drained the wound, and gave the injured man Tommy as his guide to Alice Springs, a journey that took an agonizing week. A hard man, the surveyor.

The aborigines, Tommy remembers, were a hard mob, too. The mob at Musgrave Park were bad enough; they would kill you for a reason, but there were other bands, like the Ilpi (Tommy says they are not in fact Pitjandjara, as supposed) and Malupiti around Mount Davies in the Tomkinsons, the "soldier mob," who did not wait upon a reason. "My word!" says Tommy, "dey were a bloody mad mob, dem pellas." Across the Mann Range into the Petermanns (named so with a double reason by Giles: for a patron and for the native phrase *pika mereinga,* meaning "to strangle"), was another truculent bunch, the Wintanjupiti. Their particular dunghill was at Docker Creek (recently made a reserve station) and the water hole Piltardi (not to be confused with the Musgrave Piltardi, where we had sat down for a while).

Another thing that adhered well to Tommy's memory was Hann's second-in-command, a fellow named Talbot, an American Negro.

Tommy was taking a packsaddle off a camel when an aborigine leaped out of the bush and threw a spear right through Hann's shirt. Talbot fired back with a big .44 pistol; its bullet struck a rock behind which the warrior was hiding and fragmented. Judging by the native's shrieks, Tommy said, he reckoned every bit of the bullet struck the spearman. This event gave the white man's gun a useful reputation; like the Irishman's rifle, his pistol could shoot around corners.

In later, more tranquil times, Tommy gave up camels for horses, even riding as a jockey at the race meetings every settlement, no matter how small, made as its first social institution. At one of these near the railroad when it was put through, Tommy met his first Irishmen, the navvies. He remembers yet "dem bloody nabbies pinched my bloody tucker dere."

Tommy had two wives along the way of his life, producing for him three sons, who show specifically, without the distortion of dirty statistics, how aborigines of the second generation can slip from the Old Stone Age into civilization, if they want to and go about it right. Sammy chose to be a station worker, a fringe dweller. Martin went in closer, and is now mining opal at Coober Pedy. Steve went all the way, living now in Adelaide and training white troops in desert warfare. All his sons have large families, but he has not seen any of his children for a long time. Daughters? Several; all finish now, dead. His second wife died after being bitten by a "red-arsed spider." "Going to get married again, Tommy?" I asked, expecting him to give some accounting for the young woman who was always in his shanty back at Amata. "Naw," he giggled. "Prightened it might bend a bit, hee hee."

He changed the subject quickly to food, whispering when Bob Verburgt was out of range, "You bin out wit' dat baastid Bob Perburt? Allatime eatin'. Eatin' dat hot curry. Nuttin' but eatin', eatin', eatin'. He bin gib it to you, dat curry?" He bin gibbit me, dat curry orright. That was the unidentifiable stuff he put in the 'roo stew. Tommy confided to me his favorite whitefella food is pussycat. "My word! Dat *putjikata* proper good tucker!"

After we struck camp at Pidul the men told us there was a fine stand of resined spinifex not many miles away. Their spears were at that point in manufacture where the marvelous adhesive, *keti*, was needed to fix the mulga points to the spear shafts. I wanted *keti*-making on my film, since it is the most interesting artifactual activity

201

of the desert aborigines, made all the more so because its product is so little known by anthropologists in other parts of the world. And with these pictures I would have also the use of *keti* in spear-making.

How the men knew where spinifex was being attacked by the parasite that causes the spear grass to exude its gum is one of those mysteries of the bush telegraph that lead credulous folk to believe the natives possess telepathy. We had no doubt of their credibility in this matter, and so we moved northeast across the flatlands between the Mann and Musgrave ranges at their direction. Along the way we passed a famous clump of blackboys (*Xanthorrhea, urlba* to the aborigines) discovered by Norman Tindale more than thirty years ago. Like the saguaro cactus of the extreme southwestern American desert, the blackboy is nearly indestructible in nature, living at least ten times longer than any human being would want to live. Its bole is rich in natural resin, and in aboriginal Western Australia it was exploited for that substance. Here this clump remains isolated and unmolested after thirty years by historical record and, judging by its maturity, five hundred years before Tindale came along. Surely one of the aborigines who make *keti* by the more arduous method of beating it out of spinifex might have been expected to stick a finger, at least, into this cluster.

Watching aborigines gather spinifex will set you shuddering with empathic pain, like watching subincision. The men tore the tussocks out of the sand, humped them up in their arms like soft hay, and carried them over to a flat-surfaced rock. Tjipi strode barefooted through the spinifex as we might do through dew-softened bluegrass. Even knowing he had crepe-soled feet did not stop my wincing.

Tjipi was the star of this segment of my filming. The rascal knew just what I wanted — too well, perhaps, because no one who sees the motion picture will believe I did not direct him. He would hop through the grass when the camera was on him, feigning agony — followed by an enormous aboriginal grin. He would pick up a bundle of spinifex and walk with it directly up to the camera, letting a few blades snap against the lens. And after dropping the bundle on the rock with the other men's gathering, he looked about in exaggerated scrutiny for another Found Artifact — a beating stick pulled out of a dead mulga tree — and then began pounding the grass with maniacal frenzy. A good show.

Terenyi (Bell Rock Jacky) building a *wiltja* (brush shelter); one of his wives and three of his children

George and his two wives gathering spinifex for yandying and melting into *keti* (hafting gum); beyond Giles's Titania Spring, S.A.

After the spinifex was pulverized, the three men brushed away the bulk of shredded grass and gathered the residue in old bits of cloth and, in Jimmy's case, a *wira* bowl borrowed from his wife. The next phase fell into the women's jurisdiction — winnowing or "yandying" out the resin from the minuscule fragments of grass. Each of the women had her own style of work in this, and each let us — and the camera — see her pride in her work.

After the purified resin dust had been given again to the men, the last phase begins, the exercise of a delicate skill rather like that of paperhanging. Only experience can teach this; theoretical instruction is useless. Each man took a burning brand, brought it near the pile of resin before him, and turned a small stick into the melting material. The critical element is giving the resin just the right amount of heat. Too little and nothing happens; the least fraction of a calorie too much and the resin is volatilized, turning brittle and useless.

When the job is finished, each man has a stick on which the *keti* is gummily wrapped like spun candy. This will be kept by him for whatever purpose he needs an adhesive. In our situation, the *keti* fixed hard mulga points to the soft, flexible spear shafts. I never saw stone points used in aboriginal Australia. Stone spear points do not make good sense. They are pretty, but like all pretty things, including women, they tend to break if you handle them roughly. Mulga will run you through as easily as flint. When the *keti* has been applied to both surfaces (cut, interestingly, into a miter joint), the kangaroo sinews which they have been keeping Christ knows where (they keep spear barbs inside their noses!) are brought out, chewed into thick gumminess, and wrapped tightly around the joined elements of the weapon. There! A fine spear to run through some adulterous baastid!

If it were humanly possible to tell the French anything, I should like to have them put all newly found "coups de poing" — hand axes — under a microscope to check for traces of organic material. As custodians of the classic Paleolithic implements for more than a hundred years, they have sold other archaeologists on the notion that European Old Stone Age man made it through the Pleistocene with no weapon more powerful than a sharpened rock held haftless in his hand. I cannot imagine a British Neanderthaler strolling up to a mammoth and grunting, "Ere, mate, 'old still whilst I bash you on the bonk with this 'ere coup-de-poing." *That might work with French mammoths, but surely not with any others. No doubt hand axes were used, even in Australia, for some few purposes, but not for heavy pounding or chopping. I have never had the experience, fortunately, of working with a French carpenter, but I wonder whether he would follow his traditions and pound a nail in with his fist. Probably. But the rest of the world puts a handle on the hammerhead. The trouble is the French experts will not accept any tool without waistbanding as having been hafted. The Australian aborigines do not ordinarily waistband axes; they just fit a handle to a stone axe in a lump of keti; when it cools and hardens, they have a hafted axe (like the archaeological kodj) firm enough to chop down a tree or another aborigine. I suspect the same was done in Paleolithic Europe, but the gum, being organic, has vanished like its organic users. Still, traces may be there — unless some diligent museum technician has scrubbed them off to make a more sparkling exhibit for the Sunday museum gawkers.*

Puntaru was ailing the day we moved out for the keti-gathering. Practicing for the traditional hard death of desert aborigines, he made no complaint, but just curled up in the sand, waiting for recovery or the alternative. I should say a word here too for little Paul; when we first took him on this trip he had a torn thumbnail, so we wrapped a bandage around it. His mother, Munadji, looked upon bandages the way a foot-hurt cat looks upon bandages. She tore it off, taking the nail with it. Nu? So Paul loses a fingernail. He has nine left.

Bob gave Puntaru a couple of "Aspros" — aspirin tablets — which are so potent a medicine here that I am sure the aborigines work some mapaŋpa into them. But Puntaru did not respond. We looked him over closely and diagnosed measles, a hard disease among the native people. So I told Bob I was willing to scratch the rest of the filming trip; we'd run the people back to Amata and radio the flying doctor to come take Puntaru to the Alice Springs hospital. He would have a better and shorter time of it than the surveyor who got the spear in his eye at Gnarlbo.*

* Ailments and injuries are not suffered without treatment; the bush pharmacopoeia is extensive, and, augmented with patience and stoicism, will cure anything — if the mapantjara's magic is working. White diseases need white mapant-

We had him back at Amata about the time the plane came in. I paid the men off with presents of good knives, cans of tobacco, and a couple of ten-bob notes each. Not yet having been apprised that their faces had been ground by a bloody Yank capitalist, they parted company with us in good spirits.

I had the better part of a week to wait for the regular bush mail plane to come in for its Amata stop and Bob was not scheduled to return to Woomera for more than a week, so we reasoned together on the unusual quandary of what to do with ourselves. We quickly found that we each wanted to fossick around the same place, Opparina Creek, on the Northern Territory–South Australia border beyond Mount Woodward, the mountain from which the two Inma Pabelo men had danced. My object for nosing about was the hints of historical archaeology surely present; Bob's was mineral hunting.

The going was a little rough, as it should be for any place worth the going to, and the country surrounding the creek was as sterile a region as we had seen outside the gibber plains around Coober Pedy. It should not have been so devastated, judging by the good reports of the region by the early explorers. Another problem to which I would not twig the solution until later.

Opparina is distinguished by a classic stone-cut creek bed, a fine watercourse, when the water is coursing. Actually there was more water here than I was ever to see again in the desert country. Bob led me down the creek bed to where there was — a bloody great stone and concrete dam. "Well! How the bloody hell did this get here?" I asked him. "Aw, I put a mob of the men on it when I was super at Musgrave. I thought we could make this place the center of all abo life." The idea had not panned out. There was not a single native within thirty miles.

Opparina evidently was a popular place at one time, when there was growth here instead of barren gibbers. We found leavings of all sorts — the unmistakable dung of wild camels, microlithic tool flakes,

---

jara, like old man Canning, who convinced all ailing aborigines he had proper big-fella magic when he sang over a wounded man,

> No more gammon, no more lie;
> You be better-fella by and by

and pouring him full of castor oil the while.

flint from earlier and later archaeological periods, and three singularly interesting remains — one on a tree, one on a rock, and one in the ground. The tree was an old eucalypt, a slow-grower, that had been carved with the names of visitors at least half a century ago, estimating from the overgrowth. We scraped at the edges of the names and identified the tree blazers as Hart, Jolliffe, and Davies, who sat down here in 1901. Bob knew as much about the history of the old reserve as anyone — unlike the superintendent then at the station, he visited as much of the vast area as he could, and applied himself well to what histories he could dig up in the South Australian Archives. He said Hart, Davies, and Jolliffe were in part responsible for one of the other interesting remains, the hole in the ground a few yards behind the tree away from the creek. The three explorers had buried a cache of food there, he said, and hooshed their camels over the spot to hide it from the aborigines. As soon as they departed, the natives dug up the food, as they had done in almost every case of this sort (the principal exception being the cache under the Burke and Wills "Dig Tree" on Cooper's Creek). There is no imaginable way such deception can be brought off on aborigines.

The third interesting archaeological item was badly eroding name-painting on rock overhanging the creek bed. With knowledge aforethought, we could make out the names of Hann and Talbot and the date of 1907. With evidence of Hann having sat down here I silently took the distressing opinion that the cache hole had been made by Hann rather than Hart, for Hann had tried burying food in 1906 over in the Tomkinson Range. He recorded in his journal the great regret he felt at discovering the aborigines had got away with his food without setting off a store of dynamite he had buried with it.

We ran south to Mount Harriett, good fossicking country for surface archaeology. It was here I found those incredible porcelain points in a Mudukian assemblage. I also found another anomaly at nearby Pinundi — two Woakwine points, which should not have been there, since they are Coorong implements.

By the time we worked our way back to Amata to wait for my plane, the two of us were bent into the shape of composite bows. I feared osteosclerosis was setting in. We each had found a few things of interest, but in retrospect what we were to remember most was an irony apiece. Bob's was his strong suspicion that this region held nickel; he did nothing more than record his guess, for nickel is not the sort of mineral an individual prospector can exploit. This and other nickel sources we were to traverse in a later journey into the Dead Heart, the worst of the western deserts, are bringing Australia to world attention. My own irony was not to be revealed until much later when, by an accident I cannot even recall now, four or five little puzzles and hints of puzzles fell together into a theoretical discovery that unhappily had been solved by others.

The last photography I made on this trip was at the Amata airstrip, not more than an hour before the plane came in. For some well-forgotten reason, I let Bob fill up the truck with a half dozen women and dogs to do some rabbit-hunting out by the airstrip. As it turned out, the sequence was excellent, a fine finish to my film. The women were each possessors of strong and warm personalities that came across well over the silence of the motion picture — Yaritja, Paniwa, Tjimakuda, Iripindiri, Gnoygnoy, and Nola. And the dogs, too. They did absolutely nothing so far as any help to the hunters was concerned; they simply walked about anemically, never more than five yards from one resting place to another, collapsing rather than deliberately lying down at the end of each stretch. As if they had been trained to do it, they let me establish in my narrative commentary that the hypothesis of dogs having been domesticated during the Paleolithic as hunting companions was demonstrably wrong.

Paniwa was the star of the latter part of my film, as Tjipikudu was the early scene-stealer. A woman of beautiful ugliness, a *belle laide* — if we can accept exuberant good humor to be part of beauty — Paniwa dug as the other women dug, with her iron *croba* (I would have preferred for the Paleolithicism of the thing that she use the traditional mulga *wana* instead of a "crowbar"), but she went on down into the holes long after she knew them to be *nen:u* (abandoned), just for the fun she could give me by disappearing entirely into the earth chasing a rabbit. She had no consciousness at all about her grotesquely protuberant belly, but made the shaking of it part of a little dance she did before getting down to dig into the warren for rabbits. Why do we educate ourselves at all, when we have so much evidence of the comfort, if not bliss, there is in ignorance? Paniwa was a happy woman, and I have no doubt she remained so till as close to the end as a woman with her lethal ailment can be happy. She died about eight months afterward from stomach cancer.

The plane came in, the women waved me off, and the pilot dodged the rabbit warren holes very nicely, I am alive to say. I ran out the last hundred feet of film, sweeping the camera's eye from the airstrip "terminal" — four forty-four-gallon gasoline drums — over the Amata compound and camp, and across the northern horizon to Ayers Rock, just visible. Somewhere on that last reel is part of my irony, a boy pushing a toy roller. I noticed him as Bob and I drove out with the women to the airstrip, and more or less rhetorically asked Bob about it. It was a condensed milk can with an axle fashioned out of two pieces of fencing wire turned back and twisted into a strong pushing handle. With so many other things on my mind then — the end of the trip, the women and the rabbits, the plane coming in — I was asking a question out of my subconscious. "Where did that kid get the idea for that thing? The aborigines don't have any artifacts twisted for cantilever strength."

"Aw," replied Bob casually, "I had a big garden roller here when I was running the place. Some of the kiddies took milk tins and made little toy rollers."

Fair enough. Perfectly reasonable. No other explanation was possible. So I put it out of my mind. Two other fellows had the same kind of problem in a world ten thousand evolutionary years beyond Amata and its Old Stone Age aborigines, and they did not put it out of their minds. I was not to understand it until much later, after my fifteen-year pursuit of the wild men was over, but what that boy was pushing around was a Nobel Prize.

SEVEN

ALONG
THE FRINGE

W e were into the west again, Norman and I, and once more in my Tojo, miraculously repurchased from its interim owner who had found he could not live with the grotesque innovations I had built into it as desert necessities.

This was to be our longest single field journey together, more than eight thousand miles, most of it along the corridor between the ocean and the deserts of South and Western Australia. His purpose and mine were quite different from each other this time, but happily their accomplishment depended on our visiting the same places. Norman was completing the field research for what he considers his most important lifework, the meticulous mapping of Australian tribes, living and dead. When he began this project formally forty years ago and more, the consensus of scholars was that aboriginal Australia had no tribes at all, that the natives ran over the continent like promiscuous kangaroos. His first map, published in 1940, outlined the boundaries of five hundred and seventy tribes. It was now years out of print, gone even from libraries by the hands and razors of scholarly vandals. Like all pioneer effort, this map had errors, ambiguities, omissions, and gratuitous additions by blank-hating editors he did not wish to send along to a posterity unable to make corrections. Since 1940 he had been over nearly every inhabited acre of the nation, carrying to the oldest aboriginal men in each place highly detailed pastoral maps on which he marked their remembrances of where their people used to be. Hundreds of these maps now lay among the stones and bones in his large basement workshop at the South Australian Museum, waiting to be collated into one three-feet-by-four chart and supplemented by a heavy volume of notes and commentary. The only field data Norman still lacked were on the inward side of the line I wished to travel, the clarification of the last hazy tribal boundaries.

My objective was in the controversial present, the solution for my own satisfaction of the race conflict problem whose answer for the

League of Women Voters and similar people descends from heaven in tongues of fire, a revelation not for any reason to be altered either by factual evidence or common sense, but only by the sociology of the absurd. For these people field investigation and honest inferences drawn from it signify nothing except the verification in their own minds of their immutable certainty that dissident opinion is the vicious work of racist villains. I wanted for Australia to check it all out, settlement by settlement, and compare present conditions with what I had experienced elsewhere in the world and what I had read in Australia's early documents — not only the journals and memoirs of early settlers, but the correspondence in colonial days between Australian and British administrators.

I have been called a racist, and I suppose I am; I have not the slightest time for Frenchmen and Swedes. But by Chrise I am not influenced by nonsense except insofar as endemic nonsense is part of a culture's determination to hasten entropy. I could grow my hair to my arse if I wished, but I will carry it to the grave cut at the tragus line. If seven years ago I would have been fired from my university position if I called descendants of slaves "blacks," I will be goddamned if I succumb now to pressures to use the word. If I stand somewhat to the right of Genghis Khan, it is because I think the old Khan knew how to deal with people. I doubt that any of his people threw tomatoes at him and coerced him to sign manifestos of cowardice.

I really do not claim for myself any useful superiorities, but one thing I can do excellently well is chop to flinderjigs any opponent on the race question as Joe Duffy chopped up stepladders, so long as my opponent makes the strategic error of talking logic and facts. So hear me on these things; I give you the good oil, as my Aussie mates say. I have lived among the wildest of the desert people. I have also been among aborigines who opted for total integration — aborigines who, taking thought, had slipped quietly, one family per block, into cities where their children (possibly) or their grandchildren (certainly) would be white. The very great majority of vanished aborigines we read about as having been exterminated by murderous settlers disappeared on the latter road. So too did the American Indians. No one who has not made a close study of the secret history of the American Indian would credit how massive their integration and subsequent miscegenation with Negroes and whites has been. Selling very well at this mo-

ment is a new, and entertaining, book by that most successful popularizer of romantic archaeology, C. W. Ceram, who, I am told, actually believes that white settlers killed fifteen million Indians. I expect he attributes all deaths of Indians since 1492 to whites, even if their deaths occurred through heart attack while exerting themselves with scalping knives and tomahawks. For the aborigines, two or three generations of intermarriage with whites and they are genetically lost in the white population, emerging only to win beauty contests and tennis tournaments. No one suffers from this silent melting-off of aborigines except the administrators of native affairs. One of these latter, who strictly warned me not to name him if I expected to get into his reserves again, told me he was carrying on his books several thousand aborigines who did not exist, people created neither by God nor the tjukurpa spirits, but by local agencies padding welfare and pension payments. The same fiddle caused endless trouble for American Indian agents in America in the last decades of the nineteenth century. There was no way this fellow could get rid of the supernumerary natives; if he simply, honestly, and naïvely corrected the census, shrieks of "Genocide!" would roll like thunder halfway around the world to the glassy Babel of the United Nations — and Australia might very well be put under mandate to the Republic of the Congo (Brazzaville). I know the agents of provocation in Australia well, and I say in coldest seriousness they are not nice people. There are some things I could tell you that would harrow up thy soul about this, but I will not; you would not believe me.

For the Australian aborigines all paths led to the bifurcation of two roads. One was that taken in America by the Sioux shaman Sitting Bull and the slave messiah Nat Turner; the other that chosen by the Indian judge Quanah Parker and the Negro scientist George Washington Carver. Had I been in the Indians' moccasins or the aborigines' bare feet, I would have taken the path of the violent Sitting Bull, but then I would have fought on the side of the Tories in the American Revolution against those rebellious ratbags, from Sam Adams down (or up) to Crispus Attucks. I cannot in conscience recommend any conduct of mine to anyone else. In any case my feet are in my own shoes and I have my own problems.

Norman chose to stay right out of this business. In one of our first conversations back in 1956 he told me he could see no end to

America's festering crisis of racial heterogeneity that did not involve blood running deep in the streets. He felt the terror of Thomas Jefferson hearing the fire bell in the night, and hoped he had enough safe work among his wild men to see him off the surface of this troubled planet. If I had to be concerned with this thing, well, it served me right for being younger than he and having been so bloody mad as to give up the tranquil trade of carpentry for the study of man.

Ah well, *in for a penny, in for a pound*, as the Australians say when they are determined to do something profoundly foolish. So long as I would be called upon to speak in future about the brutal conduct of Australia's whites who, rumor had it for a certainty, were killing aborigines for their shoes, I might just as well get into the thick of it. That meant visiting the line of fringe settlements too far out to be altogether civilized and too close in to be considered clear intrusions into aboriginal territory, the places where aboriginal flint was striking white man's steel, showering sparks that one day would fall into some pan of gunpowder put in their way by the professional makers of mischief.

This was a good time for the survey, if anything good can come out of fabricated bad. Australia had just been visited by my old acquaintance of a quarter-century, banjoist Pete Seeger. Pete had sung his weepy songs of guilt for uncommitted sins, inciting the Australian university students (every bit as brainless as our own) to demand importation of large numbers of Melanesians to underpin a good problem of racial conflict where there were not enough indigenous minority members to sustain it. I met my Joan when she interviewed me on her television program; the first question she put to me had to do with my views on Australia's aboriginal problem. My reply was, "What aboriginal problem? You've got only about a hundred thousand persons with even as little as one quarter native blood — you can't run a race problem on that. Wait till you get twenty-two million of them; then you'll have a problem." She told me much later she directed her public relations secretary not to send me the customary letter of thanks for appearing. But that may have been because I sang an unexpectedly unseemly song on the show.

Whatever else I am inclined to deny him, I must allow Good Old Pete Seeger (affectionately known to his friends as the Kremlin Songbird) all the winsome charm of any fifty-three-year-old arrested adolescent. Certainly he can stir up the stew. After his tour the Aus-

216

Tjonduga (Tommy Dodd) and Bob Verburgt at Poka Rockhole

Norman Tindale

tralian university students hired "Freedom Buses" and raided sleepy towns on the eastern fringe making all sorts of nonnegotiable demands of people who had not been conscious of having any racial problem. Most of these weedy children had their tails promptly kicked by the citizenry on the pedagogical principle that what cannot be put gently into one end of a student can be put forcibly into the other, but the kids did succeed in leaving much unexpended resentment. Whites who had behaved toward their darker fellows pretty much as they did toward one another, suddenly looked at the bewildered aborigines in the new light the witless students had shone on them and agreed, "Blimey! Why, the bloody sneaky baastids are niggers at that!"

I tape-recorded several colloquies between the newly enlightened whites and the newly resentful aborigines. Like any emotional confrontation recollected in tranquillity, these were distinguished by a fair amount of *esprit de l'escalier*, but to me the significant fact was that the thought lasted longer than the throb. No doubt of it: racial friction was going to become worse before it became intolerable. Even those aborigines who recognized the mindless folly of needless contention would be drawn into it eventually, for anything that strengthens the cohesiveness of an ingroup, from screaming encouragement to the football team for the good of one's university to gassing Jews for the good of one's race, becomes at last irresistible. I should hate to have her abandon so brilliant a phrase for so poor a thing as truth, but what Hannah Arendt saw at the trial of Adolf Eichmann was not the "banality of evil" but the useful mischief of togetherness. As someone — I think it was Ernest Gann — said about war, some things are necessary for mankind, like shitting.

Not many miles from our Keibara flint mine, just off the Eyre Highway to the east, sprawled the homestead of Cyril Gurney, owner of this part of empty Australia. He had heard the Tojo roaring across the stillness of the Nullarbor and was ambling out to meet us as we slid through the bulldust to his railroad-tie paddock fence. Gurney is a character — right out of the Australian Tobacco Road fictional family, *Dad and Dave*. We would talk with him later, but at this moment we wanted him to direct us to Koonalda Cave, the largest cave in the Nullarbor limestone, an archaeological site of the first interest. He pointed vaguely to the north and a faint track, and we roared off again.

219

This would be an interruption of Norman's map and my race investigation, but one does not pass up a visit to a place like this just because it does not fit into one's primary work. Not in so inaccessible a region as Outback Australia.

Koonalda is a great eroded hole rather than a cave in the usual sense. Underground it opened into a maze of passageways for miles. We slid down a cable Cyril Gurney had fixed to the top as a kind of fireman's ladder — the only improvement this place had seen since Daisy Bates so many years before slid down a rope into the antechamber forty feet below. I will not speak of the archaeology of this place, except to mention Koonalda's chief puzzle: a long pattern of parallel lines across the soft limestone of the interior walls. These have been interpreted as everything imaginable within the general explanation of religious ritual. Norman and I found their real significance.

Far into the cavern our flashlight began to flicker. Dear God. The dark in these places is like an earache — it overwhelms all other senses. Koonalda, moreover, is not one of the best places to stumble around in the dark. Its floor is like tank traps earthed over with slippery clay and the whole thing pitched into incongruous angles — and always at one side *or the other* of whatever route one takes is a lake plumbed in some places at ninety feet. Over our heads in any case. "Damn it, Tindale," I complained, "if you smoked we'd at least have matches."

"We'd have matches if *you* smoked."

"Norman, you know I don't have any vices. I'm a good boy."

"That should be a great comfort to you if we don't get out. You can suffer in happiness the wages of virtue. Look here: if I can shake this light on for a few seconds, see where the wall is on this side of the lake and we'll feel our way out. Keep talking so we'll know where each other is."

I cannot just *talk* when someone says "Keep talking." All I can think of to say is "Testing; testing; one, two, three, four" — and in these circumstances that did not seem appropriate. So I sang instead:

> *Oh come all you good people and listen while I tell*
> *The fate of Floyd Collins, a lad we all knew well;*
> *His face was fair and handsome, his heart was true and brave,*
> *But his body now lies sleeping in a lonely sandstone cave.*

"Limestone," corrected Norman. "Eocene karst limestone. And stop grizzling. If you are worried, we'll just sit here. The Gurneys will come looking for us."

"Come *on*, Norman. Can you think of anybody less likely to come looking for us than the Gurneys?"

A moment of silence.

"Well, no; not in this part of Australia anyhow. We'd better feel along the wall."

I went on with the song.

Oh, how the news did travel! Oh, how the news did go!
It traveled through the papers and on the radio.
His broken-hearted father, he tried his boy to save,
But his body now lies sleeping in an Eocene karst limestone cave.

Without any notable adventure we worked our way out, I am sometimes glad to say, feeling our way along the wall. Bound to look at sites as heliotropes are bound to look at the sun, we fossicked for an hour over the microlithic remains around the entrance of that great sinkhole that had collapsed eons ago into Koonalda Cave. This sort of activity is good for thinking, and as I pecked like a chicken among the tiny flint fragments, I solved to my own satisfaction the mystery of the strange marks on the Koonalda walls. The few archaeologists who have been here have wondered about the parallel lines, "ancient engravings in an area of total darkness." My wonder is about the minds of people who could imagine any aborigines witless enough to go down into the tortuous vastness of Koonalda without lights. I do not require much logic to account for human behavior as other anthropologists do, and after our experience the explanation was to me clear: the firesticks of those ancient visitors had flickered out like our flashlight, and they scrabbled their way out, clawing the walls as we did. Well, why did they go in, if not to engrave religious symbols? For the same reason we did: to get the flint embedded in the limestone, poorer stuff, but in the same strata patterns as protruded from our Keibara Cliff one hundred and twenty-five miles west. Occam's Razor still cuts sharp after nearly six hundred years: *Entities must not be unnecessarily multiplied.* Occam's logic requires the acceptance of· the simplest explanation accounting for all the facts of a phenomenon.

A few miles, a few minutes, and we were at Gurney's homestead once more. He was leaning, arms folded, against the railroad-tie fence. "Owr y' goin' there orright? I see yez got out orright. Shocking bloody place. I lost six sheep down there last week. The billy's on the boil; sit 'er down for a minute. Got yer old mate 'ere. *FREDDY!* Git yer tail out here!"

Old Freddy Windlass, our taciturn companion of the Keibara quest, shuffled out from behind the woolshed, gnawing on something suspiciously unspeakable.

"G'day!" I said, sitting down by the boiling billy, hitting its side with a stick to shake down the tea leaves.

"G'day!" he responded, squatting. "You bin eber pindim dat pella black shiny stone he pall prom sky? You know dat pella?"

"*Miriwa* [drop dead], you old bugger. What you doing here?"

"Helpin wit a tank."

"You still chewing on that wombat?"

"Too bloody right. *Waṛdu kuka.* Bloody good tucker, my word."

Cyril's sons, monstrous great hulking creatures, loped slowly toward us from various hiding places around the homestead. Like their father, they were attired in the vestments of dire poverty, army jackets and overalls virginal to water. Over on the woolshed platform Cyril had enough wool baled to pay my salary for years, but prosperity and disaster are the same to these "cockies," cockatoo farmers. They are what the Australians call "battlers" — like a small pugnacious boy fighting above his weight, they keep their chins on their chests against life and swing their fists furious as windmills, so that they never know whether they are winning or losing. They do not even think so much of fortune as to have a name for their position in the world. Ask them and they will tell you, "Aw, I run a few sheep, yeh," or, "Yeh, I got a few acres." Except for the automobile and radio, life has not changed in places like Koonalda Station in a hundred years. On this border between the wild land and the tamed, aborigines and whites make their first permanent accommodation with one another. No intrusion here of one race upon the other, each on its best or worst behavior as in places of clearer territoriality. What we see here is living too poor to support the luxury of prejudice.

"Jesus Christ, Freddy," I asked, "what *is* that you're eating? The arse?"

"*Uah, maṇa,*" he affirmed. "Proper good tucker."

"Yeh" said Cyril, "the Pope's nose."

Cyril's youngest, only fourteen and no more than six feet tall in his lazy slouch, grinned and whispered to me behind his hand, "I et his leg."

"You et whose leg?"

"I et Freddy's leg."

The boy was a great gangling puppy, an untrained carnivore, quite capable of consuming anything. I looked involuntarily at Freddy's leg.

"I et Freddy's wombat's leg. He thinks the dogs et it. I et it."

Cyril handed me a pannikin of tea. In the bush the owner pours. "I reckon Fred's leg wouldn't go too bad at that, you scorch some of the hair off it. If the old baastid gets any more careless how he rolls around his fire at night, I might have a go meself. Make good cracklin', I reckon. S'truth, we had an old bloke, blackfella, here a while back who got in his fire and roasted the skin off his leg. Shockin' bloody sight, my oath. Thought we'd have to shoot 'im. But he was a hard doer, and pulled out when we put a graft on his leg."

"You grafted skin back on his leg?"

"Aw, yair. Had to be a sheepskin, of course. Grew back to be a funny-lookin' thing — wool on one leg, hair on the other. Kept his leg warm, though. Got three pounds of wool off him last shearin'."

"Tell 'im about the sheep breedin,' Da," said the middle boy.

"Aw, yair. You read about them Yank doctors puttin' new hearts into people and them Rooshians puttin' new heads on. But we'll stand up to any of 'em, my flamin' oath. We crossed a sheep with a kangaroo last year."

"What did you get?" I'll go along with anybody's nonsense.

"A woolly jumper. The old woman don't have to knit sweaters no more, she don't. S'truth. Hey Freddy, why don't you take the boys and get back to work on that bloody tank?"

"Uah," Freddy acknowledged, and went to sleep.

We thought we'd better take our leave of the Gurneys if we were to have any hope of getting down to our Keibara mine by sunset with any sanity remaining. Cyril pumped our tanks full of petrol, we exchanged parting "hoo-rahs," and pulled back onto the Eyre. My reflection as we drove into the sunset was about the manifest equality of whitefella and blackfella on Gurney's station. I did not deceive myself into believing Cyril thought Freddy as good as himself. But on the other hand Freddy had his own opinion on personal evaluation.

223

That night we had our last sandalwood camp fire, and the next morning we revisited our Keibara cliff, gathering more trade flint, but nothing of special value. The tide was in and I went through the surf naked, Norman opting to clamber along the cliff boulders fallen over the millennia. I tried to break pieces off these flint boulders and found that flint is harder than steel.

The first time a man turns his vehicle out on Western Australia's share of the Eyre Highway he thinks the only way this corrugated track can be negotiated is slowly. Try that and you will know how it feels to ride a bucking bronco — one with a metal canopy to crack your skull against. No; it must be driven at speed, sixty miles an hour at least, so that your tires touch only the tops of these iron-hard ripples. You will be tempted to turn off the track and make your own road along the margin. All along the way to Madura loop the tracks of drivers who have tried the expedient; they run on the average two hundred yards, at the end of which you find either their abandoned and rusting car or the massive excavation out of which the vehicle was somehow dug. Norman recalled pulling off the track thirty years before onto a good solid flat surface and immediately hearing *pop! pop! pop! pop!* — the pistol cracks of blown tires, punctured by needle-pointed cones of limestone grown like stalagmites out of softer eroded soil. He and Jo Birdsell had to hack a path through them with axes to get back on the westward track. Aside from the corrugations (which engineering tests have proved extend twenty feet below the surface), there are potholes three feet deep alternating with bulldust soft and smothering as talcum powder. I will say only one thing further about this *transcontinental highway* between Eucla and Madura. Norman Tindale and I have traveled thousands of miles together over many years. He knows me well as a person who does not accept annoyance with equanimity, a cranky baastid who curses at the least provocation, kicking trees and tires and dogs and small children. But in all the days of our pilgrimage I have never heard him utter one unseemly word, nary a *Jesus-H-Bald-Headed-Christ*, a *damn*, or even a *golly-gee*. His only acknowledgment of unacceptable behavior of man or beast of the kind that sends me brachiating through the mulga is a hissed intake of breath, learned as a boy in Japan, and a short sharp shake of his head to clear his brain of nonsense or misfortune. In all these years, these miles, there has been only one exception: on the Eucla-Madura track. Feeling some need of support for my continuous, violent condemnation of the road as I skipped the Tojo across the washboarding, skidded it around the potholes and boulders, and slid it broadside through the bulldust, I put it to him straight *proper-fella no more gammon*: "Come *on*, now, Norman, what do you think of this bloody road?"

"John," he sighed, "I will tell you. It is a bloody fucking shit of a road, a *fair cow*."

Approaching Madura (Mirning for "rocky scarp") we groaned up a forty-degree grade to the plateau again. Norman remembered it being steeper thirty years ago; he and Jo Birdsell had to winch their trucks up the cliff face.

Madura is another cartographic illusion: a large central tin shanty for all service functions for the traveler foolish enough to be in this corner of the world's emptiness, and a half dozen corrugated iron minishanties the size of two-hole privies rented out as sleeping rooms. I felt myself suddenly in one of those deadfalls where travelers were killed for their purses on the old American frontier. We peered through the window of the "dining room" and saw on a large calendar the notice that this was all that comprised the town of MADURA THE ARSE-HOLE OF THE EARTH. Dusk had fallen; we looked toward a tank-up, a kitchen-cooked meal, and perhaps a bed off the ground, but I said to Norman, "You know, mate, I tink we bin more comportable out on dat track."

We boarded the Tojo again and sped west, bound immediately for a place called Cocklebiddy, sixty miles away. Norman remembered it as an aboriginal camp, a *ngura*, but since these places become fueling stops as the automobile bumps out the natives, we hoped for more.

So it was. In our headlights and the weak glow of its own self-generated lights the Cocklebiddy compound was much the same as Madura — a large but minimal structure housing a garage, dining room, and general store, and behind it a row of sleeping sheds like an old Mormon polygynous household — but it was subtly more honest, brighter, safer. The proprietor came out promptly as we drew up to his pumps. He looked hospitable enough for me to ask whether there was any chance of getting something to eat at ten in the evening.

"Aw, yair, mate, too right," he said, "steak and egg, steak-and-kidney pie, boiled pumpkin, proper good tucker, the lot, fit for a bloody king, yair." Gourmet cuisine on the Nullarbor! I expected at best the Australian ham sandwich with the pig's bristles sticking through the bread.

The dining room half of the all-purpose interior was walled by a panorama of aboriginal life. Even in this wild country where the culture of the white man had hardly taken any hold, this mural was an astonishing thing. We had not seen a blackfellow since we left old Freddy Windlass snoring over his wombat arse two hundred and fifty miles back; this was still Mirning land and the Mirning were all finish. But the mural was accurate, though poorly executed as art. Someone here knew the old ways.

And then she appeared — a full-blood Mirning woman, a few years short of fifty, hair and skin dark almost to blackness, and the fine white teeth of the pure aborigine sparkling in the pure aborigine's puckish smile. She came out of the kitchen wiping her hands as we sat down at a table, calling out a hearty "G'day" and recommending Australia's staple, muscular steak for muscular jaws and loose fried eggs spread on like American ketchup. We puzzled over her existence as she fried up our dinner. She had no right to be in the kitchen or anywhere else, for the last Mirning in the record died years ago and his bones were lying far over on the Murray banks.

Norman was more interested in this woman than even this anomaly warranted. There was *something*. Whatever it was grew when she brought out our steak and eggs and began talking, as evidently she did for every outsider who stopped here, about aboriginal life. Much of this was palpable nonsense, but that was orright, since we all understood tourists are persons who will be satisfied only with the spurious. There was a something for her, too; she seemed to be paying no more mind to her talk than we did to the hearing of it. Suddenly the grin broke sharply again and she exclaimed right in the middle of some flapdoodle about boomerangs, *"You Mister Dumdale — you cut my hair!"*

Norman dropped his fork handle end-first into his soppy eggs. This is one of the few emotional expressions he has learned; subconsciously useful, it lets him bumble till he recovers his self-control. The woman certainly had shaken him. "Yes," he said slowly, pulling from his extraordinary memory an incident nothing to him a quarter of a century ago and everything to her, "we called you — Eileen?"

Eileen it was, now Eileen Flynn, *née* God knows what, though Norman had her name somewhere in his roomful of journals. She was a giggler, so what she had to tell us about her life since Norman and Jo Birdsell cut swatches of Mirning hair for physical anthropology data twenty-seven years earlier took us well past midnight. She sat down with us all the while, and it was significant to me in my observational studies to see not the least scowl from the proprietor. She was the kitchen and dining-room boss and he kept out of her province.

No doubt the cutting of her hair by the two strange white-skinned men was the greatest adventure in her life at that time. She went on to greater things as the white man began to penetrate the Nullarbor in greater numbers and her own people died out. A life of wickedness followed, she told us; but she had put all that behind her now. One more example of the aching tooth of age; a man does not leave his vices — his vices leave him. She had met a white man to marry her and be father to his children and they now had children. More importantly, she had come to know Jesus. Well, fair enough. Sin is great for the short run, but for the long haul put your money on religion.

On the two sides of midnight Eileen answered a dilly-bag full of questions most anthropologists would think aimless, but each filled a small space in the interlocking jigsaw puzzle of our knowledge of Australia and its native people. Greenway: Can you still speak "the language"? *Aw, not too good now; talk Engli' too long.* Tindale: Are there any others of your people alive now? *Aw, yair, Old Jessie, she used to be at Cocklebiddy Station wit' Harold Carlisle, don't know where she is now, maybe finish, must be 'bout a hunnerd years old, I reckon.* Tindale, with his map in mind, for we were near the western border of the Mirning country: Did the Mirning people live over this way in the old days? *Aw, yair, dat my mob, Ngandatha Mirning; Murinitja close up here, proper cheeky fella, my word.* Ngandatha Mirning? Another horde of the Mirning like the Wonunda Mirning and Jirkla (Eucla) Mirning? Or is the word cognate with Ngadadjara dialect *nangata*, meaning "this one"? Early explorers got the names Meening, Wanbiri, Warnabirrie, Wanmaraing, Ikala, Ikula. So Greenway: What does "Mirning" mean in whitefella talk? *"Mirning" mean "man."* Sure; there it is again. Nearly all tribes reserve the word "man" for themselves, thus excluding all other hominids from the species *sapiens*. Such taxonomy makes ill-treatment and racism easier.

Tindale, checking on reports of polydactyly in the journals of the Elder Expedition of 1892: Did you ever hear of anyone in this country with more than five fingers on one hand? *Aw, yair, out near Mount Arid, "Six-Finger Tommy" and Jacky Donaldson.* Greenway, asking a question for Peter Aitken, still not satisfied with his mammalogical colleagues' identification of the Pitjandjara *kuḷpirpa* as the Gray or Plains kangaroo (*Macropus major*) and who suspects another species or subspecies: Do you know of a large, reddish-brown kangaroo with a very long middle toe on its hind foot, a dog killer? *Aw, yair, gulbirra, proper cheeky fella, he grabs dogs wit' his front feet and tears out dem belly, my word.* This is what we heard from the men at Yalata, and they, like Peter, were almost violent in their assertion of this being a little-known — to the white man — kind of kangaroo. But how do you classify the macropodids? There are more varieties than you can aim a *ripela* at. The Gray Kangaroo is also called the Red Kangaroo and sometimes the male is gray, sometimes red, ditto the females. More often than not one sees in print the common name of *Thylogale stigmatica Gould* spelled not "pademelon," which is correct, but "paddymelon," which is a cucurbitaceous plant. My own feeling about the *gulbirra* is that this dog killer is the western race of *Macropus rufus* subnamed *dissimulatus*. The things you get into studying anthropology.

Tindale, still in pursuit of other remnants of Barrineans: Are there any "tiny people" down in this country? *Aw, yair, two-t'ree 'way in sout,' in mountains, hard to find.* She gave us their names and where to look for them (unfortunately circumstances took us away from the extreme southwest, so we did not find them). Greenway, riding his hobbyhorse: Any trouble here between the whitefellow and the blackfellow? *Aw, no, whitefella here orright. Kids go to same schools ollasame, no more fights, no more rubbish. Used to be, onetime, no more. My daughter she speak only Engli', her children ollasame white-fella children. No more trouble like in old times. Old times, some plenty bad whitefella — not like Mister Dumdale.* Schools? Out here? *Aw, yair, little bit long way — in Esp'rance, Norseman.* "Little bit long way"! Norseman is two hundred and eighty miles west of Cockle-biddy, and the eastern outpost of inhabited Western Australia; Esperance is four hundred and seventy miles southwest. *Aw, we got wireless school here.* The School of the Air — transmitted education with two-way communication, so that children and teachers can question one another, throughout the whole of Outback Australia.

Eileen's acceptance was proved next morning when her boss gave her several further hours to talk with us. The talk and the *recherche du temps perdu* had by then drawn the two of us pretty close to Eileen, and our departure just before noon had the three of us rubbing our eyes. Few other professions condemn friends to making *good-bye* a final parting. Most of the people in this book I shall not see again.

Dumdale and I almost took the wrong track out of Cocklebiddy, but Norman's directional instinct put us right directly. One is not often presented with a choice of tracks in inland Australia. Much later, while reading a manuscript journal written by Griselda Sprigg, I learned that the new track had been bulldozed almost straight north over the western Nullarbor by her husband, Reg Sprigg, and named by him for their daughter the "Connie Sue Highway." Reg is a classic example of the Sacrificial Pioneer, one of the men in every enterprise who precede even the Baptizing Johns into new deserts but who are not mentioned in any gospels. Before I knew anything at all about Reg Sprigg I consulted with him in his office as head of the Geodetic Surveys about what in his view was the best desert vehicle for small expeditions, and it was he who recommended the Toyota Land Cruiser. I was to learn, a fact at a time, that he insisted against the entirety of geological opinion that oil existed in Australia's center, that the most ancient fossils were also in the Australian earth, and that Joan Disher was far more than just beautiful. Now oil development has proceeded so swiftly that Australia is expected to be an oil-exporting nation by the mid-seventies; Sprigg himself has found so many of the oldest, pre-Cambrian fossils that he has not merely species but genera named after him; and the Spriggs were good friends of my Joan before I met her. It was in fact Joan who gave me Griselda's manuscript — and in that journal I read of the Spriggs's flight in their small plane over our Keibara cliff mine, where they saw a whale. Never in America have I met even one man who knew even a region of his country as so many of my Australian acquaintances knew the whole of it, nor any who had their desire to bury their souls into their land. Without that there cannot be any useful patriotism, I am sure.

The Western Australian environment changed sharply some seventy miles west of Cocklebiddy in the middle of a thousand-square-mile rectangle marked on the official map by nothing but two rockholes, neither of which we saw. The Nullarbor vegetation of saltbush, bluebush, occasional mulga, ti trees, and sandalwood abruptly stopped and the weird forms of ancient flora began — two or three individuals of a species at first, then in the next two cartographic rectangles (two thousand square miles with one named place, the Jenkins Clayhole) clustering, each to dominate its particular econiche. Like so many other natural ecological boundaries, this no-man's-land was the border of two tribal countries — the Mirning to the east and the Ngadjunma to the west. So too the fauna separated; into this strange corner of Australia the great plains kangaroo did not venture, leaving the range to the whiptail and other minority wallabies, possums, and marsupial mice. No sufficient inorganic cause seemed to account for the conspired segregation of plants, animals, and man beyond clay overcoming lime and the Jurassic still resisting the inevitable Tertiary. The land was no more than a passive battleground where armies of living things had been made to fight one another by inviolable order of natural selection for the bits of precarious territory the survivors now held, prevailing marsupial mouse overcoming the giant kangaroo; the Xanthorrhoea in its grass skirt holding its spear against the alien mulga. The poet Frost was wrong; apple trees *will* eat pine cones, grass *will* kill apple trees, and everything loves a wall. A truce had been made here where the limestone plateau of the Nullarbor runs out in the southwestern loams, but now, in this evolutionary instant we call Australian history, the white man, in his function as carrier of the aggressiveness that made apes into men several million years ago, was changing everything. To speed American automobiles along the Hollywood Freeway helicopters were scanning the desert for oil — and finding it. Tomorrow we would enter gold country, where the earth itself had been torn back down to the pre-Cambrian; today, if we were to turn abruptly southwest, we would enter the one-and-a-half-million-acre region being opened to agriculture by a great American consortium.

We saw our first native Western Australian a few miles out of Cocklebiddy, a faunal victim of human intrusion — a kangaroo dead from attacking a vehicle a day or two ahead of us. He was an unusual member of his genus: large, with beautiful russet-red fur, wide flaring ears, and hind feet so black as to look like patent leather slippers, out of which protruded a long central middle claw. He was a *he*, no question, for his penis stuck out of his anus, as it does with all poor male marsupials. No question also, he was our *gulbirra*.

230

"Let's take the head for Peter," Norman suggested.

"No bloody fear," I said. "We're not carrying any kangaroo pieces eight thousand miles on *my* truck. Nothing bigger than a bloody butterfly, and that's flat." We photographed him and I suggested we sling the fellow into the bush and pick up his skull on the way back. He may still be there, for we did not get back to this place.

Finding a *gulbirra* was a rarity, but nothing so surprising as the next discovery — a stretch of bitumen road. Could such things be? I thought it a mirage, for there was heat shimmer, looming, on it, and there apparently floating was a large road grader. A man stood beside the machine, waving both arms. Out here you stop to help any man, even if he is pointing a gun at you. Coarse, tough, stubby-bearded, and nearly toothless, he grinned as he clambered aboard on Norman's passenger side. "G'day. Great Christ, it's bloody hot out here on that bloody grader. Yanks, are yez?" (I had UNIVERSITY OF COLORADO U.S.A. painted on both doors.) "Good on you, you beauties. I love the bloody Yank baastids. Remember the Coral Sea. Take me to Norseman and I'll shout yez to a round of beer."

Norman likes to go along with the Yank identification, so he left the conversation to me. "What's the trouble, buddy?" I asked. "Grader break down?"

"Naw. Just got bloody fed up sittin' in the rotten thing. I quit. Stuff it. Let the bloody baastid rot. Don't know why they want a bloody road out in this bloody place anyhow. I'm goin' to Norseman and get bloody pissed. You blokes come on with me and we'll all get bloody shickered."

I hit the brakes and the Tojo bounced to a stop. To hear such talk after the Eyre — it was not to be borne. "Out!" I ordered. "Out, you bloody bludger. No wonder this road is taking twenty years to build — lazy bloody buggers like you. *Out*, you baastid, or I'll lay this god-damned tire iron along your ear. *OUT!*"

He tumbled out, speechless for a moment, Norman in silent embarrassment pulled the door shut, and I rammed the Tojo into gear. As it leaped forward the man aimed a kick at the tailgate but missed and fell, whirling around in his inertia like a dervish. He screamed at us. "*STUFF* you bloody Yanks, you bloody baastids. You killed Phar Lap. Les Darcy! Bloody Yank bloody baastids!"

As long as I could see him in the side mirror he was on his rear, shaking his fist. "Welcome to the white population of Western Australia," laughed Norman. "He'll curse you Yanks till the day he dies."

"Maybe he'll die today. Has a good chance of it. We'll pick up *his* skull on the way back, too."

The next Australians we saw were flying easily over the salmon gums. "Wedge-tailed eagles," said Norman, continuing his habit of identifying everything new for me.

At quarter past four on this memorable afternoon we rolled into Norseman, home of 2,740 people, Western Australia's eastern outpost, the first water-supplied settlement in seven hundred and seventy miles. Of course this was Saturday and everything was shut except the grocery store, milk bar, and pub. Norman dashed into the grocery store and I ran into the milk bar as the proprietors were trying to close down operations in the great Australian tradition of dead weekends, so we managed to get some fresh food. We then rushed over to the Norseman Christian mission to lay hands on their few aborigines, but we were told no work, even interviewing, would be permitted on Sunday, and everyone was too busy this late Saturday afternoon to talk to us. Out here anthropologists are about as popular as policemen. But anthropologists never lack for contingency plans, so we looked in at the Central Norseman Consolidated Gold Corporation, whose enormous tailings (two hundred feet high and three-quarters of a mile in circumference) should discourage any individual prospector who thinks he can get gold out of the ground with a shovel. It was not just an eye-balling stop for me, since I was concurrently working on a study of the Australian frontier and its development.

For the rest of our long trip settlements were frequent, and in each we visited first the police station to present our credentials (one is not permitted to enter the edge-of-town reserve land or even talk with aborigines without proper authority) and then the local missionary, in whose charge the native peoples are usually if not always imprisoned. All along the southern line my interviewing of white settlers revealed an attitude of mind that was probably also a fact of existence: the aborigines were generally "good blokes," "good neighbors," their children well integrated in the schools; on the whole, pretty decent people — "not like your American blacks," one man told me — "but they keep to themselves."

Striking south from a curiously flyless camp on dry Lake Dundas, we entered what I call "Art Linkletter Country," a coastal strip at

232

least a thousand miles long where in imagination or reality the television personality Art Linkletter is supposed to own large land enterprises. At Esperance at the end of our south-bearing track it is a fact; Linkletter and a consortium of other American movie and television stars are developing about a million acres known as the "Esperance Miracle." Too bad — bloody Yanks mucking up a place I should so like to have for my golden years. Esperance is La Jolla before the hippies, Acapulco before the jet set, Tahiti before the French. Now the population is approaching four thousand, many of whom are not only Americans, but sheep-raising Americans. In another decade not even the bush flies will be left.

Esperance was named by the French mariner D'Entrecasteaux in 1792 when, during his part of the great search for La Pérouse, his two vessels were driven into the harbor by a gale. *Espérance* was not only his hope in this peril, but the name of one of his two tiny frigates; the other was *La Recherche,* for which he named the maze of islets hugging the south coast between Esperance and Israelite Bay. Poor D'Entrecasteaux; he was an ardent Catholic and would have become a Jesuit priest if his father had not sent him into the navy; had he landed a settlement party at Esperance, the place today would be as Catholic as New Caledonia — but he did not and it is not (he died the following year of scurvy). Esperance today is the province of the Australian Aborigines Evangelical Mission.

I must say for Ian Pedler, superintendent of the mission, that he is one of the good ones. He was very helpful to us, though he frankly declared he did not generally like either anthropologists or their "thesises." Well, I generally don't like anthropologists or their thesises either. He guided us to people we might not have found otherwise, the most notable of whom was dead — Tommy Windich, as legendary in Australia as Squanto or Sacagawea is in America. Tommy's grave is a pitiably poor thing — but it looks down upon the west beach of Esperance, a lovely view even from the grave. Of the live people, old Murray Newman was outstanding. Murray was a half-blood in his seventies, alert and full of information far past our ability to recover it, at least in the time we had. Too much of what he had to say conflicted with our information, but it had the ring of truth to it. His people — like so many others, now gone — called themselves the "Ngungar," a word to raise difficulties. Norman heard it elsewhere as "Ngunga"; so it would be heard by every educated Australian white, whose ears are just not to be entrusted with the American *r*. Who were these "Ngungar"? One tribe? So Norman thought, but Murray referred constantly to "these Ngungar here" and "those Ngungar there," the latter not really his tribesfolk, but a mob once living forty miles west along the coast at Fanny Cove (named for one of the last Tasmanian women taken to Kangaroo Island by an American pirate and freebooter a century ago). In Murray's mind there was a difference between the two groups, but logically it was indefensible. He confirmed our hypothesis that three important aboriginal demographic lines were coincident: the border of circumcision to the north, the division between the Ngungar and the Wongai tribes, and the *-up* place-name isogloss. As to circumcision, uppermost in his mind if lowermost on his torso, he said with unconvincing pride, "I never been caught." He deeply wished he had been, that was obvious, for he respected the Wongai to the point of terror. I wondered whether he lived fifty years on this remote beach because it was as far away from the desert people as he could get.

Murray said the Ngungar put the suffix *-up* at the end of their place-names, but he did not know what it meant. We did; it means "water," and it is cognate to most native names for water over the continent. My Pitjandjara say *kapi*, but that is subtly unpronounceable by Murray's southern tongue. In this southwesternmost pocket of Australia there are such places as Cobinup, Jerdacuttup, Quallilup, Dalyup, and scores of similar legacies from the natives preserved from colonial times, from the corrupted "The Pup" near Israelite Bay on the southeast to Joondalup northwest of Perth. Inland of this line, the region Murray knew as Wongai country, the place-name suffix was commonly *-ya*, as in Buraminya, Womarbinya, Curnadinia, Murtadinia, Willgonarinya, Yalodinya, and other water locations north of the Mount Arid–Israelite Bay line, none of which came within forty miles of the coast. Murray contested one of Norman's place-names — Tjitjala:ngya — which, he insisted, should be "Tjitjalup." Who was correct? Both, for the place lies right on the isogloss. There must have been some grand fights there in the old days.

This sort of brain-picking — which we conducted with a hundred other informants on our journey along the fringe — is properly the work of years, not hours. Each man has a lifetime, and it takes another man's lifetime to recover what he knows. To Murray Newman we could afford only two days. So many things we could have had from

234

him, if we had had the time.* What, for example, of the land here when he was a boy? When J. S. Roe fought his way into this region in 1848 he said the scrub was so dense "only axes could have opened a passage"; now the growth was so sparse as to be indistinguishable from that of true desert a day's journey north.

And only Murray is alive to tell about myths, as another example. He sang for us a fragment of a song about a bird which went into the bush and emerged as a woman, whose onomatopoeic *tau tau tau* I recognized from a quite differently interpreted fragment recorded so long ago by an Adelaide University team that it is on an Edison cylinder — and that was found a thousand miles away from Esperance. Did he know about the Keibara? We did not think to ask; there was so much else to recover in two days.

For as long as we had the stomach for it we worked at Ian Pedler's Mission Hotel with thirty teen-aged part-blood aborigines who had come to this hostel from as far away as Warburton. They were insufferably useless. Two of the boys had been born in the desert around Boundary Dam, one hundred and sixty-five miles straight north across the Nullarbor from our Keibara flint cliff, but they could not even remember the name of their natal country. One of them played the guitar. Norman and I shared an approbation for the old-men who were choosing in these latter days to let traditional ways die rather than pass the sacred lore to young louts who would let it rot into rubbish to be played to a Rolling Stones beat. To think that these creatures were Wongai, Ngalea, Pindiini, and Kokata — whose grandfathers terrified men like Murray Newman! Some bloody Wongai.

We left the mission and took the barely passable coastal track west, swinging inland two hundred miles to enter the narrow ellipse of the Stirling Range and its rocky satellite, the Porongurups, both part of the earth's last refuge for its primeval plant life. Here the strange grass-trees, the blackboys (from whose bark we practiced making *yaka*, equivalent to Pitjandjara *keti*), grew in whole regiments of skirted spearmen. And so many other weird floras proliferated that they did not seem to be of this earth. Even the birds were not of our

---

* Norman made a second trip to continue interviewing Murray, when I was in the desert with Bob Verburgt, and it proves this immediate point when I say I have never had the opportunity to speak with Norman about it on the occasions we had together later — too many other things.

experience. We saw a flight of the rare black cockatoos, which might as well have been pterodactyls. Driven like the last lumbering dinosaurs to this environmental wall of rain forest on a desert continent, the *karri* and *jarrah* trees were mammoths of their genus from the age of giants, eucalypts closely related to the stunted mulga, but no more like them in appearance than a lion is to a house cat. These are gray-green pillars as tall as the biggest California redwoods; one was rotted hollow at its base and I drove the Tojo through it.

So helpless these giants, and so certainly doomed. For nearly two hundred miles, from the *karri* loop track above Nornalup almost to the outskirts of Perth we drove through burning forests. The road signs calling the visitors' attention to the need to PREVENT FOREST FIRES were an impudent irony. Cigarettes here as in the United States are the innocent accused, believed beyond possibility of doubt to be the means by which forests are destroyed. We saw no other motorists and no cigarettes, but we saw farmers — lighting new fires, great roaring blazes, as the horizon all around them was burning. Here now in the west of Australia, as once in its east, it is a farmer's saying that dry-time is burning-off time. Two hundred miles of development: the *karri*, unharmed and to some degree protected, at Nornalup; the blackened bones of newly burned *jarrah*, not yet torn from the earth, at Balingup; and at last their tamed successors, pretty rows of domesticated apple trees, at Mullalyup. Again, the way of the world; those starving million mouths of India cannot eat *karri* bark — but man must live and reproduce to overpopulate the earth, so apples come in, to do as much mischief here as they did in the Garden of Eden. Curiously, the people who call most strenuously for preservation of the environment are the same people who weep most copiously for starving mouths.

Another hard paradox was leaving its archaeological mark at Collie, the only substantial settlement between Albany at the most southerly point of Western Australia and Perth well up the west coast. I did not then know that Western Australia had any coal at all, but at Collie I found that coal (though barely sub-bituminous) had been mined there since 1896. Collie had its boom and Collie had its bust, the latter brought about by the inevitable footless strike. Collie had ten thousand people once, but hardly enough now to keep the pub alive. We visited the edge-of-town reserve, not unhandsome in this pretty place, but tiny and moribund, with moribund people. Here we found Alec Rowe, who claimed to be the son of Sir John Forrest's great native guide Tommy Windich, which might have been possible had Rowe been thirty years older. His other remarks on local aboriginal history were equally unconvincing.

"Why do they tell such wicked lies?" I asked Norman as we left the camp and started north for Perth.

"They're not lying — not in any sense we understand as lying. You haven't been examining your culture map. This is New Norcia country. These are New Norcia people. Everything was taken from them when they were children — when their parents were children — and without any understanding of reality, anything they can imagine becomes reality."

Daisy Bates spoke well in her time of New Norcia, but she was speaking from the point of view that the aborigines were doomed, and the missionaries' responsibility was to usher them out gently, like terminal cancer patients. I did not, as Norman chided me, think of this as New Norcia country; that to me was north of Perth, where Dom Rudesindus Salvado built his grim mission. We would see it later.

We came to Perth at sunset. It was not this first time, my alabaster city, shining white. The sun, a fiery Chinese red sinking in the smoke of the south's burning forests, incarnadined it to rose-red, like Petra, that city half as old as time. And Perth was old in its ambience, too; by a long measure the most isolated city of anything near its size in the Western world, Perth lies somnolent and provincial and comfortable as if it were in the last century.

After settling in at the sleepy and comfortable old Beaufort Hotel, remembered by Norman from his youth, we went over to Native Welfare and carried the compliments of America and the sister state of South Australia to Mr. F. E. Gare, the governor of this enormous territory's aborigines. Gracious and helpful, he gave us the names of aboriginal informants to the north — Bob Williams in Carnarvon, Jack Councillor at Northampton, Jack Comeagain at Mullewa, and others — and passed along news we had not known, such as the latest crisis in the aboriginal communist colony established by Donald McLeod in the far north, an enterprise that would occupy my studies for years afterward.

From Native Welfare we went to the Western Australian Museum, grown unrecognizably from the Fremantle guardroom of seventy-five

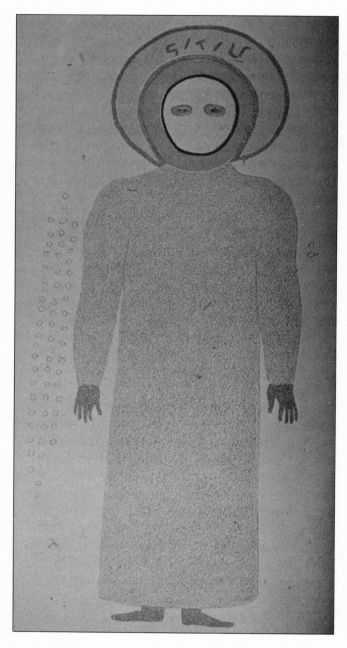

Wondjina figure (original sketch by Sir George
Grey, 1837; first reproduced in Thomas Worsnop,
Prehistoric Arts of Australian Aborigines,
Adelaide, 1897)

Old City Hall and principal hotel at Coolgardie, ghost gold town, W.A.

years ago. The museum's curator of anthropology, Ian Crawford, gave us in the Australian manner more of his time than he could really afford, showing us through the unexhibited riches in the museum's vaults which corroborated Norman's archaeological sequences.

Ian laid on a fine dinner that evening in his home for Norman and me. Certainly his most exciting news was his disclosure that with the help of scientific equipment he had solved one of Australia's great archaeological and geopolitical mysteries — the meaning of the marks on the haloed headband of a *wondjina* figure discovered in 1838 on the sheltered wall of a Kimberley cave by Sir George Grey and thereafter lost for a century. The figure, painted in ochers and clay, appeared in Grey's drawing to be a red-garmented, saint-like, mouthless person, with a sign or message in a curious alphabet on his headdress (see illustration, page 238).

Having nothing better to do with their time, cryptologists and persons even less qualified to speculate about nonsense have made actual

239

"translations" of the symbols. One, Mr. A. Carroll of Sydney, not otherwise known to philological science, communicated to his friend Thomas Worsnop (Adelaide town clerk and author of a fairly good book on aboriginal material culture) his discovery that the symbols translated clearly to *I am a great personage, or chieftain, of the north-east country of the Red Sea.* One laments the loss of so economical an alphabetical system — and wonders that still another people confused a word for "reed" as "red" in naming that treacherous body of water. A Reverend J. MacDonald of Melbourne recognized the characters unmistakably as elements of the Chaldaeo-Phoenician alphabet, whatever that is, though he did not know what they meant! Another nineteenth-century clergyman and anthropologist, the Reverend John Mathew of Coburg, Victoria, disclosed to the Royal Society of New South Wales in 1889 that the writing was Sumatran, one word transliterated to *dabai*, meaning "divinity," and was cognate to the Japanese word *daibatsu*, "Great Buddha." The eminent scholar Wilhelm von Humboldt gave as his thoughtful opinion an educated guess that the "alphabet" was not Polynesian (a safe inference, since there are no Polynesian alphabets). In more recent years Chinese writers have put forward a claim to the continent of Australia by right of prior discovery, clearly shown by the Chineseness of the figure. And there is some talk that Thor Heyerdahl will construct a wind wagon with the symbols on its sail and journey backward to the hidden source of the god. All of these interpretations except the last have been based on the drawing made by Grey.

And then Ian Crawford stepped in with dull science to put an end to these delightful speculations; China lost one excuse for an invasion, and Heyerdahl will have to build a replica of a Kansas farmhouse for a cyclonic flight to Oz. Ian told us he had just returned from an expedition to Grey's cavern, and certified what many of us supposed — that the clear outlines in Sir George's drawing of the *wondjina* are as gratuitously imaginative as the old maps astronomers used to make of canals on Mars. And most important, that the "symbols" revealed themselves under infrared photography as random cracks pushed up through the surface by innumerable coats of ocher paint laid on by generations of aborigines.

A weekend approached, and fearful that Perth might have a law forbidding the movement of vehicles on the Sabbath (everything else stops on Friday noon), we rushed on to the north coastal road. The

Great Northern Highway lies on the map like an aorta leading out of the heart of Perth, branching into arteries large and small, the arteries into capillaries, and the whole overlying a comparable system of blue veins. Red is for roads, blue is for rivers. The innocent traveler is misled into thinking he is entering a region with as rich a circulatory system as that of a freshly flayed man. In this last thousand-mile outward leg of our journey we passed through three settlements large enough to justify our stopping: Moora, whose entire male population was drinking beer in the pub; Geraldton, Western Australia's second seaport, population 12,000; and Carnarvon, the space city, population 2,957. Onslow, the northern goal of our mission, had a population of 260. As for rivers, we did indeed bump across many of them, but only two — the Ashburton and the Gascoyne — had any water in them. (If the Gascoyne had been dry, I might have driven along its bed to the old Yalgathuga Station to see whether anything was left of the first homestead, a platform built up in a tree behind a fifteen-foot fence with access by a rope, pulled up at night as protection against the savage natives of the district. Norman had built the same kind of shelter nearly fifty years ago on Groote Eylandt, for the same reason.)

All along these thousand miles we sought out aborigines as a French pig sniffs out truffles, but few were left now. On one stretch of the road we drove for two hundred and seventy-seven miles without seeing a human habitation of any kind. We might have stopped at the New Norcia mission, eighty miles north of Perth, but I was not about to take any chance of finding autos-da-fé still being practiced behind those heavy walls.

Northward, as the human population declined, the heat and the insects inclined. Before we reached Geraldton the flies floated comfortably in a shade temperature of a hundred and twenty degrees. In Geraldton we found an oasis into which the insidious American way of life had penetrated deeply enough to produce a "motel," run by a jolly fellow named Ernie. Ernie relieved our apprehension about the heat. "Aw, yeh," he agreed, "she's hot orright, but it's a cool kind of heat." On the strength of that assurance we took a tin cabin in which the temperature that night did not in fact rise much above ninety-seven degrees.

Somewhat soggy and dispirited next morning, we put reflection upon Geraldton's cool heat out of our minds and sought out the aboriginal colony, though we did not do much work. Beyond making acquaintances to be pursued later and recording messages we promised to carry to aboriginal relatives in the far north, nothing of import. Norman got a point here and a line there of tribal boundaries all but forgotten while I went off to speak with less pleasant people — the young white louts who everywhere in this sad world talk eagerly of their villainy. Yair, they had bloody good punch-ups with the abos, some of whom resented their women being bought for fifty cents a go.

It was not a matter of virtue with the complaining aborigines, but of valuation. Almost nowhere in Australia for as long as prudery allowed the subject to be recorded did aborigines oppose their women having white children out of casual relationships. The natives showed greater wisdom in this than the wowsers who deplored the practice. They believed integration began not merely at home, but in their beds, and only good has come of it. The part-blood children are accepted by whites in the Outback settlements and welcomed by the blacks. In 1860 the Reverend George Taplin wrote that the aborigines "preferred to have white children, as they were least trouble, and whites sympathised more with them." With the deed done and the children grown, repentance and honor can come, as they did with Mary Magdalene. Marriage, however, did not result often from the sexual relationship; in South Australia Norman's first doctoral student, Fay Gale, found only three cases of white women marrying aboriginal men. One of these was tragic: a full-blood native, Bert Kite, married a white prostitute, and when she refused to abandon her profession, he cut her throat and was hanged.

Three hundred miles north of Geraldton and three thousand miles from Adelaide lies Carnarvon, an extraordinarily rich town for the anthropologist to contemplate. Here among its three thousand people he can trace the whole course of cultural evolution from the Old Stone Age to the Man on the Moon. Here, on an offshore island now bearing his name, the Dutch mariner Dirk Hartog in the year 1616 (while Shakespeare was dying in England) set the first white foot on Western Australian earth and nailed to a tree the famous pewter plate (as well-known to Australian children as Plymouth Rock is known to American schoolboys) inscribed with a record of the event. Here, nearly four centuries later, the Carnarvon Apollo tracking station picked up the first electronic pulses from Neil Armstrong's radio as he set the first human foot on the moon and implanted the American flag on a landscape even barer than Dirk Hartog's. Here, at century intervals, other great exploring pioneers left more than ordinary records of their visits. In 1699 the gentleman pirate William Dampier stopped to survey the country, declared it to be utterly worthless, and wrote the first description in English of the Australian aborigines. They were even more loathsome than the country, he said; the most degenerate human beings he had seen in earlier voyages to the nastiest parts of the globe were gentlemen to these naked, black, dirty, fly-blown, and apathetic savages. Early in the nineteenth century Sir George Grey, questing for the antipodal Grail — water — found near here the trickling Gascoyne; with its water he went overland to discover his *wondjina* cave paintings. And was speared by the aborigines.

At Carnarvon's Native Welfare office we met Bob Williams, one of the memorable people in my Australian adventures. Bob's name and position as liaison man between the mission and the local aborigines notwithstanding, he was a full-blood Tjuroro, a people once located two tribes inland on the scrub borderline between the coastal natives and the ferocious desert warriors of the spinifex and sand. Tall, dark (as distilled midnight), and handsome, vital and virile in his sixties, Bob was a man of extraordinary achievements. In his youth and early manhood he had lived at times with the savage Wadjari — whose name is whispered still by the Carnarvon people — lived with them, fought with them, and took his wife from them. Converted to the true faith only four years before our visit, he already had good English, drove a Land Rover assigned exclusively to him by the mission, and was organizing the scattered pockets of disgruntled and dissident remnants of the lost tribes. Defeated these people may be, but they will still execute any aborigine who ranges too loosely through the old tribal countries. Bob overcomes the difficulty of free passage without the traditional message-stick passport by cleverly using his position as a native missionary. What Bob was doing — more for his own aggrandizement than for the glory of God, perhaps — might be compared to a Jew organizing the Arab states and converting them all to Judaism.

One day we took Bob to dinner at what we had been told was Carnarvon's finest hotel. As we were leaving the dining room the proprietress motioned Norman and me aside and warned us sharply not to bring any of "those people" in her hotel again. Norman sternly told the woman that Mr. Williams was probably the most accomplished person in this part of Australia and that he might well become the Member of Parliament for this district. And he told the woman what she had been trying to disguise — that she was herself part aboriginal. I had not noticed the fact; I was not then good enough at recognizing one-eighth part-bloods, but I should have guessed from what David Carnegie said of the integrating natives of this region so long ago: *It is marvellous how soon a tame boy comes to despise his own people, when he far outstrips any white man in his contemptuous manner of speaking about "a . . . blackfella."*

Bob was to prove our best informant on this fringe journey. For Norman, he drew in tribal boundaries as skillfully as a draftsman, speaking all the while eloquently and authoritatively of tribal and sub-tribal divisions like the Mandi, the people of the immediate Carnarvon district; the Maldjana, dominant people of the coast; the Ingara of the south bank of the Gascoyne in land now split into the Idadgi, Wirunga, and Kalegi stations, and so on, *und so weiter, in saecula saeculorum.*

For me (doing a little conventional anthropology for a change), Bob drew out of his memory the marriage pattern of the dominant Maldjana, which I put into an obfuscate paradigm:

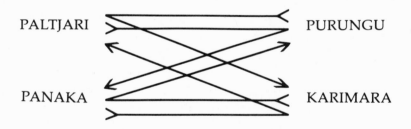

PALTJARI   PURUNGU

PANAKA   KARIMARA

Impossibly far from the central desert Aranda, the terms are cognate, but not otherwise similar, and again meaningless in their semantics. As a four-section system, this accords with what I once cherished as an environmental explanation for the causes of exogamy (the harder the country, the more complex the organization), but the more one analyzes these things, the less consistency one finds in them. Extrapolating to political systems, one must conclude that any system

244

works as long as it is enforced. It is not reliably productive to ask even so good an informant as Bob Williams whether the systemic pattern is adhered to. But talk long enough and the answer comes out. After recording hours of cyclic myths from Bob, we let him choose for the tape recorder whatever he personally thought well to preserve.

"I'll sing you some — ah, I'll sing you a loving song. What you call a 'love song' on the records.

Marungu nganli alangu mulangu mulangu . . ."

This was exciting to us for its rarity. In the primitive world emotional love songs expressing the temporary insanity of infatuation are almost never found. But here was a genuine aborigine singing a genuine aboriginal love song which I knew could not be translated into any lilac rhetoric. I asked Bob what it meant, the words being apart from anything I knew in the western desert language.

"This means this girlfriend — he is saying, 'I'll hold you like this, my girlfriend' — *marungu*, we call him, means 'girlfriend' — 'Dear, I'll hold you like this, because I'm crying' — that means *mulangu mulangu*, means 'crying.' See?"

"Why would he cry?" Norman asked.

"Well, because he loves him. See? And the girl loves him. They both love one another. That's what he means, see?"

I thought for one egocentric moment, *Dear God — can these descendants of Dampier's Yahoos have felt what so few of us advanced people have experienced — love so intense that one cries at the touch of a lover?*

In retrospect Bob's song still remains for me an astounding thing. Partly for the nonsense of the question, partly to disguise the shivers of emotion flowing up and down my spinal column (somehow I felt he did not have a right to feel what I had felt; it was much too personal, too much mine as an individual), I asked him, "Would that be a girl he would marry sometime?"

"Yeh."

"If this man were a Paltari, would that girl — his girlfriend — be a Purungu?"

"Yeh, somewhere about that."

"If he were a Paltari he wouldn't sing this song to a Panaka?"

"Na. He gotta sing it to his own. That was the rule when I was a young fellow. The law was straight then. Now they are giving the law away."

What about the old rituals? Did he know them? Yes, but some had to be let die for want of holy men to carry on their sacredness. Others Bob was himself adapting into friendship ceremonies for boys, so that everyone could know how to behave toward one another, now that the old law was gone. He strongly recalled the bad times when the local tribes, pressed on one hand by the whites and the other by desert savages, fought among one another until the white men, for the sheer nuisance of this sempiternal squabbling, threatened the extinction of all.

No, he did not know the name *keibara*, but he did know about a mythic song telling of how a bush turkey, *ba:duru*, carrying a fire in his head, was pursued to a great water by two brown hawks, the *korakorara*. No, he could not at this remove sing the song, but since we had to come back this way on our return from the north, he would direct his memory back to its recovery.

What about a red, dog-killing kangaroo, not *malu̱*? Yes, that would be *kulbili̱*, as the Tjuroro named him; the Wadjari called him *kulbirba*, a proper cheeky fellow, my word.

Next day at Bob's home, a corrugated iron cottage buried in rich foliage within a clearing of tamarisk trees, feathery fans against the heat, we met his wife. Could he have wept for the touching of her? Yes, why not? What of the fact that she was the most savage-looking female I ever had the pleasure of meeting. Short, square, five feet tall standing and four feet tall lying down, her hair bright blond and her skin desert golden, Mary Jane Williams was the embodiment of everything the coastal folk feared in the desert Inlanders. Much of Bob's status here, I felt, came from his having taken and tamed her from the Wadjari. Again, looking at her, I thought of the history of desert people, how everywhere they would explode at least once a generation upon the docile outlanders. Often they were small, less civilized except in weaponry, but fearless and understanding that attack usually won. She had command over three or four languages, exercising her authority most cruelly over *Engli*. We recorded from her two hair-raising songs, beginning with a scream, each of them, and gliding down to a howl, carrying a machine-gun chatter of plosive syllables. She asked us to play these songs to her sister, Eulie Dingo, who lived with her husband Irwin and their children in Mullewa, seventy miles inland. The songs still lie untranslated somewhere in my fifty

246

miles of recording tape. One day I will master them, but so far even transliteration is impossible until I find out where to put in the continuum the white spaces that signify separation of words. The English of her speaking is hard enough to get on paper. As introduction to the message songs she put this into our microphone:

Irwin Dingo? When you go up dere, you give message to my sister son. Dis is song I'm singin. You know dat song, my boy? See what you hear about, what I'm singin. Dat should break you up, my boy? Dat's all d'song.

Mr. and Mrs. Bob Williams at Carnarvon, W.A.

Good-bye, my boy, and good luck to yourself. Now I talka my language now to my sister. Nanagalawaladgidjangawaalumama. You hear dat? Dat will break you up. All bodies bin singin dat song an Minya's modder bin singin dat and we bin dancin under dat song, my sister. Dat's d'song, I put it trrrough. And you glad to hear dat, my sister. Op pourse you don't know what to do to you. Good-bye, my sister, God bless you.

247

To all the people we recorded on this fringe journey we offered ourselves as message bearers, to pay back something on the debt of early explorers along this desert line — Carnegie and Canning among them — who sent native carriers back to the outpost towns with the inscrutable "paper yabber."

It was a happy time for us with Bob and Mary Jane Williams, sitting in the cool of the tamarisks, drinking lemonade, meeting Bob's many aboriginal friends. We stayed long enough with these people to get further than picking their brains of almost forgotten times, to learn of their thinking as well as of their memories. In this century running downhill, we all became pensive too soon. Mary Jane would remember someone she knew in times long gone and say to his spirit, "Poor ole fella good luck to you God bless you." The old men put their past against their future and lamented, "I don't know why we turned around and threw our law away."

They wondered about us, too, and what was happening to our souls. They knew of the unimaginable scientific apparatus being installed at the Carnarvon Space Vehicle Tracking Station and the plan to put a man on the moon; but they had heard on the wireless also of what puzzled them more — the peace protesters in Perth. Were soldiers all finish? What was happening? Many of them remembered at least two wars in which Australians fought, every white man able to walk volunteering to go overseas to save England their mother, leaving Australia to the aborigines. So sad to drive through those dead little settlements in Western Australia with their cenotaphs in the square preserving the names of dead soldiers whose towns died when they died. Remembering these places and the multitude of heroes gone, all I could answer the aborigines was, "We threw our law away, too."

On another day, Norman and I drew out our *bona fides*, set our faces into the scientific scowl, and butted our way past security at the Carnarvon tracking station, past the periphery open to ordinary people, and into the heart of the place. Entrails, not heart, for a better anatomical metaphor here, for the installation of two Univac 642B computers and their adjunct electronic equipment was in progress, and the wiring lay over every floor like masses of boiled spaghetti. Though the station was being operated jointly by NASA and the Australian Department of Supply, Americans were a small minority among the Australian Engineers. Dressed in the Aussie scientific uniform of short-sleeved shirts and walking shorts, they were picking up heaps of wiring and throwing them this way and that. *Dear Christ, my ethnocentrism exclaimed, they're not letting those bloody Australians handle this stuff, surely?* I could hear them say, "Aw, she'll be right, mate." After work, some of these fellows would go back to the Port Hotel — the most highly recommended hostel in the settlement — where Western Australia's entrance to the twentieth century is so precariously recent that they have the toilet paper padlocked in its lavatory cylinder. Who in the name of good sense would want to steal Australian toilet paper, which is about as soothing to one's bottom as sandpaper? It did not help my confidence in the local personnel to look out the windows at the station and see the thirty-foot dish of the Unified S-Band radarscope swing wildly across its azimuth as its operators, for a bit of Aussie fun, shot crows out of the sky with the powerful radio pulses.

Everything was bewildering. Red and white banded poles rising around the horizon among more complicated gear were not really "peppermint sticks," as the staff called them, but sensitive space-ground antennae. That concrete mixer was just a concrete mixer, and not a disguised little radarscope. What was that thing over there, looking like a billboard to which a thousand aluminum — beg pardon, mate, *aluminium* — pie plates had been nailed? Aw, mate, that's a VHF receiver, picks up one watt of radio current at lunar distance. That C-band radar has only a thirty-two-thousand-mile range with a two-yard margin of error. Cost five million Australian — that's five million six hundred thousand American, mate. On the wall formal portraits of President Lyndon Johnson and Queen Elizabeth looked down uneasily, as if they had been up to some mischief before we entered the control room. A likely couple, that.

Outside again, we wandered around the installation. Suddenly that crow-shooting USB scope snapped across the zenith and headed its beams down — toward me, I thought. Frightened, I ran underneath its housing.

Sitting there among the struts, I thought of an incident that happened a handful of years ago, when the great minerals search began on the desert east of here. A helicopter was flapping over the empty desert, scanning for underground wealth. Suddenly its pilot saw a smoke where no smoke could be — this was uninhabited country, he

249

had been told. He changed course and flew toward the smoke, and saw beneath it a family or two of naked aborigines; since they were entirely unrecorded, they had to be uncontacted people of the Old Stone Age. In inconceivable terror, they ran underneath the sparse brush. The pilot, an Australian with the same bad habit of Americans — doing harmful good — lowered his craft upon them, blowing the leaves off their pitiable hiding place, exposing them like Adam and Eve in the garden under the sword of the avenging angel. But he brought not the sword — only cornflakes, a case of individual packages, which he threw out to the terrorized aborigines. Then he pulled up and swung away for his horizon. Next day he returned to see where his Paleolithic friends were — and found them leaping up and down, making signs of worship and joyous supplication to a benign flying god from some other Dreaming than theirs, no inimical mamu, but a bestower of gifts. They had eaten the cornflakes and found them good. Manna will enter their mythic remembrance as it did the Jews on another desert four thousand years away.

I thought too of the Woomera missile station on the other side of the desert and wondered whether the aborigines might not have a better understanding of all this than I did. As scientists (of an equivocal kind, to be sure) we were considered to be initiated males and thus qualified to be present at proper-fella big corroboree business, a privilege denied women and boys in both Woomera and the bush. We had eaten dinner there among the staff, and noticed with amusement a sharp division among the several grades of initiated scientists — founded, like the aboriginal grades, on no observable achieved distinction. The radarscopes were the power-shooting tjurunga, against which visitors were sternly warned; their antennae were the waninga (strangely similar in design) drawing down the mana from the invisible dimension. We had entered that sacred place by showing our credentials, our message sticks, passports through the tribal boundary. And finally there was the great rocket, an immense erect phallus, spraying the earth with waru fire, coloring the earth like mapanpa ocher, penile blood, raising the spirit up to the stars of the Dreaming. The gantry technicians, we were told, urinated on the rocket to make it finally effective, as the aborigines urinated on ocher to mix it into consecrated paste.

A government scientist at Carnarvon explained the complex in language as unmeaning to us as the ritual singing was unmeaning to the wati kuritjara: "*The up-link system comprises voice and digital command sub-carriers combined with the binary ranging code system developed by the Jet Propulsion Laboratory. The voice sub-carrier is derived from a 30KHz oscillator frequency modulated with voice from a 100Hz to 3KHz. The digital command update is bi-phase modulated at 200Hz onto a 1KHz/2KHz phase shift keyer, then frequency modulated into a 70KHz sub-carrier oscillator.*"

"*What the* hell *was he talking about?*" *I asked Norman a few moments later, as we stood inside the mobile trailer housing the VHF receiver control computer and watching it flash up six-digit numbers five to the second, "and what does* that *bloody thing think it's doing? I can't even* read *the bloody numbers, much less understand them.*"

"*John, we are aborigines in a new world.*"

It was right back into the comfortable, comprehensible past for us at dawn, up the bare coastal track to the outward terminus of our fringe trek, Onslow. The rich obligate cultigens of Carnarvon did not continue, as I expected; almost immediately after leaving town we found the country reverting to dry sandy soil and sparse scrubby plants. Marking the Tropic of Capricorn within a few hundred yards of cartographic accuracy was a thick line of great termite mounds, slabs of red concrete-hard earthworks built to heights of ten feet by the secretions of *Antitermes meridionalis*, named for their obedience in staying within the tropics. These were the famous "magnetic" anthills, oriented in human imagination to the Magnetic Pole, but in mundane reality set ninety degrees around to expose a broad area to the swing of the sun. *Heat and eat* might have been the motto of these voracious rascals. With omnivorous ants on one side and violent hurricanes crashing in from the sea on the other, the road to Onslow is understandably more devoid of human beings than even the Nullarbor. Not even nymphs have been seen up here.

Onslow, across the gulf from Exmouth (where those insidious Yanks are building a huge installation, described with little conviction as a "telecommunications base"), is in a sense the outpost of our civilization. No other town is more remote from other settlements, if we reckon distance by the roads one must travel. Though it was the sea base for the nuclear testing of 1953, Onslow is under the tyrannous command of nature. Tides rise to nearly ten feet (the aborigines

251

used to ride these to offshore islands) and cyclones strike with predictable regularity. In fact, the town was moved in 1926 twelve miles from its original pearling-port site to a more sheltered bay — but it still was smashed flat by cyclones in 1934, 1961, 1963, and 1965. We checked into the town's one hotel, washed in suspicious water, and were eating a minimal dinner when we heard outside a series of rapid popping explosions. Armageddon? Had the Russians struck Exmouth? What a hell of a place to die. We ran outside — to see Onslow's entire contingent of long-haired louts farting up and down the two-block main street on bloody Hondas. Stimulus diffusion brought the concept of California's Hell's Angels but it did not bring the equipment. These youths had the "blue denim trousers and motorcycle boots and black leather jackets with an eagle on the back," but instead of Harley-Davidson hogs they rode absurd Honda scooters. Jesus Christ.

What else do Onslow's two hundred and sixty inhabitants do for kicks? There is a gym, in which a muscle-nut leads a thoroughly integrated group of white and aboriginal children through useless calisthenics. Next year, karate with white canvas pajamas, twentieth-degree black belts, and bare feet. One would think they get enough exercise here running from the cyclones.

The town's one communal meeting place is a milk bar. We ventured in to drink reconstituted milk shakes, each richened with a cherry-sized lump of Australian ice cream (which comes in two flavors: dirty white and pale brown). We fed sixpences into the jukebox, filled to my taste with American country-western records peppered with the work of a few indigenous hillbillies. One of the latter was interesting enough for me to fetch the tape recorder and take it down for another sixpence — "The Steps that Namatjira Climbed" — sentiment for the tragic Aranda artist slopping over into sentimentality.

On the morning of our second day we drove out to the small reserve where, we had been warned, we might run into one of the country's "most villainous aborigines," one Louis Sampey. But Louie was orright — in fact, an excellent informant; he was knowledgeable, frank, and fearless, except for one thing: he did not want to say anything about a group known as "McLeod's Mob," to which, we had heard, he attached himself now and then during depressions in individual mischief.

252

Whatever else we have to say about it, McLeod's Mob is the most fascinating socioeconomic experiment ever to arise among the native aborigines. Appropriately, it is also the most difficult experiment to get accurate information about — it has had several chroniclers (notably Donald Stuart, who tells about it in his nonfiction novel *Yandy*) but all of them, for very silly reasons, look upon McLeod and his band benignly. Witness Kerr, working out of two M.A. theses:

Native leaders, some of them of the older generation who possessed authority derived from tribal status, and others of the younger generation who possessed newer ideas and were able to express them in English had, with the assistance of D. W. McLeod, a white station contractor, arranged several meetings of natives, mainly centered around Port Hedland, in the Pilbara area. These meetings, aimed partially at obtaining better wages and employment conditions for natives but more fundamentally at setting up communally-run pastoral stations and mining activities, culminated eventually in a strike which involved native workers from quite a few pastoral properties.

Don McLeod a contractor! The baastid has been a Communist for donkey's years. We will refer to him delicately as an agrarian reformer. What he did was to cast the dice — Australian-*kip the nob* — across the Murchison and construct a commune among proletarians more primitive than existed even in Marx's philosophy. He conceived one of those bloody brilliant ideas that the most accomplished Australian rascals come up with to keep sympathy and admiration on their side. He got himself an aboriginal liaison man, one Dooley Binbin (whom we shall meet again), rough and tough and charismatic and clever, and set about solving a mission impossible: to organize a general strike among illiterate aboriginal pastoral workers to occur secretly, simultaneously, and spontaneously along a thousand miles of northwest Australian stations. He sent Dooley to a Marble Bar storekeeper, a "good man" (read again "agrarian reformer"), who would give him for the incipient strikers a pile of calendars each with a red mark covering the first of May (when else?). Dooley was to take the calendars along the strike route, marking for the local aboriginal leader the day each calendar was delivered. The local man would then mark each day from that point every morning and when the day mark coincided with the red mark, every abo on every station would lay down his tools. The effort would be assisted by the comrades of the

Seamen's Union, some of whom could read calendars even without marks. And so it chanced that on May Day of 1946 every aboriginal station hand who was not sleeping went on strike. Unfortunately, McLeod did not issue instructions on contingency plans, so the strike collapsed on the second of May with some of the strikers going back to work and others giving up work forever.

About four years later McLeod formed his "Mob," philosophically communistic but practically monarchic, as these things go. Not to put too fine a judgment on it, the cooperative was one of those nut communities dear to Australian and American intellectuals. Before long he had about three hundred natives living together in the old way — or in the old way plus McLeod as an absolute paternal monarch. Consistency has never been a strong suit in these things; the mob so separated themselves from white Australia as to avoid even the crossing of whitefella roads — but their income derived from grubbing out asbestos, wolfram, scheelite, and tantalite to sell to capitalist warmongers to build weapons of aggression for the perpetuation of imperialist neocolonial running dogs. Tantalite especially cannot be practicably extracted from exposed iron deposits by existent technology, so back to the good old days and ways of human slavery disguised as communality. Everybody was equal, but more equal than the others were Dooley Binbin, whose "comity" of bloody great black bruisers enforced lawnorder and strict obedience in the classless and weaponless society, and of course McLeod himself. Every man Jack of the community — and every woman Jill — had to collect every day one "fruit" (a thirty-ounce fruit can) of tantalite yandied from surface iron with a magnet. No fruit, no bloody food for you that day, mate. This regimen was for the field hands; the house servants had their fruits topped up by the field niggers each according to his bloody orders.

It is the way of the world, communist or capitalist, that all economic enterprise becomes individual, one way or other. Shortly before our fringe expedition McLeod had bought several barren stations and had a treasury of an estimated four thousand dollars' worth of tantalite (and rubbish) in American gasoline drums. A succession of corporations was formed — most importantly, Northern Development and Mining Co., Pty. Ltd. How does that grab you for a Communist endeavor?

254

Ah, well. Governor William Bradford, three years after the Pilgrims landed on Plymouth Rock, lamented,

The experience that was had in this common course and condition, tried sundry years and that amongst godly and sober men, may well evince the vanity of that conceit of Plato's and other ancients applauded by some to later times; that the taking away of property and bringing in community into a commonwealth would make them happy and flourishing; as if they were wiser than God. For this community (so far as it was) was found to breed much confusion and discontent and retard much employment that would have been to their benefit and comfort.

And so it was also in the Pilbara in 1966. A young counterrevolutionary, one Ernie Mitchell, broke off half of Don McLeod's colony and marched down to Perth to get Native Welfare chief Gare's permission to revert to the policy of each getting what he bloody well earns, mate. McLeod and Dooley and the remnants of the comity and community are still noodling around the northwestern corner of the Great Sandy Desert.

We had one profitable day recording and filming Louis and Tillie Sampey, Maudie and Veronica Doughton, Jack Smith, and Dan Gilba, whose combined knowledge quickly filled in the last blank spaces on Norman's map in this region. I even felt far enough ahead of schedule to lie on the Onslow beach in the tropic sun for a couple of hours, watching a curious purple cloud growing on the northwest horizon. Tomorrow we would visit the Native Welfare office and talk to the administrators to get their view of the aboriginal situation.

But at dawn we were roaring back down the track to the south; at sunset there was no Native Welfare office. On the previous evening Norman and I had strolled up to the post office — for kicks — to read the notices posted on the door. One was a telegram, received a few hours earlier, warning all residents to get into the storm cellars, for Cyclone Shirley was spiraling in from the Indian Ocean. We looked at the damage done to man and his environment by earlier windy ladies from the northwest — buildings smashed, palm and coconut trees and people decapitated by the flying knives of corrugated iron roofs — and decided to get out of this bloody place *tout de bloody suite.* Well, not *tout,* because Shirley might accelerate and catch us out on the track, but at the crack of dawn.

At seventy miles an hour — the speed at which the Tojo becomes dangerously unstable — we were able to keep ahead of Shirley's pursuit sufficiently to get some nightly sleep. Our plan had been to strike east out of Carnarvon on this return leg, through Meekatharra and Wiluna (the jumping-off place for the Carnegie and other early exploring expeditions), and down to Cundelee Mission on the north edge of the Nullarbor. But the weather bulletins we picked up on our transceiver radio dissuaded us from getting off even so bad a track as the Great Northern Highway. Shirley had smashed Onslow with the worst destruction in five years; the Native Welfare office was one of the buildings totally destroyed; Shirley was giving signs of breaking up into torrential rains all along the western border of the desert; and all travelers were forbidden to make any deviations from the recognized roads to the east.

At Geraldton we had gained enough on Shirley to break inland ninety degrees for Mullewa and Mary Jane Williams's relatives, the Dingos. And not only the Dingos, as it happened, but such fascinating people as Jack Comeagain, Eric Papertalk, Ivy Wingo, Bessie Dingo, and Queenie Dann, a "proper Wadjari, my oath."

Shirley, moving inexorably down, began to spray preliminary rain upon us, so we hurried to the Dingos — Eulie, her daughter Bessie, and Bessie's children. Eulie was Mary Jane's sister, all right; hair gray instead of golden, but with the Wadjari ferociousness pulsing through as strongly. She sang us a few songs, though time and "too much Engli'" had erased much from her memory. One pretty little tune she sang into our recorders was a *ngunga ngunga*, a lullaby, whose lyrics translated to "Granny will beat you with a stick if you don't go to sleep." That's what makes Wadjaris.

On this tribal business, now, Eulie was more a hindrance than a help, since she insisted her Wadjari were different from other Wadjari, and in fact were not really Wadjari at all, but Nogan, which meant "Wadjari." And there were divisions like the Kurduba, meaning "Don't Say It," and the Kurudendi, meaning "Speak Like That." I should have liked to meet — and join, if I could — the Konin, whose name meant "Poor Fella Me." She could not tell us much about circumcision, because when she was a young woman, "dey nebber let woman know, dey knock woman on d'head if dey know."

Eulie was a howling success as a singer of the wilder Wadjari songs, a high C above Mary Jane at least. We took them down, with some

256

fear that the tape recorders would shatter. During one of the songs daughter Bessie sidled over and whispered to us, "Top Forty."

Bessie too was a memorable person. A big strapping handsome girl in her late twenties, she was the mother of six variegated children, all sired by different fathers of at least three different colors. But all of the kids were going to school, by Chrise. Her pride seemed to be concentrated on her ten-year-old, Irwin, who sang for me and the recorder a most remarkable song ("from Queensland," he said):

> *Oh, they chew tobacco thin*
> > *In Queensland;*
> *Oh, they chew tobacco thin*
> > *In Queensland;*
> *Oh, they chew tobacco thin*
> *And they spit it up again*
> *And it runs all down their chin*
> > *In Queensland.*

I have no doubt that happens in Queensland, having been through the state and met its denizens, but the song originally came out of Kansas in the sod-busting days.

Mullewa has had more than its share of tragedy, even for an outpost. From here several ill-fated expeditions moved off into the Gibson and Great Sandy Deserts, of which the best known for the sheer incredibility of its misfortune was the Wells Party. And here, in our presence, the foredoomed "Operation Self Service" of the Mullewa Native Council collapsed.

Aboriginal legislation passed in 1964 gave impetus to native enterprise, and out of this stimulus had grown the Council and its hopeless agricultural operation. Norman and I looked up the records for background information after we were invited to attend as guest observers the disposition meeting of the Council. On paper it looked as if the assistance given the Mullewa aborigines (who had been assured full control of the project) was not merely adequate, but prodigal. The land — a thousand acres altogether — was donated by white station owners in the district on condition that certain production minima were achieved within three years; failing these goals, the land would revert to the donors. To develop the land other individuals and organizations made substantial contributions. Father Edmund of the

Pallottine Mission gave a hundred and sixty bags of seed. Elder Smith Goldsbrough; Mort, Dalgety and New Zealand Loan, Ltd.; and the Westralian Farmers Co-op, Ltd., gave five tons of urea; this was immediately matched by the C.S.B.P. and Farmers, Ltd. G. A. Williamson and Sons donated one hundred pounds for skilled labor. Ampol, the Australian Petrol producers (whose gasoline is drawn from the same American tanks as every other Australian gasoline), gave 1,740 gallons of distillate; Ampol's great competitor BP (Burns-Philp) contributed all the oil and fuel necessary for the development of five hundred acres. Tractors and other clearing machinery were promised for a share of the produce.

At the meeting I had the tape recorder turned on, surreptitiously. Although the Native Welfare officers, invited to give their advice, did most of the talking, the aboriginal officers — President Charlie Comeagain and Secretary Eric Papertalk — understood the situation just as well and were every whit as intelligent. For both I had the highest respect — and helpless sympathy. The farm, named Tenindewa, was a manifest failure. Before seed could be planted the land had to be cleared. Clearing virgin Australian land is, apart from the problem of finding water, the single greatest obstacle to farming. With the best equipment clearing takes the better part of two working seasons and much risk capital. The aborigines' work force was fifty-three men, laboring for promises. To get the tractors, the Council had to use them first to clear nine hundred acres of the lenders' land — and then, when the tractors were needed for the Tenindewa clearing, the lenders found it impossibly inconvenient to lend them. The Council had to buy its own tractor at the inflated Australian retail price of nearly twenty-five thousand dollars — a fatal mistake, certainly, but what else could have been done? The Council was not a committee of agricultural experts, and by the time it learned that superphosphate was essential, there was no money left to buy it. The land donors had assured the Council that the least it could expect from the farm's first crop was $8,400; what it actually got was $245.66.

The meeting was a very sober one. One Native Welfare officer said the aborigines were no longer working the farm. The Council answered that the people were hopelessly discouraged, as well they might be. No one put the crippling fact into words, but everyone (including myself and Norman) knew that the donated land would revert, and that it had been given in the first place in the certainty it would come

258

back cleared and free of the aboriginal workers. In the circumstances Eric Papertalk's letter to the Mullewa whites was generous:

Many Mullewa people think we can't do anything but next year every-body will see what the Mullewa native peoples can do. . . .

We are doing our best, and if some of our people should fail, we hope the white people will understand and not criticize.

The meeting ended with the reading of a complaint by a delegation of white farmers that aboriginal dogs were becoming a nuisance.

Coolgardie is large on the Australian map. Once it deserved its representation, for at the end of the last century it was a bustling city of some twenty-eight thousand miners digging out a thousand tons of pure gold. Now the mines are closed, the gold is gone, and only six hundred people remain, boozing in the swilleries and thinking of the days of old, the days of gold, the days of '93. On one corner of the two remaining blocks stood the Denver City Hotel, by its name alone interesting to me as a Coloradan. I asked the proprietor how his hostelry got its name; he did not know, mate, he said, because he "ony been here twenty-six years."

There once were aborigines in Coolgardie, following the men who followed the gold. David Carnegie, then surveying for a prospecting organization, recorded:

Travellers on this road had been kept lively by a band of marauding black-fellows, most of whom had done time at Rottnest Jail for cattle-spearing, probably, on the coast stations. Having learnt the value of white-fellows' food, they took to the road, and were continually bailing up lonely swag-men, who were forced to give up their provisions or be knocked on the head, since hardly any carried firearms. The finest prize that they captured was a loaded camel, which in some extraordinary way had got adrift from the end of a large caravan, and wandered into the scrub. The Afghans, when they had perceived their loss, tracked the camel, only to find it dying in agony, with its knees chopped nearly in two. This was Jacky-Jacky's way of putting the poor beast down to be unloaded. Happily, after a Warden was appointed at Lawlers, a troop was sent out, who broke up the gang and captured most of them, at the expense of the life of one black tracker.

One of these thieves paid our camp a visit, but the sight of a rifle, combined with a smart blow on the shins with a stick, quite satisfied him that he had come to the wrong place.

The Golden Mile — Kalgoorlie and its satellite city, Boulder — was a little better, as it bloody well ought to be, Kalgoorlie being the second city in all of Western Australia's million square miles. The Mile once held more than two hundred thousand prospectors and their camp followers; the population is now down to a tenth of that, most of them depending for subsistence on a precarious pastoral industry and one large government-subsidized gold mine. It is beginning to grow again since the recent discovery of nickel and other minerals in the region, but you can still buy a house for two thousand dollars, and somehow the metropolis of Kalgoorlie does not impress you as being entirely cosmopolitan when you see, as I did, one nearly naked aborigine chase another with a spear only one block from the center of town.

The aborigines here are a surly bunch and we were not able to get much out of them except excited rumors that something big was going on at Meekatharra involving Bob Williams, Dooley Binbin, and a young man accused of showing sacred *tjurunga* to women and boys.

From Kalgoorlie the road deteriorates into a track up the northeast line of dead and dying gold ghost towns three hundred ragged miles to Leonora and Laverton, on the southeastern edge of the western deserts. Nothing along the track but sadness — rich red-bark mallee turning to white-bark mallee turning to scrubby mulga turning to spinifex and sand, with the skeletons of once hope-filled towns here and there to tell of better days, forever gone.

Leonora is only three blocks long and only a handful of its shops are still functioning, with the weakest possible pulse-beat. Its one accommodating inn was named the White House Hotel, and that jogged from my memory's shelf of pending cases the fact that Herbert Hoover, thirty years before he became President of the United States for the purpose of inventing the Depression, had been chief engineer and manager of the Sons of Gwalia gold mine near here. I went out there and found his house occupied still by the mine manager, who was supervising the dismantling of the dead mine's machinery preparatory to abandoning the whole enterprise, house and all. I found a side street named for him — and just as the Democrats predicted for all of America back in 1932, grass was growing in the middle of it.

But now we had the scent of sandalwood, sweet on the wind; our western desert was just beyond the settlement; and at Leonora we found a large band of aborigines, fugitives and refugees from the desert tribes — like one unfortunate, in hiding from his tribe's vengeance for having capriciously killed a man he should not have killed. We also found that another American anthropologist had established squatter's rights — literally; we saw him first sitting down at a ceremonial ground, beginning the work that would result in anthropologists being barred from further contact with the desert people. Had I known then what I know now about this fellow, I would have kicked him in the head, but in my ignorance I respected his priority.

Sidling around the periphery of his territoriality, we got nevertheless a rich haul of information from the several score natives camping around the settlement, including Wereka (sister to my old buddy Tjipikudu), green-mouthed from chewing *mingulpa* spiked with *pitjuri*, and Tenindi (a relative of Bell Rock Jacky). We felt we were home again — and we were, however roundabout our great loop of more than five thousand miles from Adelaide had taken us. Being excellent and foolish fellows, we poached informants almost not at all; still we could work legitimately, by right of Norman's old acquaintance with them, with some of the elderly men. Three of these — Billy Windun, Pindawanu, and Old Charlie — were young initiates when Norman made his first motion picture of subincision forty years ago. The immediate recognition was so strong that I seemed to share in it. And it was a nice courtesy of fate that Norman found here a group of people with an unfamiliar name — "Tika Tika" — he heard about during the Lungly Gully sweat-quest and tried to visit then (this mob was at that time out on the desert), but could not, because Bob Verburgt had broken both axles of his truck in a dry creek bed.

At Laverton the Tika Tika men were not in very good nick. They were, we found quickly, a band from the Pintubi tribe and therefore unwelcome among the Ngadadjara, dominant here. With no assistance whatever from the American inventors of racism, the Ngadadjara made the Tika Tika sit down on the ghetto edge of the clearing, and when they ventured into the prohibited area, all of them were promptly speared — none fatally, however. Norman had to take them a half mile away from the other men to interview them.

Primitive as they were, these half-dozen intruders were clever. One day, when we were working with a Tojo-load of aboriginal men beyond easy walking distance of water, the Tika Tika fellows asked us to take them out. Well, we thought, it's their skins; so we complied.

But the cunning rascals had a good thought in mind; when we pulled up at the singing circle, they jumped out of the truck before it stopped and shouted to the hostiles to come get some drinking water — *kapi* bloody *pulka*, our bloody drinking water, mind. The greedy baastids consumed thirty gallons out of my tank before they quit, and the Tika Tika blokes looked on, smiling generously and generously urging them to drink up. The ploy worked; the Tika Tika were rewarded by being allowed to sit "li'l bit close up" in camp thereafter.

We went as many times as we could to the secret daytime sings, with permission because I carried half the bloody mob in my Tojo. I got some good stuff in these sessions — three or four hundred feet of 16-millimeter color motion picture film, a recording of most of the songs, and many Rollei and 35-millimeter color still photographs. To be there at all in the sacred singing Norman and I had to be placed in the two generational circles. As a sun lover, I was not pleased to be put into the shade moiety, *Ngombaluru*; but since the shade people sat in the sun, it was orright. Norman as my "father" went into the sun moiety, *Tjindulakalngoru*.

One curiosity I had to ask about. An unusual number of men sat away from the singing every day, making spears. For their fighting, I was told; there was a distressing amount of enmity to be released by holes through the thighs. This same American anthropologist's smarmy book later declared with the sanctimony required by Consensus Anthropology that there was no spearing, that the people were all gentle, that they hated war and grew their hair long. Only white Americans settle disagreements by violent means. That is a well-known fact. Everybody knows that.

I did pinch one of his informants, justifying the theft by telling myself this fellow, a rough gentleman named Witjika, was too violent in mien for his use (he would say "utilization"). I first saw Witjika spinning a roll of human hair — *nampa* — for making a *yinka*, a man's girdle that may go to several hundred yards of spun hair, depending on how sacred the rite it is to be used for. Witjika I also recall vividly for his description of a distant journey he had made:

Comealong comealong comealong comealong comealong comealong comealong makim makim makim makim makim Mini Creek; goalong goalong goalong goalong goalong goalong goalong — PINIS!

Jimmy at camp beyond ghost gold town of Laverton, on the south-western edge of the Western Desert, exultant after a night of spear fighting

Knowing my interest in religious change, Norman told me that night, as we spoke from one swag to the other, about the totemic anomalies of the Tika Tika men. One had the Dreaming of the Pussy-cat — *putika* in their Pintubi tongue, *pudjikata* in the Pitjandjara language. Norman went on to raise a pertinent and important point: he knew a Ngangamerda man whose *tjurunga* design had literally to be dreamed, but the fellow could not make the pattern come good until the accidental sight of a Worcestershire sauce bottle in a bushman's swag gave it to him — the writing on the label. And of course it is common knowledge among Australianists that on the north Carpentarian coast gin bottles thrown overboard by the early Dutch mariners were found and used by the aborigines as sacred totems. And why not? What could be a better source of spirits?

Presently Norman began making mewling noises about an appointment he had shortly with Neil McFarland back in Adelaide to go hunting bugs in the Flinders Range, so we broke camp and piled aboard the Tojo for her last leg through the bush. We were pleased by the data we had gathered along the fringe — sorry only that we had not been able to get a coherent account of the "big business" at Meekatharra, which had even the Laverton men on socioreligious tenterhooks. Evidently it involved an initiation, an unprecedented public trial of one man on a capital offense, and an equally unprecedented Apalachin-style meeting to determine who if anyone would be the aboriginal *capo di tutti capi* of the Western Australian fringe. It would come to us one way or other, *bimeby, koara*.

My faithful companion would not have been Tindale if he could have got straight back down the track from Laverton to Kalgoorlie without one deviation of substance. Now it was to stop in at the Mount Margaret Mission, thirty miles into the southern bush from any other settlement. Nor would it have been Norman if he could have set foot anywhere without meeting an old aboriginal friend from the almost abandoned past. At Mount Margaret it was Petawara, still another of those 1933 initiates.

The deviation took us to Kalgoorlie by a track running through towns like Kookynie, totally abandoned. What a place to film science fiction movies on life — or the absence of it — after the Bomb!

Though I said nothing about it to Norman at the time, I had made a decision at Madura not to drive across the Eyre Highway again, that the Tojo should have a smooth ride across the Nullarbor on the transcontinental railway. Norman was surprisingly agreeable to the change of plan — not that opposition would have changed my opinion.

Watching the Tojo being secured by cables to a railroad flatcar, I felt glowingly altruistic, as if I had done some great kindness to a human being. Well, it *was* a kindness, even if the subject of my consideration was only an inanimate Chevrolet engine set in a chassis made in Japan by a subsidiary of General Motors. I would do the same even for a Volkswagen, peace stickers and all. What would happen to my old cobber when we returned to Adelaide and I flew off to America? To the knackers, perhaps? If the Tojo had had just a *bit* more virility, I would have put it out to stud.

In view of the other most improbable coincidences I have experienced in Australia, I was not overly surprised to meet in the dining car of our train W. H. Douglas, my favorite Australian missionary, bound for Melbourne. And I had him trapped for 1,108 miles — how I would be able to pump him! That is my bad angel speaking; actually we spent most of our conversational time swinging Irish bulls by the tail and talking about Ireland the Ould Sod.

Like Browning's "Fra Lippo Lippi," Wilf Douglas had also been a waif taken to the Church because no one else would have him. It came good for him, though, for he was happy serving God, and he served God constantly, whether he was working with his mission to the aborigines or trying to pound Australian linguistics into the white man's hard head.

So much more than I conceived possible when I decided to make a narrative out of my terse journal, religion looms now out of my experiences as the crucial force in the lives of most of the people whom I met in Australia. Everything seems to yandy down to that, under the surface of things we all suppose to be more important. And under the institution of religion, its purpose in making man more than the animal nature condemned him to believe he was. Integrity, above all, from which all other virtues grow. An unhappy unbeliever my-self — I opted for reason too early in life to change now — I so envied those who had a belief, whether in the Wati Kutjara or the various manifestations of our culture's God. Of all my experiences nothing touched me more deeply than the absurd, incoherent, but deeply emotional sermon I heard from a woman, very old, among a pitiably small band of evangelists who came into a little park across from the Beaufort Hotel one night when Norman and I were in Perth.

They were preaching salvation out of the Elim Four Square Evangelistic Church (possibly an Australian colony of Aimée Semple McPherson's California church of miracles). The Elim Four Square people — four men and the old woman with a portable organ — were in no danger of making inroads upon the evils of the world. They outnumbered their audience, which included myself and my tape recorder (carried like an attaché case with the microphone hidden in my jacket pocket). I wish I could say the old woman in her sermon had been either eloquent or organized. She was neither. By the time I got my recorder going she had gone clear through Creation and was right up to Noah in a sentence long enough to have come out of the soliloquy of Molly Bloom. Her theme was the history of sin.

They never had rain in those days it was simply dew and everybody wanted to get in the ark even animals and birds I had a sheltered life I'd walk under a hotel and pass by and not know whether a man was drunk or sober that's how simple I was in those days I did not know what sin was till I came to find the Lord Jesus Christ but when I came to find the Lord Jesus Christ I found there were a lot of things that can turn you away from the Lord when you know about them you don't get trapped I'm sorry for people who get trapped in hotels there's a hotel we'd like to have that for a Pentecostal hostel but what does it do it's bringing people out intoxicated into the streets and we've got to start preaching to them that's my hotel because I can prove that back to whom that hotel really belonged and I am that said person but because of the foolishness of man selling his birthright for a broth of beer I have missed out on that hotel but as far as I'm concerned that hotel is a Pentecostal hostel it might not be in my time but we've got upper rooms where people can come out sober-minded and we can say "Praise the Lord brothers and sisters" and they will respond in like manner so we pray that the Lord will just do that for us and next door there is a wine shop that gets them drunken and here we are good people out here in Korea little children that want bread and butter and things like that I say all these people that are on Social Service should be going into cultivating beautiful country like I saw the other day with gorgeous orchards beautiful orchards I suppose somebody's wealthy too but we don't need to be wealthy we are wealthy so we need to till the ground and we need to tin the fruit and we need to tin the peas and tin everything and it should be sent over to these children so friends I ask you to join in with us and to be very expedient in your remarks and be very sure of your grounding and be very positive how you're going to spend your money because this money has come from the Man above and He is watching what you're doing it says in the Scripture about the talents one man dug a hole and put it underneath when he came to get it up well it was all just as it was when it went under only it was a bit more rusty others had doubled their talents and so it goes if you can't give well give your own self and give your voice and give what talents you have and Jesus will see you through.

She tottered over to the little organ and in an old woman's voice, quavering like a kookaburra's call and altogether unbearably beautiful, she sang "Grieve Not, My Soul, for I Have My Saviour." Dear, dear old woman! Her religion will see her out. It will not break faith with her.

Wilf Douglas had been at Meekatharra and had brought God back from the Big Business. He was not at all eager to speak of its sociopolitical aspects, and I had to piece out his deliberate imperfections with my thoughts in some cases and with what we had heard from a score of secondhand witnesses in others.

About seventy oldmen — *wati yina* — intertribal delegates, with their wives and children, had come from places as far apart as Port Hedland in the farthest northwest and Port Augusta on the southeast line of civilization, to make judgment on a young man accused by his elder brother of having shown sacred *tjurunga* to women and uninitiated, partly Christianized men. This was sufficient cause for a smaller assembly of tribal leaders, but there was more on the agenda than a capital crime. Digging down into the situation, we found Bob Williams as the actual organizer of the council, and his reason at bottom to be his ambition to become leader of all the tribes and tribal remnants of Western Australia's fringe dwellers. Shabby business, one might think, for an aboriginal Christian missionary — to wallow in mundane ambition. But are not politicians the most moral men in our culture? To succeed, they must abandon all vices except ambition.

Dooley Binbin brought in his augmented comity from the northwest principally to see that Bob did not bring off his *coup d'état*. Old Dooley did not appear to have all the nuances of politics in hand. He was supposed to be a Communist, but he was also the nominal head

267

of McLeod's capitalistic enterprise, Nomads Ltd. With his surly goon squad prominent in the audience, Dooley opened the meet with what he felt was the one important question precipitated by the charge. "We got to decide," he shouted, "what religion we got to follow — Catholic, Country-Liberal, Labor, Church of Englan', and den dere are Christians as well." Wise in the ways of debate, he departed for a sleep after making this inaugural address, so that he would be fresh to carry his own resolutions when the others had been wearied by parliamentary squabble.

Bob Williams was more than Dooley's match. After Dooley had taken his leave, accompanied by his punch-up boys, Bob put his humble request to the elders. He outlined the difficulties and dangers they would all have to face very soon now, since mineral prospectors and developers were pouring into the Pilbara and intruding into the edges of the desert itself with their machines, their money, and their vices. He had experience in both worlds, more than any other man, and he was offering himself to all the tribes as the liaison leader. The old men were struck with consternation, for few had any concept of an intertribal leader. While the first wave of surprise rushed through the delegates, one of Dooley's men ran out to tell him of the awful thing Williams had brazenly asked — and it was awful in every sense, because it was a request for permission to commit regularly the crime of moving freely among the tribes.

Dooley, nearly mad with anger and dismay, ran back with his roused comity to the assembly and began to denounce Williams, the missionaries, the silly receptiveness of the oldmen — everything he could think of. As he ranted on, he lost all sense of propriety and began to venture into secret religious regions few in the audience were qualified to hear. Wilf Douglas, invited as *amicus curiae*, had an inspiration; he dashed over to Dooley and put his arm around his shoulders. Along the way, on the edge of the assembly, he passed one of his own mission boys who had fallen to his knees, wailing a prayer with his head bent nearly to the ground. Remember: an embrace of one man by another is a rare public act, restricted to certain related men in restricted circumstances. There is no equivalent in our own society — unless we were to imagine a formal white-tie-and-tails presidential reception at which an ambassador of another nation demonstrated his regard for the President by zipping open his fly before the cameramen. The President in such straits might well do

268

what Dooley did — fall down immediately in a swoon of unbearable emotion. Wilf later asked his mission boy what he had been praying for at the moment of crisis. "Oh, Mister Douglas, I pray for the Lord to stop Dooley from talkin', to strike him to the ground — but not hurt 'im!" These minor miracles happen all the time to Wilf, pumping even more *mana* into his status as perhaps the most successful missionary to the aborigines.

When the Meekatharra assembly had settled down, Bob Williams skillfully meliorated his request to mean that what he had asked for was only the liberty to go about freely among the tribes, preaching the right law for all men. The oldmen from Geraldton shouted to him, "Welcome!" The Jigalong mob from Dooley's country called out together, "You can come!" The southern oldmen nodded approval, and with Dooley still held in a stupor of exhausted emotion, Bob carried the day.

In a star council later the young man accused of *lèse divinité* was brought to trial. He admitted preaching the Christian gospel, but, he insisted, he had shown no sacred things to the congregation. Yes, he had played a shabby trick right out of the ancient tradition of spellbinding evangelists; he had shaken before his audience a bag, which he implied held *tjurunga*. Like Chaucer's Pardoner six hundred years before him, he had held up a bag full of sticks and stones and *hooly Jewes sheep sholder-boones, to saffron with his predicacioun*. Copping thus a plea, and helped by the knowledge that his brother's reputation for unbridled jealousy was common to all present, the young man was acquitted with a warning that he had better walk straight in future.

The fundamental question raised by the incident came up for discussion: whom should they follow — Jesus Christ or Wati Kutjara? "Who made you a *man?*" asked one oldman of the prisoner. "Jesus Christ or Wati Kutjara?" The answer came not as clear as the oldman would have liked. As an aborigine, the convert was made a man by the subincision ceremony — but he had also been baptized by the water of Christ. One traditionalist shouted. "Jesus Christ for white man, we follow Wati Kutjara!" Wilf Douglas asked to speak; he was given the floor, and he declared yet once more the resolution of the eternal paradox. Jesus Christ was for all men, he said, white and black. But there is no quarrel with Wati Kutjara, for all good roads lead to Christ.

We talked on into other things and finally retired after a New

269

Australian accordionist gave up on his demonstration of patriotism by playing polka hell out of "Waltzing Matilda."

In the morning, the twenty-first of April, we woke to see a better country than the Nullarbor; Port Pirie was imminent, I would reclaim the Tojo once again, and we would sprint into my emerald city of Adelaide before night fell. Occupied as ever with the irreligious mysticism of curiously recurrent events, I reminded Norman that this day was the ninety-fifth anniversary of the fatal return of Burke and Wills to the camp at Cooper's Creek, and ninety-two years since Giles and Gibson came to the tragic end of their journey at the Clutterbuck Hills.

At breakfast on the train we bade Wilf Douglas to fare well in his pilgrimage. He in turn told us of Dooley Binbin's conversion to Christianity, giving me as much food for wonder as for thought. After listening to Wilf, Dooley had drawn out of his personal treasury a couple of pearl-shell knives and asked, "What gave birth to these?" A rhetorical question, for he went on without pausing to hear an answer. "What gave birth to this?" — tearing up a bush. He explained to Wilf what he meant: that the shell came from the salt water, the bush came from fresh water; both — all — had birth in water. He remembered a strange thing that drew it all together: once he had been aloft in an airplane, and looking down on a watery cloud he saw a circular rainbow with the cross-shaped shadow of the plane in its center. Remembering also a text from a Scripture he did not until that moment understand, Dooley saw that all living things came from water, and that at the head of the universal fountain was the Cross of Christ. Wilf murmured, "I am the Water of Life."

EIGHT

INTO THE
DEAD HEART

M y last journey into the desert began with a letter from my old
mate, Bob Verburgt:

Dear John:

*We [he and Wal MacDougall] are still amongst the living but I
guess that you thought we had died, it's been so long since I last wrote
to you. We have been frightfully busy and I'm afraid this year will be
busier for both of us.*

*Musgrave Park [Amata] blew up again early January as the new
Superintendent tried to stop a spear fight by producing rifles and
shooting over their heads. All the white staff were immediately clob-
bered and bruises were won by all. The then Supt. packed up and left.
Jolly good show, what? My partner in crime Wal MacDougall was
recalled from leave and went to Musgrave Park to settle the people
down again and restore their faith in the nasty white man, and he
did a very good job, too.*

*I have been busy in Central Australia with a small Abo group of
ten who I made contact with in June last year. I took the Commonwealth Film Unit up to them in November and we shot 27,000 feet of
film on 35mm on daily life. Some of the sequences should be good —
spearing emus at water holes, cooking and its distribution, stone knife
and axe making, etc.*

*MacDougall and myself have been made inspectors for the pre-
servation of Aboriginal and Historical Relics. This of course suits us
down to the ground and we have made six arrests in the past month.*

*I have just returned from a patrol which was to last four weeks but
developed into nine weeks. The patrol was sent to the Lake Perceval
and Tobin area south of Hall's Creek to dump petrol for future work
in this area. Myself driving the International and the O. I. Giles Met.
Station was to drive the big Bedford 4x4 truck with the fuel. We got*

back to the Windy Corner area east of Lake Disappointment and were caught in 960 points of rain.

We were flood bound for five weeks and after several air drops of food finally got the Inter out but the Bedford is still there, and I heard today that an attempt to recover it will be made in September. Old Tommy Dodd was with me and enjoyed himself. Man, he's tough. I guess I cut ten tons of timber and shovelled 20 tons of mud to finally get out of there.

As you can imagine the country is looking colossal from that cyclone you and Tinny brought down from the north west, with spinifex 6 ft. high and all the wild flowers in bloom. The game is moving back into the areas that were virtually cleaned out during the drought.

John, why don't you come back here? Write for permits to the three states, i.e., Western Australia, South Australia, and the Northern Territory, and also write to the Superintendent of Woomera to accompany me on a patrol. He will in turn refer your request to me and ask if I am willing to take you along. Then we can arrange a trip to almost anywhere we want to go. We may even do the whole chain of waters from Ernabella to Jigalong Mission. It would be good to see you again and if you can get a permit for the North West Reserve we could take Tommy out to the Mt. Davies area and camp there for a week with Tjipikudu and Bell Rock Jacky. This in turn would help me as I have a lot of work to do there. We could extend it to three weeks if necessary, and then we could take old Tommy and the other two and do a trip up the Canning, as there are two groups of people up there that as yet have had no contact with whites.

There it was. Only a few difficulties in my way — getting money for the trip (a publisher's advance solved that) and permission from my university to bug out again. Since I am absolutely indispensable to the university — without me they had no one to teach ethnomusicology, ethnoliterature, Oceania, Australia, Culture Dynamics, and the Dynamics of War as well as lesser academic flapdoodle, and the Chair of Fascist in Residence would have to go unoccupied — the university thought it might be nice for me to hang around a bit and teach for a while, for Christ's sake (I had already put in some sunny time on an eyeball anthropology trip to New Caledonia, Fiji, and a mess of Polynesian isles since my last go at Australia).

Well. Orright, then, said the university, take the summer and fall *terms off, but you'll have to teach double load in the spring and no research grant or travel money, mind. Now puckopp and we'll have a little peace around this place, hah?*

I had by 1968 put behind me any hope of achieving my three strongest ambitions: to run the Boston Marathon, to take Salvador Dali's house at Cape Lligat away from him, and to go out beyond the Canning and discover a Lost Tribe of Aborigines. It seemed that Carl Sandburg's minima for happiness would have to see me out — to have love in the house and to be out of jail. Bob's letter revived the hope of a Lost Tribe. I cannot allow any dramatic tension to build up to the achievement of that quest; my third ambition remains just that still. On this expedition I found no lost tribe, but, as you will see, a talisman instead, of greater worth.

I had other reasons for going back to Australia in 1968. For one thing, I was homesick for the place — I even missed the bloody spinifex, God bless my soul. For another, unbelievable mineral discoveries were being made, and I wanted to see how these were affecting my aborigines. And finally, Joan had to get Down Under to do the fieldwork for her doctorate in anthropology; she had taken up a new career to further richen a life that already had the honors and achievements any one of which would have satisfied any other extraordinary woman.

Westward, then, chasing the sun on advance royalties, across 7,600 miles of Pacific Ocean and two-thirds of arid Australia to hunt for a possibly nonexistent band of pristine naked wild men who had never seen water they could not leap over.

Adelaide! How I love that city. Most of it in the last century, its central city ringed with a broad green girdle ordained by the founding settlers in perpetuity, its sleepy suburbs contiguous with each other and the outer Park Lands, twenty-one miles of white sand beach, balmy weather, and cut right off from the rest of this naughty world by the blank Nullarbor to the west, wilderness to the east, and the deserts to the north. At the Museum my friends were there, just as I had left them — Bob Edwards, back this day from the north with remarkable color photographs of cave paintings: Graeme Pretty, home briefly from an expedition to New Guinea; Mrs. Murphy, the anthropology secretary, for whom I used to scream through the Museum when I wanted anything; old Mr. Cooper, even more now the mouse with his bit of cheese among the stones, looking very old and feeble, allowing himself the merest complaint of failing eyesight and a persistent fever the physicians could not relieve; and Tartangan Boy, two years older and still unmoving behind my worktable. Only Norman was away, chasing bugs somewhere, watching moths to see them turn into butterflies.

A few weeks of gorging myself on juicy meat pies and feeble milk shakes, warming my soul among people who genuinely liked Yanks, and then my permits came through. I bought a great cylinder of maps and as much swag and photographic equipment as I could carry, and flew off for the Centre for rendezvous at Alice Springs with Bob Verburgt. Joan would follow in a few days up the northern air lane to Groote Eylandt, where she would live among wilder men than mine.

I am always a gawking tourist flying over Australia, watching the green wine-and-wheat lands of the "farinaceous village" of Adelaide browning out to desert as the rainfall line dries out, and the oddly proximate wild Flinders Range cutting off a border of practicable habitation. Except for the tiny strip-mining settlement at Leigh Creek I saw nothing of human origin below for hundreds of miles. Lake Eyre put a great ellipse of white salt on the brown desolation; there appeared to be a long narrow billabong of water in its center, for all the good it might do man or beast. We just caught the western edge of Simpson's Desert's ghastly blank, its long sand ridges looking like red finger strokes from our height of twenty thousand feet.

After nearly nine hundred miles of hostile nothingness our Fokker Friendship swung down over the guarding mountains around Alice Springs. There was Bob, on the edge of the tarmac with his big International 4x4-C-1300 two-and-a-half-ton truck, its bed covered by a new green tarpaulin, impregnated red in the back (Tommy Dodd would have said "like a red-arsed spider") from its run to the Alice from Woomera. Speaking of Tommy — where was he? And Tjipikudu and Bell Rock Jacky? Tjipi had left Amata for the Mount Davies "mine" to grub out chrysoprase; Bell Rock had walked down to Warburton; and Tommy had been left, at Bob's decision, at Amata. In writing me of the plans to take Old Tommy Bob had forgotten that our journey would be made in summer, a time of year hardly anyone in Australian exploratory history had chosen to venture out into the Great Sandy, and he just did not relish the prospect of having Tommy die out there. Oh? What about us? *"She'll be right, mate."*

Bob said he had some business in the Alice to take care of, so I went to the movies alone that evening. The one theatre in Alice Springs is a curiosity. It is a walk-in outdoor house, vehicles lacking in enough numbers to make it a drive-in, with reclining canvas beach chairs for seats, set far back from the stage. Again the frontal area for the aborigines, who ambled in by threes and fives. They sat down on the flat in little circles as if they were in the bush, and several built little camp fires until the attendant — himself an aborigine — made them extinguish the blazes with angry chatter. Another aborigine, against the rules, brought a dog into the theatre, and the attendant grabbed a spear and chased him out.

Joan came through next day and Bob drove me out to meet her. She had only a few minutes before the plane took off again, but it was enough for her to charm him into a never-ending respect for me; I could see him thinking, *There must be something in this bloody drongo if he can catch a sheila like this one.*

After the establishment of Alice Springs (first called Mary Springs and later changed to Alice Springs to honor the wife of Sir Charles Todd, who comes into the mystery of the toy roller later) in 1872 by John Ross, with Ernest Giles second in command, when Ross led the Adelaide Overland Telegraph Exploring Expedition through this place, the community was founded on nothing more than its location at the center of the continent. But this geographic fact made it subsequently the base camp of expeditions into the surrounding Never Never, none of which, however, left tracks strong enough to become permanent roads to anywhere. That task remained for the world's great road builders, the Americans, first with the nine hundred and fifty-mile "Stuart Highway" to Darwin during the Second World War. Aussies these days say they built the bloody road, not the bloody Yanks, but it is a well-known fact that Australians will say anything for a drink.

After loading up with canned food and two new tires, we began our expedition by running a dozen miles up the Stuart Highway and then cutting ninety degrees west on the Mount Doreen Beef Track, a narrow bulldozed path servicing a few cattle stations huddled around the Alice.

Civilization stops so suddenly west of the Alice that it was an extraordinary event for us to meet another truck a couple of hundred miles out. Another Banal Impossibility: it was Bill Johnson. I had never expected to meet Bill Johnson on this planet; he was one of those legendary figures of the Inland's folklore who may or may not exist — but if I had expected to meet the legendary image of Bill Johnson, I should have seen him as a wild-eyed maniac with a beard like Osawatomie Brown, a pair of hedge shears in one hand, a can-opener in the other, and a kipper tail hanging out of his mouth. In the legend he spends nearly all his time in the deepest bush, making surveys (his position is number-two field surveyor in the Common-wealth); drives a Land Rover kept as unblemished as a vintage auto-mobile because he precedes it on foot wherever the bush is higher than the bumpers, snipping off brush that might scratch its paint; and lives on dried apples and kipper snacks. The bush traveler fortunate enough to strike one of his track markers can recognize his handiwork because he always has an aluminum kipper snack tin nailed above his blazed mileposts. As an actual person he is a wicked fraud, an indictable impostor. No nut he, but a gentle, pleasant, soft-spoken man of sixty-two, showing signs of madness only in admitting he liked Americans. I mention Bill here with apprehension, because the legend has him infuriated with Len Beadell, the maniacal road maker, who described him (without naming him) as being a bit mad — what with the spinifex-clipping, the apples-and-kippers diet, and his habit of retiring at two or three in the morning and pulling out on the track again at five.

We spoke of Beadell. Bill exhibited no real animosity — another exaggeration of the bush, this grudge — toward Beadell; Len, he said, did great service in bashing tracks through the emptiest spaces of the Inland west — from Alice Springs' southern track at Victory Downs Station an irregular thousand miles west to Carnegie Station, and from Warburton Mission north to a point near the Canning. Indeed this was an accomplishment to rank with any road-making in the history of vehicular transportation. With a half dozen men, a grader-scraper and bulldozer, plus a couple of supply vehicles, he made the only continuously visible tracks in all of that million square miles. But, said Bill, it was a pity he chose to grade the track a foot below the desert surface. When rain strikes any desert region, from Los Angeles to Cairo, it finds inadequate watercourses and so must cut its own, raising hell with the ecology — "as we know it." Fair enough. Beadell admitted as much. His "roads" — especially the "Gunbarrel Highway" — had to be built to supply the Giles Meteorological Station and a few cache points for the Woomera Weapons Research personnel, and there was no other way to build them. They were, Len said, intended to be markers, bench marks on a map, orientation lines for those who had to travel this country and who could not distinguish Crux from Carina in the night sky. What matter if the rare cloud bursts washed four-foot gulleys down his track? The better to see it by. No one, he boasted, could drive across the Gunbarrel Highway without seeing it.

The last settlement we were to see on the thousand-mile outward leg of our journey was the aboriginal reserve station of Papunya, one hundred and eighty miles west of Alice Springs as the desperate crow flies, more by our irregular track. Papunya was on the Plutonian periphery of mission and government native reservations orbiting the Alice. I intended to make some systematic observations here on intertribal culture contact, for this was an artificial meeting place for very diverse groups — confirmed bludgers of partly tribalized aborigines and the genuine myalls — wild men who crept in and out like stealthy dingoes to snatch food and women and run away. Papunya has always been an outstation since it was established by the Hermannsburg Mission to bring the untamed people gradually into marginal civilization. There is nothing else between here and Jigalong, half a continent westward across the desert.

Whatever ideas I had about laying on some instant ethnography were entirely aborted by the time we bounced over the rough track of the outlying reserve property to the tiny iron shanty identified by a sign over the one narrow door as the reserve office. Along the way small groups of aborigines had waved us down to demand peremptorily in a locally concocted pidgin of Pitjandjara and English that we hire them for photographs. *"Pikita po' pai dalla? Mani pulka wia!"* ("Pictures for five dollars? Not much money!")

"What the hell is this?" I asked Bob.

"Aw, some bloody commercial film units have been here and at Yuendumu making documentaries. They hire on a pack of these bloody bludgers, strip them down to their arses, and make out they're right in from the Stone Age. These bloody no-hopers would perish if you took them three miles from the commissary. I nutted out a good title for one of those films — *Brown Skin and White Tits.*"

This was an allusion incorporating the title of Percy Mountford's best-known film, *Brown Men and Red Sand*, and the white skin among

279

the golden tan occasioned by the women wearing brassieres in the ordinary way of living.

Bob had to slow almost to a stop to traverse a dry gully and one aboriginal man jumped upon the running board and stuck a fly-clouded head in the window — my side. *"Pikita?"* he screamed. *"Pai dalla wia — kutjara kutjara dalla, uah?"* ("Five dollars no — four dollars yes?")

Bob chuckled and I growled all the way to the Papunya compound. Pulling up at the reserve office to report in, Bob told me to stay in the truck and keep an eye on a furtive pack of villainous-looking men standing about thirty yards off the fence. Inside the enclosure a small group of very bushy aborigines squatted, obviously frightened of the others. Bob stopped to have a natter with the myalls. They were slow to recognize him (all white faces to them looking alike), but once they pegged him they jumped and swarmed around him like one of their own. He said something to them just before he pulled himself away to go to the office that upset them grievously. One began crying.

Bob came out again in a few minutes with one of the administration officers, a pleasant-looking Scots chap who was to be our escort in our inspection of the reserve settlement.

The settlement seemed to be mostly administration housing — and damned fine housing it was, too. Probably only the Americans in a secret installation outside Alice Springs had better. All the cottages were air-conditioned, and all had Braemar Solar Heaters on the roofs, looking like radar scanners. Hot water for bathing. He took us in his quarters for a drink — Bob and I taking lemonade — and told us about the place and its philosophy, so far as he understood it, which wasn't very bloody far. Reading between his unspoken lines, I deduced that Papunya was grossly overstaffed — about one officer for each ten of the thousand aborigines squatting at various places in the reserve. But where were the administrators? I didn't see any in our tour. In their cottages drinking beer in the cool of the air conditioners. Yes, a pity; but then the people were incorrigible and quite dangerous. Best to leave them alone.

Outside again, we drove past the huts built for the natives. A housing project, lines of tin shanties, rather like an army camp. Again, all empty. The place looked like a scene from *On the Beach*, nothing alive in sight, dust and dead saltbushes blowing around the dirt streets. All the wood door and window frames had been torn out.

"Can't understand these people," said our guide. "We build them these rather nice little homes and they pull out the fixtures for their camp fires and go off squatting in the bush. Strange."

Of course they did not occupy the houses. There were so many of them that there must have been one death at least early on — and that meant evacuation, just as at Umeewarra. We see the practice all over the world. Our American Navajo used to abandon a settlement after a death, and not so long ago, despite their sophistication. It is the same ancient and universal fear that makes us put ghosts in old houses.

Bob said later, "I told Giese [Northern Territory Aborigines Administrator] to build houses with just a concrete slab floor, four steel corner posts, and a corrugated iron roof with a smoke hole in it. They could make their own brush walls and have their fire in the house. And when somebody died, they could burn the brush walls to drive the spirit out. In a week they would have been back in."

The few aborigines we saw around the settlement carried spears and ferocious scowls. I scratched the interview plan. To ask this hostile mob any questions about anything would be like going into Harlem and interviewing door to door about the residents' own experiences with heroin.

After we left Papunya and got on the slowly vanishing western track again, Bob told me about the little band of natives sitting in the protective demesne of the reserve office. They were the remaining members of eighteen previously uncontacted people he had found in August 1966 in the trackless country west of Lake Macdonald's salt pan, two hundred and fifty miles out from Papunya. Bob had spotted their smokes — one column having been put up by the band's women, gathering *mirka* ten miles west of their camp and twenty miles west of their men, who were vainly hunting *kuka*. There was some game in the area, but in loose sand country human beings move slower than snakes, and kangaroos easily stay at a safe distance. Bob found the men first. They were of course terrified by the truck, but he shouted to them in Pitjandjara, "Don't run! Don't be frightened! I am Pitjandjara — I am Puruna!" One of them, parading his courage, came up, put his foot on the truck, and ran away again. All rattled their spears at the truck, since anything that strange had to be a materialized *mamu mamu*, a "debbil debbil," which according to religious rules could be intimidated by a spear or the hook-end of a *miru*. Bob then took down his heavy rifle and with three quick shots brought down three

281

kangaroos. This, now, was something in their line of work, and they came up to admire this strange unmoving *kuḷata* (spear) that shot crackling bursts of *yiṛi* (points) by some form of *mapana*.

Thereupon the men went well beyond the limits of what they thought either pleasurable or prudent, and got in the back of the truck to be carried back to the women. They were all promptly sick. In aboriginal Australia courage is not in the guts.

When the women caught sight of the great *mamu* thundering across the sands with the heads of their men sticking out of its maw, they dropped everything, including their infants, and ran away. When they could run no longer, Bob rounded them up and persuaded them no harm could come to them. The men had a serious palaver about Bob's suggestion that they come in to Papunya, where there was safety — and foods whose variety and quantity they could not imagine. They agreed at last, and, under the leadership of their oldman, were taken in. The old leader was then gravely ill (he had been in the camp when the others were food-hunting), but he became for the trip a grim-lipped, all-wise, indomitable Moses — until he got his people settled in at the reserve, when he promptly took his earthly leave and went to join Wati Kutjara in the night skies.

At Papunya, Bob continued, the people fell into the middle of some very bad business. Although they came from the vague Pintubi country, they were set upon by the resident aborigines — Pintubi, Ngalia, Aranda, and Pitjandjara principally — who, like all wary antagonists, bridling dogs or human beings, kicked hell out of uninvolved newcomers.

"Well," I asked him, "what did they want from you just now? Looked like you let 'em down."

"They wanted me to take them back to their own country. But I can't — the administrators won't allow it. Now that the abos are citizens, the policy is to civilize them."

No doubt of that. The Papunya people already had the vote — I saw on the reserve office fence a political poster urging the support of one candidate for the Northern Territory council. In a couple of years, probably, the Communists would be pushing for aboriginal self-determination, with a seat — or a camp fire on the floor — at the U.N.

"What's going on at Papunya anyhow?"

"The Pitjandjara are trying to take over the place. They claim the

282

reserve as Pitjandjara country and the other tribes have got to knuckle under to them."

"But that's not Pitjandjara country — it's Kukatja country."

"Hell it is. The Pitjandjara outnumber the Kukatja, so it's Pitjandjara country. And now the bloody Pitjandjara baastids have pushed the super into forbidding any of the other abos to hunt on the reserve — it's their 'sacred ground,' they say, and so everybody is on food rations. Nobody does a damned thing except show up for three meals a day."

"The old story," I observed, not very profoundly.

"The government people at Papunya are scared shitless. These abos are hard-goers. They know a punce when they see one. And then you get administrators like the Musgrave Park super who take out rifles and fire over their heads. These baastids ain't silly. They know bloody well no white man is allowed to fire at them, so they just walk up, take the guns away, and beat their arses with them. Christ, if you pull a gun on a man you've got to shoot him or he won't have any respect for you."

"Ever hear of Sergeant-Major Harry Alford?"

"Naw."

"Alford was the only regular policeman in Adelaide a hundred and twenty-five years ago. Aborigines were killing the outlying settlers all over the bloody place, but the Protectors had laid down the rule: no white man was to fire at an aborigine unless the aborigine not only had his spear in his woomera, but had it in the air."

"Jesus!"

"Yeh. You could fire a gun only after you were dead. Well, Alford — he was as tough as our Texas Ranger Frank Hamer, who got Bonnie and Clyde — put the Protector under arrest and made him walk in front when Alford and his deputies were going after a mob of abos who'd killed a twelve-year-old boy. The poor kid had obeyed the law — he waited until the mob had thrown their spears — and then he lifted his father's heavy rifle and killed one of them."

"Didn't they spear him?"

"Oh, yeh; he was dying when he shot. Well, anyhow, Alford got the Protector out in front when they caught up with the killers, and told him not to worry — the deputies would fire back just as soon as the abos speared him. Baastid was on his knees screaming for the police to fire first."

"I never read about that."

"You won't ever read about Indians killing American settlers, either. Not fashionable."

At Papunya we were already far past the beef track and following Ernest Giles's path on his first expedition into the interior in 1872. His Glen Helen, in fact, lay east of Papunya. It was not a good path to follow for any distance. Giles's map of that first probe into the Inland shows his trail wandering like the path in the probability statisticians' model of entropic behavior, the "Drunkard's Walk," crossing and recrossing itself aimlessly, as he looked for water to keep his expedition going. It didn't go. His horses died, his companions came as close to mutiny as anyone could go on dry land, retreating to their last water base, and he alone was pushing on, trying to see on the horizon some topography promising water. At the Ehrenberg Range he turned back, almost exactly ninety-four years before our own arrival at that line of scrub-engulfed hills. And there was no more water there now than there was then.

The land leading over to the Ehrenbergs — at least fifty square miles — was burnt off. I wondered what could have started the fire.

"Old woman," said Bob. "About two years ago the abos had a bad time out here and they had to abandon an old sick woman. They left her under an overhang in the Ehrenbergs with enough food and water to see her out. But she got right on her own hook, went crook at her mob for leaving her to die, and went on living by herself. She burned off the flat to roast goannas and rats. May still be out there someplace. We see fires now and again."

Good on you, old woman, I thought; *I'd like to shake your hand. You're more a man than those damned Papunya bludgers.*

The Ehrenbergs are a travesty on mountain ranges, but at least they are a boundary for the western badlands on an otherwise flat and featureless vacuity. What David Carnegie wrote in 1898 of the flat margin setting off the interior sand ridges on the other side of this dry wilderness serves well to indicate the unchanging character of the country. It was for us as it was for him:

From lat. 26° S to lat. 22° 40′ there stretches a desert of rolling sand, not formed in ridges like those already described, nor heaped up with the regularity of those met further north. "Downs" I think is the only term that describes properly the configuration of the country. "The Great Undulating Desert of Gravel" would meet all requirements should it be thought worthy of a name. In this cheerless and waterless region we marched from August 22 until September 17 seeing no lakes, nor creeks, nor mountains; no hills even prominent enough to deserve a name, excepting on three occasions. Day after day over open, treeless expanses covered only by never-ending spinifex and strewn everywhere with pebbles and stones of ferruginous sandstone, as if some mighty giant had sown the ground with seed in the hope of raising a rich crop of hills. The spinifex here cannot grow its coarse, tall blades of grass — the top growth is absent and only round stools of spines remain — well was it named Porcupine.

Occasional clumps of mulga break the even line of the horizon, and, in the valleys, thickets or belts of bloodwood are seen. In these hollows one may hope to find feed for the camels, for here may grow a few quondongs, acacia, and fern-tree shrubs, and in rare cases some herbage. The beefwood tree, the leaves of which camels, when hard pressed, will eat, alone commands the summit of the undulations. As for animal life — well, one forgets that life exists, until occasionally reminded of the fact by a bounding spinifex rat, frightened from his nest.

Looking closer at the desert, trying to get behind Huxley's turned pictures, Bob and I found much to justify objectively what we both as desert lovers found subjectively. Even in the spinifex we saw patches of the rare scarlet Sturt's Desert Pea (*Clianthus dampierii* to the botanists, *maḻu kuṟu* — "Kangaroo Eye" — to the aborigines); wild or desert holly, a startling mimic of our Christmas bush; and great quilts of Purple Pussycat Tail. Nights in camp were beautiful — sharp, clean air, stars overbright, and the delightful feeling one gets at watching artificial satellites sailing slowly overhead and knowing they are the closest things to you from the outside world. Lying on our backs in our swags, the fire dying to embers, we watched the skies, seeing as many as five different earth satellites a night, and nutting out between us from their direction, speed, and point of disappearance in the earth's shadow, whose they were.

Australians fiercely love their sky, in some measure because visitors from the northern hemisphere regard it as an inferior sort of sky whose best stars and constellations peek in as visitors from the north. Australia's most distinctive constellation, the Southern Cross, is unrecognizable by Americans unless they see it on the Australian flag;

even the Aussies confuse it with the False Cross. The names are as dull as the figurations — Telescopium, Microscopium, Horologium — and over all, the Milky Way, so strong in the south, spreads its dusty light like smog. The aborigines know it well, like all night people, and I wondered what they thought when they saw a man-made satellite swimming through the familiar stars. Does it worry them?

"My oath," said Bob, "it scares hell out of them, too right. First one I saw out with the abos got them jumping up and down like a mob of euros. They thought I might know something about it — the whitefella has changed everything else. So I squatted in the sand and drew a picture of a rocket with a stick. Said there was a mob of torches on top — that's what made it shine; then I raised the stick the way a space rocket goes up — slow, then fast. I made the rocket go around and around on the flat — I wasn't going to muck up the gen by going into the earth-is-round business. Works just as well like a wheel. That was orright, they reckoned. Then a few months later at Musgrave Park with the same mob on Guy Fawkes Night the super set off some fireworks. As soon as they saw the Roman candles go up they started jumping up and down again, shouting 'Rocketa! rocketa!' I reckon the word has got around pretty well by now."

"Speaking of rockets, what about this rocket we're supposed to be looking for around Lake Perceval?" (At Woomera I learned Bob's official mission was to fossick in the Sandy for a rocket, and thought it best not to say anything of hunting down aborigines.)

"Aw, it's their big one — the F4 Blue Streak. Supposed to go out over the Indian Ocean, but this one went down somewhere out there in the sandhills between the Canning and the lakes."

"Reckon we'll find it?"

"Naw. Shouldn't think. They gave me a two-hundred-square-mile grid where they think it is, but I don't reckon we'll find it. Not a hope."

"You say the Blue Streak is a hundred and four feet long?"

"Yeh."

"Our truck is about fifteen feet long?"

"Yeh. Bit longer."

"If they can't find a hundred-and-four-foot rocket, do you think they could find our truck if we broke down out there?"

"Shouldn't think."

"Wouldn't they search?"

"Aw yeh. Been looking for that rocket for two years now. Never give up, that Woomera mob. Every once in a while they shoot a jet out that way. Can't see nothing from a jet, of course."

"No helicopters?"

"Naw. Helicopters ain't got the range."

"How long you reckon we'd last if we got lost with the radio out?"

"Couple of days, maybe. Maybe a week, if we get the water topped up on the Canning."

"Well, that's real comforting."

"She'll be right, mate."

Len Beadell's confident assertion that his Gunbarrel Highway could not be missed proved out well. We nearly broke our axles when we hit it. And we hit it at an intersection of not much and nowhere, a place called Sandy Blight Junction, commemorative of the eye disease prevalent in this part of the continent. Almost as important as the trails he bashed out of the bush are his location plates, incised on aluminum plaques and fixed to trees (where there are trees) or to empty gasoline drums (where there are no trees). At Sandy Blight Junction the plate was crucified to a whitewashed post growing out of a gas drum. It read:

SANDY BLIGHT JUNCTION

Latitude S. 23   11   58
Longitude E. 129   33   35
ROADS MADE BY
THE GUNBARREL ROAD CONSTRUCTION COMPANY

NORTH.   *Vaughan Springs ? m.*
SOUTH.   *Giles 252 Miles.*
  EAST.   *Haasts Bluff 170 Miles.*
        Alice Springs 309 Miles.
  WEST.   *Canning Stock Route 350 Miles.*

LEN BEADELL
17 August 1960

We turned north. We would stay on Len's track (or alongside it, where erosion made the "road" impossible) all the way to "Gary

287

Junction," its northern terminus. This would be our last contact with Beadell's trails — or any other — until our return from the trackless great eyebrow of salt lakes — Lake Blanche, Lake George, Lake Auld, Lake Perceval, and Lake Tobin — the region where we hoped to find the rocket and the wild men.

The desert beyond continued monotonously — flat, featureless, a sea of spinifex with here and there a patch of mulga like flotsam. Sixty-three miles north of Sandy Blight Junction there rose out of the spear grass what at this distance appeared to be a solitary brown hill. I threw the binoculars on it and saw it was — a truck! derelict, burned out, oxidized to henna by flame and the slow burning of decay under the sun.

"Frank Quinn's," Bob said. "He was running a cache for us out on the Canning. Not his fault. Burning out a truck is easy when the spinifex is up — the seeds stick to the manifold and if you don't stop every couple of miles, or even if you do, sometimes, up she goes. Wal MacDougall had his truck burned out last year."

Quinn is another bush identity. He lives on the desert, usually standing alongside his buggered truck. He runs contracts for the government at ten cents per hundredweight-mile, a sustaining but not profitable rate, and his trucks are too old for the work. He carries no radio, since he was severely reprimanded for using foul language on the air. So he is reported in passing by stations in inhabited country, and rescuers (most often by plane) locate him beyond the last place he was seen. I had seen him about twenty-five miles beyond Lungly Gully with a broken axle on an earlier trip, standing with his part-aboriginal son. I was the first person by in four days. "G'day," he had said, "ow'r y' goin' mate orright?"

The spinifex here was still low and hadn't given us any trouble so far, mainly because Bob had installed a triple sliding screen in front of the radiator and another encasing the exhaust pipe and manifold.

We struck our first water since Alice Springs at Jupiter Well, bored by a party led by Bill Johnson a couple of years ago in an oasis two hundred and forty miles west of Sandy Blight Junction. We put its location at 126°15′ East and 22°35′ South, which brought it awfully close to David Carnegie's Family Well — about five miles, as nearly as we could judge. But his location was ambiguous; our map makers drew his placement from his text, though his own rough map puts it well out of the way, at 125°54′ East and 22°40′ South. You cannot rely on any of these maps, old or new. The National Mapping Department was still selling official charts of the desert areas discrepant enough to compare to an American map setting Chicago in the middle of Lake Michigan. At least the Mapping Department has the grace to label its charts *POOR; Compiled from reconnaissance, sketches, etc.*, with *Relief data incomplete.*

In the Australian Inland there are no credulous or even trusting travelers; one makes one's own maps, using the official charts as a base only, the errors and omissions emended by information from many sources, especially aboriginal.

But striking Carnegie's 1896 trail was a satisfaction. I felt at last I was getting into the deepest desert. Stop the truck anywhere now, walk a few yards into the bush, and you could be certain you had put your foot down where no white man had trod before. We had crossed only one trail since leaving Sandy Blight Junction — the wheel marks left by Reg Sprigg's Land Cruiser in 1965. If you have the least common sense in Outback travel you will have forearmed yourself with information on who had been in the region you propose to enter, from the earliest comer; when, why, and whether he had made any mistakes either in his journey or his journal; and how to identify a vehicle or a transport animal by its tracks. Your life depends on it.

You must not on any account let the wits literally be scared out of you. Not far off our track in the Sandy Blight area, two aviators named Hitchcock and Anderson landed for some reason near Lake Mackay while searching for Australia's Lindbergh, Kingsford Smith, in 1927. When their plane was found by a ground searching party it was in working order and could have been flown out but for the heavy brush. The two aviators spent their time, strength, and lives chopping out the vegetation, finally going mad from fear and shock. One drank gasoline, the other engine oil; both died. All they had to do was start a brush fire downwind — it would have taken out the obstructing bush. Even if it kills you, the bush is not all that hard to master, and those who let the bush kill them are not held in high repute by the dinkum Inlanders. In that greatest of Australian bush books, Tom Collins's *Such Is Life*, the rowdy bullocky (bullock-team driver, who carried supplies to the Outback in conditions of great hardship) Mosey shut up a less experienced but better educated companion who had been praising the courage of Burke and Wills by sneering,

Wills was a poor harmless weed, so he can pass; but look 'ere — there ain't a drover, nor yet a bullock driver, nor yet a stock-keeper, from 'ere to 'ell that couldn't 'a' bossed that expegition straight through to the Gulf, an' back agen, an' never turned a hair — with sich a season as Burke had. Don't sicken a man with yer Burke. He burked that expegition, right enough.

. . . They give him a lot o' credit for dyin' in the open . . . but I want to know what else a feller like him could do, when there was no git out?

Bob had the opportunity to do some impromptu track-reading at Jupiter Well. This was an important place for us, since it was a depot, a cache of supplies, one of a half dozen or so in Bob's huge patrol region. We had filled our big tanks at Papunya and had enough gasoline and water to take us to Well 35 on the Canning and the cache there, but we always topped up when we could. One follows aboriginal practice in these things — eat and drink when water and food appear; forget about eight, twelve, and six o'clock feedings; twelve and six o'clock may not come for days, and the cache at Jupiter Well may not be there.

As soon as we were within sight of the well itself, almost hidden in the heavy brush that surrounds natural water, Bob grew coldly tense. "Somebody's been here," he said; "cover's off. Some mug threw the cover off. Christ knows what's down in the water. Fucking thing may be poisoned."

We drew up to the well clearing and I got out first and went over to pick up the cover, a piece of corrugated iron in a frame.

"Let it be! Don't touch it! Be snakes under it! Give it a bash with a stick, run 'em out."

The limb-cribbed well shaft was too dark to see the water clearly; it seemed to be down nine or ten feet. I got a pail from the truck, tied a line to it, and dropped it down, giving the rope a snap as the bucket fell so that it would strike the water open end down. The water was full of the usual muck open water holes fill up with on the desert — birds, bugs, centipedes, a few unidentifiable things bloated to puddings. But there was something else.

"Petrol!" Bob swore suddenly. "Bloody petrol. Some bloody cow

dropped a petrol line in here. And I think I know who it was. I wonder . . ." And he jumped up and ran into the bushes — to another
clearing, I guessed, where he had hidden the gasoline cache. Right
on all counts; cursing, which suffices in the bush to express usual and
expected annoyance, gave way to howls and screams. He came back,
furious.

"If I catch those baastids I'll fix their fucking arses so they'll have
to shit through their ribs. Fucking bloody Frenchmen. They did it
again. A hundred and seventy-six gallons of petrol — four drums.
Gone. Fucking Frogs."

I asked the usual silly question. "How do you know who it was?"

"What the bloody hell do you mean, how do I know who it was?
Come look at the bloody tracks, will you, for Christ's sake!"

I followed him to the clearing and saw depressions in the sand. A
number of shod feet — no aborigines these — had shuffled around the
area and there was a network of vehicle tracks.

"Look at it, will you? Look at the big-wheeled track backed up to
where the drums were. See? The truck went in light and came away
heavy. Now that's a Bedford with sand tires. Over there is the track
of a Bedford van. Sand tires. And you ought to be able to twig Toyota
tracks." Well, yes, I knew that much.

"These baastids robbed my Windy Corner depot last trip. I read
the tracks and had Woomera investigate — three Toyotas, a Bedford
van, and a Bedford truck, all with sand tires. They belonged to the
oil people licensed to prospect this area — a team of two Australians
and five fucking Frenchmen. Fucking shitheaded sons of bitches.
Anybody who'd rob a man's stuff out here is a murderer. John [sud-
denly sober], I'm going to kill those fuckers if I find them. I'll drop
them with the Enfield. No good fucking around with arrests."

"Why would they want to steal gasoline?" I asked for a second
silly question. "Doesn't their company supply them?"

"Too right their company supplies them — but the company makes
them keep a record of their own stuff. They steal my petrol and
haul it to Alice Springs and sell it to some shithead there."

"But a hundred and seventy-six gallons of gas wouldn't fetch
them more than about eighty dollars Australian — and since the
guy they'd have to sell the stuff to would know it was hot, they
probably wouldn't get half that. Figure it. Divided among seven of
them, the take would only be five or six dollars each — for hauling

a load all the way to the Alice. Hell, that's not stealing — that's not even working. Why would they do it?"

"How in Christ's holy name can anybody say why a fucking son of a bitch of a Frenchman does anything. They're *Frenchmen* — can't you understand that? They're not *people!* We're getting some ratbags in this migrant program — the Eyties got their Mafia going, the bloody Greeks copped all the grocery shops and delis, the bloody Yugos'll stab you for your bloody boots. But you can understand them. They're shitheads, but they're human beings. Fucking French baastids. I'll kill them, Christ help me."

A couple-three hours past Gary Junction I saw a homemade sign, just higher than the spinifex. We stopped. On a rectangular piece of metal cut from a gasoline drum the word BILLILUNA, and beneath it, 300 MILES. No road, no track, no trail; nothing but the spinifex flat.

"That's odd," I remarked to Bob. "What's that thing doing out here?"

"Billiluna is the first station to the north, about a hundred miles south of Hall's Creek. Abandoned now, I think. Used to be the top end of the stock route. This is the Canning."

The Canning! My Royal Road to Romance! It should be paved with yellow bricks or gold. But nothing — not the least break of any kind in the spinifex sea, just this sign pointing to a ghost station three hundred miles away. Aren't all romances like this?

We crossed the invisible Canning track and struck into the heart of the Great Sandy, reaching Well 35 before I had time to think properly on the men who had come this way so long ago, few as they were. The true explorers, the first comers, were Forrest far to our north, on a route from the Overland Telegraph Line through Hall's Creek to the coast at King's Sound, in 1873; Warburton in 1873 also, on a route very close to ours, making lethal charts of his track and its features; Giles on his two expeditions of 1874 and 1875 — all of them trying only to cross the hideous desert to the coast, not trying to probe into it. The north-south pioneers were David Carnegie, whose 1896 route we had crossed near Family Well; the ill-starred Wells expedition of 1896, the first to hound that chimera of a stock route up the Sandy; and finally Canning and Trotman at the turn of the century, actually making a line of useless wells and the unusable Canning, whose crazy intention was to open a path for cattle drives between the rich tropics above Hall's Creek and the gold fields below Wiluna.

Well 35 had water but for anything else it was an abominable camp, its wretchedness a function of the heat and the humidity sweating out of the unusual vegetation grown up from Cyclone Shirley's unprecedented rains. We were now in the land of temperatures steadily rising above 110° as one went farther into the sand. I was not able to record the highest temperatures we were to suffer from in the weeks ahead, for my thermometer broke after the first 120° reading a couple of days later — but they were higher. Twenty years earlier I had recorded a 124° top in Death Valley — an official Army reading, since I handled the meteorological duties for Camp Irwin on the valley's edge — but I never experienced heat like this.

"If you want to get any messages out, you'd better get on the blower now," Bob warned. "After tomorrow we go out of range." We had been making daily reports to the Giles Met Station, but from this place onward contact would depend on luck of atmospheric weather conditions. Bob's suggestion came welcome to me; I had been dubious about the propriety of sending personal messages through what after all was a stodgy government medium. I therefore put the message to Joan — a simple statement of longing — between the lines of a mundane report, shot it off three hundred miles to the Giles Met Station, which relayed it through its powerful transmitter four hundred miles northeast to Alice Springs, whose Flying Doctor station rebroadcast it another eight hundred and fifty miles to Darwin, from where it would go on as a radio telegram to the Angurugu Mission on Groote Eylandt, a final four hundred and thirty miles. How wonderful this patchwork inland communications network! But Joan told me later she had got the message, with its interlinear meaning decoded, from an aboriginal woman who had picked up the Darwin leg on her transistor radio and made it public in a tossing boat in the Gulf of Carpentaria on the way to Chasm Island, where Joan and a party of twenty-three aborigines were to visit rock paintings in old ritual caves. "Miss Joan!" the aboriginal woman announced, "you husbin' he sure bin tinkin' 'bout you!"

At Well 35 we went immediately to Bob's cache of six drums of gasoline. It was intact; the Frenchmen had not managed to work their way out here. We topped up the gasoline and water from the wonderful well. The preserving aridity of the air had scarcely allowed the ancient equipment left by Trotman to rust. The well itself was covered, the water good, and twenty-eight feet of it in the thirty-three-foot shaft. The troughs out of which camels and a few head of cattle had drunk a half century ago were in good condition; so also the utility pole implanted at an eighty-degree angle with its pulley on top — through this the hardy working camels had pulled the ropes which hauled up the heavy buckets of water to fill the stock troughs before I was born. The camel story is too long to tell here, but it is a fascinating one. Without camels this part of Australia would not have been won. But when Herbert Hoover brought in his Panhard automobiles the camels' day was done; they were turned loose on the desert's edge and had gone feral. No one knows how many still wander their nomadic ways, but we had seen their tracks for hundreds of miles paralleling our own trail from the Northern Territory border, though they were even more careful than kangaroos to keep out of sight. They are bloody ugly, nasty, stinking, vicious, dangerous, and misanthropic brutes, and I say good on them. Like my Aussie mates, I admire a battler, even if he is a baastid.

I bathed that evening, during the night, and before we broke camp next morning, as if I thought it was my last opportunity for total immersion in this world or the next. Bob, inured to bathless desert life, poured a few score gallons over himself. We filled our shoes as well — makes them doeskin-soft and cool for the time before evaporation turns them brittle again.

Shortly after dawn we packed up and pulled out into the desert's core, choosing what we hoped was a clear sand ridge valley up to Lake Auld. Our imagined fear for water at Well 35 began looming as a reality not many miles out; the radiator hose broke and we blew out nearly six gallons before we could cool the radiator enough to touch it. A hell of a start in man-killing country. At midday we came upon a native rockhole in a patch of clay; by our maps, it must have been the native well called Tarkutju. It was dry. We used the place to set up a communications effort. We had not seen any other human beings for hundreds of miles, and ahead of us were hundreds more with no known people, unless Bob's suspicion of an uncontacted band was right. So, like the radar men who beam prime-number pulses through the atmosphere into outer space hoping — or fearing — for a reply, we gathered up handfuls of brush into a large pile on a rocky flat (to obviate igniting the spinifex), poured a couple of gallons of gasoline mixed with oil on it, and sent aloft a message of our presence to anyone out there who could see it. If there were aborigines in the distant bush, they would see the smoke, no doubt of it; and they would know someone was at Tarkutju.

I saw the reply first because I was wearing Polaroid sunglasses, which made visible clouds the naked eye cannot see. Clouds I saw, not smoke; clouds were suddenly forming in the northwest. And when the reply grew enough in volume, I could see through the binoculars that the clouds were forming at the top of thin lines of smoke. A few minutes later another smoke went up farther to the northwest, on the other side of Lake Perceval, perhaps twenty miles away from the first answering smoke. Probably the women of the group, making their response. The three smokes — ours and those of the aborigines — formed a scalene triangle pointing sixty miles toward us from the dry lakes. On a California freeway, we could have been upon them in forty minutes or less; out here in the sliding sand, looping over the sand ridges like a sidewinder snake, we followed the smokes all day, camping at dusk at a red clay shelter Bob knew as Picture Cave Hill.

We woke to the smell of smoke. Picture Cave Hill was on the edge of a red clay cliff looking far down to the whip-shaped line of salt lakes. We saw that the aborigines' fires had spread, met, and were now racing before the northwest wind across the plain toward us. It would soon strike the sand ridge valleys below where we stood and run down them in fiery fingers. This had to be the end of our search; we could not go forward to the fires and it was going to be a race to stay ahead of them.

Even on the run the anthropologist has work to do. I photographed the ochered paintings on the shelter walls and a weatherworn law-stick *tjurunga* that had been left standing in a recessed corner. In an obviously sacred place like this a communal *tjurunga* could not be taken away as an abandoned object, though early explorers (who could not have been expected to know better) and certain contemporary anthropologists (who could) carried them away. David Carnegie found some of these on his route — "some strange carved planks hidden away in the bushes, which unfortunately we were unable to carry." He wrote about them later to a knowledgeable amateur archaeologist, a Mr. W. H. Cusack in Roebourne, who replied,

The implement you allude to is used by the Mopongullera [mapantjara!], or Rain-Doctor, at their ceremony which they hold annually when they are making the rain. They are very rare, as there is only one every two hundred miles or so in the country. They are generally left at the rain ground, where you have found yours, or placed in a cave, where the only one I have seen in twenty-five years was found. They are the most sacred implements they possess.

The paintings on the roof of the shelter were the most colorful I had seen anywhere: an endless serpent of white pipe clay, its body speckled with spots of red ocher, twined intricately around itself over the whole of the shelter's red ceiling. It was hard to photograph because of the short focus I had to work within and because of the shadows in which it lay, so I used film prodigally on it — four cameras loaded with different films, shot at various exposures. The prodigality resulted in some excellent pictures; one of these is now the background for the titles in my film *At the Edge of the Old Stone Age*.

The fire was moving other creatures besides ourselves. We saw a troop of nine kangaroos swinging gracefully through the spinifex with no regard for our attention; to them fire was the worst of all evils.

We fled also, choosing a valley rather to the north of our approach line, for two reasons: it sliced through a segment of the quadrangle given Bob by his Woomera superiors as the probable landing area of the Blue Streak rocket, and it was a straighter route to the safety of the Canning country. How ironic, I reflected; my previous trip aborted by fleeing water, and this one rubbished by fleeing fire. It was a bitter disappointment to get so near to our people and miss them, just a thousand miles out from Alice Springs, but it could have been worse. As we spun our wheels away from Picture Cave Hill, I looked down on the far plain to the one appreciable land pass through the three-hundred-and-fifty-mile stretch of salt lakes. Through that pass the doomed explorers Charles Wells and George Jones walked, halfway between Separation Well, where the expedition divided, and Discovery Well, where their bodies were found after five abortive searches by Larry Wells alone.

Although my thermometer was gone there was evidence beyond that of our senses to tell us we were in a natural furnace stoked above one hundred and twenty degrees. We had repaired the broken radiator

296

hose and cleared out the spinifex seeds, but we were getting only two miles to a boil, and each topping of the water system meant a loss of a couple of quarts at least. The measured straight distance from Picture Cave Hill was not much, but our route took us through a real maze of sand valleys and ridges; sometimes we had to run ten miles down a sand trough to find a ridge low enough to blast across; sometimes a probing run like that would end in a bowl of insurmountable hills and we would have to go back. Each mounted ridge cost a gallon of water, and there were ten times as many ridges as the map showed — two hundred and nineteen, by count; and since we carried only seventy gallons of water, the country was impossible to cross in summer. What we had to do was run the engine dry, waiting after each ridge for it to cool down again.

Replicating Carnegie's experience, Bob found one unrecorded water hole, a couple of feet in diameter, at a point nearly two hundred miles from the last water source. It had been dug — like the others of its kind — repeatedly by the aborigines, and at this point in its prehistory, it was eight feet deep. Bob climbed down and scrabbled around the bottom for water, finding at last a little moist earth and the bodies of a fall of birds that had gone into the hole looking vainly for water. When birds die of thirst it is time to be concerned. Bob got out his charts and marked in the water hole. This place now became the second location in its hundred-square-mile map rectangle, the other being a previously identified rockhole known as *Kumba*, whose worth is weighed by its name, which means "urine." Bob named his discovery *Tjumpu*, "Left-Hand," his own name among the aborigines.

An interesting thing, this; that the aborigines should think left-handedness so important as to name a man for it. Walter Gill mused upon it in his Petermann Journey, *noting that* tambu *among the Aranda means both "left-hand" and "tabu," and that in Indian belief the left hand is the hand of tabu. My oath, Walter! Out in Polynesia, the homeland of the* mana-tabu-noa *complex of spiritual power, the word is again* tambu *and pronounced so. Our orthographic representation, lacking the nasal, comes from an arbitrary spelling of early missionaries. Going beyond that "outsight," we wonder again whether this is another tie of the Aranda to the Polynesians.*

Our plans were Bob's business, and generally I did not interfere with his decisions, but here I made one suggestion in which he concurred: "Stuff the bloody rocket; let's get out of this bloody place." His mind reacting like a touched steel trap, he replied instantly, "Good-oh," and we turned tail and made for the Canning again.

Between Wells 38 and 37 we pulled back into the sand valleys off the Canning to have a look at a cave shelter discovered by Bill Johnson and named beautifully by him "Glory View Cave" for its magnificent aboriginal religious paintings. One of these was an insigne of the Red Ocher Men — a charcoal Greek cross on a yellow-ocher field within a red-ocher circle.

It is astonishing how little is known by outsiders of the Red Ocher Men. Many whites who have learned almost everything else of aboriginal life have not even heard of the Red Ocher Men, so well enforced is the omertà *among even those of the aborigines who wish the whole organization ended. Anthropological books on the natives and their social organization do not mention the cult and the working missionaries seem not to understand it (even if they know of its existence), yet this aboriginal equivalent of the Southern Ku Klux Klan and the Sicilian Mafia works almost by itself and without opposition to conserve the old moral system of the desert and to make it quite impossible for any native to adopt Christianity fully and still remain an aborigine.*

The cult is nearly universal in Australia; in my own experience (guided, I freely admit, by some extraordinary luck), I saw its trail extending over a great rectangle from Kalgoorlie in the southwest to Coober Pedy in the southeast to Alice Springs in the north to Broome in the northwest.

In the deserts the Red Ocher cult moves right across the whole land in the course of a year, carrying its own ceremonies and myths, touching all tribes in its path, and working as a kind of ecclesiastical circuit court embodying all processes of the religious judiciary. The function of the cult is to punish lawbreakers — not so much the perpetrators of everyday misdemeanors like spear fights and wife-beating, but those felons who blaspheme the laws incorporated in the myths. If, for example, the young man on trial in Meekatharra had really shown the tjurunga *to women, his only chance to escape the Red Ocher Men would have been to flee from his tribal jurisdiction and live in a city or large, well-policed town among other fugitives from their honor and their heritage.*

Sometimes these fugitives are run down, but apparently for extortion, since they are considered no longer to be of use or harm to their people; their souls are irrevocably lost. Bob said the appearance of the cult in an area is held secret from all but the most prestigious of the oldmen, the incorruptible pillars of the tribe. When the intangible wave of the Red Ocher movement comes to a tribe, the wati yina choose the executioners on a basis of demonstrated responsibility, fidelity, and probity. New myths and rituals are sold from a possessing tribe to a receiving one; the chosen men sing and dance secretly in preparation for a general corroboree. Security can be inferred safely, because the sinners do not anticipate the time of penance, which comes during the general dance. A ring of dancers is formed, the dance begins, and continues until at a signal the transgressors are thrown into the center and badly beaten. Deliberate killing is not so often practiced nowadays for the same reason the Klan does not lynch so frequently. But a beating can be worse; the brother of Teddy (the fellow in Lungly Gully with the phonograph and the broken-armed wife) was beaten so savagely about the head that he suffered serious and permanent brain damage.

Women are also punished, but less publicly. Bob said one of these woman-killings brought him into a subtle conflict with the Red Ocher Men, a conflict he won brilliantly. Sometimes it is hard to remember Bob is a policeman first of all. In his first year in that capacity he came through Amata and heard about the death of a young aboriginal woman. Bob knows the aborigines well enough to understand there are no deaths from undetermined causes. Barring fatal accidents (infrequent in a culture of minimal material content) or environmental collapse, a child making it through its first year is well and truly launched for a half century or so. The reserve nurse told Bob she had been summoned to the native camp to see a young woman who had suddenly been taken ill. The girl appeared to have great difficulty breathing, with severe chest agony, but the nurse's examination showed no injury, nor did the woman complain of any. But she died in a few hours, poor thing, just the other day; they live so hard a life, don't they? Well, asked Bob, where was she buried? Oh, the men took her away; I suppose she was buried according to their pagan rites. Good-oh, said Bob, but he was sufficiently suspicious to go drop a flower on the departed's grave. But there was no new grave in the aboriginal equivalent of consecrated ground. Ah, Watson; very interesting indeed — not given a proper burial. Bob looked into the potter's field, where an executed felon might be expected to lie. And there he did find a fresh grave. Deputizing a reliable staff employe to exhume the body while he arranged a hunt to keep the men away, Bob was able to examine the body by flashlight that night. His examination was rather more thorough than that of the nurse; he lifted a breast and found the ribs broken and signs of internal hemorrhage. It was a clever means of execution; her dispatcher had laid the girl on the ground, lifted her breast, knelt on her chest, and broken the rib cage. He knew the station nurse would never do anything so improper as to look under a young lady's breast, and the girl herself could be relied on to say nothing; if she had not lived with honor, she at least could die honorably.

A lesser law officer would have required the oldmen to deliver up a scapegoat for punishment. As a Native Patrol Officer, Bob was under oath to support his culture's law; exceptions could not be made without his giving his own law away, which would have rubbished both him and his law in aboriginal eyes. And a cult enforcement of the traditional native law could not be countenanced. Somehow this business had to be stopped, and a few months in jail for the killer would not affect the next death dance. So what he did was to bury the body again — but reversed in the grave. He and his deputy then filled the grave again, leaving it just short of appearing undisturbed so that he would be well away and forgotten in context by the time a native man noticed that the appearance of the grave was not entirely right.

When that discovery occurred, another conclave of the oldmen was held and the body again exhumed. Finding the body end-for-end must have been soul-shaking to them. Bob said he had a year of smug self-satisfaction while the oldmen had a year of severe worry about who — or what — had turned a dead girl around in her grave. At the year's end — the term Bob set for their punishment by mental anguish — Bob called the men together and told them what he had done, warning them they must never do a thing like that again. No more did they.

We went on to Tjalkiwarringa Soak, thirty miles south of Windy Corner, out of the sand ridge country. The land is rich here; let the focus of your eyes blur a little and you might think yourself in southern New Jersey in summertime. Possibly it was not so rich as I remember; I may have been reacting to its comparison with the spinifex

300

and sand hell we had left west of the Canning. Aborigines might well be living here, for there was much mulga in seed (an edible staple), wild tomato (*kumparataba*), and *ngaru*. It was rich here as well in bird life — red-backed chats, blue-wrens, charms of finches, and exaltations of budgerigars. I have a particular fondness for these creatures — known to people who do not know better by the French word *parakeet*, to white Australians as *budgies*, to ornithologists as members of the species *Melopsittacus undulatus*, and to the natives of the western deserts as *kilykilykari*, a lovely word. Budgerigars, I am convinced, are the most intelligent of all brainless animals. Several hundred of them may fly together in a tight cloud of brilliant green through the fringes of the desert, all changing direction when one of them — a leader, perhaps? — gives an undetectable signal, as suddenly as a school of those tiny, communally frenetic tropical fish of the Bermudan waters when fright takes them. It is hard to confine a budgie to a cage after seeing what they do as free spirits. No matter how valid the theory of survival, I am always enraged by the wilder of the aborigines, who hurl throwing sticks into a formation of flashing green budgies, popping the fallen into their mouths, and chewing them whole, bones and brains and bunions, like so many owls with beaksful of mice, and spitting out the bloody feathers.

From Tjalkiwarringa Soak we turned westward again into rough sandy plains to check on two other aboriginal water holes — Walalukuna and Patjuntja, the one thirty miles west of our track and the other another twenty miles south. Again the signs were encouraging, and I began to blow on hope's embers; perhaps we would yet find a mob of wild people out in the Mount Madley area, sixty miles across trackless sand hill country. It was not to be. At Patjuntja Bob emerged from his regular evening inspection crawl under the truck to announce that the front differential was cracked and leaking oil at a serious rate. The Mount Madley adventure had to be canceled, and with it my last chance to fulfill my purpose on this trip into the Dead Heart.

Bob roused the Giles Meteorological Station on the transceiver and explained our trouble. Understanding immediately that our truck could pack up at any moment, Ron Roberts (the Giles superintendent) said he would sent out a rescue team in the station's new Land Rover with ten gallons of oil and a fluid plastic sealer; if we possibly could, we were to get back on the track at Carnegie Road Junction, running then as far as our oil lasted. The Giles track over to Carnegie Road Junction was one of Len Beadell's last efforts and had been kept in good condition as a major military access should the Chinese threat to the north explode. If we had to get our vehicle buggered in the bush, this was the best bush to do it in. In ordinary times, that is; in extraordinary times it could be as bad as any other. It was just below Tjalkiwarringa, at a featureless place called "McAuley's Swamp," that Bob and Tommy Dodd and Ron Roberts were nailed down for five weeks. Bob and Tommy remained with the vehicles, working to get the smaller one out, while Ron — an important man in the Woomera-Giles establishment — walked thirty-six miles to the nearest place a rescue plane could land.

Driving skillfully and carefully so as not to wrench the diff into more cracks, Bob got us back on the Gunbarrel safely. No matter where we stopped now, the Giles rescue vehicle would find us — not, we hoped, at night on this single-lane track.

Work went on the while. This southern trail to the Giles Met Station, four hundred miles away, took us across the path made in 1876 by the explorer for whom the station had been named. His Alfred and Marie Range lay in sight to the east, and to the west a place fate was reserving for me later, when I had time to make what was for me my greatest archaeological find. The names Giles affixed to this undistinguished land were drawn principally from the group of scientific amateurs who financed his expedition, except when he drifted into a romantic mood. Then he went back in mind to Edgar Allan Poe and christened clumps of bushes *The Tarn of Auber*.

Even more winsome names lay southward across the Beadell track, devised by David Carnegie in his expedition of 1896–1897. Winsome, but tragic, some of them — *Charlie's Knob*, for instance, named by Carnegie for the head of Charlie Stansmore, his offsider, who was to die on that journey. We have met the aborigines' Wati Kutjara; this double-peaked pile of rubble Carnegie named Mounts Gordon and Everard. In his journal Carnegie listed briefly the sources of his place-names, forever to remain on Australian maps:

MOUNT ELPHINSTONE, after my cousin

ERICA RANGES, after one of my sisters

STANSMORE RANGE, after poor Charlie

302

*MOUNT WEBB, after W. F. Webb, Esq., of Newstead
    Abbey, Nottinghamshire*

POINT ROBERT, after my brother

MOUNT LANCELOT, after another brother

MOUNT COURTENAY, after my brother in law

POINT KATHERINE, after my sister

*MOUNT DORA and MOUNT ELISABETH, after two
    of my sisters*

SOUTHESK TABLELANDS, after my father

*MOUNTS ELGIN, ROMILLY, STEWART, after three of
    my brothers in law*

MOUNT ERNEST, after my brother in law

MOUNT BANNERMAN, after my sister in law

Carnegie could have named much of Australia without exhausting
the resources of his family, but once in a while he went off into his
own fantasies, during which he skewered the topographical points
with names that have persisted because they were not understood* —
Thryptomene Hill, the Young Range (because to Carnegie it did not
look very old), Patience Well (commemorating five days of digging
by his whole party to find water), and Jew Well (because the natives
at that place looked to him like Jews).

The only recent intrusion into the area's nomenclature is an in-
appropriately negligible butte named Mount Beadell; Len deserves a
better monument.

A little while before the party from Giles met us, Bob and I inter-
fered with nature and ecology to play God — or perhaps Setebos
would be more correct — in rescuing a goanna from the Yaltaputa
Rockhole, another of those three-foot aboriginal water holes. The
poor baastid had slithered down into the water without giving provi-

* The Post Office, Australia's naming agency, does not overlong hesitate to
alter names for respectability; "Charlie's Knob" is now officially "Charles Knob,"
suffering a double alteration, one for the vulgar diminutive, the other in line
with a policy against possessives. "Hall's Creek" is now "Hall Creek." The
G.P.O. still sees nothing amiss with having two Lake Victorias in New South
Wales.

dent consideration to the need of getting out again. There he was, submerged to what passes in a reptile for shoulders, hanging on to a tiny ledge. I broke a branch from a shrub, hooked it under him, and pulled him out. A pretty specimen of one of evolution's early attempts at a human being, this sand goanna (*Varanus gouldii*) met Finlayson's description well — a "beautifully coloured lizard with a delicate lace-like pattern of purplish-brown on a pale yellow field." The poor bugger was so heavily waterlogged and cold that he couldn't get up off his wrists when I laid him gently in the hot sand. If the eagles or abos don't get him first, perhaps he will grow up to kill small kangaroos.

The Giles Land Rover met us two hundred and thirty-five miles out, when we were on our last fill of differential oil. Bob poured the plastic sealer in along with a fill from the new ten-gallon oil can, we all had a *kapati* and a can of fruit, and started for the Giles station. Our rescuers were Mick Doyle, the chief meteorologist, and Ray Goldfinch, the cook's offsider and a real frontier thumper.

It was midnight when we saw the lights of Giles, the one source of unnatural illumination in fifty thousand square miles, and beyond comparison my favorite constellation in all the Australian night: five stars on the northern horizon:

When we arrived, the men of Giles were passing the two-thirds point on their regular evening ceremony of getting pissed on beer — a sort of boozy evensong. When Bob introduced me as an American, two or three of them draped themselves over me in a warm blanket of alcoholic friendship. *Plonk prens.* "More fuckin beer," one of them called out to the volunteer barkeep. "Nunky pays for all, right, mate? Fuckin bloody right." *Nunky pays for all* — the British phrase from the Second World War translating to "Uncle Sam will buy it for us." What the hell; I'd shout the baastids a round, and did, taking lemonade myself. Putting on a sad, morbid frown, I explained, "Stomach cancer." Nothing else will excuse a man from drinking with Australians. I do not like drunks; I have no tolerance whatever for vices I do not share. Bob rescued me quickly, noticing I was beginning to simmer. He stayed on to talk with them; I took a shower — one of the most enjoyable in my life — got a couple of large bottles of lemonade from the cook, with ice, and retired to an air-conditioned cabin reserved for VIP government visitors, to luxuriate in clean sheets. I could still hear the beery shouting from the lounge, and one short declaration won my heart. They had been arguing the sea, an understandable if inappropriate topic in this desert. Someone made the usual remark about the superiority of the British navy. Then the scream of refutation, with the traditional Australian sanguinary adjective displaced by the American copulatory equivalent, which (judged by its prevalence out here) they had recently discovered: *"What the fuck do you mean? The fuckin British weren't IN the fuckin Coral Sea — wasn't it the Coral Sea that pulled Australia out of the fuckin SHIT? FUCK THE FUCKIN BRITISH NAVY!"*

Ah, the dear men! Someone remembered America's finest hour, and was grateful to her. I suddenly felt fond of the desperate drunks, though I couldn't possibly approve of the fuckin language.

I grew fonder of them in the week that followed. We had not intended to stay that long, but next morning an inspection of the differential and the other viscera of our truck revealed it to be on the forward edge of terminal illness. To survive, it had to be given a massive organ transplant, viz., an entire front end — wheels, axle, suspension, and differential. The diff alone had thirteen cracks in it. Donors for that type of replacement winnowed down to one: Wal MacDougall's truck, now in Woomera. Ron Roberts made the request for its cannibalization in the morning's radio contact with the Weapons Research Establishment. The plea was granted, but with the caution that the front end would have to come overland. Three days at the least. It was in fact a week, for the man who drove up the supply truck was overcome by what we used to call sunstroke at Coober Pedy, and he had to be rescued.

The waiting week was my first leisure in many years. I read all the readable books in the Giles library — including *The Double Helix* by James D. Watson, the story of the Nobel Prize–winning discovery of the DNA structure — fate teasing me again. Nothing else in the library was new; this had been donated by Mrs. W. C. Wentworth, wife of the federal cabinet minister for aborigines, the only woman ever allowed to enter Giles.

To keep this nine-man contingent docile (no appointee was allowed to remain at Giles longer than six months), the government assuaged the appetite for women by surfeiting the appetite for food — and I ate back many of the twenty-five pounds I had lost on our expedition so far. Eating, reading, and playing chess, with a few sorties into the Rawlinson Range — that was my week. As scientific boffins, all the professional staff were chess players, a common *non sequitur* among scientists, army officers, Jews, and other professional intelligentsia. I must have played a hundred games without a loss, coming away with the chess championship of a million and a half square miles of inland Australia.

Some surely damned person once said to me when I was anticipating some pleasurable thing, "First thing you know it'll be over." I have suffered the truth of that ever since. First thing you know it will be over, even life. So the first thing I knew, that Giles sojourn was over and we were tearing down the southern track toward the Warburton Mission. *Was the truck in good shape now? I asked Bob. Aw, yeh; the chassis's cracked and a couple of spring leaves, bearings are making some noises, things like that.*

Jesus — with that you are going into the bloody desert again?

Aw, yeh; she'll be right, mate.

We expected less congeniality at Warburton than we had at Giles, though Giles has the accurate reputation of being the hardest place to enter on the whole continent. We were not wrong. Trouble had seeped into Warburton from the outside, trouble generated by political subversives working upon the soft-headed innocents who in quieter times used to weep over unwed mothers and stray cats; from the explosive conditions on any mission station over whose gate hangs the admonition NO PRAY, NO EAT; from herding together people from inimical tribes in a cornmeal mush democracy imported from the United States; from the unforeseen disabilities of the freedom forced upon the natives by civil rights legislators; from the genetic drive the aborigines share with all other human beings to be just as bad as they are permitted to be; and most of all, from the lack of firm control in a missionary whose own drive seemed to be to make a martyr of himself for whatever denominational heavenly kingdom he subscribed to.

The missionary was gracious enough to us, I will admit; but his home was something that might have been conceived by those early Christian nuts, the fourth-century North African Circumcellions, eager for martyrdom, or the lunatics who had themselves literally immured standing up within the enfolding bricks, praying until they drowned in their own feces. He complained, as if it were a duty, that

306

the natives were taking his fence and the house itself apart for fire-wood, but what he could do about it he was at a loss to say. As a man of God he could not do what Bob or I or a hundred other bushmen would have done — kick their arses, just for starters. He did not even have the language to accompany arse-kicking.

Griselda Sprigg in her unpublished manuscript described the place exactly as we saw it — religiously filthy, with scriptural slogans burned into the walls; the amiable but overwhelmed missionary; confused teachers laboring in a school with a useless curriculum; and about three hundred aborigines living on Payments-for-Praying and the small cash remaining (after mission expenses were creamed off) from child endowment and old-age pension benefits. Fun City in the desert.

Violence was bubbling, its banked heat shimmering like loomings on the desert. Warriors strode through camp, all armed with deadly spears, looking for smaller groups to attack and not showing whites the deference whites are accustomed to. Bob told me that in his last visit someone hurled a spear through the back of his truck. When spears are thrown at Bob Verburgt, it is time to *look out for the locomotive*. In our brief stop at Warburton I stayed within five seconds of the Enfield racked above our seats in the truck. On our first evening there six aboriginal men, more trusting and less wary than myself, were speared. Bob said that was nothing; last Christmas twenty-seven men had been speared in a free-for-all.

Everything was ashes in our mouths at Warburton. After word spread through the scattered camps of the aborigines, the men who knew Bob and me came in and sat down around the truck. They agreed conditions were impossible and they were astute enough to know the fundamental trouble was flabby administration, religious and secular. A couple of the men said there were a few families, bush natives from the other side of Walalukuna, who were crying to be taken back to their wild country. Well, fine; we could have the satis-faction of giving a few people at least their freedom — it would be crowded in the truck bed, but this vehicle had carried dozens before, and we could put in a week with them, observing and photographing them living in the unspoiled traditional way. Bob knew the policy was not to reverse integration by moving aborigines back out into the desert, but he changed the radio crystal to contact Kalgoorlie and radioed for permission to repatriate the group, pleading urgency. *No!*

the low-echelon welfare officer replied; *we're not running a bloody taxi service for bloody abos.* That is not the way to speak to Mr. Verburgt, as the fellow discovered a blistering moment later. *All right, then, you can have a "your responsibility" authorization if they agree this time to stay out there. But check with Mr. Dunlop; we understand he is using them as informants.*

Mr. Dunlop? Ian Dunlop of the Commonwealth Film Unit? What was he doing here? Was he in fact here? Yes, said the missionary when we put the question to him. Mr. Dunlop was editing his motion picture and needed these people to clear up some points of food-gathering and tool-making. That was that; we could not possibly exercise a "Your Responsibility" warrant when two branches of the federal government were involved.

Ian Dunlop's presence was another heart-sinker for me. Poor fella me. I had gone out into the desert three times with a French 16-millimeter Bolex camera backed up by an ancient Bell and Howell with less than twelve hundred feet of color film to make a motion picture of native life, using hairpins and chewing gum and bits of bailing wire to dub in sound, using stills for occasional background shots, and expecting to print 90 percent of the film instead of the usual 5 or 10 percent — and then someone brings Ian Dunlop to this particular place at this particular time.

I have no animosity toward Dunlop; my heart-sinking was based on the comparison of my pitiable resources with his unit — a full crew of trained cameramen, technicians, assorted Erks and Turks, modern sound-synchronized 35-millimeter motion picture camera and a cartful of tricky lenses and other gimmicks, and twenty-seven thousand feet of film run off upon an uncontacted band of natives whom Bob had found for him on an earlier expedition. As a matter of fact, said the missionary, giving the screw a turn, Mr. Dunlop was showing some of the film this very evening.

What to do but go along? When the formal lecture began I was flattened again; Dunlop's research unit had found buried in the archives of the Melbourne Museum a voice recording of Australia's anthropology pioneer, Sir Baldwin Spencer, made in 1901, and motion picture films made by Spencer among the Aranda in 1912. I am as envious as any other man, and this kind of fortune falling on some other baastid was beyond the bearing. Then Dunlop introduced his own film, with the usual prefatory regrets for its not being better.

I have strong opinions on how ethnographic films should be made. To begin with, these things are made for all time, not for the current fashion. Consequently, they must avoid gimmickry — like the old still portraits of the paterfamilias standing stiff with his derby held over his chest or the more recent publicity portraits of entertainers with their greased heads entering the picture from the lower left corner, bearing a pipe. Zoom lenses, when they must be used, should be used as a substitute for the time-wasting separate lenses — no whisking in and out to give the audience stomach-wrenching Cinerama views. And above all, nothing cute. Dunlop seized upon — with his camera, I hasten to say — the breasts of a mother suckling her child. He had more footage on the lady's mammary glands than I had in everything I had photographed in all my picture-making — from the right, the left, the top, the bottom, every direction except out through the tits. Jesus. Sure and tits are lovely things in themselves, but they are not much use in an ethnographic film.

In photographing the daily life of people in a primitive culture — or, for that matter, in any culture whatever — one must not demand multiple takes. The subjects do not understand needless repetition of a natural act, and if they do, they never repeat it properly. You photograph what you see, and if you miss it, serves you right for having such rotten luck.

Nor should the cameraman attach himself like a bloody barnacle to his subjects. He should at most use two cameras, one far enough away to encompass all the subjects (one may be doing something unobtrusive but ethnologically important on the edge of the main action), and he should keep the goddamned camera still. "Motion pictures" means exactly that — the photography of motion. It does not mean moving the camera as in the hand-held craze popular nowadays. The second camera should be set up rather closer to the subjects to catch action the farther camera cannot see. A little necessary motion of the camera permitted here, but no cuteness, no focusing on tits for human interest. Leave the damned tits alone; half of the human race has them and the audience can be expected to know what they look like in general. In the specific there are differences, but the differences are for a woman's lover to know.

Feet are nearly as strong a fetish for ethnographic film makers as breasts. Let a group of primitives start to dance and the camera zooms in on the jiggling toenails. As an ethnographic film viewer, what can

I learn from a close-up of toenails? My interest is in the entirety of the dance, so that it can be related to the events and beliefs on which the dance is based.

Above all, the ethnographic film should be honest. One must not give Paleolithic ladies, desperately trying to become like their white sisters, pai dalla *to take their bras off. Give them the* pai dalla *and take the bras off after you have finished the filming, if that is your bag.*

It all comes down at last to the essential purpose: ethnographic films are for learning, not entertainment. The photographer should be a craftsman but not an artist. In a word, NO PULLSIT.

I went into the room apprehensive and with my heart sunk to the bottom like a Cartesian devil; I went out almost angry that Dunlop had wasted a band of pristine aborigines I had just driven over two thousand miles to find. And the final, insupportable irony was the discovery that all of his twenty-seven thousand feet of film was in bloody black and white. Could not afford color, he said.

Early in the morning, while the aborigines' tiny camp fires were still burning, Bob and I filled our tanks and moved out, with a last slow cruise around the camps, observing everything, like a couple of cops on patrol. Here, more than three hundred miles from Amata, we found old friends from previous work in the Musgraves — Paul Porter, a hulking six-footer, recovering from six spear wounds, Bell Rock Jacky, and Bell Rock's daughter Nia of famous memory. What a change a couple of years and desert adversity had wrought upon Jacky and Nia! Bell Rock looked twenty years older. He was gray-grizzled and nearly blind (trachoma was blinding nearly 70 percent of the natives when I first met them), no longer able to go into his beloved bush. He was imprisoned now by circumstances at Warburton, needing the help of prayer and handouts to support his children, now increased to thirteen. Nia, the temptress, was married and carried an infant in her arms. Her figure was gone; her breasts pendulous, a temptation neither to lecher nor cameraman; she was closer to being a *minymapalpi* (old woman) than an *ipi longkara* (girl ready for marriage). First thing she knew, she would be finish. Bell Rock came up to us with a .22 caliber rifle, his life savings in a little room, buggered — he had bashed the bolt almost flush with the rifle stock, objecting to its unaesthetic protrusion. It was beyond our power to *pixim.*

"Finish," said Bob. Poor old Bell Rock, his *ripela* and his daughter ruined, his admirable feistiness gone forever.

What were my own discouragements to his? I was in hock to three publishers for advances spent on this expedition with the dead-horse work of writing ahead of me; I was so lonely that I found myself retreating to my fantasy land of California in the twenties (Bob was giving me funny looks when I'd dream off in the cab, singing "Ramona"); I had found nothing of real value; before I knew it, I would be back trying to put knowledge and wisdom into the hairy heads of students growing dumber and more smart-assed every year; and everything seemed to be rubbish. From my view Bell Rock was worse off; from his view, this was another phase in an inevitable life of decline. He knew nothing about the theory of it, but he knew that man's function once he had reproduced himself was to die. To die and not to be remembered. The name of a dead man was instantly expunged from the language, even words containing a syllable of his name were tabu. Finish.

Our first camp out of Warburton was a pleasant relief from the rubbish at the mission and my depressing philosophy. In the bush life was day-to-day, tucker from the cans, incomparable billy tea, lazing against the swag and watching the firmament turn slowly, and revivifying in our mind the remembrance of things past, always more joyful than the real experience. Curiously, our talk was never of women, though the two of us were at the very least normal men with normal appetites. We looked forward to seeing our women — first thing we knew we would be in their arms, and for now, life was good.

We bore east toward Giles off the Warburton north track with the intention of probing into a trackless region of possible aboriginal occupation. There were rockholes west beyond the Rawlinsons, and where rockholes existed, there could be aborigines. We had no real hope of finding any of our wild people, but it was part of Bob's duty to inspect the water sources. We could have followed Giles's track crossing the Alfred and Marie Range and over to Butjar, the outlying water hole, but the truck was again making importunate protests against rough country. The crack in the rear differential was larger — not bad yet, but one must cosset a crack in the diff as one must cosset a fracture of the skull. It was the long way around, therefore — past Wati Kutjara, Charlie's Knob, Mount Beadell, across the dry lake

Breaden, through the Baker Range and the Todds to the Giles track and then sharply west again over the Van Der Linden salt lakes and finally across trackless country to pick up Tika Tika, Yalara, and a few other small rockholes, ending at Butjar. Having even less confidence in nature than I have in human beings, I did not myself think this trip wise. A fair amount of this country was rocky, denuded of enough earth to lay down a track. If we should get stuck here, no one could find our trail. As it happened, we lost our own trail, though Bob had been in this country twice before. We never did find either the Yalara or Tika Tika holes. "To hell with 'em," Bob ruled, after we had run in great spirals over the rocks, "we'll pick 'em up on the way back" — the bush way of saying we would never look for them again. So we belted on toward Butjar.

For about fifty miles on the flat we bounced, each with a different degree of confidence, until we passed between the undistinguished red rubble rock of the Clutterbuck Hills on the left and a less distinguished outcrop on the left, nameless. My confidence was better established than Bob's, for about eight miles from Butjar, as nearly as we could guess, the truck hit an unusually hard-based spinifex hummock and came back to earth with the steering wheel whirling in sudden freedom from its function of guiding the truck. Buggered. Bloody buggered.

Ah, well. She'll be right. Bob delved into the steering assembly and found that the Pitman arm had snapped. A small thing. We would just establish our position by the maps, radio Giles, Giles would relay the message to Woomera, Woomera would contact supply in Adelaide, and the broken part would be replaced. It was just past noon; supply would shoot out a jet fighter plane, a bit under a thousand miles in a couple of hours, and drop the part. She'll be right.

But Bob's maps, which he kept in a three-foot aluminum cylinder, were missing. *Left the baastids at Giles. Baastid.* No matter, for I had duplicates. I got them out — or rather, I got it out, for during our Giles sojourn I had taken the four pertinent maps for the remainder of our journey and glued their contiguous edges into one large map, cutting away the irrelevant edges. The edges held the coordinate identifications; I had lines but no numbers. The maps were useless.

And then out of the past reached the hand of Ernest Giles. I am an unbeliever in such things when I allow myself to fall into the deceitful trap of reason, but on this trip there were so many weird coincidences

312

of our being at a certain place on the anniversary of an early explorer's presence that I have not mentioned them. I have followed Mark Twain's implied guidance: truth is stranger than fiction, for fiction must stick to possibilities. Nevertheless, when I allowed myself to feel without thinking, so often I have felt the presence of Ernest Giles. Whatever the circumstances, I had in my swag a Xerox copy of Giles's own map of this region, and that gave me the lost numbers. We got on the blower, raised Ron Roberts at Giles, told him our need and location — and then, again suddenly, malignant fate took control: our radio packed up. We had no confirmation the message had been received.

It was the third day in the Clutterbucks. I was sitting, naked and alone, under my groundsheet set up as a shadowing fly at the top of the first of the Clutterbuck Hills, scanning the eastern sky for the rescuing plane three days overdue. I had time and the mood to think sober thoughts. We had six gallons of water left in our tank, and we could not leave the truck to search for the Butjar hole, for the law of the bush is that one stays with one's vehicle. And judging by the other water holes we had seen, Butjar was probably dry.

We — they — were all bloody mad. Bonkers. Crackers. Every man who had ever come into this infernal bloody country. Look at me for a start. Certified by four university diplomas to have some bloody sense, and sitting naked on top of a two-hundred-foot pile of Jurassic rubble in Australia's Gibson Desert, watching for a rescue plane forty hours overdue. If the old mathematician Archimedes with his Brobdingnagian geometrical paraphernalia could implant one leg of a cosmic compass in this hill and swing the other around in a circle with a radius of three hundred and twenty-five miles, I would be the immobile center of more than three hundred thousand miles of bloody desert, an area as big as all the Atlantic seaboard states from Maine to Florida, with not a single permanent white resident, and if you count only sedentary inhabitants of any color, nobody at all. Mad? Right around the bloody bend, my flaming colonial oath.

Through the binoculars I could see Bob Verburgt, three-quarters of a mile out on the spinifex plain, orbiting slowly on his arse around the disabled truck to keep under the thin shade while he read for Christ knows how many more times the Australian Women's Weekly. *We* had read and thrown away all our paperback junk novels — polluting the bloody desert, my ecological-freak students would say — except a copy of Henry Cecil's Portrait of a Judge which I had been saving against a time of enforced leisure, but the other day a bloody dingo had raided camp and run off with it.

At this distance Bob's head looked overlarge and fuzzier than my eyes usually see things. Bush flies. I had my own hundred or two settled on my face and back and buzzing lazily around my head, but Bob at the truck had the main encampment of this most vexatious of the world's flying creatures.

Bob Verburgt, in whose competence I had placed my bloody life. Except for the venerable Wal MacDougall, now pretty much in retirement, no man in the entire history or prehistory of Australia had traveled more miles across the desert surface. To talk with him you would suppose him to be the sanest of human beings — though I had been a shade juberous about that back in Alice Springs when he tried to communicate in Pitjandjara with an immigrant Italian waiter who could not understand my American-accented English or Bob's Austrine. If I hadn't thought him compos mentis I wouldn't be out here with him now, would I? But just look at him, will you? Just get on the bloody man. His wristwatch slides from his palm to his elbow as he brushes flies from his face — he lost a fifth of his body weight during those five bogged weeks at McAuley's Swamp when he caught food poisoning by eating meat from cans ruptured in an airdrop. On the trip before that he had to leave his two companions with their crippled vehicle at Well 35 on the Canning and blast his way alone fourteen hundred miles to Alice Springs for replacement parts; then too a radioed call for help had brought no response. And he does this for a salary of $3,750 a year. Of course, he does this because he has a deep need to do this. With the small man's hatred of big things, he attacks them — men, trucks, or deserts. He goes after them like a dingo after rabbits.

I put the glasses down and the truck disappeared in the spinifex and casuarina. How in hell would a search plane find us from a thousand feet if I couldn't see the truck from two hundred? A worry. Last night I took out my journal to log the day's notes. Bob had snorted, "You know what you ought to write in that thing for today? Two bloody words: Fuck all." I agreed, wrote them in, and crawled into my swag. Just before sleep took me I thought that death hunted

314

explorers and anthropologists this time of year as if this were open season along the Styx. Two days ago we recalled the death of David Carnegie sixty-six years before; fifteen days ago it was the seventy-first anniversary of Ernest Giles's death; and tomorrow would be exactly sixty-eight years since the passing of poor Charlie Stansmore.

If I had been sitting here on 23 April 1874, I could have seen below me in this little plain two men, one bound for his appointment in Samarra. On 21 April in that year the two men, Ernest Giles and his companion, poor, foolish Alfred Gibson, in hopeless circumstances on Giles's first attempt to penetrate the desert to the western coast, left Jimmy Andrews and W. H. Tietkens at their last base camp in the Rawlinsons and struck west in a desperate reconnaissance for water. Giles recounts in his Australia Twice Traversed *the tragically ironic conversation he and Gibson had when they set out:*

. . . I remarked to Gibson that the day was the anniversary of Burke and Wills's return to their depot at Cooper's Creek, and then recited to him, as he did not appear to know anything whatever about it, the hardships they endured, their desperate struggles for existence, and death there, and I casually remarked that Wills had a brother who also lost his life in the field of discovery. He had gone out with Sir John Franklin in 1845. Gibson then said, "Oh! I had a brother who died with Franklin at the North Pole, and my father had a deal of trouble to get his pay from Government." He seemed in a very jocular vein this morning, which was not often the case, for he was usually rather sulky, sometimes for days together, and he said, "How is it, that in all these exploring expeditions a lot of people go and die?" I said, "I don't know, Gibson, how it is, but there are many dangers in exploring, besides accidents and attacks from the natives, that may at any time cause the death of some of the people engaged in it; but I believe want of judgment, or knowledge, or courage in individuals, often brought about their deaths. Death, however, is a thing that must occur to every one sooner or later." To this he replied, "Well, I shouldn't like to die in this part of the country, anyhow." In this sentiment I quite agreed with him, and the subject dropped.

Two days later Giles and Gibson came to what must have been this very place (though Giles's account, edited by a fanciful British publisher, is ambiguous, and later writers, reading the country by the maps, certainly mistook the Clutterbucks for the Alfred and Marie Range, which I could see behind me on the horizon). As the two men

315

lamented their absolute inability to continue west, Gibson's horse concurred by falling down dead. Giles put Gibson on his own horse, gave him a compass he could not read, and sent him back to the base camp. Back — as they both supposed; but Gibson became confused after leaving Giles, turned west instead of east, and disappeared forever. That was on 23 April 1874, exactly thirteen years to the day since Burke and Wills had set out in the wrong direction from their base camp at Cooper's Creek, the camp abandoned by their companions within hours of the return of Burke and Wills from the north — within hours on the same day, after waiting four months.

On the fourth day we woke with the sun, as everyone must do where the sun is a tanning lamp thrust in your face. But this morning there was a great shadow in front of the sun. I blinked my way to consciousness and resolved the shadow into the form of an aboriginal man, naked but for the merest wisp of a groin rag, standing above me with his hand full of spears.

It would have been no shame to admit to some apprehension, but it was too early in the morning to be frightened, and by the time I was sufficiently awake to entertain such an emotion I realized this naked fellow, for all his spears, was more scared of us than we were of him. If that had not been true, he would have shown himself sooner. He must have heard our arrival four days before. Three days of agonizing before he screwed up the courage to visit us.

I called out to Bob, "We got visitors."

"Yeh, I know," Bob shouted back from his swag, twenty yards or so from mine. "I've had my eye on that baastid ever since he came in sight. He's got his old woman with him, too. See her?"

I looked around and saw the woman — a girl, really, young and handsome, standing a safe distance away in the spinifex. Seeing us both awake and fearing we might shoot him first and ask his intentions later, the man strode off into a clump of heavy brush and planted his spears, butt end down. Returning, he displayed the sign of friendship — fist pointed toward us, fingers down. Bob responded with the sign for "Come here" — repeated swimming motions with one hand.

Bob picked up the lingo easier than I did, and after we had fed our visitors (always the best means of establishing good relations), he began winkling information out of the man's head. His name was Kanaki; his woman was Puratnya. He said nothing about it, but it

316

was obvious that the two had married illegally and were hiding out from their tribespeople over at Butjar until her pregnancy had advanced too far to be terminated. (Abortions are performed by beating on the stomach.) They would then return, she would be beaten, he would take another spear through the leg to accompany the two scars he already carried on his thigh, and life would be as it had been.

Kanaki was the eternal male in this contact of two cultures and four people. He knew damned well he wasn't impressing me or Bob with his head held haughtily high. But he had seen a truck before; his wife had not, and to her it was still a *mamu*, for all its being apparently dead. Our own appearance could not have offered her a great share of security; we were pretty bloody scruffy-looking by now and we both must have handled a score of artifacts she knew not of and therefore feared greatly. They both jumped when I put my hillbilly tape on the recorder and the voice of Leapy Lee came out of the little brown box singing "Little Arrows." But people learn fast; by early afternoon they both were gaining a confident accommodation with this strange new world.

A full minute before I heard anything at all except the crash-diving buzz of the bush flies striking through the barrier of Flyaway, Kanaki turned his head suddenly to the south and fastened his eyes to the horizon, every sinew alert. Though we heard nothing, we knew what he was hearing — the motor of an airplane. Bob and I sprang up out of the dust, he to fetch the Very pistol, I to unbolt the rear-view mirror from the door of the truck, drag out my cameras, and generally run around like a chicken with its hat off.

Probably these young people, Kanaki and Puratnya, will live to be old in their country, to see the children of the child swelling now in her womb, but they will never experience a more memorable day than that. Frightened as they both were of the truck, when the light plane appeared and dropped down toward us after my mirrored sun caught the pilot's eye, they both ran at the truck and clung to its side like a fly to a kangaroo's fur. He kept control of his voice but she began a ululating howl — "*oooooooooooo*" — broken by a series of staccato yelps and quick screams when Bob shot off orange flares from the Very pistol. While Bob fired into the sky I was aiming my Bolex and Rollei and Pentax at the swooping plane as it made a couple of preliminary low circles around us. When it cut out of the orbit and skimmed overhead I could see one of the three men inside holding open the door and another running off a motion picture camera at us. Our two aborigines must have thought we were shooting invisible streams of *mapana* at each other.

One of the Very flare fireballs fell burning to the ground, igniting the spinifex. Another terrible thing to frighten the aborigines — and us. This was a real danger, and I put down my cameras, tore down the groundsheet I had stretched out from the truck as a shade, and ran out to try to smother the blaze. Then the plane began to drop things, the more to terrorize the aborigines. An inner tube first, filled with water. It should have been no more than half filled, so that it would have bounced and rolled upon landing; but being full, it exploded. So much for the water we needed. A sack of food came next from the plane, now skimming only a few feet above the spinifex. I was afraid the pilot was considering a landing in what looked to him like a wheat field. If he had tried that, he would have stretched his plane into a half mile of fragments.

One of the dropped objects was small but heavy, well wrapped, with a cloth streamer to signal it was to be examined immediately. In a situation like this a message more often than not requires a quick visual reply. We recovered the parcel and tore it open. On a sheet of foolscap paper inside the bundle (whose weight was in the new Pitman arm), Ron Roberts had written:

Bob & John:
    Sorry about the delay, fellows, mostly caused by rough weather closing the Alice airport for a complete day.
    Have been really worried about your water situation, and am dropping a tube full, just in case you are short.
    Have not been able to contact you on radio and assume your set has packed up completely.
    If you are not at Giles by Saturday afternoon, will come looking for you by truck.

    1. If you are all OK wave your hat in circles above your head.
    2. If you need assistance by ground stand with both arms extended outward.

    Am hoping like hell that this is the correct part.

The best of Aussie luck,
Ron

We waved our hats vigorously, and Bob then pointed to the truck and to the west, several times. I was puzzled for a moment, and then understood he planned to go out to Beadell's track on the other side of the Alfred and Marie Range rather than the way we had come in. This made good sense, even though the new route was across virgin country. We had left only intermittent tracks on the rocky flats behind us, and the only man who knew the way through here was Wal MacDougall, ill at Woomera. Bob was afraid that the Giles men would lose themselves if they came in that way by truck, assuming another misfortune with our vehicle.

The plane swung back once more, closer; we could see Ron clearly — and also the meteorologist Mick Doyle. Ron threw out a final object, the plane picked up speed and altitude, and flew off south again. We ran over to see what this last drop could be, and found it was a half-gallon can, well swaddled in white masking tape, and identified in heavy black labeling ink as

ICE CREAM FOR JOHN

Bob had the new Pitman arm installed in a quarter of an hour; we packed up, put the two aborigines inside (for our new route took us through Butjar, where they were camping), and roared off again. The path to Butjar was terribly rough. Bob was driving, as usual; next to him sat Kanaki; next to Kanaki, Puratnya; and between Puratnya and the other door, I sat. I mean to say we sat to begin with. When we struck the basketball-sized boulders clustered like bubble gum in a vending machine down the Butjar track, our buttocks did not often make firm contact with the seat, except when we bounced down from the roof of the cab. I held on to the door frame with my left hand, the bottom of the seat with my right, with no hand free to do anything at all about Puratnya's heavy left breast flopping over my right shoulder. For a couple of reasons this ride would be as memorable for me as it was for Kanaki and his bride. What they thought of this put me on the defensive further than I had been since Freddy Windlass gave me the business about the meteorites at Eucla. They must have thought we — and all other *walypela* — to be bloody mad, bonkers. Why make (or had we captured it?) this monstrous *mamu truka* to ride on when even a child could outwalk it with no misery at all? Since they did not ask, I did not initiate an explanation.

Kanaki had assured us there was *kapi pulka* at Butjar. It was not *pulka* and only partly *kapi*. It was mostly the slimy dregs of a water hole nearly gone dry. The surface green was ideal for photography but bloody rotten for drinking. Even Kanaki — *he used to it* — had dug out a sump to strain out some of its nastiness. We could not work from so small a resource to get enough water for the return to Giles, so we compromised by bailing out directly from the Butjar pool and picking out by hand the largest and nastiest of the quick and the dead and the dying among the organisms polluting the dead pond.

We bade our friends — for they were friends by now — to fare well as we left them sitting under the portal arch of their branch-and-brush *wiltja* and pushed west. *Pulukari*, mates!

Although this was quite unfamiliar territory, we knew it was passable, for Giles had come through here from the west two years after the Gibson tragedy. We were still on his track when we crossed north of the Alfred and Marie Range to Len Beadell's road. We were safe now; from here it was four hundred miles to the Giles Met Station, but the track was well defined all the way, and if the truck held up, we would be in Giles with a day to spare. If we had another breakdown, we would be where the Giles rescue team could easily find us. Our poor desert-broken vehicle would be put in adequate running order by the Giles mechanics to get us down the eastern track to Amata, thence to Victory Downs, Coober Pedy, and Woomera, and I would shortly be in my Emerald City of Adelaide once more.

Still following the Giles expedition track we hit Beadell's road near a place known to the aborigines as Wrakina, not far enough from the Gunbarrel to make a stopover dangerous. Wrakina was little known; indeed, I believe this is the first time its name has been put into print. It is a large claypan, and because of its isolation and obscurity, we were sure fossicking would be good. It was worth half a day at least. I still wanted to find an australite, and knowing Giles's maps and journals well, it would be worth that time just to put down my feet where his had been.

My poor luck held on the australites; Bob found one, I found none. But there was more here than australites. I found a sherd-bagful of flaked stone tools and two Kartan choppers. Norman would be pleased to know his archaeological sequence extended this far west.

With my brain out of gear and idling, I had nothing in mind when I saw protruding from the brittle clay surface a half inch of something just the slightest bit too regular to be natural. I kicked it loose and worked it out with my fingers and a rock lever. It was larger than the aboriginal tool I expected it to be; it came out of the earth reluctantly. Rough and red, like nearly everything else in the desert soil, I could not identify it until it relinquished its roots entirely, like an extracting tooth.

It turned out to be the blade of a very old hatchet, broken at the

Hatchet dropped by Ernest Giles on his 1876 traverse of the Australian continent

top. Now this was a tool of my trade and I consequently knew something about it. Four inches across at the blade and about the same length vertically, it was the kind of tool known as a broad-hatchet, shaped rather like the surveyor's hatchet adapted by the North American Indians into the tomahawk. It was a hand-forged tool, which dropped it securely into a time-slot. Carpenters are among the most

321

conservative of craftsmen, retaining tools basically unchanged for thousands of years. Cradle saws common in the time of imperial Rome are still used in the New Hampshire backwoods; I have a kit of bronze chisels going back further still in design. But drop-forged and hand-forged hatchets disappeared in Australia about the end of the third quarter of the nineteenth century, for complex but compelling reasons. This hatchet, therefore, must have been dropped here from eighty to a hundred years ago. Corroboration of the time it had rested embedded in the Wrakina clay was easily inferred from the extreme degree of rusting and pitting, in some places three-sixteenths of an inch into its surface.

One does not venture into country so barren and hostile that every entry is an expedition, without knowing who else had been there and when. Bob came over and looked at it; without saying a word, he knew whose party had put this broken hatchet here. "That's a National Treasure, John," he said soberly. "I'm afraid you'll have to give it to me."

"My ass. This is going out of Australia in my pocket, and Christ help anybody who tries to take it away from me. I'll kill for this thing. You just run along and find some more australites, *na?*"

"Orright, orright. Don't do your block. I reckon you deserve it."

Bob knew more about maps than I and he knew only one expedition had crossed Wrakina — and at precisely the point where we were standing in a time when hand-forged hatchets were carried. Capricious fate, who had dealt me so many cruel disappointments, had suddenly given me something, the best something, to balance the scale. Ninety-two years ago, on 24 June, a man passed by here, a man whose death we memorialized on the nearby track ten days ago on our way in to Butjar: Ernest Giles.

NINE

THE END
OF THE TRACK

I saw my wild men a last time, not in their desert heartland, but at Amata, which now had become a station on the fringe. No matter how barren, isolated, or primitive a place may be, one is not able to support its identification as part of the empty desert when a trail of broken and abandoned automobiles marks the track into it from Alice Springs. Civilization had come to the Pitjandjara tribesmen. The dead automobiles were theirs, bought each by a family head with the pooled resources of his relatives. They were the rubbish of an aborted millennium, these cars, ending a hope scarcely any white man was aware of.

This was what that roller was about, the toy Bob Verburgt and I saw being pushed over the Amata sands. I saw the one and took Bob's reasonable explanation for it, his garden roller. But when Joan returned from Groote Eylandt she brought back photographs of similar rollers, pushed not only by boys but by grown men. And she brought with them their latent function: they were symbols of a native movement of revitalization, a marginal cargo cult from the Oceanic islands to the east, a promise of emergence. All religions began this way. Hundreds of them had sprung up in the islands since the war in the Pacific, all promising a literal revolution by which the earth would heave, burying the white man, and giving his "cargo" (material possessions) to the native peoples. In Australia there had been an anticipation, an adumbration, of the millennium when the first hordes of American soldiers began to pour through all of the southern Pacific. For the first time the aborigines had seen people of their own approximate color on an equality with their white mates, dressed the same, some carrying higher rank, many driving the war trucks. As the Essenes predicted Christ, so the Negro soldiers predicted the coming of Mammon.

The millennium came for the aborigines in the last years of this century's sixth decade. Suddenly, by no means they could understand, the aborigines became citizens. Their work would now be paid for at the same rates white men received, they could buy liquor openly, they could purchase *motoka*, everyone — men and women alike — old enough in appearance received the same pension as superannuated whites. It had indeed come about — the oldman in government named Rations had died, finish, and a new oldman named Pension was ruling. But like all others, this millennium revealed itself as not worth the having. If they had jobs on the fringe stations, the aborigines earned whitefella wages, but white employers no longer hired the unproductive blackfella.* So the newfella high wages became no wages at all, and the working native had to become a bludger, a parasite. As the god-men had said, liquor proved to be a pleasant-tasting poison; it killed directly and indirectly — by making a man incapable of staying alive in the desert, and by causing more spear fights than they had ever known. As citizens, the aborigines who had accumulated purchase money for the *motoka* could no longer be protected from used-car swindlers who freighted moribund automobiles from Adelaide to Alice Springs, few of which stayed alive long enough to get the blackfellas back to Amata. Even the Pension was bitter, for by giving women the status of men, the entire social system collapsed with nothing to take its place. Their dreamed wealth was an undreamed poverty. All, all rubbish.

Crime founded Australia; gold and its pursuit established her stability as a nation; and by that eternal paradox of economics that makes coal more valuable than gold, Australia's lesser minerals made her wealthy. But for the discovery of gold, the vast state of Western Australia, as large as the United States east of the Mississippi, might still hold only enough people to fill a few football stadia. Before the discovery of gold in the west, it took sixty years of strenuous effort to build Western Australia's population to thirty-nine thousand. But in all those long golden years Western Australia produced less wealth from its earth than the first two years of mining operation in the one iron field known as the Pilbara. "Incredible" is an abused word in this adjective-glutted age, but no other can fairly be used to describe the

---

* The common notion that aborigines make good stockmen is fallacious folklore; they are poor stockmen. Bob and I rounded up some seventy head of cattle on the hundred-square-mile Amata paddock after the aboriginal cowboys swore there were none there.

discoveries in Australia in the last decade, most of them in the last three years. With American capital and enterprise developing these fields, unprecedented change is coming to the great Outback. The Americans do not work on the cautious principle of slow exploitation; they are building ports, railroads, and towns with swimming pools and similar amenities to hold mining populations of thirty thousand within a few months in each area. To say the face of Australia is being changed more drastically in this decade than it was in a hundred previous years of normal growth is to state the matter conservatively.

When Joan read in Norman Tindale's Groote Eylandt journals of "the black earth" he saw in great profusion wherever the surface had been disturbed, she asked him why he had not recognized it as manganese. "Because," he answered candidly, "I had not studied geology in 1921." Pursuing butterflies, Norman overlooked the richest deposit of manganese in the entire world.

Persons who had studied geology and who had their doctorates in the earth sciences did no better. As late as 1955 the immense "reddish cliffs" noted in 1802 by the mariner-discoverer Matthew Flinders as running continuously for many miles along the eastern coast of Cape York Peninsula were not accepted for what they had to be — deposits of bauxite — because it was not possible for bauxite to be so plentiful. But it was bauxite — three billion tons of it, 30 per cent of all the aluminum ore in the world.

On our expedition into the Dead Heart, Bob Verburgt and I had our troubles with the outriders of the oil men. We might have been more tolerant, accepting their misbehavior as a small annoyance for an industry that in a handful of years moved from producing nothing to producing many billions of barrels of black gold a year. Following oil and aluminum and manganese and iron, rarer minerals are being extracted in quantities that could make Australia one of the richest and strongest nations in the world — if only the Australian minds could be emptied of the strange notion that they are compelled to follow by historical imperative the reiteration of American errors. Mount Isa in Queensland, to take one of many examples, is the world's largest producer of lead, zinc, and silver; the surrounding country, once dry, empty, and barren, is becoming another southern California.

The discoveries were inevitable — and also the manifold evils of their wealth. "Put it away, Mr. Clarke," exclaimed Governor Sir

George Gipps of New South Wales, when the first piece of discovered gold was brought to him, "or we shall all have our throats cut!"

At Amata the cutthroat mineral was not gold or manganese or even the nickel still waiting to be torn out of the Mann Range; it was chrysoprase. Chrysoprase is not a useful mineral, in the sense that you can do anything with it except make money. It is a semiprecious stone whose value increases tremendously along the road of the middlemen. It is rubbish to opal, but again paradoxically more valuable, since it is a mimic. A pound of chrysoprase dug out by the aborigines and sold to the Amata superintendent for thirty cents might wind up in America via China as three thousand dollars' worth of "jade."

Another irony: Bob Verburgt discovered the chrysoprase near Mount Davies, but got nothing at all from it except a reprimand. He had notified the authorities of his find and sent along his plan for its exploitation: recruit the North West Reserve aborigines to work at the mining under his direction, for he had most of a lifetime of experience in prospecting. His plan was negated by the then premier of South Australia, who had other ideas. Bob told me that the new men didn't know what the bloody hell they were doing; that they were going to exhaust the mine with at least twenty years of chrysoprase still in the earth; that they had so little knowledge of grading and mine preparation that one of these days there were going to be fatal cave-ins; that if the green stone were not so hard going down the aboriginal gullet they would confuse it with some vegetable and eat the bloody stuff. And when he said "they," he was not restricting the antecedent of his plural pronoun to the natives. The Department of Aboriginal Affairs had sent out great mobs of bloody experts on one thing or other, nearly all of whom made their safe return to Adelaide their greatest achievement.

So this last visitation to my people was an appendix, a subscript, of my more substantial earlier work. I literally flew in and flew out again to examine one thing only: the progress of a unique native enterprise, a laboratory experiment in economic evolution conducted communally on a capitalistic basis.

Before leaving Adelaide for the central north, I visited the Department of Aboriginal Affairs to talk with the administrators about the project into which so much hope and labor had been sunk. They reaffirmed the foundation of the experiment: it was to be wholly aboriginal in management, production, and marketing. One goes into the Department of Aboriginal Affairs with one's hat in one's hand, so I did not tell the administrators they were bloody mad baastids and that the project was mischievous beyond the imagining. Bell Rock Jacky sitting at mahogany tables with financial tycoons? Arm-breaking Teddy conducting delicate negotiations?

Well. I listened and nodded enthusiastically as the organization was described to me. "The Amata Society," as the working group was to be known henceforth to all men (and bloody women too, for the love of Wati Kutjara), would be open to all aborigines acceptable to the native council and possessing an initiation fee of ten cents. The government would interfere in no wise — except to make a few initial suggestions and to require that decisions voted by the cooperative society's members in their democratic meetings held every fortnight would be carried out — this to insure the integrity of democracy against men of tribal power. Democracy? They were going to run a commercial enterprise by democracy? As well try to run a government by democracy. Bloody mad. If I had been asked to advise on this point of management, I would have suggested that the first order of business be the institution of the death penalty, to be exercised capriciously and without recourse to appeal, by old Kata, who would also make any other productive legislation he saw fit. But that was not what the government had in mind. Kata would have one vote — if he paid his ten cents initiation fee. So would Teddy's broken-armed and cheeky wife. So would Teddy's mad brother. One man, one vote. Jesus H. Thorny-Headed Christ. Nevertheless, eager as I always am to make a mistake, and never in any way prejudiced against any man or his absurd notions, I flew off to Amata to see how the noble experiment was faring.

Somewhat to my astonishment, I found first that I was not awfully *grata* in my person — not because I was who I am, but because I was anybody. Without dwelling on the matter, the administration people revealed that *things were crook in Tallarook and a bloody sight worse in Bourke.* There had been a half dozen superintendents since I had last visited the reserve. All the staff people I had known were gone, replaced by a triple-sized contingent of twenty-four persons I knew nothing about, either through acquaintance, reputation, or notoriety. One thing I saw wrong immediately was the number of white personnel; they now constituted a self-sufficient, viable community that needed no interaction with the aborigines for its stability. The new superintendent, I must say (despite the difficulties for me of which he was necessarily the agent), was a man whose only deficiency was being too well qualified to hold so menial a position in the Department of Aboriginal Affairs. He was young, powerful in physique and in personality, a university graduate (which accomplishment made him nearly unique in the whole state organization), and a former police patrol officer in New Guinea. Moreover, he was a man who wanted eagerly to learn and to do a good job in his assignment. The trouble of course was that nobody knew how a good job could be done, for there is no solution, simple or complex, to the problem of bringing Old Stone Age people into the Atomic Era. *Kulila.* Tasol.

Dave Hope, the superintendent, was most genial and cooperative, even more so as we got to know one another. But he was caught in a trap of conditions imposed by the amorphous administration in the higher echelons; for me that meant there were no accommodations in either the overpopulated compound facilities or in the aboriginal camp. The natives were restless, as we used to say in anthropology, and the Department did not want any outsiders in there to stir them up. Orright; I radioed for the weekly mail plane to pick me up on its next visit; meanwhile I would reluctantly accept the hospitality of the Hopes. I should have preferred to hump my bluey into the bush, to waltz my matilda, but that was not permitted. Orright.

The Amata Society saved the day — the week — by giving me a chance to crowd in a notebook full of information. It had given its permission to four men to work in the mine, replacing four others now working. Dave had to ferry the men out — and back, since the diggings were a hundred and thirty-five miles east along the Giles track.

This track was now as commonplace to me as the moon must be to astronauts. What there was to see had been seen and described. There was little for my remembrance until we reached the mine, little-bit-close-up to the track in the hills rising upon Mount Davies. Bouncing through the bush in Dave's new Land Rover, we could see the miners a good distance before they could be surprised. Ten of them there were, some supine and some prone, around their fires. The Appalachian hillbillies' sacred song came to my mind: *Mother's not dead, she's only a-sleeping, patiently waiting for Jesus to come.* Our communal capitalist enterprisers were not dead, for they stirred and moved enough to keep out of the fires; perhaps they were waiting for Jesus. They sure as hell were not working. Dave had to act upon compulsion of his duty; since the miners of late had not been taking out enough chrysoprase to come near paying expenses, the Department of Aboriginal Affairs had authorized him to pay the men a wage for "preparing the mine for production." The men were obviously not doing what they were being paid to do, so they had to be poked a bit. "Come on, you fellows," Dave complained, "we are not paying you to sit around all day. Come on, now." They were not in truth sitting around; they were lying down, some on their backs, some on their bellies. A few of the latter exerted themselves enough to roll over to accept the rhino, the gelt, the stuff. I thought but did not say, *Teitu nara! Wait a bit! Did this order to work and this wage mean the state, despite its manifesto to the contrary, was intruding upon the ideal, communal, and cooperative aboriginal democratic Amata Society after all?* Dave did not speak to the point until later, but I knew some of his superiors might have justified the action — I had heard it in every Australian city since 1956 where, in my position as a visiting scholar, I had to suffer intellectuals: *These defects are unavoidable in the first phase of the new society, in the form in which it comes forth, after the prolonged travail of birth, from capitalistic society. Justice can never be in advance of its stage of economic development, and of the cultural development of society conditioned by the latter. But as soon as the victorious proletariat captures power and the instruments of production, the state will wither away. They have nothing to lose but their brains, and they have a world to win. Wala? Miriwa.*

Embarrassed, Dave volunteered an answer to my unspoken criticism. "Of course this is a handout, but what can we do?" *Not a thing, Dave; not one goddamned thing, if you want to survive. If I were in your shoes I would kick the arses of this mob and say unto them,* "UP, you lazy baastids. Nyurulu yawiyawu. *Pick up your instruments of production and hop to it. No bloody work, no bloody eat. From each according to his bloody orders.*" I do not think I would last long in civil service.

One of the men who condescended to roll over to have his wages stuffed in his pockets was my old pren, Tjipikudu. He was somehow different; not aged, for there had not been time for that. Aged in spirit, perhaps? Time is not a factor in eroding one's soul. With me I had color prints for all the men and women whom I had photographed on my last trip. I gave Tjipi his, and he was tickled black with it, giggling in that winning aboriginal way, and showing it to the others in his cupped hands, as if what he had was his naked soul, caught like the spirit butterfly in the hands of Mr. Scratch.

I looked into the mine shafts — just holes sunk to a maximum depth of twenty feet, the point at which the sides were liable to cave in. (Bob had been right in his prediction; Dave said one man had been killed recently in a cave-in.) On the surface beside each shaft lay a sack with chrysoprase in it. I examined handfuls of the stuff. Rubbish. Bloody worthless junk. Not a good piece anywhere. Talking long with Dave at our camp fire that night (and later with Dick Rudling, the arts and crafts supervisor at Amata), I had confirmed what I had expected: the "preparation wages" were too close to what responsible work would bring to stimulate the men to do anything at all.

The four men we loaded aboard for the Amata return included George — of famous memory at Lungly Gully. He too had changed. A loser in his campaign to become Big Chief Shitstick of the integration movement, George was slipping back into the old ways, and looking the better for it. The three other men blossomed back in the bush to their traditional integrity. Young Larry was a superb hunter, and the other men — George, Billy, and Jacky — deferred to him whenever the stalk was difficult. We were making a long hunting trek of our return, no hurry. All the men took a share of the game on their own. George ran after a bounding joey which fled from its mother's pouch after she was killed by Billy. Apparently George had improved his racing ability since our run. I was sitting in the back of the truck on this leg, Dave requiring a guide as we scouted through the bush on a digressive pilgrimage to the sacred Lake Wilson area, and I took the terrified joey into my lap and arms. He was a great hulk of a lazy bounder, legs about eighteen inches long, ready to be evicted from the external womb. The poor little bugger shivered in fright, though I cosseted him. I do love 'roos; it is a pity they are so edible. What would become of this little fellow? How long would he live after we returned to Amata? A day or two while the primitively cruel children played with him, sticking him with toy spears? I hoped not so long. I could not intrude with the suggestion, but I prayed George would whack out its brains quickly (as he indeed did, before that day's dinnertime).

The Lake Wilson excursion pleased me immensely. The hard salt lake, an ellipse of about one hundred and fifty acres, lay in a saucer rimmed by low but spectacular mountains. What a place for a natural cathedral! I have never seen more impressive primeval scenery anywhere else in Australia; one certainly felt that here was the Dreaming. Without the belief and the tradition behind me, I was here immersed in greater religious awe than I had felt in tiresome Bernini's piazza at Saint Peter's among billions of Italians screaming in holy frenzy as the Pope wiggled a sacred finger from a window.

At Lake Wilson I satisfied one of my nagging ambitions. I found an australite. My good fortune was in their religion; the aboriginal tabu excluded most trespassers, and the lake's surface was unhunted. Billy escorted me around the lake's crusted perimeter for our half-day fossicking. When we returned to Dave's truck I had my one australite; he had thirty.

For me, a last hunt on the return to Amata. The bed of the truck was piled with kangaroos and wallabies, making for a while a comfortable couch for me and the other three back-riders. Each feature I saw from this point of vantage — animal, vegetable, and mineral — I asked them the name of: "*Eni ni watjala?*" Soon they fell into the game of teaching the *walypala pu:rpa*, plucking me by the arm to point out this and that, naming it in Pitjandjara.

We had one amusing moment on the way back. The men spied a 'roo, far off in the bush, beyond the range of their slight .22 *ripela*. They asked Dave to bring it down with his heavy gun. He took down his rifle, crept a few yards toward the 'roo, assumed the prone firing position, shot — and missed. Even at the range of two hundred and fifty yards he should have been able to fell the animal, but then how could he hit anything in the commotion the four men were kicking up in the truck? The back-riders were hanging over the side like green sea voyagers in a critical attack of *mal de mer* and George hung out the window of the cab, hysterically beating the door panel. Chundering? No, howling with derisive laughter. What was so bloody funny? *Look at the silly* walypela, *lying on his* nyuntjinpa *to fire a* ripela, *instead of walking with it shaking, the proper-fella way!*

Back at Amata, I had another, sadder experience with the New Ignorance, George's this time. Still trailing a few dissipating ragged clouds of civilization, he was contracting to buy a great bloody Bedford truck. The owners of a station outside the Alice had towed it here, and here it sat, waiting for George to yark up the last few dollars of the seven-hundred-dollar purchase price. George had nearly all the money now, drawing upon the resources of his family and relatives, the results of a year of labor for most of them. He asked me proudly what I thought of the vehicle. Holy Mother of God. It was a bomb, a bloody wreck. Its bed was bent in a graceful downward curve in the dorsal region, like a sway-backed horse. In pride of place on the otherwise empty flat bed reposed the truck's engine. What did George know about repairing and installing a motor? Damn-all. In the United States a junk dealer would not have hauled this thing away for nothing; George would have had to pay for its removal.

Cannot the Department of Aboriginal Affairs prevent the sale of this rubbish to innocent aborigines? Not any longer, mate; the aborigines are free, enfranchised citizens now, their constitutional right to be swindled at last guaranteed to them. Once in a while Providence exercises the right to overrule the affairs of men. The last issue I had seen of the Alice Springs newspaper carried an item about a fatal automobile accident along the Papunya track. Two white people had sold an aborigine a *motoka*; in preparing it for delivery, they had replaced the good demonstration tires with cleanskins, baldies. On the delivery trip one of the smooth tires blew out, overturning the car, and killing one of the whites. Providence had an eye in the same area after Bob and I had passed Papunya on our trip into the Dead Heart, though we did not find out about it until long after our return. Almost on our heels the brother of Australia's first aboriginal university graduate (part-blood) died of thirst. Another banal irony: Charles Perkins, the show native of Australian Communism, calling for black power in Sydney; his brother in the bush perishing for water.

Another buggered vehicle sat rotting beside George's Bedford — the communal truck of the Amata Society, chrysoprase merchants. *What 'appened dat fella one?* Well, you see, Teddy the arm-breaker got real crook at the decisions made by the democratic processes of the last board meeting of the society and took the truck out and deliberately burned out its bearings and fried its cylinders to show all and sundry that direct individual action can put a spear up the arse of democracy any day.

I spent a last morning with old Tommy Dodd. What was to become of him in this new era? What need for a liaison man when the *walypela* was no longer in a governing position? He had made me a

334

present — a wooden figure he had carved, a Mountain Devil lizard, the *mineri*. I had a gift for him, too — an electric blue necktie with pink spots.

On our last run to the airstrip, Dave Hope cut his way across an undulating sea of rabbits, a hundred times as many as I had expected, and my expectation was a hundred times as many as the experts on rabbit control had expected. So much for interfering with nature.

The plane dropped down on schedule, a Beechcraft Twin Bonanza piloted by a woman, Christine Davy. As always, the low flight over the Australian desert thrilled me; how I do love that terrible nothingness! We landed at Ernabella also, where the superintendent, Bill Edwards, met us with a picnic basket for tea and crumpets under the wing. Wal MacDougall was there, too, for my unexpected pleasure. And by sunset I was in the swimming pool at the Oasis Motel in Alice Springs.

The truncation of my Amata visit gave me a week before Joan was to arrive from Groote. I had a surprise for her which may be worth the telling to cheer this last chapter at the end of my trek into the deserts. When last we met at the Alice, when she was off for Groote and I was leaving for the Dead Heart, I weighed one dinner short of two hundred pounds. I was now down to one hundred and sixty, a weight I have kept since that day.

There may be some readers of this last adventure who have interest in the American fad of somatic art, losing weight. I will tell them a wondrous thing. Not only am I lighter by two bowling balls and a large bag of Kitty Litter, but I can kick the arse off a much taller emu than ever I could in my youth. Do I diet? Indeed not, madam. I eat any bloody thing I have a mind to, and delight in calories, which to me are units of goodness. I will tell another wondrous thing: for twenty-three years I suffered from stomach trouble; not three days passed together without my being nauseously ill. I could not drink tea, eat homemade bread or porridge, or any of the other lovely Irish peasant foods I grew up by. Twenty-three years sick on a quick and regular schedule. Nothing helped — not expensive bloody doctors who ran tubes down my throat and up my arse, not nuns who prayed for me.* Some days I chundered on Gelusils.

---

* They did, too, dinkum, four of them in a National Science Foundation Summer Institute for College Teachers of Anthropology I directed the year of my second Australian trip. I was confidentially told of their solicitude for their poor

But at once and together these two miracles occurred: I lost weight and my stomach trouble. Ever wary of the *post hoc, ergo propter hoc* fallacy, I experimented with the changes in my diet forced by our desert privations. The trouble turned out to be milk. I am told now that all women know this, and I do not venture to dispute their prior

---

old teacher too late to thank them. They will read this, I know: Thank you, Sisters, your prayers for my physical if not my spiritual well-being were answered — for a change — and in gratitude, I give you this recipe for the bread I can now make and eat. It comes down in my family, with some American enrichment, from the slums of Dublin:

Recipe for Greenway's Bread

This recipe makes three large loaves and a half dozen rolls.

A rich bread, particularly resistant to staleness. Especially delicious as toast. Best eaten warm from the oven with a cup of strong tea.

The Makings:

YEAST:	2 packages (dry yeast dissolves best)
SUGAR:	4 or 5 heaping tablespoons, to taste
SALT:	2½ heaping tablespoons
EGGS:	6 large
BUTTER:	¼ pound
MILK:	1½ pints
FLOUR:	about four pounds

The Making:

1. Dissolve yeast in ⅛ cup of warm (125°) water.
2. Melt butter. Mix all ingreedymints together in a blender, except the flour. Add flour to the liquid mix a sifted cup at a time, in a five-gallon sketti pot, using a stout stick (a three-foot length of unpainted broomstick is ideal). The rising of the bread will be helped if you heat the liquid before adding the flour, but be sure you do not make the mix so hot the damned thing will bake before you put it in the oven. The idea is to excite the little unicellular yeast organisms, not to fry them.

   Mixing must be smooth. This gets to be arduous after the third pound of flour is mixed in. A sexual division of labor is advisable here: lay women may call in their husbands for assistance with the mixing; nuns may call in the priest. Mixing is finished when the dough is a smooth ball — about the size of a soccer ball — that no longer sticks to the inside of the pot or the fingers. (What are your fingers doing in there anyhow?)
3. Let the dough rise in a warm place (be very careful of using a warmed oven — remember the little yeast buggers). Cover pot with a porous cloth. I do not know the function of the cloth; it is traditional, and must not be messed with. The first rising is complete when the dough is a bit more than double the size of the batter ball; another guide is the level of the top of the risen dough — first rising is achieved when the dough just starts to drop from convexity.
4. Punch the bread down, literally; knock hell out of it.
5. Let rise again to about ¾ the size of first rising. If you can control your impatience (the entire process from mixing to mouth is about six hours), let it rise more.

knowledge. But when I used to get sick, I drank milk. When I became sicker, I drank more milk — fattening milk. But out on the desert we had no milk and I had no illness and my weight began to drop. And I drank pannikin after pannikin of billy tea, satisfying a childhood lust for the stuff.

Anthropologists have commented for a hundred years on the curious culture of the East Africans who herd cattle but don't milk them. Recent investigations have shown that these tribes have a high degree of lactase deficiency which leads to an inability to digest lactose. The deficiency is genetically transmitted. (This leads me to speculate further on whether it also accounts for those tribes which mix blood of the cattle with milk before drinking it — I know that ox blood used to be used as a flocculating agent in wine-making, so maybe it breaks down the lactose artificially in a similar way?) Anyway, the significant point is that the cultural sanctions of these people stop them from suffering the effects of drinking milk, not their knowledge of enzymes, their purpose, their molecular structure, or anything else. I can't get into China to test it out, but their tabu on dairy products may be similarly linked to genetic factors.

I asked Vic MacFarlane about the milk theory when he came through Colorado on his way to his cold desert studies. He looked at me in amazement. "You weren't drinking milk, surely? Don't you know adults are not equipped to digest milk?" I lamely admitted I knew very little about metabolism and milk beyond the fact that the adult body does not readily manufacture chrysoprase or whatever the hell it is that breaks milk down. And if women and everybody else already knew what I was supposed to have known, why the hell didn't they tell me about it instead of letting me go on being sick and fat

---

6. Meanwhile prepare the bread pans by swabbing thoroughly with butter. The pans, I mean.
7. Take dough out of pot and knead. This means punch hell out of it again (to kill any live yeast), fold like taffy, and shape into loaves, each half the height of what you want for the final, baked loaves.
8. Let shaped loaves rise for about half an hour.
9. Bake in preheated oven at 400° for ten minutes, then reduce heat to 350°. In about 25–30 minutes the bread will be light brown on top. Test by poking a clean knife into the bread; if it comes out clean (without dough adhering), other cutlery can be inserted.
10. CAUTION. Do not rubbish this recipe by using stone-balled, black Russian, high-yellow Hungarian, or other faddish flours. In mixing, be careful of allowing long hair, lice, or other organically grown materials from falling into pot.

and disagreeable for half my life? *Nungkarpa.** All I knew or cared about, I told Vic, was that my weight was quite stable at one hundred and sixty pounds, I could eat as much of any bloody thing I wanted, and I had not once been stomach-sick since coming out of the Dead Heart.

I will probably never find my Lost Tribe of Wild Men; I may never see many of my desert friends again; but if all I gained from my fifteen years pursuing the aborigines is my discovery about milk and Ernest Giles's hatchet, it will be sufficient.

---

* I must have discussed this business in one of my lectures, for a former student of mine, himself now a professor, has just published, with far more scholarship than I thought he had in him, a most impressive article entitled "Lactase Deficiency: An Example of Dietary Evolution," in the October–December 1971 issue of *Current Anthropology*. I recommend it highly, if only to demonstrate how difficult and complex all these problems are, and how conscious I am of simplifying them. Incidentally, the name of the author, my former student, is Robert D. McCracken, a bloody great Irishman.

EPILOGUE

In the third week of May 1971 my green mountain town of Boulder exploded. When I came to this place in 1957, after my first trip to Australia, it seemed to be a good place to begin my golden years. (I might then have considered Australia as my last home, but at that time there was only one department of anthropology in all Australia, and one professorship.) So close to the foot of the Rocky Mountains that its western side rose from the mile-high plain upon the mountains' instep, Boulder had been built through the love of its pioneer settlers from a barren rocky flat almost as bare as Sturt's gibber desert to what visitors called one of the most beautiful and peaceful small cities in the United States. In those days I used to like to drive my Australian guests up the precipitous dirt road swinging spirally up the side of Flagstaff Mountain and let them look down upon the city — colorful pioneer houses surrounding a central business district of restrained commercial architecture. In summer one could see little of this, for the trees, each brought across the plains by the settlers, buried every man-made thing in green — or in fall, green and golden aspen.

But in ten years all that changed. The population of less than thirty thousand (some were children of the first settlers) had grown rowdily to nearly eighty thousand. The university, a red-tiled outcrop of ocher among the green, was approaching a student population of twenty thousand. Some small friction warmed the natural antipathy between the university's gown and the cowboys' town, but not much; occasional letters to the stodgy local newspaper about the evils of fluoridation, that sort of thing. My first memory of police action then was being stopped by an old-style western posse, tracking down two immigrant killers of a policeman. There was one long-haired student at the university, known with intolerant amusement as "Jesus Christ."

341

During the middle years of that decade the ammunition for the explosion began infiltrating the town, a little at first and then more, transients and specious students, noticeable but not worrisome, until suddenly we were shaken into awareness that there were hundreds of them — scattered groups no longer but a solid population in physical possession of the Hill, the once-stylish shopping block adjoining the university. Within this rootless drifting crowd of idle nomads, identifiable subgroups formed — ten of them at least — from the diffident, experimental, idealistic students on the fringe to the dead-heart wild men, the STP Family (named for their unifying drug DOM — 2, 5-dimethoxy-4-methylamphetamine, a powerful hallucinogen).

These people had not been robbed of their gods and their traditions like the New Norcia people; they had thrown them away. Obsessed with amulets, food fads, drugstore magic, they were as anomic and credulous as any New Norcians. Incompetent, like the hangers-on of Ernabella, in any skill or craft, like them they depended for survival on handouts or thievery. Like George of the Sweat Quest lacking pride or will, doubting their own untested manhood (dey nebber bin cut), taking hallucination for insight and madness for *mana:* what were they? Parasites? Harbingers of the new American male? Or *ludi naturae?* freaks in fact as in name: an evolutionary dead end, a willfully regressive subculture so maladapted to the social environment that it must in the course of nature wither away?

The last, I hoped. But their numbers kept growing. I discovered that Boulder was known to the underground as Freak City, U.S.A., that it was a depot for much of the marijuana traffic coming up from Mexico to split east and west to the coast cities, that there were perhaps a hundred heroin addicts on the Hill, some with an addiction of five hundred dollars a day. As one police officer told me, "They can't beg that much — they can't even steal that much."

The city's crime rate shot up to an incredible level. The STP Family alone, its nuclear group only thirty-five people, were arrested for two hundred and forty-one crimes in six months (serving an average of one and a half days in jail per capita), and known to be involved in many times that number, including two murders. These worst of the freaks were animals. A hospital attendant I was speaking with later while guarding one of the STP women being pumped out of an overdose of Speed (Methedrine) told me that the most nauseating experience he had suffered in nearly three years in the emergency ward was having to cut the trousers off an STP man near death from an overdose — they had not been off his body in two years.

Early in 1971 the Hill became impassable; it was crowded like Times Square on New Year's Eve with drug merchants and their customers making deals. The police established a substation — and that was the fuse to the explosion. On 22 May the disparate freaks joined forces and hit the police. Two police cruisers were destroyed and the officers beaten; the freaks then took over the Hill, burning, looting, smashing shops and automobiles. That was on Saturday night. Late Sunday afternoon came the confrontation.

I had had my own troubles as an unreconstructed straight. Some months earlier I was warned by several students that my class of nearly six hundred which I was teaching in the Flatirons motion picture theatre (no classroom on campus being available for an enrollment of that size) was going to be hit next day by militant protestors because I had not only announced I would not allow "free cuts" for a scheduled moratorium, but that I might set an examination for which absences due to participation in treasonable activity would not be accepted. I delivered into the hands of the university president that afternoon a letter conveying the information, my reassertion that I would hold class, and my expectation of protection. Since he had already come obediently down from his office to tell a crowd of students in the quad that he was in strong moral opposition to the war, I did not expect much help. (There must remain some university presidents who do not equate opposition to the war with indifference to academic freedom. But I wouldn't know where to look.) So I dropped an eighteen-inch tire iron in my briefcase.

What happened next day I do not like to think about. The class was indeed hit. I came within a literal fraction of a second of killing one of the protestors. The university police (whom I had posted one of my teaching assistants to call) refused to help for fear of instigating a confrontation. My students showed their intention of joining the Silent Mush by pulling in their shoulders. After I drove the protestors out, I decided: Shit — if I have to defend my class alone, I'm going to get some authority.

343

Shortly thereafter my motivation was reinforced by an incident in which a young girl was caught by a gang of freaks one block from the school. They cut her ears off. *By God*, I thought, *that's enough*. So I applied for membership in the Boulder Reserve Police, a group that has full police functions but without regularly scheduled duty hours or (for 80 percent of its work) pay. If it is called in for riots, each man gets $3.50 an hour.

Wonder of all wonders, they accepted me. I shouldn't have done it in their position; anyone but a university professor. It was hard going, and I thought too little of my chances to tell anyone of it. One of the command officers who interviewed me summed up the obvious objections. *Well, frankly, you are not very big and you are well over the optimum age. This can be very dangerous business. Your application shows that you taught judo in the Army. That was twenty-eight years ago. Do you think you can still defend yourself?* I didn't tell him that in my opinion judo and jujitsu and karate are a load of crap, no more use in a real fight than Mrs. Murphy's arse. I just told him, *I'll fight you for your job.*

So on the second evening of the riots I stood, with nine other reserve officers and two regular policemen, on the front line of a human barricade we set up to oppose entry to the hill of the freaks. Twelve of us faced at fifteen yards across the street three hundred freaks. Moving among them, giving advice and encouragement, was a man of the cloth, a minister, in beard and pipe; he had been their chaplain for months. *Please, God*, I prayed, *let him be there when the trouble starts. He is not really Your servant; he is not Your true pren.* But a God who does not listen to the righteous cannot be expected to listen to me, and the minister of the faith moved off. Then, as darkness fell, when they had worked themselves into a rage by shouting and chanting and dancing (like my wilder Pitjandjara), one of them took out the streetlights by striking them into an overload with a strobe. Then the rocks and other missiles came. Their women had been making what I call tampon bombs during the three hours we stood in confrontation; we had seen them, sticking hoses into the tanks of automobiles parked in their territory, sucking out the gasoline and pouring it into wine bottles, stuffing the bottlenecks with gas-soaked tampons and kitchen matches. One of them struck me on the shoe and broke, the matches failing to ignite on the leather. I was hit by two or three rocks. Our second line, three regular officers about twenty yards behind us, shot out cover for us with tear-gas rifles, and we moved on them. I will say only that the freaks did not achieve the purpose of their battle cry, *"All we want's the Hill, kill the pigs!"* We busted them.

At our regular meeting the next week a lieutenant of the regulars came and told us, "There is no way I can tell you how much you guys mean to us. I don't know what pushes you. We couldn't have handled it alone. It was Pearl Harbor for us, but they didn't know it. I didn't see any of you who didn't do a good job." This pleased me especially, for the lieutenant and I at one point held another street entrance to the Hill, the two of us alone in a steady shower of rocks hurled out of the bushes on the edge of the university grounds across the street.

Police work is excellent training for the anthropologist. We see all of life in our culture, necessary if you expect to understand life in another society. Some of it is funny. A rough humor, perhaps, but it is a rough life as a policeman in America or a nomad in the western deserts. Just before my time, two officers were called to assist in an illness emergency. When they arrived (in no more than four minutes; that is the usual limit of time expenditure between call and arrival), the ill person, a very old woman, was not only dead but cold dead. Her relatives were keening and screaming for the police to do something. Well, what the hell. One of them gave her mouth-to-mouth artificial respiration, useless, but harmless, and comforting to the relatives. But with her muscles dead, he blew her up like a balloon — and the poor dead woman farted. They lost another measure of reputation for the police by collapsing in helpless laughter.

I was talking to the fellow who gave the mouth-to-mouth the other night. Another officer had shot two armed robbers a couple of days earlier. We were wondering what sentences might be handed down. Probably none, we agreed. "Well," I said, "at least they have something to make them remember what can happen to armed robbers. A shot in the hip is awfully good for the memory."

"Don't I know it?" asked the officer, and showed me his wallet, which had a hole through it. "When I got shot in the hip, that's where it went out." I had forgotten that.

Anthropologists are able to dissociate death from reality if it occurs among a primitive people. They understand and justify cannibalism and head-shrinking so long as they are done by Jivaros. They should see violent death as a policeman sees it. On the first of this year,

1972, New Year's Day, I went on patrol cruiser duty at ten-thirty in the evening. Two detectives carrying investigative equipment jumped in with me. "What's up?" I asked. "Homicide — Gregory Canyon."

We got there in a hurry, and a police sergeant already on the scene led the detectives to the body. It was a young girl, an obvious straight, twenty-one years old, naked except for one pulled-down stocking and part of a blouse, beautiful. No mutilation, but obviously raped. Somehow mutilation is easier to take; a mangled body is less human. All she had was a small hole in her left breast and only a teaspoonful of blood beneath it.

It was established later she had been hitchhiking — her car had broken down. On the fourth of January a twenty-three-year-old woman accepted a ride from a man when her automobile refused to start. She was stabbed twice in the breast. Another similar attack in our green mountain town a week later. Last Monday night, Valentine's Day, I was driving night cruiser. On the border of my district I saw at the same time that another officer driving on the contiguous border saw it, an automobile, drifting down a hill on the wrong side of the street, backwards, lights out. We both turned on our revolving red emergency lights and closed in on it. Two young women. "What's the trouble, ma'am?"

"Oh, damn, we ran out of gas."

It was only a few blocks along the main north-south street to a service station. As they walked they could think about the need to keep an eye on the fuel gauge. "Can you give us a ride?"

"Sorry." It is normally against regulations.

"Shit." They stood in the street and waved their thumbs at an approaching car.

"Don't you know it's against the law to hitchhike?" asked the other officer.

A scowl and they got back on the sidewalk and walked off. We got in our cars and drove away. I thought I'd look in on them a few minutes later. There they were, thumbing again. I stopped, reported the contact and location on the radio, and went over to them. "Didn't we tell you it is illegal to hitchhike?"

"Well," one of them whined, "why get uptight about it?"

"You girls hear about that rape-murder in Gregory Canyon last month? Doesn't that affect your thinking at all?"

346

"Oh," she grumbled, "I know it's dangerous, but if we don't get home quick our dinner will get cold."

"Aaaah, don't argue with him," said the other one.

What's the good of being an anthropologist, understanding people? Or a policeman, trying to keep them safe from their own folly? In the elections for city council following the riot, all but one of the candidates elected called for restrictions on the police; the man with the heaviest vote advocated an end to prosecution of "no victim" crimes and harassment of the transients, who, he said, "are just nice kids out to see the country." The council has since cut the sheriff's budget so severely that half of the sheriff's patrolmen had to be laid off. I am now also commissioned as an unpaid deputy sheriff. A member of the city council declared the riot had "resulted from strict enforcement of the laws, rather than weak enforcement." Laws? They have given the law away.

My Australia is in trouble, too, not because of losing her soul, but because her friends are losing theirs. I know Prime Minister Gorton flew to Washington in 1969 to ask President Nixon when, if at all, would the United States help Australia in threatened invasion from what we call the Far East and Australians the Near North. One of my students asked a little while ago, "What will *you* do if Australia is invaded?"

"I'll go back and die with my people."

So I will. I believe patriotism lies with one's culture, one's people, not with one's land. If the land holds your spirit as part of itself, as the Australian desert holds at once the Dreaming ancestors and the spirit of the men and women living on it, one can love it. I have no feeling for these bare rocks to my west; I cannot feel any spirit residing beneath the piñon and juniper; none of these crags holds any Wati Kutjara. The Hill teems with crazy dingoes in the university, my colleagues cringe before them; in city hall, our leaders truckle, as they do in Washington. These are not my people. What mates I have in this country are policemen. Like bushmen, they know life at its simplest and direst. When a split-second decision may mean life or death, when there is no time to waver or obfuscate or make-believe, a man must keep his values clear. No *pullsit*.

I see my old friends, now and then. Norman has been through here twice since I was last in his country, and I hear he will return next year. Norman is as reliably perennial as one of his *Hepialidae*. Some of my visitors, my friends, I cannot speak of here, since they did not enter my narrative. I will mention one only as an example: Professor V. A. Bailey, professor of physics at the University of Sydney, father of a family of pure geniuses, including the former junior chess champion of Australia, a Rhodes Scholar. Professor Bailey was honored here by the university and brought over to be given a Roman triumph after a satellite brought back proof of a theory he had held alone through years of contumelious opposition.

I bought a color television set to honor our Apollo astronauts, pleased to contribute through the purchase tax a pittance to help the moon shots. I was watching the liftoff of Apollo 11 when I answered a telephone call from Denver. It was Mick Doyle, the meteorologist from Giles, who saw me last out of the rescue plane at the Clutterbucks. *What the hell are you doing here, mate? Getting married to a Yankee sheila. Well, good on you! One for one! I'll drive in and pick you up.*

Mick and I postponed the inevitable reminiscences while we watched the Apollo telecast. The separation of the second stage over northeast Australia brought in a descriptive commentary from a meteorologist observing on Cape York. The old Australian twang — and Mick shouted, "I know that fellow — he's an old mate of mine." A small universe.

When Eagle went up with Apollo 11, we were told the flash of the separation engine burned the Australian night sky to a pale ocher. I had received a couple of weeks earlier a correct but painfully written letter from Joan's Groote Eylandt brother-in-law Budji Lalara. What better time to respond than this — to ask whether he saw the fire of our Eagle rising through the sky of his Dreaming, our Eagle going up to meet with the Eaglehawk of his totem?

Those problems I carried unresolved from Australia are solving themselves, one by one. Norman was involved with two of them; he helped with one solution and hindered the other. The hindrance, a long time ago: I had taken from an archaeological burial a kangaroo tibia split down the middle and sharpened to an awl point at the distal end. I asked him what the hell it was used for, since I had never read of any such thing. Probably held a ball of fat, he said, to give sustenance to the spirit of the dead man on its way to the Dreaming. Fair enough, and so I spoke of its function to students for years. But after my last visit to Australia I was reading the memoirs and diaries of the founders of Adelaide and came across a gruesome vignette of history. A hired man to John Wrathall Bull went out to placate a mob of restless aborigines; out of sight of the Bull homestead he was struck on the head and left unconscious for Bull to find. He died soon after his employer found him, apparently of an internal injury, but no wound was evident. John Wrathall Bull was more careful than the Amata nurse who examined the moribund woman, for in the belly-folds of skin he found a tiny incision the shape of a new moon. Bull tracked down the mystery and discovered the murderers and their weapon — a bone exactly the size and shape of mine. The aborigines had inserted the bone while the man lay unconscious, pushed it up just under the skin of his chest, and turned it down into a lung. One small drop of blood to wipe off the belly. Joan has informed me that the natives of Arnhem Land did the same sort of thing, assisting the psychological killing magic of the ancient pointing bone by sticking it into a victim's neck under the earlobe and turning it into the carotid artery. A weakening of faith here in the old *mapana* power to kill, but a reaffirmation of the belief that the *mamu* help those who help themselves.

The problem Norman helped to solve is one of so many that persist in an anthropologist's work, growing in complexity, over the years. When I first met Norman I told him of my interest in cultural determinism, the philosophy that nearly everything we do is actually done by culture without our realization. I hoped he could contribute some evidence. He did. "Did you know that for two thousand years the design of spoons preserved the ancient form of a pectin shell at the end of a wooden or metal handle? No designer seems to know about it. The design changed because of metal shortages in World War I." No, I had not known about that at all, but from then I pursued the idea, finding it still persisted, but almost unseen — the barest vestige of the pectin joint carried in handle design. I found the same process going on in the design of cup handles. Of course the same discovery had been made long ago by the great Egyptologist Flinders Petrie in his study of the inorganic and unrecognized evolution of vase handles, and by General Lane Fox Pitt-Rivers in his research into design changes in the British army rifle.

Two years ago on their visit to Boulder, Mrs. Tindale had us to dinner, elegant with heirloom silverware she had brought with her. One look at an anciently curious spoon gave on the instant the key to tie together all those things I had seen on the desert, from the milk-tin toy roller to Watson's book on the DNA molecule structure. The handle of this spoon was two strands of silver wire spiraled together like the serpents on a caduceus; why thus, the functional

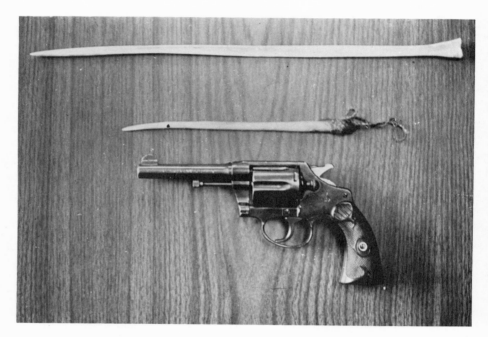

Forty thousand years of weapon evolution: killing bone, pointing bone, and .32 calibre Colt revolver

why? Because silver is too soft to be a stable single-strand handle. Twisting gives it the necessary strength. If the boy at Amata had built the handle of his toy on one strand of fencing wire, it would have bent upon striking the first rock in the path. But he twisted it — an independent polygenetic invention. The big remaining problem in advanced biogenetics after the settlement of the DNA composition was the form of the molecule. It had to be spiral, but a simple stair-case of the adenine, guanine, thymine, and cytosine bases attached to phosphate esters and pentose sugars and garbage of that sort was neither strong nor stable. The solution in retrospect is simple — the Double Helix, a simple twisting of the strands. I have been told that twisting strands is not only simple, but known by everybody. The aborigines twist human hair into religious twine. Small imagination there. But twisting for ductile strength and twisting for rigid strength are quite different things; the former is traditional among the ab-origines, the latter is not. The difference at any rate was enough for a Nobel Prize. This small but intriguing problem has a relational twist as well; Sir Lawrence Bragg, who contributed to the solution, was born in Adelaide, grandson of Sir Charles Todd, one of the founders of Alice Springs, and Alice Todd, for whom Alice Springs was named.

Australia keeps calling to me, sometimes loudly, sometimes in a whisper, as with the Todds and Bragg and the Double Helix. Twice on national television I have heard my own recorded voice singing Australian songs — each time a complete surprise, the old records I made during my first visit having been peddled through a succession of unpaying agents.

How poignant the call when it comes with tidings of tragedy. Dorothy Tindale dead, dear rough-hewn Dorothy, craggy in her soul as the Musgrave Range, so heart-winning in her person.

Old Mr. Cooper dead, gone into total blindness and unable to climb Mount Remarkable, just as the galley proofs of his monograph on Hallett's Cove, his lifework, arrived.

Sir John Cleland dead; I shook his frail hand, one of the first to be thrust into Australian anthropology, on my second visit, when he was ninety years old.

D. F. Thompson dead, nearly the only Australian I did not like, but then no one else did either. Poor baastid; he was the only Australian soldier in the Second World War to be done nearly to death with a Neolithic axe, in New Guinea. It was a hell of a job to find anybody to write his obituary; *de mortuis nil nisi bonum.*

Gruff old cigar-chewing T. D. Campbell dead, the man who had taught Joan stagecraft at Adelaide University and who had been so kind to me at the museum. And what about my other mates? *Ubi sunt?*

Hwāer cwōm BobVerburgt? Left the service, I heard through a mutual friend. I have not been able to find out what happened to him. When we parted at Amata Bob was enmired in personal problems, not of his own making.

Ron Roberts, superintendent at Giles, gone also from the service. No word from him in nearly two years. Where do they go, these bushmen, at last?

Gordon Inkatji, assistant to Wilf Douglas in teaching Joan and me Pitjandjara, Gordon Inkatji, who remembered his father telling of the first automobile in the central desert and how the people wondered whether it was a visible *mamu* or a moving hill — lost a leg in a spear fight.

Wal MacDougall, builder of Ernabella, with Bob Verburgt, the master bushman, half of the police force of nearly a million square miles of inland Australia, retiring from the service six weeks from now.

Jo Birdsell, disillusioned like myself with the new generation of anthropologists, trying to Go Home Again.

Vic MacFarlane, his years of work rubbished by this smarmy, sanctimonious, smart-assed new generation, not because of any fault in it, but because the discovery of why men die in the desert was supported by the United States Army and therefore was unethical.

Young Wally, that boy on the forward edge of manhood, who did so well to prove himself during our filming trip into the Mann Range — arrested for burglary of the Amata commissary. Did he go to the Adelaide jail to become civilized, like Harry?

I want so much to know about all of them; the vanished men of Giles, who made me a half gallon of ice cream and dropped it into the spinifex near Butjar; and others whom I remember so fondly but who stand outside my narrative of desert journeys.

Bob Verburgt told me a strange and beautiful thing one night as we sat looking into our camp fire between the Warburton Range and the Rawlinsons. Once, he said, when he was at Yalata, he showed the Ngalea people there a piece of a branch from a tree growing in their country south of the Musgraves, a poor fragment of a poor tree that somehow had fallen into his truck. They all burst into sobs, weeping for their lost country and the remembrance of it.

I know that feeling. I know it as Hube Trotman knew it — that

rough and unsentimental bushman who dug the wells for Canning —
and his aborigines, whom he heard express it in their little English,
"*I am heartcryin' alonga dat country.*"

PINIS — FINISH

INDEX

361